Tigers of the Snow
and Other Virtual Sherpas

Frontispiece. Arriving in Sherpa country, Khum Jung Village, northeastern Nepal, near Mount Everest, 1986.

Tigers of the Snow
and Other Virtual Sherpas

AN ETHNOGRAPHY OF
HIMALAYAN ENCOUNTERS

Vincanne Adams

PRINCETON UNIVERSITY PRESS

PRINCETON, NEW JERSEY

Library of Congress Cataloging-in-Publication Data

Adams, Vincanne, 1959–
Tigers of the snow and other virtual Sherpas: an ethnography
of Himalayan encounters / Vincanne Adams.
p.   cm.
Includes bibliographical references and index.
ISBN 0-691-03441-9 (cloth : alk. paper)—0-691-00111-1 (pbk. : alk. paper)
1. Sherpa (Nepalese people).   2. Ethnology—Nepal.   I. Title.
DS493.9.S5A33   1996   305.8′0095496—dc20   95-4618

This book has been composed in Janson

Princeton University Press books are printed
on acid-free paper and meet the guidelines
for permanence and durability of the Committee
on Production Guidelines for Book Longevity
of the Council on Library Resources

Printed in the United States of America by
Princeton Academic Press

10 9 8 7 6 5 4 3 2 1

10 9 8 7 6 5 4 3 2 1
(Pbk.)

For Maggie

Those Himalayas of the mind are not so easily possessed.

Anonymous

In spite of a persistent fiction, we never write on a blank page, but always on one that has already been written on.

Michel de Certeau,
The Practice of Everyday Life

Contents

x · Contents

Illustrations

Acknowledgments

It seems fitting that a book that argues that Sherpas are both "intrinsically real" and "imaginatively produced" by the desires of others should begin by acknowledging those persons whose peculiar desires have helped forge it. I thank the Sherpas whose desires were particularly influential in my efforts to write this book, including Da Yangin Sherpani, Ang Tshiring and Chanda Sherpa, Mingma Tenzing and Doma Sherpa, Kandro and Ching Nuru Sherpa, Ang Tashi and Lhakpa Dorje Sherpa, Lama Onchu and Ang Phuti Sherpa, *thawa* Phurba Sonam Sherpa and *thawa* Ngawang Thondup Sherpa, *lhawa*s Nima Tshiring Sherpa and A-Tutu Sherpa and their families, *minung* Phu Dorje Sherpa, and the family of Pemba Dorje Sherpa. Numerous other Sherpa families in Kathmandu and Khumbu extended great hospitality to me and offered me many conversations about their personal lives; I am indebted to them. I hope they will receive this ethnography as a way of furthering my relationships with them, and that they will see some form of their desires in these pages.

The manuscript for this book went through many revisions, and I have had many critical readers and reviewers who contributed greatly to it. In the sense that this book is only virtually a single-authored ethnography, all these readers deserve great thanks for helping me clarify my insights in it, but none should be held responsible for any part of it. They include Ronnie Frankenberg, Krishna Bhattachan, Louisa Schein, Holly Anne Hyde, James Fisher, Robert Desjarlais, Sherry Ortner, Paul Rabinow, Aihwa Ong, Mary Anglin, Stacy Pigg, Abdellah Hammoudi, John Kelly, Gananath and Ranjini Obeyesekere, Michael Gallo, Lawrence Cohen, Rena Lederman, Kaushik Gosh, Quetzil Castaneda, and several anonymous reviewers. Special thanks are owed to Pat Pannell for her careful editing of one version of the manuscript, and also to the Tibet scholars Geoffrey Samuel, Mark Tatz, Richard Kohn, Donald Lopez, and Matthew Kapstein, who have read or discussed portions of the manuscript concerning Buddhism. I am grateful to Martha Kaplan for subtitle suggestions. I also extend warm thanks to my colleagues, one and all, in the Department of Anthropology at Princeton University for their insights, which (sometimes probably unbeknownst to them) greatly influenced the ideas here, and for their ability to create an atmosphere of collegiality and support still filled with great intellectual challenges. The influence of earlier teachers is also evident in this book, and I am grateful to them for their attentiveness to my ambitions; they include Gerry Berreman, Jack Potter, Nancy Scheper-Hughes, Fred Dunn, and Leo Rose. Thanks also to Mary Murrell at Princeton University Press, and to Jane Lincoln Taylor for her editing. Finally, I reserve most heartfelt thanks for my husband, John Norby, for his unceasing support, his desires, and his willingness to share in the joys and hardships of my life as an anthropologist.

I extend thanks for the generous funding that was provided to me for research in 1986–87 by the United States Department of Education Fulbright Doctoral Dissertation Research Award Program. Research funds from the Department of Anthropology at the University of California at Berkeley also aided my research in 1986–87. Funds for research in 1982 were provided under a grant obtained by Ivan G. Pawson from the National Science Foundation.

Orthographic Note

SHERPA is a spoken dialect of Tibetan. Many believe it is most closely derived from the Kham-pa dialect, which would be consistent with written histories that claim that Sherpas came from the Kham-pa region of Tibet (Macdonald 1979). Others (including Matthew Kapstein, personal communication) suggest that it may be more closely related to western Tibetan dialects, based on grammatical cases. As a spoken dialect, Sherpa has many words that have no written form. Wherever I have been able to find the Tibetan spellings of Sherpa terms, I have offered transliterations (following Das 1983, Samuel 1993, and Matthew Kapstein, personal communication) in the glossary at the back of the book, but the Sherpa terms appear as phonetic transliterations in the text. (Sometimes the Tibetan spelling is close enough to the pronunciation; in these cases, I have used the Tibetan spelling in the text.)

I have used pseudonyms, not real names, for almost all the Sherpas discussed here, and I do not indicate which names are real. Readers should assume that, unless the name of a Sherpa has already appeared in print (and even in some cases in which it has), I have used a pseudonym. Finally, readers should know that there are not many Sherpa names, Sherpas often have the same names, all of them use the surname "Sherpa," and they often change their names at different times of their lives. The Sherpas who reappear at different times in my text have the same names each time they appear, but this does not mean that each time a similar name appears, it refers to the same Sherpa.

Readers should also note that "Sherpa" is synonymous with the occupational role of Himalayan assistant trekking guide. I have used the capitalized name "Sherpa" to refer to the ethnic group, and this form of the word is also used as a surname for these persons when and where they need one; I use the uncapitalized word "sherpa" to refer to the occupational role.

Many of the quoted passages from interviews were originally recorded in English, or were translated into English while I was in the field. English is often the second or third language spoken by Sherpas, many of whom speak, with varying degrees of proficiency, five or more languages.

Tigers of the Snow
and Other Virtual Sherpas

1. Pasang Lhamu Sherpa.

Lament for Pasang

IN 1993, one of the first sights one saw outside the Tribhuvan International Airport in Kathmandu, Nepal, was a faded billboard with a picture of a smiling woman named Pasang Lhamu Sherpa. Above her head, it read, in English: "May the Spirit Live On Forever." Below: "San Miguel pays its respectful homage to Pasang Lhamu Sherpa on her sad demise." An outline of the Himalayas and Mount Everest sat to the right of her portrait, and on the highest peak was an image of the Nepalese flag. The message continued: "Her undying Spirit will continue to inspire us now and forever after, and we pray to the Almighty to bless her soul with eternal Peace." The billboard was put up by the official sponsor of the "Nepalese Woman Mt. Everest Expedition," the San Miguel Beer Company—for "San Miguel Sagarmatha [Everest] 1993." On the far right side of the billboard, commanding much more space than Pasang Lhamu, were an oversized bottle and can of San Miguel Beer. The top of the bottle even jutted above the frame of the billboard. The fine print and somber words offered in memory of Pasang Lhamu seemed diminished by this bottle, so large that it seemed to come to life, enticing passersby to have a celebratory cool drink in honor of her achievement.

Pasang Lhamu Sherpa reached the summit of Mount Everest with five other Sherpas, all young men, on April 22, 1993. The first Nepalese woman to accomplish this feat, she was thirty-two years old, a wife, and the mother of three children. It was Pasang Lhamu's fourth and last attempt. There was another, foreign, expedition team with radios at the base camp, and news of her successful ascent was transmitted first to New Zealand, via a satellite device placed on the peak of Everest by New Zealand climbers. From New Zealand word was relayed to Nepal that she had succeeded. Word traveled fast to me as well. Within a week, I got a call at my home in New Jersey from a Khumbu Sherpa living in New York, who, knowing that I was a friend of Pasang's, described to me her achievement, and conveyed to me the sad news of her death.

After fifteen to twenty minutes on the top, three of the men climbing with Pasang Lhamu descended quickly to the South Col, more than eight hundred meters below the summit. Pasang Lhamu descended more slowly with two other Sherpas, Pemba Nuru and Sonam Tshiring. Pasang, our Sherpa friends said, was fortunate in that, although she walked slowly, she never suffered from the effects of altitude. On that climb, Pasang and her companions all walked so slowly that it took them more than a full day just to reach the top after leaving the highest camp that morning, and so they had had to bivouac for the night just eighty-eight meters below the summit on the way down. The next morning, Pasang Lhamu sent Pemba Nuru down in order to get oxygen. She stayed behind with Sonam, who had been coughing blood since the day before. But Pemba Nuru never found them. In fact, no one made contact with Pasang Lhamu or Sonam Tshiring again; bad weather made it impossible for climbers at lower elevations to locate them with binoculars.

This seems like a fitting place to start this ethnography of Sherpas, on the way down the mountain, in praise of Pasang's achievement and lament over her demise. It is the other story of Sherpas of Nepal—the one less seldom told, of not simply the astounding achievement of these Himalayan folk but the great cost of this achievement as well. Starting here, I am able to ask questions about the cost, and questions about who authorizes the expenditure of life and who profits from it. This story, I submit, requires the telling of a tale not simply of Sherpas, but of Sherpas and their Western friends in Himalayan encounters.

I first met Pasang Lhamu through her siblings seven years before her great achievement. Her younger brother Ang Gelu had offered to be my tour guide on my first visit to Nepal in 1982 upon learning that I lived near his brother, Dorje, in San Francisco. Ang Gelu also wanted to travel to the "States," and envisioned me sponsoring his visit there. After meeting Ang Gelu in Nepal, and later, Dorje in the United States, I met their sister, Pasang, in 1986 soon after I arrived in Nepal, loaded with gifts from her brother in San Francisco. I was their courier. Pasang's husband, Lhakpa Sonam Sherpa, ran a trekking agency, so it was easy for me to find her when I got to Kathmandu. When I met her in 1986, Pasang had absolutely no interest in climbing mountains. Indeed, few Sherpanis (female Sherpas) did. We spent time together at meals and on shopping trips in downtown Kathmandu, talking about the trials and tribulations of her life and mine as we wound our way from the butchers' section of the city to the fashionable new supermarket. In 1987, she told me about the new home she and her husband were planning to build on a large lot in a nice part of the city. But she was dogged by her lack of energy and general poor health. She told me that ever since the tubal ligation she had after giving birth to her third child, her health had declined, and now she was always suffering from thinness, colds, and diarrhea. By 1993, however, Pasang had completely remade herself, or so it seemed to me from the photos, for she had put on weight, was visibly athletic, and was full of smiles, like one who had found her niche in life. She had been to Everest four times, the last time all the way to the summit.

A search party led by Pasang's husband found her body, three weeks

2. Transport of Pasang Lhamu's recovered body over the Everest glacier.

after she was lost, frozen in the snow at the South Summit, only eighty-eight meters below the peak. The body of Sonam Tshiring was never found. I thanked my friend for telling me the news, and I felt my eyes mist over as I thought about Pasang's children and realized I would never see her again. As I hung up the phone, I thought of all the other people I had met in the Khumbu whose fathers, sons, or brothers had died in the same way, and wondered why Pasang Lhamu had wanted to climb. Her incentives were certainly not simple or obvious to me.

Climbing was not expected of Sherpa women in general, nor did Pasang Lhamu, in particular, need the money such climbs could bring. In fact, although she received sponsorship from San Miguel Beer and a host of other agencies, including, ironically, the Nepal National Life and General Insurance Company, Ltd., she and her husband's company organized and paid for more than half the cost of her expeditions themselves. This was no small amount of money. Her final expedition cost her family more than Rs. 1,900,000 (19 lakhs, or $38,000).

It was not until I arrived in Nepal a few months later that a possible motivation for her climbs became apparent to me. Her acclaim as the first Nepalese woman to reach the summit was overwhelming. Her husband's company had become a center of national and international attention and, with the momentum of public support, organized the Pasang Lhamu Mountaineering Foundation in her memory. Her commemorative portraits could be seen on the walls of local trekking shops, magazines, and billboards throughout Kathmandu. Even Daman Nath Dhungana, the Nepalese Speaker of the House of Representatives, approached me at a Sherpa festival during my first month back in Kathmandu in 1993 in order to tell me about his involvement with the Pasang Lhamu Mountaineering Foundation, devoted to honoring this brave and admirable Nepalese woman for her heroism. "It is very important for all Nepalese people that we honor her," Dhungana said, "because we have many national heroes but very few national heroines. Especially, we should honor her for her bravery and courage as a woman." It was not common for members of Parliament to attend Sherpa festivals, but he went to this one at the request of Pasang's husband and brother-in-law, who had also invited him to be a member of the board of the foundation. With his help, the new Nepalese government had gone out of its way to honor Pasang Lhamu posthumously. They called for a national day of mourning and parade for her funeral. Her blackened, lifeless body was carried, high atop a palanquin, through the streets of Kathmandu, and they awarded her the Nepal Tara, the Nepal Star, a title awarded to only three other persons in history.[1] Schoolchildren, class by class, approached her corpse and placed wreaths over her head in the grand stadium where the parade terminated, where her body lay in state for an entire day.

The existence of a desirable image of Pasang Lhamu Sherpa, the first Nepalese woman to reach the summit of Mount Everest, satisfies the needs and interests of a variety of people. The San Miguel Beer Company, the Nepalese Speaker of the House, the Sherpas described in this story, and the anthropologist all look to her image as an icon for what it can say about and for Sherpas and themselves. This image can increase the sale of beer, arouse sentiments of a gendered national pride (and thereby raise support for politicians), and contribute to a highly reflexive international fame for Sherpas. Finally, it provides me, in a highly personal way, with one of the transnational configurations of Sherpas for this ethnography.

During my 1993 visit to Nepal, soon after her death, I was greeted at the airport by her brother-in-law. Later that night, Pasang Lhamu's husband showed me photos of himself and his wife traveling abroad, her last climb, and the recovery of her remains. It was not a pleasant evening, for he was still visibly distraught over her absence. Pasang was noticeably missing from her domestic scene. Her children watched television in the side alcove of her spacious new home in the nice part of the city. I ventured the question that had vexed me since I heard of her death months before. I asked him why Pasang Lhamu wanted to climb Everest. He told me then that neither the money nor the subsequent fanfare of the Nepalese government was the reason for her climb. The latter, he said, was a totally unanticipated outcome, and not necessarily one he or she had wanted, for it had politicized her death. So I asked him again why she *did* climb, and he responded simply, "She wanted to!" He also loved climbing and had even planned to accompany her on the ascent attempt. "After all," he said, "this is what Sherpas are famous for."

We sat a while longer, looking at photographs of her in an album. One remarkable oversized and framed photo of her standing with Sir Edmund Hillary (one of the first two persons to reach the summit of Everest back in 1953), his hand on her shoulder, filled up the wall space behind the sofa where Lhakpa sat. "That is one of my favorites," Lhakpa said, pointing to the wall photo.[2] We drank beer (San Miguel, of course), and he told me about their last trip to France, the Alps, Versailles. . . . But the large photo over his shoulder would not let me stop thinking about her motivation, and about how I might do justice in my ethnography to just what he said about her, that "she wanted to." How could I make sense of this desire? It was obvious enough to Lhakpa and to the other family members in the room why she climbed. It seemed as if it should have been obvious to me too. But I kept looking at that photo looming, nearly life-size, just behind Lhakpa as we sat in his enormous living room, and wondered what role the presence of my world had played in her motivation.

It was people like Edmund Hillary who introduced climbing to Sherpas, for no Sherpas had climbed Himalayan peaks before Westerners recruited them as guides and porters for their own Himalayan expeditions. In fact, they had considered it taboo; the mountains were gods and goddesses. Yet now Pasang, too, was part of that special club of elite Westerners and Sherpas who had achieved national and international renown for "summiting" Everest. Was this simply all there was to her desire, and what cost her her life—a mimesis in which Sherpas had become "like" the West or had dutifully lived up to the expectations Westerners have had of them? "This is," after all, "what Sherpas are famous for," Lhakpa had said. Somehow this explanation seemed too obvious, and therefore incomplete, as if her motivation had already been scripted by Westerners and was consequently missing some essential quality that could define it as "Sherpa." Surely the idea that one climbed because one "wanted to" belonged, originally, to Westerners, I thought. It could only belong to Sherpas secondarily, like secondhand clothes. His comments reminded me of the famous aphorism of Sir Edmund Hillary, that he climbed Everest "because it was there!" The challenge, the adventure—surely he had simply "wanted to" climb Everest too, and here I was being told that these were obviously Pasang's motivations. Yet even if Pasang had adopted this perspective, I thought, a Sherpa's own motivation would also have to lie elsewhere and be saturated with notions of cultural difference. Buddhist discipline, I hoped, or even some special relationship to the mountain, a goddess, would explain it. At a minimum it would have to be explicable via notions of exploitation, false consciousness, or even "staged authenticity," which would make Pasang somehow different from those Westerners who initiated the business of Himalayan expeditions. What sort of creeping ethnocentrism was it, I thought, that could let me see in these Sherpas only those qualities that reflected my world? If I probed long and hard enough, I was sure to come to the truth about her climb, and I would be able to explain it in this text. I would surely find the "true" Sherpa behind this Westernized construction. But Lhakpa was telling me precisely that it was not elsewhere, that I should look no further to understand Pasang Lhamu. There was nothing more hidden than that which was presented as a fact by him: she simply wanted to climb, no matter how much this made her look as if she was only an image in a mirror reflecting my own culture. It was a surface appearance that contained all the "truth" I needed to know, and it was clear that her motivation was, by all accounts, much the same as that of Hillary.

In this book I explore, by way of a more general inquiry into the creation of Sherpa identity in the Western imagination and the persistent anthropological and Western desire to find a site of authenticity beyond the Western gaze, what led Pasang Lhamu to get involved in the high-risk, high-profit, image-making, and body-breaking business of mountaineering because "she wanted to." I try to discover what the answer to this question can tell us about ourselves, about Sherpas, and about the relationships between us. To talk about why Pasang Lhamu climbed Everest and what made her image of use to so many people, one must first analyze the obvious role Westerners have played in "creating" the Sherpas I came to know in late-twentieth-century Nepal—by most accounts, thoroughly modern Sherpas, especially in their desire to climb the Himalayan peaks. I thus begin by stepping back in time and beyond the borders of the small Himalayan country of Nepal to examine the history of Sherpas' involvement with Westerners—an involvement that created relationships linking the West to these Sherpas' home region, called the Khumbu, at the base of Mount Everest. Although Khumbu Sherpas are small in number (they make up only about three thousand of the twenty-five thousand or so from the Himalayan region), they have become more closely connected to Westerners than have other Sherpas (and arguably other Nepalis in general) because of their location in the high Himalayas near Everest and their work as migrant laborers in Himalayan India on British, European, and American expeditions as early as the turn of the twentieth century.

The perceived qualities of Sherpa greatness among Westerners, like the Himalayas themselves, have been both "actual and ideal," in the words of Agehananda Bharati (1978), and these qualities figured prominently in the creation of the Sherpas I came to know beginning in 1982. But whereas this book starts with an examination of the Western impact, and the impact of the Western gaze, on Sherpas, I hope that by the end of the book readers will see the impact of Sherpas on Westerners like me. Deeply bound up in that recognition is the idea that we are present in them and they in us (at least those of us who spend time with Sherpas); the distinctions are blurred between a Sherpa who is beyond our gaze and a Sherpa who is constructed by it. If one were to turn to an exploration of where, beyond the impact of "the West," one might find motivation for Pasang Lhamu's climbs—for surely her desires were also somehow her own and not simply those imbued in her because of her relationship with Westerners—one would still find the ineluctable presence of the West in her life and other Sherpas' lives.

This book reveals that becoming what Westerners desire is built into the ways in which Sherpas are expected to be similar to Westerners, who have brought them modernity in such things as climbing Himalayan peaks for sport. But becoming what Westerners desire also demands that Sherpas remain different from them; difference is built into the possible ways of "being Sherpa" that are taken as more "real" than those created in or by the West. I argue that a logic of mimesis governs this interaction, in which surface appearances in such things as representations of difference or such simple statements revealing sameness as "she wanted to" become the location of authenticity. They conceal no more true ways of being Sherpa than that appearing on the surface. But mimesis is not organized and narrated solely by the West, nor are Westerners the first through whom mimesis has been accomplished for Sherpas. Today, Westerners arriving in Sherpa country often do so with the intention of achieving some sort of epiphany in which they will be better climbers, better Buddhists (or simply more spiritual), or more in touch with the socially intimate way of life displayed by Sherpas, just as anthropologists arrive hoping to find "true" motivations in the agency of Sherpas who are beyond our construction. Westerners often find this epiphany among Sherpas because Sherpas actually give these opportunities to Westerners, being able to mirror Western desires. One of the most spectacular results of this interchange, however, is a reversal of the mirroring between Sherpas and Westerners. Sherpas recruit Western Others to become their sponsors (*jindak*), "lifelong" friends, and supporters who provide them with gifts, money, advice, employment, and more, in response to Western desires to become part of "the Sherpa world." Anthropologists are seldom exempt from this seduction. They too enter into mimesis with Sherpas, into an ontological becoming of that which is Sherpa—that which anthropologists take to be "more real than reality itself"—in order to find themselves. In the process Westerners become mirrors reflecting Sherpa interests and desires.

Exemplary of this mutual seduction is Tashi's story. A year after Pasang's death, a Sherpa visitor named Tashi sat in my kitchen in New Jersey, telling me about her betrothal to a Sherpa named Kansa from Khum Jung village, where I had lived. She explained that he was on his way back from England as we spoke, having been sponsored by the duchess of York to visit and reside in England for eight months. My Sherpani guest showed me a photo of him dancing at a going-away party he attended with the duchess. "She went trekking in Nepal last year. My fiancé was the guide. She was doing charity work," Tashi said. "She had a very good time on the trek and now she says that she loves Khum Jung village more than any other in Nepal. And, after her trek, she invited Kansa to visit her." It was a common story, and one I heard frequently about other Sherpas, from other Sherpas and from Westerners who had gone trekking in Nepal. How many Americans, British, French, Swiss, Canadians, Germans, Italians, New Zealanders, and others had I met who had entered into special bonds with their Sherpa friends, I asked myself. So many had become sponsors for these Sherpas, inviting them to live and work in their home countries, and even returning to Nepal to trek with them, that I could not keep track of them all. I was excited myself at the type of social connection this particular encounter described by Tashi represented. "Your Kansa seems quite lucky," I said to Tashi, wishing I myself had a duchess for a sponsor. "Yes," Tashi said, "she said that she wants to come back to Nepal again, for her work, and we will help her then too."

On the way to that point in this text where one finds Sherpas who seem to be more than passive victims of Western interests, I try to avoid falling into the trap of reading these seductive Sherpa acts as instrumental acts of staged authenticity (i.e., performing Sherpas deluding gullible Westerners for handouts; therefore revealing "inauthentic" culture). Why are such acts not fruitfully analyzed as "staged authenticity"? Because this concept presupposes that there is a way of being more "authentically" Sherpa, and I try to show in this book that that cannot be found. I suggest instead that the Janus-faced analytical construct of authenticity/inauthenticity needs to be reconsidered. I also try in this ethnography to avoid the pursuit of a set of Sherpa behaviors that appear to be more "authentic" than those that have made Sherpas resemble Westerners, for example in things like climbing Everest. Most Sherpas who want to climb Everest do so at least in part because of the Western interest in having Sherpas climb Everest, but this does not mean that other arenas of Sherpa activity are therefore more "authentically" Sherpa than those that emerge from Western modernization. I frequently encounter Westerners who lament the loss of an original Sherpa, who feel that Sherpas who have become Westernized are somehow no longer as "Sherpa" as they could be. I suggest here that a Western set of behaviors in Sherpas is as authentic as any other; what is important in this realization is not simply that Westernization occurs (for surely this has been discussed ad nauseam), but rather that these behaviors force one to think of Sherpa culture as located not in Sherpas sui generis but in the relationships they have with others, such as with the Westerners I describe in this book. This enables us to think about how these behaviors are marked as relationships of power, desire, and, in the case of the Sherpas, seduction. This, too, I take to be an analytical approach emergent from my relationships with Sherpas; I presume not only that my experiences with them are the contingencies from which these insights arise, but also that the relationships that tourists, development agents, and anthropologists have with Sherpas are not necessarily similar to those such persons have with other people elsewhere in the world. Seduction (and other ideas) may characterize the particular encounters in the Himalayas of which I speak here, but it may not characterize the encounters ethnographers, tourists, and development agents have with the Others they meet elsewhere. Finally, the problem of authenticity in notions of cultural difference resurfaces here: arenas of Sherpa lives that many Westerners take to be beyond the gaze of the West, such as those demarcated by such potent markers of difference as Buddhism or shamanism, are also, I show, engaged in strikingly visible ways by Western interest. While this makes these arenas equally susceptible to being called "inauthentic"—made so by the "corrupting" gaze of the West—I argue that such accusations are only viable if one presupposes a distinction between authentic and inauthentic culture. I propose to move beyond that distinction. An account that refuses to apprehend relationships in these terms must itself then use different terms to describe them; I am compelled by the multiple contingencies of Western social theory, Buddhism, and Sherpa shamanism to deploy a notion of virtual identities, explained below.

This book is, first, about the West and its impact on Sherpas, and Sherpas here are initially presented as objects through which Western discourses are spoken. More than in their relationships with other non-Sherpa Nepalese, Sherpas in their relationships with Westerners have created the type of situation in which Pasang Lhamu Sherpa would want to achieve international fame by climbing, even at the cost of her life, and in which even death could be used as a form of transnational cultural capital profiting many people in many ways. I define "the West" as the whole complicated and pluralistic set of relationships Sherpas have had with modernization inspired and paid for by Western nations and organizations through tourism, charitable development aid, and anthropology. It is not simply the individuals, it is the entire apparatus by which Sherpas have become visible to and involved with persons from all over the Western hemisphere.

In this totalizing use of "the West" and "Westerners," I aim to convince readers neither that the Westerners are all of a type nor that the West is a singular, homogeneous entity. Rather, I use these terms as a way of situating the analysis reflexively and identifying its specificity from the outset. To borrow from Anna Tsing, I introduce this discourse "to show its very specificity, not to universalize from it,"[3] and to reveal its ability to see the West from a Sherpa perspective. What is not gained by taking this perspective is insight into the ways Sherpas think of and deploy notions of difference between Westerners. Sherpas do sometimes categorize Westerners in terms of specific differences between them, based most often on nationality. (Germans are thought to behave predictably differently from Israelis, Americans, Italians, British, French, and so forth. Sherpas also categorize Westerners on the basis of different occupations: hippies are thought to be different from development agents, mountaineers, and anthropologists, even if these distinctions are less important than those based on nationality.) But in many ways these distinctions made by Sherpas are persistently forced to give way to homogenizing perspectives, which make most of the relationships Sherpas have with these Westerners of a single type—a type that approximates the sponsorship relationship and creates a virtual Westerner who could be a sponsor. What is gained by focusing on the generalizing construction of the West deployed by Sherpas is a sense of the specificity of Sherpa relationships with these people, as opposed to others with whom they are also in contact (Tibetans, Indians, and above all other Nepalese). I pursue these identities created out of engagement with the West not simply to "know" Sherpas, but also, inevitably, to "know" those reflections of Westerners like me that one finds in Sherpas.[4] In doing so, I realize there are other aspects of Sherpas' lives, and other ways in which they have been constructed (e.g., especially by the Nepalese state), that I do not address here.

I begin with a focus on the Western impact on Sherpas, but a goal of the book is to show that accommodating Western interests for a particular sort of Sherpa is part of who Sherpas are. I hope that by the end of the book, readers will see that the relationships between Westerners and Sherpas have been reversed, and that Sherpa discourses speak through Westerners. I also hope that by the time the reader starts to realize that he or she is no longer witnessing (through the text) the creation of modern Sherpas by the West, but rather the Sherpa creation of a virtual Westerner who meets his or her own Sherpa needs, it will be unclear where the boundary is between who Westerners would have the Sherpas be and who they truly are. The culture that floats between the two groups of participants includes the representations of Sherpas that have been produced by Westerners and found their way into Sherpa lives. My ability to speak about Sherpas reflects the intentions of Sherpa subjects speaking through my text and through relationships of seduction I have had, and have, with them. I inform my ethnographic method with an awareness of the mimesis that moves from them to me. Thus, what begins as a theory that looks like a Western abstraction imposed by me on Sherpas will, I hope, by the end appear as a theory that emerges from Sherpa practice. Sherpas invite us to step into their world and experience an Other way of life in order to learn about our "true" selves. They also offer us a way to slip back into our world by becoming the idealized "Sherpa-ized" Westerners of whom they dream. This approach, which discovers Sherpas as agents, in the end leads me back to the West, for the Sherpas' engagement with Westerners strives to maintain links between themselves and their Western Others, in part through practices Westerners call distinctively Sherpa. This process operates epistemologically in the same way it operates ethnographically, as a "practiced" theory.

To explore what I mean by mimesis, I begin with the question: Who are the "Tigers of the snow"? Invoking a phrase used by Rey Chow (1993), I ask not simply what is the "violence of representation" done by this title awarded to Sherpas by Westerners (since it is questionable that death can in all cases—particularly for Buddhists—be called violence), but also by what mechanisms and with what profits have Sherpas become self-willed "Tigers of the snow"?

MAKING TIGERS OF THE SNOW: MIMESIS

According to tour brochures circulated by the Nepalese government Ministry of Tourism in the 1990s, Sherpas were, one and all, "Tigers of the snow."[5] The title "Tiger" was created in 1938 by the British mountaineer H. W. Tillman for those Sherpas who distinguished themselves by climbing to an altitude of twenty-five thousand feet or more during a British expedition.[6] These Sherpas were awarded the bronze Tigers Badge (also called the Tiger Medal) in a ceremony honoring their assistance to the British climbers. The ceremony also recorded the names of those exemplary Sherpas for future reference. According to one American expedition and Sherpa enthusiast, the title "Tiger" was "a precious symbol of ability"[7] that was recognized by European, American, and British climbers. The British, in particular, wrote affectionately about their "loyal Tigers," without whose help, they claimed, they would never have been able to attempt their ascents to glory.[8]

The term "Tiger" signified for Westerners an exotic and respected beauty, an animal once the most prized trophy of subcontinental colonial safaris.[9] This image, at once wild and dignified, has continued to invest Sherpas with a bizarre mixture of qualities. Representations of unlimited endurance and enviable skill are coupled with representations of a will subordinated to and bent in the service of Western desires. Both attributes flourish within the same constructed identity. The tiger represented, for the West, a beauty that was admirable enough to merit ongoing attention. Yet the beauty of the tiger could be admired for its qualitative difference from the West, and in that difference the tiger was seen as dangerous unless tamed, or placed in service to the West. The tiger and its image

3. The Tigers Badge, awarded to Sherpas who succeeded in climbing, as high-altitude porters or guides, to an elevation of twenty-five thousand feet or more on British expeditions.

encompassed that aspect of the subcontinent which, for the sake of its own betterment, needed to be controlled and then saved by the West.

As Tigers, the Sherpas were intriguing and admirable enough to be preserved because they were exotic—which eventually came to mean Buddhist, mystical, highly compassionate, hospitable, and seemingly embedded in endless webs of endearing social relationships that were enticing, even sexually so. Yet woven into that web were also attributes of difference centered on the Sherpas' perceived poverty and need. These undesirable attributes were deemed to result from the "wildness" and "primitiveness" of their "natural" living conditions, which needed to be tamed by the West. Sherpas became, in the eyes of the West, a slate on which Westerners could write their own desires in the language of need and lack. Unlike real tigers, which were hunted and made into trophies, Sherpas were offered interventions of another sort. These came first in the form of mountaineering jobs, which allowed Sherpas to put their "natural" talents to "good," rather than wasted, use. Later, they arrived in the form of charitable development aid, which built hospitals, schools, airstrips, water systems, and government facilities. These enabled Sherpas to remain healthy, educated, available, and disciplined so as to enhance further their "natural" talents as servile employees, as admired and skilled mountaineering guides, and, subsequently, as purveyors of spiritual knowledge and socially intimate tourist attractions—*Others* through whom Westerners could find *themselves*.

The mixed Western imagery of the tiger as possessing on the one hand skill, stealth, intrigue, beauty, and endurance and on the other hand the subordinate qualities of an animal probably made the initial reception of the title among Sherpas somewhat ambiguous. The indications of this become most apparent when one considers the variations on the tiger theme in common discourses through which Westerners came to know Sherpas—that is, in particular, the discourse in the Sherpas' religion of Buddhism. Therein, *tag*, the tiger, is portrayed as the wrathful animal ridden by the goddess Chomolongmo (mother goddess of the universe, otherwise known as Mount Everest). As an animal, the tiger is thought to be less capable of Buddhist enlightenment than humans are because it is less able to use its sentient mind (*sems*), being overwhelmed by undesirable emotions such as greed, anger, and ignorance. The tiger is often used as the figure on which spirits are sent out of homes or villages in Buddhist exorcism rituals (*dozonggup*), a figure that the laity often sees as embodying demons and harmful spirits.[10] Sherpas born in the year of the tiger are considered problematic marriage partners because of their emotional volatility. At the same time, this particular animal is known through the Buddhist tale of the tigress who enabled the bodhisattva Gautama Buddha to exercise compassion by offering his body to assuage her hunger when he found her starving yet still nursing her cubs. In another famous representation, a tiger is held on a strong chain by a Mongol, and the image represents, in disguised form, the three great personages of Tibetan Buddhism. The Mongol is symbolic of Manjusri, the chain of Vajrapani, and the tiger of Avalokitesvara; together they form the triad of wisdom, power, and compassion. The tiger is also iconographically depicted as one of the four protectors of Buddhism, along with the bird (*garuda*), the snow lion (*senge*), and the dragon (*duk*), but is particularly remembered for its compassion. These qualities of the tiger are rewritten in Western accounts of Sherpas' compassion, revealed in acts of hospitality and graciousness toward foreigners and in an uncanny willingness to risk their lives in order to save foreigners while on treks and expeditions.

Despite the polysemy of the tiger image, its positive qualities articulated in the relationships between Sherpas and Westerners came to reign. Many Sherpas themselves, under the gaze of Westerners, expressed desires to become "Tigers" on early expeditions. Tenzing Norgay, the Sherpa who, alongside Edmund Hillary, was the first to reach the summit of Mount Everest, said about his earlier climbs, "All of us who reached Camp Six in 1938 were later awarded the Tiger Medal, with the ranking entered in our record books; and since then the Himalayan Club, which is the chief mountaineering organization of India, has issued them to all Sherpas who have performed comparable feats on other expeditions. I was proud and happy of course to be among the very first Tigers."[11] Considering again that, before the arrival of Western mountaineers, Sherpas were loath to climb to the peaks of mountains for fear of disturbing them—mountains were, after all, gods and goddesses—Norgay's stated desire to become the sort of Tigers Westerners had in mind (for he talks about becoming a Tiger by achieving the Western standard for this title) marks his effective mimesis with a representation created by the Westerners for whom he worked. Norgay's enthusiasm was not uncommon in the years after his achievement. Another Sherpa from the Khumbu, Ang Rita, had reached the summit of Everest (and a host of other high Himalayan peaks) eight times by the 1990s, each time without oxygen tanks. Sungdare Sherpa from Pangboche village in the Khumbu reached the summit five times before his death in 1989. Young Sherpas of Khum Jung village, where I lived, looked forward to the day when they would be given a chance to reach the summit themselves, and all of them recounted stories of Sungdare, Ang Rita, and others as Sherpa heroes.

By the time I first went to live as an anthropologist among Sherpas near the base of Mount Everest in 1982, their more than eighty years of involvement with Western visitors was worn, like their down parkas and hiking boots, in obvious ways. Sherpas no longer spoke about their desire to become Tigers, but they were still clearly interested in becoming the type of Sherpas Westerners desired, and in that construction of self one could still see the same qualities historically found in the image of the Tiger.

The project of creating a Sherpa with these qualities was begun by mountaineers and Sherpas as early as the turn of the twentieth century. It was perpetuated by development-aid programs that followed closely on the heels of mountaineering tourism in the Khumbu region, beginning in the 1960s. The modern Sherpa who was defined by his or her relationships with Westerners had to be desirable enough to merit endless amounts of financial support from Westerners, yet disciplined enough to reproduce the perceived needs on which donors themselves came to depend for sustaining their role in the region. To be Sherpa in the eyes of the Westerner meant to be in need and, equally important, to be amply *deserving* of aid. In the same way that the image of the tiger given by Westerners was taken up by the Sherpas as an identifying icon that designated a Sherpa subject imbued with the needs of the West, the development agencies produced constructs of subjectivity that were embraced by Sherpa recipients. "Our children have eyes, but still they are blind," wrote one of the older Sherpa headmen of Khum Jung village to the Himalayan Trust in the early 1960s, in order to convince the trustees of the Sherpas' desire for Western-style schools.[12]

For Sherpas of the Khumbu involved with Westerners, to remain distinctively Sherpa once meant to possess the qualities of admirable exoticism and enviable skill attributed to the Tiger. In the 1990s, it still meant to be different in all the ways the West desired—exotically spiritual and unfailingly hospitable, yet endlessly needy—different enough to warrant a tourist visit and to warrant being "saved" by the West. It also meant being similar to the West in all the ways the West desired—to want to become educated in schools where English was the medium of instruction and to develop a consumer need for those things the West could provide, including medicines, Western Ph.D.s, and Mercedes-Benzes ("proof" of successful development for both many Sherpas and many Westerners). The Western-Sherpa relationship worked to separate the Sherpas out as different and superior not only to other Nepalis but also to other "non-Western" colonized and formerly colonized people.

In exploring the paramount role that the three most visible Western agencies of modernization in the Khumbu, namely mountaineering tourism, development (particularly medical development), and anthropology, have played in the construction of Sherpa identities, I have found that one of the primary mechanisms therein has been a type of mimesis. Mimesis is usually defined as the process of copying nature; it also refers to the creative process of imitating human action as art—in this case representations of Sherpas that arrive from the West—through acts that reveal the nature of the self by way of the Other. Mimesis is imitation of nature in art,[13] but I use the term here to define a process of identity construction—the imitation of what is taken to be one's "natural" self by way of the Other, through whom one's constructed identity is made visible to oneself, not necessarily through art but through a variety of representations. The Others of concern to me in this book, through whom Sherpas construct their identities, are Western visitors with whom they have had relationships since the advent of Himalayan tourism at the turn of the twentieth century, and who have been active producers of textual and other images of Sherpas. Again, this does not exhaust the possible contexts that could be analyzed in an ethnography of Sherpas. It is, however, the one I have chosen in order to elucidate the particular effects of an index of cultural difference and sameness, an index through which Sherpas came to be known by me.

Sherpas' mimesis is reflective of the Western imagination. Sherpas do not simply become like the Other by incorporating the "modern" offered by the West into their lives; they become like that which the Other desires to see them as, in a set of perceived cultural differences and similarities that make the Sherpas larger than life, more real than reality itself. Eventually, I hope to show that the logic of mimesis and seduction that compels so many Sherpas to be "better" at being Sherpa in ways defined by the West also compels them to engage in mimesis in ways that are not simply defined by the West, but also found in cultural practices of Sherpas that they know define them as "different." It is through these Sherpa practices of being "different" that we eventually see how Westerners also engage in mimesis with them—finding themselves through Sherpas—and not simply with their imagined version of Sherpas.

Mimesis is explored by Paul Ricoeur (1981) in reference to Aristotle's *Poetics*, in a manner that focuses on the issue of intertextuality. Aristotle, he says, "tells us that tragedy seeks to imitate human action in a poetic way."[14] Ricoeur argues that the text, which is by nature removed from the speaking context where meanings are shared and specific, takes on opportunities for polysemy.[15] The tragedy, for example, reveals the possibility for imitation of human nature that offers the reader something that is more real than real—a creative imitation: "*mimesis* does not mean the duplication of reality; mimesis is not a copy: *mimesis* is *poiesis*, that is, construction, creation. Aristotle gives at least two indications of this creative dimension of *mimesis*. First, the fable is an original, coherent construction which attests to the creative genius of the artist. Second, tragedy is an imitation of human actions which makes them appear better, higher, more noble than they are in reality."[16]

The same mimesis is possible via the ethnographic text. Our relationship to the text is filled with possibilities for interpretation and understanding, based on the text's metaphoric ability to become something larger than life, more real than real. The reader (or, I suggest, the recipient of the text's images), he says,

> understands himself in front of a text, in front of the world of the work.[17] To understand oneself in front of a text is quite the contrary of projecting oneself and one's own beliefs and prejudices; it is to let the work and its world enlarge the horizon of the understanding which I have of myself. . . . Thus the hermeneutical circle is not repudiated but displaced from a subjectivistic level to an ontological plane. The circle is between my mode of being—beyond the knowledge which I may have of it—and the mode opened up and disclosed by the text as the world of the work.[18]

In the world of Sherpas and those who have written about them, a similar mimesis is revealed. Sherpas engage with Western representations of them, which begin as texts and end as images, in a manner that opens up and discloses ways of being Sherpa—ways created in the Western imagination but based, after all, on real experiences of Sherpa life. This mimesis is the creative imitation of that which is constituted as "Sherpa nature" once it has been produced in representational forms for them. It occurs via the intertextuality of Sherpas (constituted by their texts, literally) and via the plethora of relationships they have with Western Others who carry these representations with them, as images, to Sherpa country. In this sense, mimesis goes beyond simple textuality (even though textuality is of particular concern to the act of writing an ethnography). The text, because decontextualized, produces images that become potent signifiers of who Sherpas are. Sherpas become intertextual when they engage with these texts or their images via mimesis—when they interpret themselves as that which is given in the texts. My book, too, ineluctably decontextualizes by the act of inscription, even if it inevitably becomes recontextualized by Sherpas' engagement with it.

The mimesis of Sherpas with Westerners involves demands for Sherpas to become like the West itself. In this sense, mimesis is like that which Taussig (1993) invites us to see.[19] This mimesis is not simple mimicry, for it demands that Sherpas become culturally exotic and different from the West in ways that are deemed distinctively Sherpa. Yet this mimesis is also accompanied by that which Homi Bhabha identifies as "mimicry" in colonial regimes, even though its roots are in mountaineering and development relationships, rather than colonialism (among other things), which leads to some important departures from Bhabha's model. "Colonial mimicry," Bhabha writes, "is the desire for a reformed, recognizable Other, as a subject of a difference that is almost the same but not quite."[20] Bhabha's sense of the *ambivalence* of the colonial discourse, which results in a flawed reproduction of the colonizer in the colonized and is contingent on colonial enunciations of difference, is similar in some ways to the Sherpa experience. Sherpas have been made to be like, but at the same time unlike, those "moderns" who have brought them hospitals and trekking jobs. Bhabha argues that imperfect outcomes of a very racially charged colonial reproduction among the colonized are an inherent part of colonial discourse. They produce an ambivalence that itself poses a threat to colonialism. The colonized subject is engaged at once in mimicry and mockery, since the subject can never be fully colonial, and as such is able to reveal the alienation inherent in the colonial vision of the Other. However, this ambivalence does not wholly "rupture" the discourse, Bhabha notes, because it ultimately "becomes transformed into an uncertainty which fixes the colonial subject as a 'partial' presence . . . both 'incomplete' and 'virtual.'"[21]

For Sherpas, a similar discourse has been articulated not through colonialism but through modern industries of mountaineering and cultural tourism, development, and anthropology. A Sherpa has been "fixed," and is both incomplete and virtual in the eyes of the Westerners who produce him or her, and ultimately in his or her own eyes as well. Sherpas are constructed to be not simply what the Westerner is but what the Westerner desires, and are therefore incomplete. By incomplete, I mean always different from the Westerner, often as subordinates (like the colonized, Sherpas can be servile on expeditions and are thought to need modernization).[22] And despite desires to make Sherpas into "moderns" through development, Western discourse about Sherpas has never enabled them to be wholly "the same" because of concurrent Western desires for cultural Otherness in Sherpas, whether as innately gifted climbers, highly spiritual Buddhists, or villagers familiar with more intimate and "seductive" ways of life than Westerners believe are available in the West. In this latter sense, however, the Sherpas were not perceived as simply incomplete, but rather as incompletely the same yet "more complete" in fact than Westerners, who, in turn, began to look to Sherpas in order to complete themselves. I explain this in relation to Bhabha's analysis below.

Sherpas were also made "virtual." By virtual, I mean several things, again, I believe, in a departure from Bhabha. In Middle English, "virtual" meant "possessed of certain physical virtues,"[23] and this definition certainly applies to the image of Sherpas held by the West. In this text, I am interested in all sorts of virtues attributed to Sherpas by the West and by themselves, including those identified in Buddhism and shamanism as articulated through Westerners; Sherpas are attractive because of certain perceived skills that Westerners admire and wish they possessed, whether physical, spiritual, or social. But "virtual" also suggests some degree of being unreal, in a simulated sense—emergent from an interplay of imaginations or technologies, or creative representations. For example, a virtual image can be defined as an image that seems to be real but is not. Technically, it is the image that can be seen in a plane mirror of a "point from which divergent rays (as of light) seem to emanate but do not actually do so," because the rays, like the point seen in the mirror, are reflections.[24] Like the rays of light that seem to emanate from the point that is not "really" there in the mirror, certain qualities of being, certain essential Sherpa characteristics, are deemed to emanate from the virtual Sherpa, the "nonexistent" point. But in the case of Sherpas, it is not that those qualities cannot be found to exist, outside the mirror behind the viewer, but that the viewer accepts their distillation in a mirrored image, and the virtual image from which they radiate, as the only "reality." So, whereas the "real" for Bhabha in the case of colonial mimicry is always the Westerner whom the colonized can only approximate by being virtual, virtual Sherpas have no original in the West, only in that which was produced in the relationship between Westerners' desires and Sherpas' desires to meet them. Virtual Sherpas are not seen, in this sense, as "almost real but not quite"; rather, virtual Sherpas are taken to be more "real" than reality itself. Those images become the simulations to which Sherpas in contact with Westerners strive to live up. The residual category of "reality" left over in conventional configurations of "virtual" is one that I suggest needs to be rethought. In this book, a virtual reality is not juxtaposed to reality proper; rather, a virtual reality persistently interrupts our versions of reality by imposing on us an awareness of who, and what desire, creates that reality as *more* (or less) real.

The idea of virtual Sherpas also poses alternative ways of configuring ethnographic subjects, for the concept of "virtual" is an attempt to collapse the difference and distance between "Otherness," identifiable as "real" cultural differences, and the producers of such Otherness, whose desires for authentic difference create the Others we take to be "real." The notion of a virtual identity is one that, by definition, always leads back to the producers of Otherness, without undermining the idea that cultural differences (or sameness) are in some sense "real." At the same time, "virtual" takes on more meanings by the end of the book—meanings that emerge from the mimetic displays arising from lay conceptions of Buddhism that make the differences between the self and those beings outside it illusory, and from experiences revealed through shamanism of "becoming" Others, whether spirits or Westerners. A virtual world is one in which the boundary between the real and the "not real," just like the boundary between the actual Other and the Western construction of the Other, is momentarily lost.

The absence of a colonizer among Sherpas in Nepal has not eliminated regimes of mimesis from either development or tourist capitalism. Mimesis is made possible through the production of desires for an Other who can be subjugated and admired for being both almost like (an approximation of), yet totally different from, the Westerner. This process is clearly at work among Sherpas. The discourse of difference enunciates the inferiority of the Sherpa, like that of the colonized, but it also articulates the desire of the Westerner/colonizer in love with those deemed "noble" by him or her. In this, Sherpas were and are also "noble" and therefore capable of being both servile and admired—in fact, loved. In the process, Sherpas engage both in mimesis and, to a lesser extent, in something similar to, but different from, the mimicry Bhabha sees in colonialism. In the act of becoming Other, the Sherpas did not and do not have an original, as the mimic does (in the colonizer); rather, they have the image of the Sherpa created by Westerners in their accounts of life among the Sherpas. This goes far beyond mimicry and works differently, as mimesis, for mimicry is about copying, whereas mimesis is about ontological becoming via the representation.

Finally, Sherpas engage in something quite different from the mockery Bhabha sees in colonialism. The mere presence of the subjugated mocks the colonial regime because the subjugated can never be complete in the terms defined by the colonizer. I contend that, in place of such mockery among Sherpas, one finds instead a type of seduction. Mockery ridicules the colonizer and hopes to eliminate him or her, but seduction enfolds the Westerner and the Sherpas he or she meets—in a desire not to eliminate those who construct these discourses, but rather to keep them around. Whereas "difference" in colonialism sparks hypocrisy and inhumanity and strives to drive away the colonizer and his or her discourse through which power circulates, "difference" in late modernity strives to preserve the discourse of "Othering" through which power circulates. This power is not necessarily repressive even if it works in violent ways; it is, following Foucault (1973, 1979, 1980), productive.[25] Mimesis among Sherpas is not about repression but rather about production of the self as a way of being—about the move beyond subjectivity to ontology, even if its effects can produce death.[26] Cultural representations of difference and sameness are the crux of ongoing development aid and tourism, both of which are desired by Sherpas and Westerners and both of which are the regimes that "discipline" them. The representation of cultural difference and sameness among Sherpas thus becomes highly charged with problems of authenticity and authorship, since these are the discursive objects through which mimesis with images of "Otherness" becomes saturated with power.

VIRTUAL AUTHENTICITY: AN ETHNOGRAPHY OF HIMALAYAN ENCOUNTERS

I explore authenticity as a general problem that has been received by Himalayanists in particular ways at the end of chapter 1. Here, I only suggest that I would move beyond the conventional configurations of "authenticity" that one finds in much of the literature on both tourism and Himalayan peoples, precisely because they so often cast people as "impression managers" who are thought to be engaging in borderline deceit, deluding gullible Others who do not know any better. (This is not to say that no Sherpas engage in deceit, for surely there are some who do.) But this approach posits that only behind the backs of Westerners (especially Westerners who are potential benefactors)—"backstage"—do the Sherpas' "true" behaviors and identities emerge. Here, that which is produced for Western Others is thought somehow to "belong" to those Westerners, to be somehow directed by them, and to be a forgery and modification of Sherpas' private intentions. (How could this be a site of inauthenticity, I ask, when finally we see Westerners are produced by Sherpa seductions?) For me, the relationships Sherpas have had with Westerners have had a much more profound effect on their subjectivity than impression management recognizes in its reduction of Sherpas to performers interested only in external display for Others. I hardly think it would be fair (and in fact think it would be offensive) to say that Pasang Lhamu died on Everest simply because of a "staged" performance aimed at impressing Westerners. To see her behavior that way is to deny the Sherpas' modernity any sort of legitimacy, and to leave unanswered important questions of power and the role of representations in it. My goal is to show that her desire to climb Everest was as Sherpa as all of the behaviors described in the chapters on Buddhism and shamanism (which many take to be the locations of a pre-Western, and therefore uncorrupted or more pure, Sherpa), and hence no less authentic than any other way of being Sherpa. But to deny the presence of Westerners in *any* of these behaviors is, I feel, to engage in a more dangerous form of denial, one that ignores the important role played by those who would represent Sherpas for public consumption and to whom Sherpas have aspired.

There are many ways of being virtually Sherpa, and all of these ways are invested with the presence of Westerners and the West today. What does this accomplish in terms of method? Does this move us beyond the persistent demand to see Westerners as producers of "difference" and "sameness," or does it simply reiterate precisely that demand? Although I suggest in chapters 2 through 5 that Sherpas bring to their engagement with the West something "different" from that which the West offers (e.g., that revealed in Buddhism or shamanism), I attempt to avoid a move toward reessentializing their Otherness or recreating for readers a more "authentic" Sherpa in contrast to that which is a result of Western involvement (or the desires of the ethnographer). These other ways of being Sherpa are simply not the same thing that the West offers, but they are still influenced by Western interests. I suggest that one cannot presuppose an essential identity for Sherpas (historically prior to and somehow outside the demands of the West today) because the West, including anthropology, is inextricably bound up with those differences; again, those resulting ways of being Sherpa are no more or less authentic than any other. One alternative, then, might be persistently to make it clear where the "differences" that are illustrated here arise from, thus persistently drawing our attention to both Sherpas *and* Westerners.

The discourse that demands authenticity suggests the attribution of culture to either Sherpas or Westerners, but not both. Pasang Lhamu's husband told me that she climbed Everest because "she wanted to." How easy it would be to presume that his comment evidences a false consciousness—a consciousness unable to see the "truth" about the Sherpas' exploitation by the West. How easy it would be to presume that his comment was simply staged in response to what a Westerner would want to hear about Sherpas—a comment that masks another falsehood (that Sherpas really do not like to climb and do it only for the money). To probe for deeper meanings of Pasang Lhamu's Everest achievement is to posit that her husband's belief that she did it because "she wanted to" is somehow a site for inauthenticity, and that only persistent hunting for the truth beyond the surface appearance will provide us with an accurate rendition of Sherpa life. How hard it would be to do justice to that statement as meaning just what it says. But this is what Sherpas say; this is how I must bring their voices into my text. Doing so forces a recognition that Pasang's desire as stated by her husband is also constructed by my design. The same is true for Sherpas who present themselves to the West as Buddhists or Himalayan villagers more in touch with an intimate way of life than we can experience in the West. Their presentation of self is as authentic as we will find; there is no more "authentic" Sherpa beyond these versions, despite the presence of Western interests in at least partially scripting these versions of "Sherpaness," for the closer one thinks one gets to such a site of authenticity, the more Sherpa culture reveals processes described here as mimesis and seduction. Recognizing "virtual" Sherpas is an approach that aims to move beyond the discourse in which culture is owned by one group or another, and to move beyond a theory emerging only from the West. We need a virtual theory, or a theory of the virtual, that contaminates conventional ways of dealing with sameness and difference. In this book, I look to Sherpas' Buddhism and shamanism, and to the presence of Western interests therein, in order to make sense of the virtual.

The Sherpa identities described herein should be seen as dynamic constructions, always resonating between the constructions emerging directly from their iconic presence in the West and those emerging from other institutions, such as Buddhism and the local practices of reciprocity found in shamanism with which Westerners have been involved, each of which offers its own notions of mimesis and seduction. Why do I focus on these institutions? Whereas ethnographers studying historical and cultural convergences among other Himalayan ethnic groups living in the border regions between Buddhist Tibet and Hindu Nepal (yet within the geopolitical domain of Nepal) turn immediately to the processes of "Sanskritization," "Hinduization," and "Nepalization" that have been at work for the last two and a half centuries,[27] ethnographers of Sherpas and other Western observers have consistently turned to the practices of economy, polity, and religion that emanate from the Tibetan cultural area, practices that at one time formed the foundation of a Tibetan state.[28] Of all these, the Tibetan religious practices of Buddhism and shamanism have become the most visible to the West and important to the Sherpas over the past century as Sherpas have faced a potent set of demands from the West. Here again, one might speak of a Western gaze upon Sherpas that does not simply see, but also produces that which it wants to see. In this case, it has always seen Tibetan Buddhism and shamanism as institutions that influence Sherpa identity more heavily than Hindu and Nepalese state institutions.[29] This is another way in which the West and its interests, not only in the Himalayas but also in Tibet, in Buddhism, and in Tibetan forms of shamanism, have actually come to be more important influences on Sherpas than the Nepalese state or its demands for Hindu practices. Thus, instead of focusing on Nepalese institutions of state or nation, I focus on Buddhist institutions and local practices of Tibetan shamanism with the hope that readers will not fall into the trap of adopting a tourist-eye-view of Nepal that imagines Sherpas as the majority in the country, and the Solu-Khumbu region as the center of Nepal's national life. Rather, I hope readers will recognize that although Sherpas are a minority ethnic group in the ethnically plural nation-state of Nepal, which has a population of more than fifteen million, and although the Solu-Khumbu is one of seventy-five districts in that nation-state, this ethnography is not about Nepal. It is about Sherpas and the West, particularly the virtual Sherpas "created" under the gaze of Western visitors striving to become Sherpa, and the mimetic acts between them. Again, we end up in a cultural Möbius strip constructed between Sherpas and Western Others that already identifies which aspects of Sherpa lives will be treated as worthy of study because they have become more visible than others over the years of encounters with Westerners.

This is also not a "traditional" ethnography of Sherpas because my focus is not on Sherpas but on their relationships to people like me who choose to write about and "represent" them. Readers will not find lengthy descriptions of all aspects of Sherpa lives—their polity, economy, material culture, kinship systems, agricultural cycles, or the "imponderabilia of daily life"—in this book. I direct readers looking for those sorts of facts to the numerous ethnographies already written by anthropologists in the past thirty years, along with numerous journalistic and travel accounts that have offered ethnographic information as the unproblematic "truth" about Sherpas. I have not presented an ethnography that offers more-accurate "truths" about the Sherpas than these accounts. This ethnography is about the whole problem of locating "truths" in a world where truth is made impermanent by seduction—a seduction through which Sherpas become visible to Westerners and through which Westerners come to know themselves through Sherpas. I have chosen to write an ethnography of encounters rather than an ethnography of Sherpas because I want to highlight the way in which seductive representations of Sherpas (like those ethnographies before mine) have become mixed up with Sherpa identities today. I want to highlight the way in which Sherpas and Westerners seduce each other, intertextually and extratextually, making my method a sort of ethnographic mimesis with my experiences of Sherpas—a creative imitation of real life, inevitably making it more real than reality itself. Virtual identities by definition always refer to the fact of their production. In this sense, I undertake that which de Certeau offers as an insight about Foucault: "[Sherpa] procedures are not merely the objects of a theory. They organize the very construction of theory itself. Far from being external to theory, or from staying on its doorstep, [Sherpa] procedures provide *a field of operations within which theory itself is produced*."[30] Virtual Sherpas inhabit Shangri-la, insofar as such a place can exist anywhere that qualities that we deem to define a "Shangri-la" actually exist, and insofar as it is always in some sense a product of our imagination. By the end of the book, readers may find this perspective itself peculiarly "Sherpa," because it reflects fundamental approaches to reality found in Sherpa modernity and Buddhism, or because it idiomatically expresses the impermanence upon which sha-manism remarks.

As an anthropologist, but more importantly as a Westerner, I am not immune to the seductions of both Sherpas and other Westerners in our transnational interactions. My representations of Sherpas are necessarily synecdochic—my individual relationships with Sherpas on which these ob-servations are based are a part that in some ways describes the whole set of relationships Sherpas have with Westerners. In this sense, I treat anthro-pology as the Sherpas I know would treat it, as part of the apparatus of modernization emergent in their lives, even though it is clear that anthro-pologists have often focused on and participated in other aspects of Sherpa lives than tourists, or mountaineers, or charitable development workers have. But I have found it impossible to extricate myself as an observer, a chronicler, and a friend of Sherpas from the history of Western anthropo-logical involvements with Sherpas, wherein these others were also observ-ers, chroniclers, and friends, whether tourists, mountaineers, development agents, or anthropologists. My very presence in the Khumbu was config-ured by the relationships that that history brought into existence and by the effects of the representations of Sherpas made by other people. Sherpas are a moving target whose course is attuned to Western interests in their culture and their persons; anthropological accounts have found their way into Sherpa lives. It is not merely that what I can write is conditioned by my relationships with those Sherpas I came to know—a, by now, banal insight. It is also that those relationships we have are referenced in the history of Sherpa involvement with Westerners as a whole through mod-ernization, and through searches for experiences of the self via the Other. My effort to locate an authentic Sherpa or Sherpa culture in existence be-tween the years 1982 and 1993 leads me to conclude that Sherpa culture is at least in this sense a process of engagement with others like myself, with Westerners. In some important ways, then, my work among Sherpas was not unlike the work of other Westerners, anthropologists or not, for all of our presences have had a role in making Sherpa culture what it is today because of our positions as Westerners among them.

The persistent desire among anthropologists to distinguish themselves from development workers (though not all of them), and especially tour-ists, breaks down—in the first case because the anthropological impact (via representations) is not distinguished from the developmental impact on Sherpas, and in the second case because tourism and anthropology both come to Sherpa country, according to Sherpas, in pursuit of the same things. Anthropologists have typically made a point of avoiding interfering with the lives of those they study (and rather claim to be interested in preserving them), but they often fail in this when their representations (as ethnographies) actually find their way back into the lives of those people in dramatic ways. Here Sherpas make explicit the insights anthropologists have at some times failed to recognize. In the second instance, anthropological claims to being engaged in something different from tourism are also challenged by Sherpas, to whom the desires for "Otherness" among both anthropologists and tourists have always been rather indistinguishable. The fall of these demarcations enables me to take more seriously the idea that a study of Sherpa culture and identity entails at the same time a study of the presence of the Western interests, culture, and identity among them.

The second insight gleaned from Sherpas and Westerners occupying the same cultural terrain typically called "Sherpa" is that, rather than seeing Sherpa culture as a set of fixed traits that we could think of as existing regardless of who was watching or recording them, I have found it more productive to capture this relational aspect of culture by noting that Sherpa culture is in constant conversation with Western interests. Above all, those Western interests have been defined by concerns with authenticity, in part as a result of a history of ethnographic attempts to locate and describe Sherpas for Western readers, and in part because it is precisely with Westerners that the issue of authenticity becomes important for Sherpas, who, sensitive to the desires of those who visit them, recognize the need to be(come) ever more authentic. The history of anthropological involvement with Sherpas is in part a history of attempts to locate authentic Sherpas; in turn it is also a history of anthropological attempts to locate an authentic anthropology.

Anthropologists Representing Sherpas

"Between Peace Corps workers, development specialists, and anthropologists, you foreigners know more about us than we know about ourselves," Ang Tshiring Sherpa said to me, after learning that seven groups of Westerners had been studying Sherpas during 1986–87. Ang Tshiring himself was an acute observer of Westerners, conducting business with hundreds of them each year through his trekking agency in Kathmandu. His comments pointed to another aspect of my relationship to Sherpas. Although anthropology does not always focus on intervention, it is often caught up in the mechanisms of surveillance used by Westerners to study those it constitutes as "different" (Escobar 1988). The anthropology of Sherpas is thus frequently about a way of knowing Sherpas, and like tourists, journalists, and expeditioners, anthropologists have created a Sherpa familiar enough to be known, yet different enough to be worth studying.

Edmund Hillary once said that "the Sherpas have so many characteristics that we, as Westerners, like to think we have: They are tough, courteous, tolerant, cheerful."[31] This statement is about Westerners seeing in

Sherpas qualities they admire in themselves; it is also about their attribution to Sherpas of "virtual" characteristics that may or may not ever have existed. Anthropologists have also participated in this swift double imaging of Sherpas by simultaneously seeing what exists and creating what does not because it is desirable. And Sherpas have engaged in mimesis with anthropological imaging as well. Here, I note that the anthropological discourse surrounding Sherpas has centered on knowing Sherpas and, inevitably, on finding a way of knowing the anthropological self.

Like other groups, the Sherpas have frequently served as a convenient mouthpiece for "speaking" anthropological theory. Unlike other groups, however, who have become a site for the localization of specific theories (Appadurai 1986), Sherpas have become a site for many different theories. In some ways, a history of anthropology of the Sherpas follows a discursive genealogy of anthropology itself; Sherpas become something of a mirror of production for ethnography. Christof von Furer-Haimendorf, for example, produced a lengthy ethnography on Khumbu Sherpas in 1964 called *The Sherpas of Nepal: Buddhist Highlanders.* In the tradition of most British social anthropologists of his era, he seems to have had two aims. First, he was interested in documenting a Himalayan peasant life that he thought might well disappear with the changes promised by involvement in a global economy. On this front, Furer-Haimendorf was far-reaching, providing volumes of information about many Himalayan groups. The debate over authenticity begins with him insofar as, despite complaints about the accuracy of some of his information, he has served other anthropologists' interests well, particularly those looking to provide historically situated observations from which to argue for linear views of social change, or those looking to provide correctives to his versions of Sherpa culture.

Second, Furer-Haimendorf looked to the Sherpas to demonstrate the utility of a structural-functionalist approach in ethnography. From him, we get a picture of hardy Himalayan traders practicing transhumant agriculture, people whose religion, politics, beliefs in the supernatural, marriage practices, and attitudes about community organization formed a complex and integrated, bounded whole—a functionalist whole where everything, even spontaneous nonsense, had a socially stabilizing purpose. Like British mountaineers, Furer-Haimendorf reproduced Sherpas as "Hail! Well met!" sorts, worthy of praise and admiration for being able to survive in a harsh climate where the annual growing season was only three months long. His functionalist interests in Sherpa strategies for economic survival were also the focus of his second book, and the questions posed therein about survival at high altitudes have continued to inform research on Sherpas from the standpoints of both geography and human biology.[32]

Anthropologists from continental Europe who wrote about Sherpas argued against the British penchant for Radcliffe-Brownian interpretive methods by focusing on the Sherpas' literary history. Michael Oppitz and Alexander Macdonald, for example, both situated Sherpas squarely within the Tibetan cultural and historical domain. Their works (especially Oppitz 1973) challenged the idea that the Sherpas could be understood as an isolated, functionally integrated group, contending that the Sherpas' own literary history provided a much richer explanation of social institutions and change than a sociological theory of functional relationships could provide. That history revealed structural transformations within social institutions that were neither explained by nor observed in an ethnographic focus on the nonliterate culture in a slice of life called the "ethnographic present." Above all, these authors' works provided an important correction to the existing view of a nonliterate, peasant Sherpa culture. However, this correction tended toward the construction of a "real" version of Sherpa history, meaning one located in reliable, literary sources believed to provide more-accurate "truths" about Sherpa society than those hitherto produced by an anthropology focused on the nonliterate public.[33] That "real" (and by this I also mean "authentic") Sherpa was the Sherpa comprehended via Buddhist texts written in Tibetan script.

In any case, such use of the Sherpas' own literature do not figure prominently in subsequent ethnographies about Sherpas by well-known anthropologists from the United States. Both Robert Paul, in *The Tibetan Symbolic World: Psychoanalytic Explorations* (1982) and articles (1976a, 1976b, 1979), and Sherry Ortner, in *Sherpas through Their Rituals* (1978b) and articles (1978a, 1978c), offer ethnographies of Sherpas in which anthropological discourse takes center stage. Critics of their books have noted that Western intellectual metanarratives are substituted therein for the literary sources of the region. For Paul, the Tibetan Sherpa psyche is obtainable via Tibetan literary sources but is best parsed by Freudian theory rather than by the complex theories about consciousness available in Buddhist literature, even if he relies on Buddhist texts for data on Sherpa rituals. In Ortner's book, Sherpa secular and sacred rituals are analyzed vis-à-vis Western social theory, which can be traced genealogically from Durkheim and Marx to Turner and Geertz, bypassing the literary interpretive sources available among Sherpa or Tibetan Buddhist scholars themselves.

Ortner's second book, *High Religion* (1989), again offers a highly theorized account of Sherpa history. Following Pierre Bourdieu (1977), she weaves a fascinating ethnography of the history of the founding of monasteries in the Solu and Khumbu regions to show how culture is practice. This is demonstrated through case materials documenting parallels between myth and practices—stories about, and a record of actual occurrences of, actual conflicts between brothers and their resolution through support from external parties, including deities and even the Nepalese Rana state. In each case, conflict resolution resulted in the founding of a monastery. This insightful historical account of a Sherpa *habitus*, which explains the role of external sponsors in Sherpa business and cultural negotiations, deals with many of the issues examined in my analysis here (and I think many will find a resonance),[34] except that I focus on relationships with Westerners as opposed to relationships with deities or the Nepalese state. Ortner devoted a small amount of discussion to the ways in which "Sherpa-ness" as viewed by outsiders was played out in Sherpas' internal relations; I have devoted a whole book to them. Still, though Ortner's second book does draw on the works of European scholars who themselves relied on literary Sherpa sources, her own text offers little in the way of Buddhist conceptual insight into the processes of monastery founding itself, such as the role of the sponsor in liturgy, or the written discussions of such things as merit (*payin* or *sonam*), which are bound up with Buddhist views of monasteries.

In both Ortner's and Paul's texts, there is a tension between the use of theory to elucidate the Sherpa material and the use of Sherpas to elucidate difficult theory and demonstrate its utility. I view their lack of emphasis on Buddhist literary sources and interpretations, perceived by some as particularly Ortner's greatest weakness,[35] not as an omission or a failure but as an attempt to understand Sherpas from lay perspectives or as lay consciousness. It is just as problematic to assume that literary Buddhist sources offer the only truths about the Sherpa psyche or Sherpa society as it is to ignore them entirely. Richard Kohn (1988), for example, translated the entire Mani Rimdu textual ceremony (the same ceremony used by Paul and Ortner in a number of their studies), contributing greatly to the literature on Buddhism from the Sherpa region. However, few Sherpas are as well informed about the ceremony as Kohn is. In fact, much of the ceremony he translates is never seen or heard by lay Sherpas since it takes place within the monastery, from which the public is excluded, and most Sherpas cannot read Tibetan.[36]

The question of authenticity is not addressed by Ortner or Paul, but is implicit in their approaches, however different their approaches are. Authenticity for Ortner in particular seems implicitly not to be about the use or nonuse of literary materials, since she begins with the assumption that authenticity of "lay Sherpas" is not found in texts accessible only to elites anyway. Rather, Paul's and Ortner's implicit assumptions about authenticity are displaced onto the problem of method: what method will elucidate more clearly the truth about Sherpas? It is not "which Sherpa texts" that is being asked, but "which Western texts"? And both find answers in different literatures. But the question of to what degree the literary sources serve as guides to what is desired of an "authentic" Sherpa still needs to be explored, for if it is overlooked almost entirely one would never know what local meanings were also being erased. Even when literature about Buddhism is used, the question of being able to interpret these materials by using Western theory resurfaces. My own approach to the issue of literary sources has resulted in an ethnography that recognizes a great dependence on scholars (both Western and Tibetan) of Tibetan Buddhism who have devoted themselves to translating and interpreting Buddhist texts, many of which are useful in studying Sherpas, just as Sherpas are dependent on such persons. But my approach remains thoroughly situated in lay perspectives that use textual insights in ways that are often inconsistent with textual truths. I try to show both how literary and esoteric knowledge informs Sherpa lay perspectives and the degree to which it does not, as an issue of authenticity. In the works of Ortner and Paul, as in my own, one does find Sherpas who are constituted in obvious ways by their relationships with Buddhism, but not overdetermined by the esoteric literary views of Buddhism itself. But unlike Paul and Ortner, I have tried to inform my ethnographic method with a perspective derived from lay Buddhist views. Virtual Sherpas are, in this sense, not simply the product of mimesis as we (Westerners) know it, for Sherpas' mimesis is also about ways of being Buddhist as Sherpas teach us about it, and these are known textually.

That Sherpas are aware of Westerners' desires for more-authentic versions of Buddhism in Sherpas, and that they engage with these desires through mimesis, is discussed below. Because the Sherpa engagement with Westerners is a focus of my text, I approach the question of "which Western texts" somewhat differently than do Ortner and Paul (and others). I suggest that because this ethnography is also about Westerners, it is important to engage Western texts that elucidate something about Western processes of engagement with the Other. Thus, I have turned to texts on mimesis and, later, to critiques of modernity and the problems of objectification. But just as I suggest that it is hard to talk about Sherpas without talking about Westerners, I find that it is hard to talk about Western theory without setting it into critical conversation with its practice among Sherpas. That is, just as Western representations find their way into Sherpa lives via mimesis, so too does Western theory travel to new sites where it takes on new meanings via Sherpas. Mimesis begins to look quite Buddhist, and objectification becomes the problem that Sherpas and Westerners try to overcome by becoming involved in transcendent relationships with one another.

It is surprising that although Khumbu Sherpas have been regularly involved with Westerners and other foreigners for almost a century, and intensively so for more than thirty years, these relationships have rarely formed the primary basis for anthropological analyses of Sherpa social life. Only in the past several years have any ethnographies covered Sherpas and their involvement with Westerners inside Nepal. Furer-Haimendorf produced a third book on Sherpas in 1984, *The Sherpas Transformed*, based on a brief period of fieldwork in the Khumbu. He notes therein that the distinctive qualities that made Sherpas so intriguing and admirable to him thirty years earlier seemed to be disappearing in the 1980s. Rather than seeing Sherpas as modern participants engaged in the transnational economies of the world in ways involving much of the same work Sherpas did even prior to the 1950s, he laments their loss of distinctiveness; he is romantically nostalgic for an era in which Sherpas seemed to be captured succinctly and timelessly. He was compelled to write in 1984, for example, that

> anthropologists are supposed to give impartial accounts of the people they study, uninfluenced by the values of their own society and their personal likes and dislikes. I am conscious, however, that it is difficult to follow this rule when re-studying a people one has learnt to love and admire. During my early fieldwork among Sherpas [1953] I had succumbed to their charm and had come to regard their society as one of the most harmonious I had ever known. I admired their gaiety and friendliness, their tolerance and kindness towards each other, and the piety which urged them to divert large parts of their scarce resources to the establishment and maintenance of religious institutions, and the creation of architectural monuments which not only served their spiritual needs but also added to the attraction of a scenery of unparalleled magnificence. In writing about the present situation in Khumbu, I cannot veil the feeling of disappointment and sadness to see this seemingly ideal society and life-style transformed by the impact of outside forces which disrupted the delicately balanced social fabric and undermined the traditional ideology that had dominated Sherpa thinking and conduct for countless generations. Happiness is a phenomenon difficult to measure, but my subjective impression is that the Sherpas I knew in the 1950s were happier than they and their descendants are in the 1980s.[37]

Still employing an implicit functionalism, Furer-Haimendorf suggests that with the changes brought by tourism to Sherpa lives, their culture has all but disappeared, and foresees their society's imminent collapse. He views the increasing number of intermarriages between Sherpas and Westerners, for example, as one example of the breakdown of Sherpa society and the demise of their culture. Furer-Haimendorf's books and the ways in which they have been received by Sherpas (some negatively) further sparked my interest in the Sherpas' own involvement in an intertextual production of their identities.

Fire of Himal, the first ethnography of Sherpas written by a Nepalese scholar, Ramesh Kunwor, appeared in 1987. Surprisingly, even though much of his material was derived from his work as a liaison officer for mountaineering expeditions to Everest, Kunwor did not make this the focus of his interpretation of Sherpa culture. Rather, his book is informed by a functionalism-oriented set of questions about the Nature-Man-Spirit complex and a distinction between Redfieldian "great" and "little" traditions. In many ways, the book itself reflects the image that many high-caste Hindu Nepalese hold of the Sherpas as quaint mountain folk whose relationships to nature and to spirits, though complex, are easily understood. Kunwor's book is another example of the yearning for cultural difference found in Furer-Haimendorf's work. Implicit in his work is a nostalgia consistent with broader Nepalese interests in promoting a sense of cultural distinctiveness for the tourist market, where exoticism is highly valued. That Sherpas distribute his book from their trekking offices in downtown Kathmandu indicates a mimesis with representations emergent from interactions with Nepalese, but I do not focus on that particular set of relationships in this ethnography.

Finally, James Fisher presented an ethnography of Sherpas in 1990 that went a long way toward situating Sherpas in a contemporary transnational setting. He used data from a journal he kept while on one of the Hillary "School House Expeditions" in the 1960s, and contrasted these with fieldwork he conducted over short visits with Sherpas from 1974 through 1988. His book relocates the discourse of anthropology of Sherpas considerably, by showing how reflexive the ethnographic process always is (even if it is not disclosed) and by showing how Sherpas actually engage with a variety of modernizing influences, particularly those of a Western-style education, in the contemporary setting. Fisher is reluctant to pass judgment on either the loss of a distinctive culture or the benefits of Sherpa participation in modernization. But Fisher does not go far enough in recognizing the complexity of the relationships between Westerners and Sherpas, in which Sherpas become intertextual, via mimesis, with Western representations. In fact he does not question that relationship at all; he treats the Western impact on Sherpas as a rather "straight" story of modernization, in which Sherpas adopt our values and leave behind their old ones, or in which they hang onto their old values and practices, setting them alongside new Western and modern ones. Much is left out of his account of the significance of the presence of the West in Sherpa lives in ways that muddle the idea of difference between Western and Sherpa culture, and that make even the desire to see an "uncorrupted" practice of "traditions" a reflection of the presence of Westerners.

So, why do we need yet another book about Sherpas? This book is not directed at refuting or confirming other ethnographies—that is, I do not say that other representations of Sherpas are true or false. I want to show that the whole notion of the Sherpas, hitherto taken for granted in most ethnographies, is troublesome. This becomes particularly apparent when one looks at whose interests are being served by various representations, and at the outcomes of representations of Sherpas among Sherpas themselves. This book is thus an intervention that hopes to shed light on both how I, as an ethnographer and a Westerner, am never really able to be absent from the persons that I write about in the text, even at the level of the presentation of Sherpas' difference. More importantly, it is an intervention that attempts to show how a Sherpa might be always present in— always in critical engagement with—my attempts to write an ethnography, wherein my notions of authenticity and "truth" about Sherpas are persistently moving toward the virtual space between us.

In this account, I draw from my experiences with Sherpas beginning in 1982, when I lived in Khum Jung village for five months. I returned for thirteen months of doctoral work among Sherpas from the Khumbu during 1986 and 1987, dividing my time between the Khumbu and Kathmandu, where increasing numbers of Khumbu Sherpas were moving for part of the year or permanently. I returned again to Nepal in 1989 and 1993 for shorter visits focused on other projects and, because I was drawn back into Sherpa events and affairs, draw from those experiences as well. My collection of Western representations of Sherpas in diverse locations (travel accounts, magazines, newspapers, commercial products, and so forth) also dates back to the early 1980s and has been greatly aided by friends and relatives who clipped and cut anything they found with the name "Sherpa."

My interest in representations and their effects stems from a more general interest in questions about intertextuality in the social sciences, particularly its call for a more reflexive, more historical stance on the part of anthropologists.[38] This stance has promoted a heightened sensitivity to how discursive representations become worthy of study in their own right.[39] As Gupta and Ferguson (1992) point out, the more one tries to locate an essential version of identity, the more one's gaze must shift to those who produce the Other as an essential creation. Anthropologists in particular cannot exempt themselves from this mandate, even though it renders the challenge of producing representations almost paralyzing. I deal with this problem in my text by showing that representations of Sherpas are the outcome of two processes: conversations and experiences I have had with Sherpas, and the inevitability that those conversations and experiences were already constructed by the mutual gazes of Westerners and Sherpas in existence long before I arrived on the scene. My scrutiny is deliberately turned toward those relationships, not away from them. Again, to avoid at least that degree of reflexivity would be to make myself transparent as the producer of those "truths" through which power circulates. But the problem with an approach that shifts the authorship of identity to the ethnographer in this way is that it runs the risk of denying the subjectivity and the agency of those actual Others who are constructed.

Accordingly, an account of representations of Others can easily fail to recognize the engagement those Others have with these representations.[40] Thus, a major focus of my book is the responses of Sherpas to these representations and how they lead to virtual identities.

A word can also be offered about my use of the term *transnationalism* in this text. I owe an intellectual debt to the authors of a volume of the journal *Theory, Culture, and Society*, who, in publishing the proceedings of their "Globalization and Localization" conference, helped me appreciate Appadurai's attempts to reconceptualize the cross-regional, cross-cultural, cross-economic, and cross-political movements of people and cultures today in terms of transnational flows instead of globalization-localization terms. The utility of the terms *global* and *globalization* is that they denote those trends in the world that are universalizing, while the terms *local* and *localization* denote the geographical specificity of these globalizing effects. The problem with these terms, however, is that they lend themselves easily to Western ethnocentrism.[41] When does the local become the global and vice versa? Is Tibetan Buddhism globalizing, or is it, as the qualifier "Tibetan" connotes, a local phenomenon? Certainly, the Sherpa monks I knew who traveled to the West to teach Buddhism believed the former. Nevertheless, Buddhism is treated as local, or regional, in most Western ethnographies, while capitalism and Western rationality are viewed as the only globalizing apparatuses. *Transnationalism* is a term that promotes a focus on a politics of identity played out through cultural practices, and one that recognizes the difficulty of claiming that any of these processes is "global" or "local."

ORGANIZATION OF THE TEXT

I have organized this book so that an exploration of representational media about Sherpas comes first, and an analysis of the mechanisms at work in creating virtual Sherpas comes second. The first chapter explores some of the many virtual identities of Sherpas found in representations largely produced in the West. Here, I am interested in the qualities and characteristics of so-called typical Sherpas created in the Western imagination via experiences Westerners have had with actual Sherpas. Specifically, Sherpas are seen as stoic and hardy mountain guides, pious and superspiritual Buddhists, and, finally, villagers through whom Westerners believe they can experience a sense of social "embeddedness," a "reenchantment"[42] via the Other that they believe has been lost in the West. I also briefly demonstrate how Sherpas mimetically engage the many images of themselves found in popular cultural resources, which I explore at greater length throughout the rest of this book.

The first chapter is mainly concerned with the nature of the images produced; the second, third, and fourth chapters address the mechanisms that make the internalizations of these images visible. The processes of mimesis and seduction do not operate solely within the contexts of tourism, medicine, Buddhism, or shamanism, as discrete arenas of cultural practice, but are located throughout these somewhat disparate areas of Sherpa life. The second chapter focuses on the first two of these, on the creation of virtual Sherpas through mountaineering and in the medical programs offered by Westerners. I am interested in the mechanisms at work in this construction of a Sherpa identity enabling Sherpas to become everything Westerners desire of them. Sherpas could become modern only by retaining, with some modifications, the qualities of "traditional" life that made them appealing. Exploring this issue, however, leads one to the realization that the mechanisms at work in relationships between foreigners and Sherpas do not all originate in those encounters. If the imperative to modernize means remaining traditional, then the imperatives already in place *within* these traditions must be addressed as well.

In the third chapter, I explore Buddhist institutions involved in constructing Sherpa identities, Buddhist institutions that are themselves in full conversation with Western interests. Analyzing the mechanisms of creating virtual Sherpas at work in Buddhism means examining how Buddhism itself can become a site for authenticity when juxtaposed to the modernity of Sherpas' mimesis with Westerners. Buddhism is configured within Western discourses in ways that affect its meaning for Sherpas. Consequently, I look at the type of Sherpa created through an engagement with Buddhism, and how the presence of Westerners informs that relationship. Sherpas take on roles within their monasteries similar to those they hope foreigners will take on with them—they sponsor monasteries as *jindak* and hope to recruit foreigners to sponsor them (again, as *jindak*). The forms for being exemplary Buddhists reveal some, but not all, of the same principles underlying Sherpa relationships with Westerners. Becoming a pious Buddhist, however, means becoming more capable of recognizing the lack of a permanent or essential ego-bound self—in other words, it means recognizing the inability to identify a singular "authentic" site of subjectivity. This closely resembles the discourse about ideal identities I have deliberately adopted in this text.

An authentic Sherpa subject cannot be found in the "modern" Sherpa, and the idea of a singular "authentic" subjectivity becomes even more elusive when one reviews Buddhist versions of the ideal "Sherpa." In the fourth chapter, I consider another important potential repository for Sherpa authenticity. Westerners arrive looking for experiences of Otherness among Sherpas and, in that Otherness, a place where they hope to experience intimate social relationships of reciprocity and seduction.

Often they find this in shamanic practices, which they film, document, and participate in. Instead of locating an authentic Sherpa beneath various constructions, I find instead an unfixed dialogic Sherpa identity that is always changing with social relationships.[43] Shamanic episodes similarly challenge notions of a fixed and authentic subjectivity. Shamanism involves mimesis of that which the Others—in this case, spirits—desire, and this mimesis is always contingent on the social relationships that bring the need for shamans into existence. Mimesis at this level is quite like that found in the relationships Sherpas have with foreigners and their representations of Sherpas, because it, too, involves aspiring to ideal identities. Even at this most "traditional, exotic, and authentic" site, the Western gaze is found. The "shamanic tours" sold to Westerners not only become places of authenticity, they become places where techniques of seduction and mimesis actually enable one to see how virtual identities can be as real as any others. Chapter 4 also suggests that the desires for authenticity in ethnography are inextricably bound up with the processes of writing texts and the fixing of identities as abstract truths—truths that ultimately are commodifiable. The more desirable Sherpas become for their exotic difference as holders of secret, shamanic knowledge and as providers of "enchantment," the more virtual Sherpas actually become, but at the same time, and ironically, the more desirable this type of Sherpa becomes as a site for authenticity. Ethnographies cannot capture such authenticity because authenticity is always a product of the relationship between observer and observed—a consequence of the desire for the authenticity that always slips out of our grasp in transient relationships, which are never fixed for long over time or in space.

I look at Sherpa relationships with images in the fifth and final chapter by exploring the concept of an economy of meanings among Sherpas. This analysis requires a focus on the notions of labor and economy among Sherpas. I argue that the economy depends on the profitable use of images of Sherpas by both Sherpas and Others. Foreigners are brought into relationships of reciprocity with Sherpas through the same mechanisms of simulation and seduction that are used in shamanic events. The images used are those created in the Western imagination and those that are internalized aspects of many Sherpa subjects today. But, I suggest, this cannot be read simply as either the staged performance of Otherness or that which presupposes a "staged" identity present in the commodification of images of Sherpas or of "who Sherpas are supposed to be." Rather, it must be read as an invitation to rethink the notion of an economy in ways suggested by theorists who see (or have tried to see) culture as productive.[44] An economy of meanings rather than a capitalist commodification of images is operating. There, the idea of virtual Sherpas becomes a more tenable location for a mobile authenticity. It becomes clear that the economy is contingent both on shifting meanings and on the labor involved in perpetuating the social relationships through which variable meanings of Sherpas' identities are created and proliferate.

I conclude the book with a brief summary of the main issue raised by my analysis. This is an ethnography that hopes continually to interrupt attempts to frame the Sherpas as "different" or, conversely, as "the same" by using ourselves as the template for their modernity, while still recognizing our presence in them. I discuss the ethnographic production of cultural difference and the response of Sherpas to this endeavor. I offer a discussion of how an ethnographic transnationalism can offer opportunities to recognize notions of power and subjectivity that are potentially different than those traditionally employed by the ethnographer. At the same time, I acknowledge that all these notions of "difference" are inevitably repositioned within a Western ethnographic gaze; their existence is, in part, contingent on that gaze. This, I suggest, is one way to answer the question of why Pasang Lhamu wanted to climb Everest. It is a way of making meaningful her husband's claim that she did so because "she wanted to." The process of constructing cultural difference in order to grasp the identity of Sherpas like Pasang Lhamu is thus like trying to find the beginning or end—inside or outside—of a Möbius strip in a world where culture moves back and forth in ongoing social relationships between Sherpas like her and Others like me.

CHAPTER ONE

Sherpas in Mirrors

MIRRORS

> [Aside from utopias], there are also, probably in every culture,
> in every civilization, real places—places that do exist and that
> are formed in the very founding of society—which are some-
> thing like counter-sites, a kind of effectively enacted utopia in
> which the real sites, all the other real sites that can be found
> within the culture, are simultaneously represented, contested,
> and inverted. . . . I shall call them . . . heterotopias. . . . I believe
> that between utopias and these quite other sites, these hetero-
> topias, there might be a sort of mixed joint experience, which
> would be the mirror. The mirror is, after all, a utopia, since it is
> a placeless place. In the mirror, I see myself there where I am
> not, in an unreal, virtual space that opens up behind the surface;
> I am over there, there where I am not, a sort of shadow that
> gives my own visibility to myself, that enables me to see myself
> there where I am absent; such is the utopia of the mirror. But it
> is also a heterotopia insofar as the mirror does exist in reality,
> where it exerts a sort of counteraction on the position that I
> occupy. From the standpoint of the mirror I discover my ab-
> sence from the place where I am since I see myself over there.
> Starting from this gaze that is, as it were, directed toward me,
> from the ground of this virtual space that is on the other side of
> the glass, I come back toward myself; I begin again to direct my
> eyes toward myself and to reconstitute myself there where I
> am. The mirror functions as a heterotopia in this respect: it
> makes this place that I occupy at the moment when I look at
> myself in the glass at once absolutely real, connected with all
> the space that surrounds it, and absolutely unreal, since in order
> to be perceived it has to pass through this virtual point which is
> over there.
>   —Michel Foucault, "Of Other Spaces"

The process Foucault describes in looking at himself in a mirror is uncannily like that of Sherpa shamans who "see" their own spirit reflections in
ritual mirrors. After entering into a trance, they look into polished brass
plates that serve as mirrors, and seeing spirits therein, they "become"
them. Foucault's experience with the mirror enables him to recognize that

his presence is at once affirmed and denied by his reflection therein, since the mirror can "reflect" a reality only by creating a virtual, "unreal" reality on the other side of that glass. Foucault's "heterotopia" presents an interesting possibility—a space where the utopian meets and challenges one's accepted notion of identity, while still providing that very identity with a sense of its authenticity. There are many heterotopias, he claims, and many share this overlapping of a virtual, imagined, possible, and somewhat contradictory space with another space taken to be more real. If identity could be thought of as a space, then the Sherpa identities presented in this text, and my own identity as author of this text, might be described as heterotopias. Like Foucault's mirror, my text is the place where I am reflected in the Sherpas I write about who are on the other side of that text and those identities. But, whereas Foucault's mirror reflects in one direction, the mirror between me, as a Westerner, and the Sherpas permits reflected visibility between different onlookers. It is in texts such as this that Sherpas also discover their manifold virtual presence, in which their own identities are affirmed and denied.

Mirrors of identity originate in the confluence of many interests and desires we see articulated in representations of Sherpas drawn by both foreigners and Sherpas themselves. At the most superficial, Orientalist level, foreigners' representations of Sherpas reflect Western desires for an imagined Other, revealing the invented space beyond the reflective side of the mirror where a "Sherpa" embodies qualities that viewers wish to find in a mirror image of themselves—possessing all the qualities they see and admire in Sherpas. Conversely, Sherpas find their own identities reflected back to them through such representations, as they actively seek relationships with the foreigners standing behind them looking into that mirror.

When two-way mirrors are created in the space between self and other, identity and its authorship are called into question. And if authorship of identity is the alleged essence of authenticity, then for Sherpas authenticity has to be examined in its articulation through tourism, mountaineering, anthropology, and the many culture industries engaged in the production of representations of Himalayan life. The following chapters will explore the apparatuses through which virtual Sherpas have been created; this chapter focuses on the characteristics of these constructed identities and how they are mimetically apprehended by Sherpas. It explores the "mirroring spaces" of representation, from British images of climbing Tigers to Western desires for intimacy with exotic and spiritual Sherpa Others. It explores the qualities of identity attributed to "traditional" and "typical" Sherpas that bounce back and forth between foreigners and Sherpas in a surface play of desires about who, exactly, the Sherpas are.

Representations: The Reflected Qualities of "Sherpa-ness"

> The [Sherpa] girl had a beautiful, strong Asian face. She must
> have been carrying at least forty pounds in a woven basket on
> her back. As she walked along, she sang a mournful, wordless
> song, over and over. I was much taken with the melody, and
> wished I had enough of an ear so that I could sing it, too. From
> time to time, she said something like "eeuk, eeuk" to her beast.
> They were walking at such a delightfully slow pace that I tagged
> along. . . . I met an American woman who had been leading
> trekking groups in Nepal and asked her how the Sherpas had
> changed over the last decade. She told me that the young ones
> didn't know the dances anymore, and quoted something some-
> one had said to her: "The Sherpas are going to become part of
> the modern world. They can't be kept up here in cages like
> animals in a zoo just to preserve them." That is certainly right,
> but one hopes that much of what has been so fine in that society
> will be saved.
>
> —Jeremy Bernstein, "The Himalaya Revisited"

Upon reading this passage from a *New Yorker* article, written by a Western
journalist in 1986, one wonders whether there is something hyperreal
about the Western apprehension of Sherpas. The Sherpas, to many who
write about them, seem to be more real than real, and to make their chroniclers' lives seem, somehow, simulated or less real.[1] Nearly all the passages
found in Western writings about Sherpas, with few exceptions (and there
are exceptions), convey similar sentiments. Often, representations of Sherpas reveal the authors' desire to become like Sherpas themselves, as the
passage above evidences the writer's wish to sing the Sherpani's song, to
walk at her pace, and perhaps to hang onto her way of life for himself. This
romantic depiction of Sherpa reality is also seen in descriptions of Sherpas
performing amazing feats of heroism or physical endurance. This has been
particularly true of accounts of Himalayan expeditions, wherein physical
endurance and skill are equated with Sherpa identity:

> Tired from their climb and baffled by the bad visibility, the two men strayed too
> close to the edge of a bluff and when the snow underneath gave way, they
> plunged thousands of feet to their deaths. On the other rope were three men—
> two Germans and the renowned Sherpa, Annullu, who had first made his name
> with us on Everest in 1954. Only after a terrible struggle were these two men
> able to make their escape. At one stage the two Germans slid off in an avalanche
> and only a superhuman effort by Annullu was able to prevent them from being
> swept away.[2]

The most remarkable stories of this sort were disseminated by Sir Edmund Hillary soon after his successful ascent of Mount Everest. He told one story about a Khum Jung woman, the wife of a village headman, who was nine months pregnant but did not want to miss her opportunity to meet Queen Elizabeth at a Kathmandu garden party, so she began the 180-mile trek to the capital. Halfway through her journey, she delivered her baby "in a tiny tumbledown wayside cottage" within just one hour. Soon thereafter, she resumed her journey and arrived at the garden party in time to meet the queen, whom she called the "headman of many villages." After the party, Hillary had to rush the woman to a hospital for treatment, as her afterbirth had not yet been entirely expelled. She recovered from this trauma, however, in only twenty-four hours! Hillary concluded his story by noting that, "in Sherpaland, the 'weaklings' die quickly; only the tough and hardy can hope to survive."[3]

Himalayan expedition accounts offer numerous passages attesting to the natural physical capabilities of Sherpas.

> As carriers they are unsurpassed, for they are brought up to it from their youth. When quite small children they learn to carry loads, fetching and carrying water and grain for the upkeep of their homes. . . . That these people think little or nothing of traversing [the nineteen-thousand-foot Nangpa-la pass] is clearly shown by the fact that there is a continuous traffic across it for five months of the year, and that among the travelers are frequently seen women carrying their babies and small children on their backs.[4]

Similar accounts were written by members of the first successful Everest ascent: "It is not Da Namgyal's *nature* to give in, but it was only too clear that we should not be able to continue much farther. . . . Da Namgyal said he could do no more. I knew him too well to doubt it, for there is no stouter-hearted and less-complaining man."[5]

The *National Geographic* accounts of Sherpas for the English-reading public have also been a prolific source of imagery attesting to the innate hardiness and physical gifts of Sherpas, specifically in regard to their natural ability to climb mountains and carry loads:

> Up they climb! As sturdy as their menfolk, Sherpa women develop lungs and legs attuned to the heights. Unperturbed by thin air and rugged trails, they carry heavy loads for a mountaineering expedition.[6]

> A young Sherpani reflects the natural gaiety of her people. She weighs about 85 lbs, yet can carry an almost equal weight during 15-mile-a-day treks.[7]

> With lungs and legs at home in high altitude, the men of Khumbu came to the world's attention as loyal Himalayan porters. And little wonder that they became famous. Feats of superhuman endurance are not exceptional in the Sherpa way of life.[8]

These representations have not diminished over the years since the first days of British and European Himalayan climbing. After the death of Pasang Lhamu in 1993, numerous accounts of her achievement appeared in international journals, and they frequently attested to the seemingly innate will of Sherpas to climb the peaks, despite their fear of them. For example:

> Sherpa is the name of a mountain people. The name designates an assistant guide or a high-altitude porter. . . . At thirty-two years, this family woman, born in a Himalayan village reached only on foot, had the will to place herself atop the mountains. Like many Sherpas, she ran a trekking agency with her husband in Kathmandu. "Twenty-five percent of my alpinist clients are women. You know, they are as strong as the men, and without a doubt, they have the advantage of strong will," she said in a passionate tone. "Without experience, it is possible to get to four thousand meters. Above that, one has to be very prudent. First, one must spend two nights at that altitude for acclimatizing, then ascend five hundred meters and spend the night adjusting, and so on," she advised. But Pasang, like all Nepalese in this respect, had a fear of the mountain. This monster with a heart of stone had already taken the life of one of her younger brothers, who was a guide. But she was prepared, sadly for her fate, to sacrifice her life for glory on Everest, for a simple minute of eternity on the roof of the world.[9]

In another example, we again hear of Sherpas' intimate link with mountaineering:

SHERPAS: MOUNTAIN MEN OF NEPAL

> Nepal is home to the Sherpas who live in the mountainous terrain and engage themselves in various productive activities. The most important being trekking when the season is right. They make their livelihood and income from this tourist business albeit with a single-minded obsession. They are a hardy and tough breed of people who live a hard and arduous life. So much so that there is no room here for the faint-hearted. Sherpas are usually hired by trekking agencies to work as guides and sardars. Meaning there is nobody to replace their invaluable service to this particular aspect of the tourism industry. Moreover, they form indispensable members of expedition teams to the snow-clad peaks and mountains. It seems only they can challenge and defy the breathtaking heights in order to put other men on top. Being unusually capable in form and disposition the risk of life-and-limb is reduced to a minimum.[10]

Even Chinese tour brochures made use of the potent images of Sherpas created at least partially within the Western imagination. In one tourist magazine (written in English, presumably for English-speaking foreigners), an article is entitled "The Sherpas: Hardy Folk of the Himalayas."[11] The perceived worthiness of the Sherpa character and the simulated versions of Sherpa identity that foreign desires generated produced a virtual Sherpa who was loyal, hardy, reliable, skilled, capable of superhuman physical feats, and, above all, good-natured about the demanding work. Although the imagery incorporates more than even the aforementioned qualities, they were sufficient to elicit great praise in accounts ranging from documentaries to ethnographies and journalistic illustrations.

The potency of such perceived Sherpa qualities was not overlooked in the early days of Sherpa expedition work, and is not overlooked today. In places far from the Himalayas, the name "Sherpa" is used as a profitable trope. For instance, in 1986, a software firm from California's Silicon Valley announced a new software product, the Sherpa Data Management System. This product would guarantee users of computerized design systems that they were dealing with only updated, correct versions of their own work. Although many human Sherpas have died on Himalayan expeditions, Sherpa *software* "virtually assures that slip-ups will not occur. . . . Key to its flexibility is Sherpa's inclusion of a sophisticated data-base management system that enables an engineering organization to provide Sherpa with essentially all the information needed to manage files—regardless of the nature of their contents or physical locations."[12]

Reviewing accounts from British and American climbers, like the following from an American expedition, it is easy to see how this particular "virtual" Sherpa arose. "Jimmy Roberts has charge of the Sherpas and manages them beautifully. . . . I believe that if put to the test some of the I.Q. numbers of the Sherpas would be quite high. They possess keen memories and can remember such minute details as where something is packed in the more than 900 boxes we have brought with us."[13] Like those Sherpas who kept track of reams of information while leading foreigners up the peaks of mountains, the Sherpa Data Management system would also allegedly "take the pain out of . . . data management."

In 1985, as I was preparing to travel to Nepal to carry out fieldwork, I learned that "Sherpas" would be attending the 1986 summit meeting of world leaders in Bonn, West Germany. These Sherpas were related to those of Nepal only by the use of their name, a potent mobile signifier of qualities Sherpas were thought to possess. They helped the "summiteers to a successful summit" by doing most of the position writing and planning for the event.[14] At the summit meeting a year later, "Sherpas" again appeared: "While the summiteers slept, their aides (known as Sherpas) toiled until 4:30 a.m. on a statement."[15]

Sherpas, in the eyes of many Westerners, are unfailingly capable. Out of sheer loyalty and a love of pleasing others—again, the perceived qualities that Westerners felt made the Sherpas more than equals—Sherpas are always expected to do their best and succeed where others might fail. The British have been particularly fond of the Sherpa trope. In 1990, while living in England, I discovered one of its newest automotive successes, the

Sherpas on way to summit

SUMMITS, like the one that opens in Houston this weekend, are good for the self-esteem of the participants, particularly for the small group of officials known as sherpas, who prepare the way for the meeting by deciding on an agenda and writing a draft of the communique that will be issued when it is all over. Sometimes the event conforms exactly to their script and the leaders need turn up only to eat dinner and have their picture taken. This one is different, however, being more unpredictable, as the page one story shows.

The sherpas are also good for the occupancy rates of their national airlines. During preparations for the Houston summit they have met in San Francisco, Paris, Washington DC, Newport, Rhode Island as well as Houston. It is hard work, particularly catching the right connection to catch

KEITH DOBNEY

Sir Robin Butler: in competition with the Treasury's Nigel Wicks

the meeting at Newport.

The summit participants are the leaders of the G-7 group of nations, plus the EC, which means that all the sherpas are either drawn from the top drawer of their respective bureaucracies or are about to be received into it. For instance, Karl-Otto Pöhl, who seems likely to become the best known central banker since Montagu Norman, was cast as a sherpa when merely a promising young official in Bonn.

This time, President Mitterrand's interest is looked after by Jacques Attali, the well-known novelist and president-elect of the European Bank for Reconstruction and Development.

Britain is represented by Sir Robin Butler, the Cabinet Secretary, and Nigel Wicks, one of the second permanent secretaries at the Treasury (there are four). The Treasury man's job is to check that the Cabinet Secretary does not step on his patch. "I always seemed to have a scuffle with the Cabinet Secretary when he interfered in Treasury matters," recalled a retired sherpa.

Mr Wicks is well qualified to perform this role, even against an experienced adversary like Sir Robin, who gives his hobby as "competitive games" in *Who's Who*. Mr Wicks, who was 50 three weeks ago and ought not to have long to wait now for his knighthood, is not quite as lean and hungry looking as he was when he represented the UK at the IMF in Washington DC between 1983 and 1985. But he is cagey, nimble and energetic – not a man to miss a trick by lingering over the lunch table.

A grammar school boy (Beckenham and Penge GS), he became the Prime Minister's principal private secretary when he returned from Washington and it would be a bold gambler who bet against him succeeding Sir Peter Middleton as permanent secretary of the Treasury.

If he is shown on television during the Houston summit, he is the one at Mrs Thatcher's shoulder with very dark hair and the accomodating smile.

The contempt in which the Institute of Directors holds the establishment appears to be evoking a similar response. Informed last week that the institute intends to put its full weight behing John Major's proposal for a "hard Ecu" as an alternative to a single European currency, the man from the Bank of England murmured: "Oh dear".

4. *Sherpa* as a "floating" signifier; summit meeting aides-de-camp are called Sherpas.

Sherpa Van. The first one I saw was depositing passengers atop mountains in Wales. I later noticed advertisements for the vans in English magazines and newspapers, with claims that they were particularly useful for carrying loads, or persons, up the most rugged types of mountain terrain.

In 1990, a "Sherpa alert" was sent out to *Forbes* subscribers, who could then be solicited for participation in a new investment fund. Called the

Sherpa alert

Marketing appellations often reveal themselves to be the height of fancy. Take Häagen-Dazs ice cream, for example—an exotic, Euro-sounding name, which, like the product, was manufactured in New Jersey. Topping the list today is Indosuez Asia Investment's "Himalayan Fund," a new closed-end offering that will pioneer investing in Bangladesh, Nepal, and Sri Lanka. However, the fund will concentrate a hefty 75% of its assets in India.

The fund, to be listed on the London Stock Exchange, is designed to attract Indian and European investors. Those who remember their geography doubtless will recall that Bangladesh and Nepal are northeast of India—and that Sri Lanka is well over 1,000 miles south of the Himalayas ... a long trek even for this lofty-sounding fund.

5. The potent signifier of *Sherpa* is used to attract readers of *Investment Vision*, the magazine of Fidelity Focus, FMR Corporation.

Himalayan Fund, it was offered by Indosuez Asia Investment and named for its goal of exploring interest-earning potential in Bangladesh, Nepal, India, and Sri Lanka. That the Himalayas are used as the logocentric orienting device for the fund, and that its advertisement calls for a "Sherpa alert," demonstrates the dominance of these signifiers over many others found in the South Asian context. "Sherpa" serves as a trope for the Himalayas, and as a mobile signifier for all those qualities perceived to be embodied in virtual Sherpas. Some of the most prominent qualities of this signifier are loyalty, reliability, and the promise of success.

The qualities thought to define the Sherpa identity are encapsulated in the Sherpa name, which then serves as a figurative way of talking about the characteristics thought to be typically Sherpa. Once removed from Sherpas themselves, their name takes on a free-floating character and can be affixed to software products, summit aides, and multipurpose vans. In an economy of meanings, the name "Sherpa" has great value, for it signifies the rugged, the loyal, the skilled, and the infinitely capable—qualities many consumers in the West find attractive both in people and in the products they purchase.

The characteristics discussed thus far, however, are only a few of those imputed to and emblematic of virtual Sherpas. When a hyperreal physical heroism or endurance is not reported, other "natural" Sherpa qualities usually are. At the top of this list are those aspects of the Sherpa character identified with heightened spirituality and inherent good nature demonstrated through hospitality. One repeatedly finds accounts of the naturally peaceful and friendly character of Sherpas in expedition accounts. From a Britisher, we learn that

> an arrangement which seems to give mutual pleasure in Himalayan travel is that each man is cared for by a faithful follower, who brings him his tea in the morning, lays out his sleeping bag at night, helps to carry his personal belongings and generally spoils his Sahib. (This Hindi word, denoting superior status, was used between us on the expedition, when necessary, simply to distinguish between members of the party and the Sherpas.) My own retainer was Pemba, a quiet and hefty lad with more than usually pronounced Mongolian features, his thick tresses wound in a massive "bun" and worn on the side of his head. Pemba was by repute one of the stoutest-hearted of our Sherpa team and was a most likable chap; we very soon understood each other well enough.[16]

In another account, we find their good nature again:

> All evening we were entertained in gay and lighthearted fashion. We bandied tales with old friends, drank much good *chang* [home-brewed rice or barley beer], and watched vigorous Sherpa dancing; the air was full of song and laughter. All of my party were brought in to partake of the food and drink. I can't remember a pleasanter evening or having felt more clearly that we were really being accepted into the Sherpas' hearts and lives. It was late when we finally said good night and stumbled our way homeward under a star-filled sky.[17]

From the Americans, we learn more about Sherpa character: "Inside, stretched out on Jake's sleeping bag in the dark, was Nima Tensing, who had been the personal Sherpa for both Lute and Jake [who had just died]. Nima was a stocky, tough looking, yet sensitive little man, with an ugly scar over one eye. But when he smiled—and he smiled often—all that he was inside opened up, and his decency and his innate kindness reached out like a soft hand to touch those around him."[18]

The *National Geographic* appears to have found in Sherpas an endless source of fascination, particularly when it comes to their uncommon spirituality. Over the years, Sherpas have served as an attraction for readers, who travel through the pages of the magazine to the farthest reaches of the globe and witness through the ocular lenses of photographers those qualities of "Sherpa-ness" reportedly experienced by others. Here, one finds a Sherpa whose hospitable and friendly character is attributed not to genetic endowment but rather to Tibetan Buddhism: "Sherpa grace, selflessness, and generosity under pressure come from Tibetan Buddhism. Sherpas believe that life is an endless cycle and that a holy life guarantees reincarnation as a human, rather than as a snake or dog. Sherpas earn religious merit by their gentle thoughts, by practicing nonviolence, doing good deeds, spinning prayer wheels, and offering gifts to lamas. Religion is a daily, if not hourly, practice."[19]

The same attributes are found in travel and journalistic expedition accounts: "As GS [George Schaller, the naturalist] commented, 'A Westerner would have slunk off and kicked stones [after a disappointment]; you have to admire the Sherpas for being so open about everything'—so open, so without defense, therefore so free, true Bodhisattvas, accepting like the variable airs the large and small events of every day."[20] "Wonderfully, Jang-bu laughed aloud, as did Dawa and Phu-Tsering [all Sherpas], although it meant wet clothes and a wet sleeping bag for the head sherpa. That happy-go-lucky spirit, that acceptance which is not fatalism but a deep trust in life, made me ashamed," one American writes.[21]

The enticing and alluring character of Sherpas is as often conveyed through descriptions of the place where they live, because it is a Buddhist place, as it is through descriptions of the Sherpas themselves. Here is the place where Sherpas live: "Around the monastery hovered an air of calm and meditation. Prayer flags fluttered in every yard. A long stone *mani* wall repeated in chiseled letters the ancient words, *om mani padme hum*, 'o the jewel in the lotus!' invoking the patron deity of Tibetan Buddhism, who is envisaged as in a lotus blossom."[22] Another author notes:

> Everyone, at some time, has a vision of a fabled valley cradled in high mountains, where the harsh realities of existence are unknown. In his famous novel *Lost Horizon*, author James Hilton imagined such a place; his name for it, Shangri-La, has become a synonym for all such places of retreat, peace, and beauty wherever men imagine them. For me, the closest thing to a real Shangri-La exists in exactly the setting of Hilton's novel, in unforgettable Solu-Khumbu, a high world of the Sherpas, below Mount Everest in distant Nepal. There, in a winding ribbon of emerald valleys, each more beautiful than the last, is a paradise into which outsiders have only begun to stray. The glistening summits of earth's highest mountains watch over it. To the devout Buddhist Sherpas, they are mighty deities.[23]

The same traits appeared in a 1994 Internet communiqué response to a user's query about air travel into and out of the Khumbu's main airstrip at Lukla:

The issue is the weather. If it stays clear there is no problem—but if clouds roll in the flights can't go. If you miss your scheduled flight because of clouds then you go to the end of the waiting list [for the next available flight]. This is extremely frustrating unless you have absorbed some of the local Buddhist culture and see it as an opportunity to practice Patience. Having said all that, you have got rocks in your head if you let this difficulty put you off visiting this amazing and enchanting part of the world. It can truly change your whole outlook on life. The scenery is simply stunning, and as one of the last places to see Tibetan Buddhism in practice in everyday life, the Sherpa region is a rare and precious jewel.[24]

One can also find representations of Sherpas' intrinsically appealing social character in the writings of ethnographers:

The Sherpas, a people of Tibetan language and culture, dwelling in the high valleys of the Mount Everest region, are best known for their role in many of the great Himalayan mountaineering ventures. Yet, their skill as intrepid climbers and high altitude porters is not their most important accomplishment. More remarkable is their achievement of having developed a pattern of life rich in social, aesthetic and spiritual values, irrespective of the harshness of their habitat close to the world's highest mountains.[25]

We shall always think with gratitude of the Sherpas of Khumbu, whose generous hospitality, friendship and good humour made the time spent in Khumbu a pleasurable and often moving experience. The completeness of the rapport we soon established seemed all the more gratifying as long years of anthropological work have taught us that comparatively advanced populations are frequently more resistant to the inquisitiveness of outsiders than primitive tribal societies. But among the Sherpas there was never any difficulty over personal relations. Farmers, merchants, and learned lamas welcomed us in their houses in the same open-hearted way. They shared with us whatever they had, and allowed us to participate without restraint in every social and religious event. Once we had set up house in Khumjung, people of the village and from neighboring settlements would drop in as frequently and as casually as in other houses, and this gave us an opportunity of repaying some of the hospitality we were continuously being offered.[26]

In many ways, the Tibetan diaspora, the growth of Western interest in Tibetan Buddhism, and the political visibility of Tibetans in a transnational arena have contributed to the increasing desire to find in Sherpas not only a spirit of hospitality purportedly disappearing in the West but also a heightened spirituality derived from Tibetan Buddhism. When it is

6. PowerBook advertisement, Apple Computer Corporation, which makes skillful use of Tibetans and Buddhism to sell the product.

possible for a Spanish rock-and-roll band to achieve stardom on the basis of their number one hit single and compact disc called *Ai Dalai*, written about the plight of the Dalai Lama and Tibetan refugees,[27] and for Apple Computers to attempt to boost sales of its PowerBook computer by associating it with the Tibetan Buddhist monastery of Ganden, then Sherpas, too, as Tibetan Buddhists, indirectly come into the spotlight. The Sherpas of Khumbu, as a group, are seen as yet another reservoir of spiritual insight and knowledge.

When Michael Tobias, a producer and mountain climber, created his 1991 series *Voice of the Planet* for United States television, he selected the Khumbu's Tengboche Monastery as the filming site. He recruited William Shatner to play the show's narrator. Shatner was flown to the monastery for the film, and he delivered his lines from within a monk's quarters. In the series, Shatner played a "middle-aged, disillusioned ecologist who goes to a Tibetan monastery both to relieve his ennui and to track down a computer hacker who has been breaking into his university work and variously taunting and inspiring him. At Thyangboche [Tengboche], he encounters a hand-built PC [supposedly assembled by a Sherpa monk] that is energized by a spirit called Gaia, the name for the ancient Greek goddess of the Earth."[28]

Gaia, who turns out to be the mystery hacker Shatner's protagonist is seeking, is played by Faye Dunaway. She is the spiritual equivalent of Mother Earth, rendered more "real" by her appearance in the tantric monastery, where spirits are plentiful and the distinction between actual deities and imagined ones is blurred. The sultry and flirtatious, but never actually seen, Gaia becomes the ecologist's obsession, and, in the end, his teacher. Gaia's message—that the world needs to be saved through environmentalism—is ultimately successfully communicated to humankind, thanks in large part to the monastery in Nepal and to the Sherpa monk from Tengboche, who is able to build an amazing computer in his monastic hermitage in the Khumbu. The hyperreal quality of Sherpa identity emerges in the show's deft portrayal of this Himalayan culture as both more primitive than that of the West (the Sherpas are thought to remain in touch with Mother Nature and her rhythms) and more advanced (in that they have produced a computer with artificial intelligence, and are "in tune" with nature because of their spirituality).

Tobias, the author and director of the film, was inspired by his own pilgrimage experiences. He was educated at the University of Tel Aviv and "spent time at St. Catherine's monastery. He lived in a cave, and studied Greek, Hebrew, and Russian and the iconography of the area."[29] He said of the project that it grew from "the obsession with ascension, and how the physical qualities of human existence—like hiking up a mountain—are so poetically utilized as metaphors for the ascent of the soul, of the spirit."

His film, like other representations of a perceived Sherpa Buddhist spirituality, is a vivid example of the way in which Sherpa identities are invested with a reality that is more real than real. In fact, it is the idealized image of the monastery and its real monks who appear as actors in the film (portraying inhabitants of Shangri-la) that authenticate the television program's message. The monastery and monks are actually there, and the film records this. But the monastery and its Sherpa monks also exist as a type of Shangri-la that is made to seem more real in comparison to the obviously simulated Gaia and the computer through which she speaks. The ability for a simulation to authenticate other social constructions derives from the perennial desires of Westerners to find in Sherpas (and Tibetans) a small piece of Shangri-la. But this is a Shangri-la that exists, and a camera proves it.

Just as the perceived physical skills of Sherpas are used in tropes by industries far removed from the Sherpas themselves, so too are perceived images of Sherpas as highly spiritual and hospitable used by outsiders for their own purposes. In the transnational markets where Tibetan Buddhism now has high visibility, there are more and more sites where one observes "Sherpa-ness" being used as symbolic capital serving Others' interests. The Ministry of Tourism of Nepal, for example, makes ample use of the perceived qualities of Sherpas, with their high name-recognition quotient, in its brochures used to lure tourists into the country.[30] In these brochures, the images of Sherpas as hardy mountain climbers are also reemergent.

> If you have seen the world and want to see more, we offer you the real Oz . . . the interior of Nepal. . . . The Sherpas, "the Tigers of the Snow," live in the Himalayan region up to an altitude of 15,000 ft. . . . This place is the home of the legendary Sherpa, who have won international renown as the most sturdy climbers with indomitable will to scale the peaks. . . . Days could be spent hiking and visiting the Sherpa villages. . . . Thyangboche [Tengboche] Monastery, Khunde Hospital, Khum Jung Hillary School. . . .[31]

> Mani Rimdu . . . is an important and gorgeous ceremony of the Sherpas of the Khumbu Region. It is held annually at Thyangboche. . . . The masked lamas dance in the courtyards of the monasteries at the presence of the Head Lamas and other Lamas. . . . On [another festival] day, the Sherpas perform their monotonous but highly rhythmic folk songs and dances known as *Sheru*. During feasts the villagers offer their famous *Chhang*, very tasty, fermented home-brewed beer.[32]

> Thyangboche (3867 m): This is the site of a famous Buddhist monastery presided over by a reincarnate Lama. The monastery is set on a wooded ridge completely encircled by snow peaks and dominated by the trio of Everest, Lhotse, and Nuptse.[33]

In many accounts, Sherpas' physical strength is coupled with the hospitable character evident in their willingness to help foreigners scale the peaks: "The first successful ascent of Sagarmatha [Everest] by Sir Edmund Hillary and Tenzing Norgay Sherpa had far reaching effects for the Sherpas. Hillary greatly admired their cheerfulness, gentle natures, and bodily strength, and knew that without their help mountaineering expeditions would struggle to reach their objectives."[34]

Non-Sherpa Nepalese journalists and writers both reveal and capitalize on the same qualities Westerners identify in Sherpas. One account contains a photo of three Sherpanis carrying loads suspended in baskets from straps over their heads. Beneath them, the caption reads: "Hardy Sherpas in their natural element." The text recounts the regional appeal of Orientalist representations of the Sherpas' religion as mystical and as full of superlative wisdom: "Their lord and god is Buddha, the 'All Knowing One' and their lives are inextricably bound with the rituals and mystics of Buddhism. Religion forms the core of their mundane lives and becomes in deaths, sicknesses and ceremonies a focal point of concern."[35]

The perceived desirability of being Buddhist in the Himalayan tourist economy cannot be underestimated. The streets of Bodhinath, the Buddhist mecca on the outskirts of Kathmandu, are lined with foreign Buddhists making pilgrimages from their Western homelands to the holy places of Nepal. When a four-year-old reincarnate Buddhist lama was brought from Bhutan and placed on his throne in a Kathmandu monastery, more Western Buddhists were in attendance than Nepalese, Bhutanese, or Tibetan Buddhists. In the inner rooms of the monastery where the lama was enthroned, it was the Western Buddhists who organized the throngs of Nepalese, Tibetan, and Bhutanese visitors who came to pay him a visit. Similarly, the yearly celebrations of Mani Rimdu (commemorating Buddhist history and cosmology) at the Khumbu's monasteries have been populated with crowds of foreign trekkers in bright down clothing and mirrored sunglasses for many years. They angle for good seats from which to view the dances and to capture them on film or videotape. Foreigners are given innumerable privileged audiences with the lamas, something local Sherpas seek for themselves and are commonly granted. By 1987, documentary videos of Sherpa festivals were made regularly by foreign Buddhists.

The appeal of Buddhism in international markets is felt not only by those who simply seek adventure and cultural exoticism. It also attracts those seeking spiritual knowledge and a way to enhance their lives through practices of self-realization. Numerous American books, from Peter Matthiessen's accounts to those of Jeff Greenwald, recount tales of spiritual growth through trekking in the Himalayas. Greenwald wrote my favorite such book, entitled *Shopping for Buddhas*. His mission described therein—

to purchase a small bronze Buddha in Kathmandu—reveals an extent to which Buddhism has become a transnational and extremely profitable attraction. He writes:

> But no. I wanted it all. I mean, if I was prepared to spend a couple of hundred dollars for one of these gods I wanted as much for my money as possible. Wisdom. Compassion. Protection. Peace of mind! And, for sheer devotional value, ounce for ounce, nothing beats a Buddha. . . . I'm inclined to believe that the majority of Americans who hear the word [hero] still think primarily of John F. Kennedy, Billie Jean King, or Superman. . . . Forget about heroes. The ones we want to watch for now are the bodhisattvas.[36]

Buddhism as a transnational currency can be found far beyond the Sherpa community, and far outside Nepal. In 1985, a group of Japanese tourists and trekkers went to the Khumbu to recruit Sherpa carpenters, stonecutters, painters, monks, and lamas, to bring them to Japan where they would reproduce a scale model of the Traxindu Monastery in Solu-Khumbu for Japan's Little Museum of the World (devoted to recreating scale models of various architectural and cultural exotica from around the world). Importing all the materials and builders of the monastery from the site of the original, the Japanese obtained an "authentic" version of a piece of Buddhist Nepal for their own backyard—an event the Sherpa monks claimed was important for the Japanese "because they are also Buddhist."

The qualities of Buddhism with such international appeal are affixed to Sherpas in ways that equate a "generic" Sherpa with a "generic" notion of Buddhism. Peter Matthiessen, in his National Book Award–winning work *The Snow Leopard*, about his journey in the Himalayas with the naturalist George Schaller, subtly intertwines his notions of Zen Buddhism with the "innate" qualities of Tibetan Buddhist Sherpas. In the process, he also invests Sherpas with the Protestant work ethic so admired by Westerners.

> On the school veranda, Jang-bu and Phu Tsering build a fire to dry sleeping bags, which are turned each little while by Dawa and Gyaltzen. Like all Sherpa work, this is offered and accomplished cheerfully, and usually Tukten lends a hand, although such help is not expected of the porters and he is not paid for it. The Sherpas are alert for ways in which to be of use, yet are never insistent, far less servile; since they are paid to perform their service, why not do it as well as possible? "Here, sir! I will wash the mud!" "I carry that, sir!" As GS says, "When the going gets rough, they take care of you first." Yet their dignity is unassailable, for the service is rendered for its own sake—it is the task, not the employer, that is served. As Buddhists, they know that the doing matters more than the attainment or reward, that to serve in this selfless way is to be free.

Because of their belief in karma—the principle of cause and effect that permeates Buddhism and Hinduism (and Christianity, for that matter: as ye sow, so shall ye reap)—they are tolerant and unjudgmental, knowing that bad acts will receive their due without the intervention of the victim. The generous and open outlook of the Sherpas, a kind of merry defenselessness, is by no means common, even among unsophisticated peoples; I have never encountered it before except among the Eskimos. And since, in prehistory, the nomadic Mongol ancestors of both Tibetans and native Americans are thought to have spread from the same region of northern Asia, I wonder if this sense of life is not a common heritage from the far past.[37]

Is it Buddhism, or something more innate, something more than a pre-Buddhist common cultural heritage, that makes Sherpas so ethical, hospitable, and dependable in the eyes of Western Others? Or is it (or is it also) the very gaze of Westerners on the Sherpas described above that prompts their success at being "typical" Sherpas in all the ways desired by the West? Matthiessen continues, revealing the inextricability of his own gaze and desires for his own spiritual growth from his perception of the Sherpas with whom he travels in the Himalayas: "These simple and uneducated men comport themselves with the wise calm of monks, and their well-being is in no way separable from their religion. And of course they are all incipient Buddhas—we are too."

In 1987, the Sherpa monk Phurba Sonam from the Khumbu's Tengboche Monastery taught a course entitled "Masks, Mandalas, and Mountains" to students at Colorado University. Phurba Sonam thereby joined the ranks of numerous Tibetan Buddhist lamas and monks who have engaged in the transnational teaching of Buddhism. In Colorado, one could see how the currency of transnational Buddhism translates into tourists wishing to visit Nepal—often to meet Sherpas and to get to know them more intimately. One of Phurba Sonam's Colorado students said she "enjoyed the class with Phurba Sonam more than [her] other classes. 'I wouldn't have come from four o'clock to five each afternoon if it wasn't worth it. I really want to visit Nepal now."[38] The presence of Tibetan monks and lamas in Western sites does more than simply reflect the expansion of their dharmic interests—as bodhisattvas would have it. It is not simply a marketing of the dharma by Buddhist scholars. These Sherpas' presence in Western sites is also the result of a space having been cleared for them to fill—a space created around the Western image of persons from a spiritually gifted culture, a Shangri-la.

A review of the reflected Sherpa qualities produced in the representations emerging from relationships between Sherpas and foreigners would not be complete without reference to the desirability of Sherpas as exotic Others through whom experiences of intimacy are possible. Foreigners arriving in the Khumbu and experiencing briefly what they see as a "Sherpa" way of life are often taken by an overwhelming desire to become like Sherpas themselves. In 1966 Desmond Doig defined this desire to become like Sherpas when he described his relationship to a particular Sherpa he had come to know over the course of his long visit in the Khumbu:

> Change will come to the Sherpas. Perhaps someday they will move south again, forsaking their remote villages for less demanding climes. It could be. Except that I have experience of my friend, the artist Pasang. He came with me to Calcutta, began painting again, and then, just when his pictures were in great demand and he was on the verge of profitable fame, he grew homesick. One morning, most unexpectedly, he announced he was going home. And he went, back to Shangri-La. I would follow him if I could.[39]

Westerners envision the ability to become like Sherpas by becoming intimately involved with them in a social relationship that they perceive as having special qualities: "We have brought them a deal of money, but between these people and ourselves a relationship has been clearly established that is something more than a material contract. These men are 'engaged' also in the moral sense of the word, and they bring us not only their muscles, but also their willingness, their pleasure and their participation . . . for deep within them is a taste and an aptitude for exceptional activities."[40]

The intimacy sought with Sherpas is usually one that desires mutuality, to bring Westerners going to the Himalayas a new spiritual awakening. Sometimes the intimacy sought with Sherpas ends up being sexual. Here one finds the ultimate seductions between foreigners and Sherpas—foreigners seeking to experience epiphany through a physical interaction with Sherpas, and Sherpas wanting to become like and unlike Westerners, or that which is desired by the West, through bodily accommodation. The hospitality, for which Sherpas are world famous, is extended even to this degree.

Tourism in the Himalayas was described to me by several tourists and tour operators as the women's equivalent of men's excursions to Thailand—a "sexual vacation." Tales of Western women, in particular, who arrived in the Himalayas and had sexual relations with their Sherpa trekking guides were rampant. This less well known image of Sherpas as sexually attractive focuses on their being physically strong, exotically different, and "safe" in their remoteness from these trekkers' homes, families, and other sexual relationships. These stories were fueled in part by ethnographic accounts documenting a number of relationships between foreign women and Sherpa men, many of which resulted in marriage. For example, one ethnography reports:

There is concrete evidence that a number of Sherpa women have lost their husbands or fiancés to foreign women. Such evidence relates of course only to affairs which led to a permanent relationship, for fleeting adventures are clearly not on record. . . . Recently, [Temba,] the son of . . . one of the prominent elderly men of Khumjung, fell in love with a European girl who had come with a trekking group of which [Temba] was the *sardar*. To the distress of his family he left his wife and lived in Kathmandu with the foreign girl who had a child from him. It is said that his wife went to Kathmandu and tried in vain to persuade her husband to give up his mistress and return to Khumjung.[41]

The details of this passage were hotly disputed by the Sherpas involved, but the image of Sherpas as sexually attractive was not.[42] Western tourists go to the Himalayas—a place that, because of Western history, is already charged with a romantic sensibility for Westerners—and they are taken into monasteries where the religious iconography is filled with the vivid sexuality of tantrism.

Many-armed and many-headed gods and goddesses are everywhere posed in passionate sexual embraces. These images are thought to reveal a secret of "true satisfaction"—the sort of secret one can only find in the Orient or in the place of Others. The trek experience, which takes tourists far from the realm of their everyday Western lives, becomes a site for exploration of the unusual and the exotic, and an experience that compels an exploration of the self. On top of the image of the Himalayas as a place that affords one the ability to experience uncommon and heightened physical sensuality, the desirable image of Sherpas as hospitable and always accommodating is usually also embedded in most Western imaginations even before the Westerners arrive in Sherpa country. Once in the Himalayas, these tourists' desire to experience a heightened self-awareness via the Other ends in the culmination of both their admiration and their expectation.

In a "Doonesbury" cartoon strip by G. B. Trudeau clipped for me by an American colleague in 1986, one finds the character Mike sitting on his front steps in conversation with J.J. about a woman at Mike's office named Marcia who had a "singularity party." Mike says, "Funny you should ask [about Marcia]. On Friday she left for a two-week trek from Nepal to Tibet." "What?" J.J. inquires. Mike continues: "She's arranged for a Sherpa, porters, the whole bit. And she's doing it all on her own!" "That's nuts," J.J. says. "What's she trying to prove?" "That she can enjoy some of life's great experiences by herself," Mike tells her. "Going to Tibet is Marcia's dream trip, but she'd always held out for doing it with some perfect companion. Taking the trip alone symbolizes her new acceptance of her life as it is." In the next and final frame of the strip we are shown Marcia in

Nepal, with her guide, standing in front of a Buddhist monk (who is depicted as Sherpa or Tibetan), and Marcia is saying to her guide, "You heard
me. Ask him if he's married."

The underlying premise is that the Himalayas are charged with romantic sensibility and are a place for self-realization. Often the self-realization
that is achieved there is one that is pursued through intimacy with Sherpas.
It is as if the hyperreal qualities of Sherpas are a means by which foreigners
seeking self-realization are able to find a more "real" version of themselves.
Here, the notion of a relationship of intimacy with Sherpas is desirable for
its ability to provide tourists with an enchanting and "penetrating" experience of the Other. It is not enough merely to admire Sherpas from a distance; one must become part of them in this physical way. Mimesis involves finding oneself through the skin of the Other, and for many of the
Sherpa/Westerner couples, such relationships have led to marriages and
families. Thus, seduction works to the mutual satisfaction (in most cases)
of the parties, and that is why it is seduction and not coercion or exploitation. A surface image becomes the reality of a Sherpa physical presence
seduced in relationships with Westerners—the Others through whom
such images are produced and sustained.

BEING VIRTUAL SHERPAS

> This time, no matter what type of difficulties I may face, I am
> determined to conquer the Everest.
> —Pasang Lhamu, in a public announcement
> before her final Everest ascent

The value of the name "Sherpa" has not been lost on advertising agencies
and publishers, who recognize it as a storehouse of cultural capital. Neither
has it been lost on Sherpas themselves. I posit that mirrors held up by
Westerners showed Sherpas who they were "supposed" to be, as they saw
reflected therein images of themselves that could embrace Western interests. But more can be said. One must still demonstrate that Sherpas in fact
internalized these images. In the next three chapters, I explore how views
of Sherpas as physically gifted, as uniformly spiritual and hospitable, and as
desirable for their intimacy and sexuality are both deeply embedded aspects of Sherpa identity and the inevitable consequence of a long-standing
conversation between Sherpas and Westerners. In the remainder of this
chapter, I offer evidence of particular Sherpas' engagements with these
images, beginning with that of Sherpas as sexually and intimately attractive, and then turning to those of Sherpas as religious, good-natured, and
endlessly accommodating. Because it demands more attention, I examine
the image of Sherpas as strong, hardworking, highly skilled, and desirable

employees in the next chapter, where it is seen as one part of Western modernization.

The image of Sherpas as desirable Others through whom sexuality and romance can be found is associated with the idea that Sherpas are keepers of a mystical and rare capacity for social intimacy that has somehow been lost in the West. This is a logic that is most clearly revealed in shamanism. It is also revealed by Sherpas in stories they tell about their relationships with Westerners. Embedded in these accounts is both evidence of the internalization of Western desires for a specific type of Sherpa and Sherpa commentaries about these interests. One account involves an elderly woman who went trekking with a daughter in her late teens. Their sardar was a Sherpa who was married and had several children. After the sardar had become well acquainted with the trekkers, he was asked one night by the mother to sleep with her daughter. The daughter was inexperienced and her mother thought this would be the ideal way (both romantic and exotic) for her to enter the world of sexuality. The sardar declined, but convinced an unwed cousin also on the trek to take his place, which he gladly did.

Another case I heard several times was about an American woman who went trekking by herself up to the Khumbu. She was quite affluent and she had paid for a "fully outfitted" trek, complete with sardar, two Sherpa guides, a cook, a kitchen helper, and four porters. The sardar, guides, and cook were all Sherpas and salaried employees of the trekking agency with whom she had booked her tour. But the porters were young, poor Tamangs (a different Nepalese ethnic group, from a lower elevation in the Himalayas), hired on a daily-wage basis in the remote region to carry loads up and down mountains. During the trek, the woman became attracted to one of these porters, thinking he was Sherpa—a misconception (on her part) with which he apparently played along. She invited him into her tent one night to consummate her sexual desires. The next morning, she insisted that the cook serve her lover the same meal of egg and toast prepared for her, rather than the bowl of porridge porters usually received. This continued for the rest of the trek. When the woman returned from her journey to the trekking agency office, she had nothing but praise for the excellent service she had received, and she told the agency owner that she planned to go trekking again next year. However, she specified that for this next trip, her Sherpa lover be hired as the sardar guide rather than as a porter. The agency staff, befuddled and amused, tried to hide that they did not even know the porter's name, since he had been hired in the field and was a Tamang. Nevertheless, they promised to do their best for her and she left satisfied. For the Sherpa narrators, this story serves both to "Occidentalize" Western women and to reproduce the Sherpas' own virtual image as sexually attractive, as persons with whom intimacy is sought. It reinforces the internalized vision they have of themselves as inherently appealing to Westerners, so attractive, in fact, that other ethnic groups in Nepal would even try to "pass" as Sherpas.

Although this story generally provoked laughter, other tales containing images of Sherpa romantic or sexual appeal were charged with more anxiety than humor—particularly those recounted by local women. I was told by several different young Sherpanis, for example, that they feared losing their husbands to foreign girlfriends. Before his marriage to a Sherpani, Tendi Sherpa from Khum Jung had been sponsored by his American girlfriend to visit the "States." She had also assisted him with a little money "now and then," according to Tendi. After marrying, upon mentioning to his wife, Sonam Kenchi, that he was considering making another trip to the United States, "maybe to work" this time, she became upset. When I asked her about this later, she told me she was worried that Tendi might leave her to become the husband of "that American woman" who was "so rich," even though Sonam had already borne their first child. In a defiant stance of her own, she insisted, "I had many proposals for marriage from foreigners, myself. Five times. Three American men, one from England, and one from Swiss." Sonam, who ran a tea shop and spoke English well, did have many close foreign friends, so I did not doubt her. "They ask me to come to live with them in their country." "Why didn't you marry any of them?" I asked. She smiled demurely and eventually responded, "I didn't like those men," laughing a little more, I guessed, at the thought of leaving the Khumbu. "My sister needs me here. I am Sherpa. I don't want to live outside. Here is my life. This is my life."

Ironically, although intimate relations between Westerners and Sherpas pose a threat to some (like Sonam Kenchi), local accounts of these relationships only reinforce the idea that Sherpas are inherently attractive to Westerners. As another Sherpani asked while we were walking in the streets of Kathmandu one day, upon observing a Western woman who had married a Sherpa from the Khumbu (one of six Westerner/Sherpa couples I knew personally), "Why do so many Western women want to marry Sherpa men?" "I don't know," I replied. She then offered her own explanation: "Maybe Sherpa men make better husbands than Western men."

In some ways, images of Sherpa intimacy and sexuality have only been made more visible by their contestation. At each turn of the debate, the notion of Sherpas as romantically and sexually attractive has been inflated rather than eliminated. Generally, this image has been affixed to Sherpa men, but it has also been grafted onto Sherpanis—always, however, in ways that reflect a need for female sexuality to be morally as well as physically appealing to Westerners. For example, expeditioners and Sherpas circulated stories about young Sherpanis who spent an inordinate amount of time at the Everest base camp. Women who were not climbers themselves generally were not hired for prestigious positions on expeditions and treks, but rather were relegated to the positions of porter, animal porter driver, or kitchen assistant. I was told that, in those capacities, some Sherpanis stayed at the base camp for extended visits, during which they became sexually involved with Sherpas and foreigners alike. The Sherpani who had questioned me about Sherpa/Western marriages informed me that foreign, Sherpa, and other Nepalese men preferred sexual relations with Sherpanis to relations with other "Nepalese" women because the latter were not disposed toward embraces or passion during lovemaking, whereas the former were. But an image of Sherpanis as disreputable women of "easy virtue" is problematic for Sherpas, whose interest in maintaining a positive view of Sherpa sexuality is inseparable from their interest in preserving images desirable to Westerners.

One case that highlights the tricky moral balance involved a British climber, Mike, who became sexually involved with a Sherpani from the Khumbu named Tshiring Drogar. Mike spent a lot of time in the Khumbu and entered into a relationship with Tshiring after many years of friendship with her family. Their love affair began when one of her brothers died while on an expedition with Mike, after which Mike took great pains to ensure the family's receipt of the insurance money due them. Mike, who, when not climbing mountains, read a lot of nineteenth-century romantic classics, talked to me about his relationship with Tshiring Drogar. He saw her as a character out of a Thomas Hardy novel, someone like Tess of the D'Urbervilles, whose romantic development was marked by a transition from peasant to urban life. Mike believed Tshiring was aware of the possibility of romantic love, even if her community was not—defining such love as a privilege granted those whose lives were not of necessity consumed with meeting the survival needs of the family. His concerns revealed the subtle way in which the Western interest in intimacy with Sherpas more often revolved around quests for spirituality and self-realization than around romance and passion. But in this case, one also sees the ways in which Western men envision a type of sexual morality in Sherpanis that is patterned on a more general set of Western expectations for Western women—innocent, monogamous, genuine. Their story also reveals Sherpa efforts to reinforce among Westerners their image as people who already practice this sort of sexuality.

Mike learned that Tshiring was pregnant with his child while he was in Kathmandu. There, he was barraged by a host of Sherpa men who told him he did not have to take responsibility for, or admit paternity of, this child. They assured him that Tshiring Drogar's baby could belong to any number of other men, since Tshiring was often observed "hanging out" at the base camp for expeditions, an assurance less likely given to a Sherpa. Mike had in fact left a plane ticket for her to accompany him to Kathmandu when he left in the spring, but she had not gone after him. He actually wanted this baby, a son, very much, and told me how it represented a sort of synthesis of his life, since he lived half of each year in the Khumbu and half in England, drumming up support for more expeditions. It seemed he finally had found a way to have a family, which he had thought would be impossible back in England. He had already planned to have his child's birth registered at the Khunde Hospital and with the British Embassy, to ensure British citizenship, and had purchased a duffel bag full of baby clothes that he planned to take to Tshiring. He decided that he could marry her in the Khumbu and leave her there while he lived abroad half the year, soliciting sponsorship for more expeditions. A few years later, after Mike had continued to sponsor the child, Sherpas noted that the child bore no resemblance to him and concluded the boy was probably the result of another relationship Tshiring Drogar had had, with a local man. This incident, which I witnessed in 1987, was related to me again in 1994 by Sherpas who had moved to Kathmandu from the Khumbu. Apparently, even this sort of image of Sherpas as attractive for intimate social relations (like those of family) was judged by Sherpas to be worth preserving, reiterating the moral issues surrounding that sexuality in a way Westerners could also approve of. The discourse among Sherpas concerning this aspect of their image encompassed both the perceived immorality of uncontrolled female sexuality and the desirability of unrestrained male sexuality.

The image of Sherpas as culturally exotic, spiritual, and hospitable also came into circulation in relation to Sherpas' apprehension of foreign desires concerning who they "should" be. Owners of Sherpa trekking agencies, for example, have reproduced images of Sherpas as exotic and welcoming in a spiritually satisfying way. Here are excerpts from three tour brochures (each from a different agency):

> Nepal—The Holidayland with a Difference—Offers everything, all within a short range. Snow-covered mountains and ancient pagodas vying for one another on the sky-line. Medieval cities and typical villages. Superb cuisine and shopping at incomparable prices. Resorts and hotels in spectacular settings. And all around the smiling people hospitable and friendly and free. Come to Nepal and be at peace with yourself and the world.[43]

> It is much more than the nostalgia of those early tweed jacketed, hob-nailed booted explorers of the world's highest mountain that keeps drawing people to this area. Certainly the mountain itself attracts—the highest point on earth will always do that as long as it remains accessible. It also involves a combination of outstanding mountain scenery, stone-walled fields and houses, slate roofs, and above all—to those who know them—the Sherpas. These hardy traders, farmers and now climbers who with patience, understanding and a barrel full of humour

also manage our treks. A trek to the Khumbu provides a great opportunity to learn something of their culture and how they have adapted to living inside the Sagarmatha (Everest) National Park—and also how the park has adjusted to its inhabitants.[44]

A typical day on a trek: Usually you will walk for about three hours at an easy pace, stopping to talk to local people on the way, passing the time of day with traveling monks, or photographing the mountains, the occasional wild animal, brightly coloured birds and numerous and varied flora. Occasionally you will stop at a tea shop or be invited into a local house for *chang* (barley beer). Lunch may be beside a river, or in a mountain meadow. Sometimes it will be a hot meal, either fresh or tinned meat, boiled potatoes, soup, chapatis and cheese, and always a welcome cup of tea. New sights and spectacular country unfold as the day progresses. You can always count on something unexpected happening: a meeting with a band of traders and their mule train, a sighting of a Golden Eagle, monks building a *chorten* (religious obelisk), or perhaps bumping into the local doctor who shows you his herbal potions kept in leather pouches.[45]

In 1994, one could find posted on public kiosks and announcement walls in the Kathmandu tourist centers an advertisement for a "Traditional Sherpa Cultural Event"—an evening of Sherpa dancing and food, explanations of traditional Sherpa customs and religion, and a special experience of the renowned Sherpa hospitality. One needed only to call the number at the bottom of the advertisement to make a reservation for this Sherpa experience. Was this an example of "staged" culture, no longer something "authentically" Sherpa even though it had billed itself as exactly that?

In 1987, one could find Sherpa trekking sardars at Sherpa festivals clearing a space for benches in the center of crowds to ensure the best view for their tourist groups. Alongside them, one could observe wealthy Sherpas videotaping their cultural ceremonies for future use at their own parties. Several Sherpa trekking-agency owners in Kathmandu had begun to talk about starting a fund for a Sherpa museum, where tourists and young Sherpas would learn about Sherpa culture—religion, festivals, clothing, food, *chang*, and so forth. It might even include a photo history of their role in trekking and mountaineering, I was told. One supporter also suggested that Sherpas from Solu-Khumbu living permanently in Kathmandu, who had raised funds to build their own Sherpa *gomba*, or monastery (run by the Sherpa Sewa Kendra, a welfare/community affairs society), institute a dress code for all events there. He remembered that one well-respected man from Namche village, whose son ran a trekking agency, had attended a festival the year before in his traditional attire. "Last year," he recalled, "Ang Pembu came in a suit and tie. When I looked at both of them [the Namche man and Ang Pembu], he [the Namche man] looked so nice, with so much good character with his big *chupa* [traditional formal-dress robe] and the *tsampa* [mixed-grain flour] sprinkled on his shoulders [for luck]. Ang Pembu just looked like a skinny little guy, like *anyone*, brushing the *tsampa* off of his lapels. . . . He looked so bad." He told me that the next year he would wear his own *chupa* and traditional hat, and he would dress his children that way too. "If we make a formal system, then everyone will dress well and they will feel good too. It will look better also. We could use new fabrics instead of the old hot wools. They will hold elections soon for the Gomba Executive Committee, and we will try to get someone in office who cares more for preservation, conservation, of culture than presently." He also wanted to videotape the entire festival for his children the next year; that way, he said, he could show it at his own dinner parties.

Sherpa publications are sites for the representation of Sherpas attentive to Western desires. These texts are made available to foreigners entering the Khumbu. One such text from 1987 was a short pamphlet by Mingma Norbu Sherpa describing Sherpa culture. Mingma was educated to work in the Khumbu by the Himalayan Trust (founded by Sir Edmund Hillary). He became the region's park warden for a short period of time. After obtaining a graduate degree from a New Zealand university, he worked as chief administrator for a national trust devoted to development ecology (the King Mahendra Trust), and after receiving a second degree, from a university in the United States, took a job as a full-time expert for the World Wildlife Fund. His pamphlet describes the "way of life, festivals and religion of Sherpa people" in fifteen pages. He included at the back of the pamphlet a list of cultural "dos and don'ts" to be observed when traveling among Sherpas and distributed it to tourists at the national-park checkpost. He wrote, "Sagarmatha [Everest] National Park has become almost as famous around the world for its native inhabitants the Sherpas, as for the high altitude peaks which lie within its boundaries." He devoted a few sentences to each category traditionally deemed significant by Western anthropologists in defining a way of life: People, Family Life (notably remarking that Sherpas have nuclear families), Religion, Religious Buildings (material culture), Yearly Cycle (festivals, agriculture, and trade), Festivals, Cultural Tips, and a Glossary of useful Sherpa words (ten words in all). Thus, through what might be considered "postcolonial" eyes, this modern Sherpa subject offered his vision of his culture to the world in a manner that, as Ashis Nandy (1983) and other writers have noted, objectifies culture in the same way that the self is objectified by Western scientific inquiry. Culture is objectified for these Sherpas who live it but also write about it. Mingma Norbu's selection of categories to detail Sherpa culture reveals a mimesis with representations by Westerners, and explains a great deal about an "authentic" Mingma, himself a modern Sherpa.

The Tengboche Rinpoche (*rinpoche* is an honorific title meaning "supreme one"; here, it refers to the abbot of Tengboche Monastery) also published a small booklet in English called *The Stories and Customs of the Sherpas*, for distribution to visitors at the monastery. It contains a religious history of the Khumbu, a brief introduction to Buddhism, and an introduction to various Buddhist practices, including prayers, public ceremonies, and educational techniques. He also provides an overview, like that in Mingma's pamphlet, of the major Sherpa rituals and customs. These Sherpas engage in their own text making, both to promulgate their own versions of identity and to reiterate those notions of "Sherpa-ness" already perceived as praiseworthy by Westerners. The creation of images of Sherpas by Sherpas themselves is a mimetic product, since what is chosen for presentation to foreigners is largely already determined by the tourist gaze and established as a necessary accompaniment to the tourist experience. But in a mirroring wherein the West configures and produces a Sherpa Other based on what it sees, the very act of offering such texts to foreigners could be read as further evidence of the "characteristic" hospitality that is an important component of Sherpa identity and seduction.

A museum established at the Sagarmatha National Park headquarters in the Khumbu offers a photographic tour of the Sherpas' social and material culture. There, one finds passages from Furer-Haimendorf's early ethnography of Sherpas, along with old photographs included in his text. When the Tengboche Monastery built its small museum for tourists (intended to complement the *rinpoche*'s cultural-guide pamphlet), the *rinpoche* requested the help of a Canadian photographer. She lived at the monastery while creating the museum for the public and writing (with a Sherpani) the book the public would receive, suggesting general topics of interest to foreigners, as well as categorizing and ordering materials in a way foreigners could understand. The "packaging" of Sherpa culture so that it is attractive to foreigners pervades the very sense of "Sherpa-ness" experienced by these new Sherpa authors of their identity. So whose culture was it reflecting? As I interviewed villagers about various events, I was told repeatedly that if I wanted the correct answer to questions about Sherpa culture I should consult Furer-Haimendorf's 1964 book. One Sherpa who was my age asked if I could get him another copy of that text, which contained photographs of his grandfather that he himself did not own. His first copy had been lost and he wanted to obtain another to keep as a reference.

What was interesting to me about all this was that the authorities Sherpas often cited in describing themselves were those representations of Sherpas found in the writings of Westerners. The qualities of Sherpas depicted in representations of expedition work, in folklore about trekking and tourism, and even in anthropology are the distillation of perceived differences between Sherpas and Westerners. But the exoticism of their religion, hospitality, and even traditional medicine (including shamanism) is perceived by Sherpas as important to their economic and cultural survival. The versions of "Sherpa-ness" mirrored by Westerners for Sherpas have consequently become indistinguishable from those that Sherpas themselves now reproduce for Westerners. To say in their own voices who they are, Sherpas consult Others' representations of them. Moreover, to establish the *authority* to say who they are, Sherpas turn to accounts and discourses of identity in which their stories are already told by Westerners. The realization that these multiple and mirrored representations of Sherpas have been embraced by them to establish their own authentic presence led me to question the location and construction of authenticity.

AUTHENTICITY AND THE CONSTRUCTION OF DIFFERENCES

> In spite of the deceptively vast quantity of statues displayed in the windows and on tattered blankets covering the sidewalks outside of the major hotels, most are chintzy rubbish; the ill-conceived abominations of a tourist-trap industry. . . . Only by being relentlessly pushy in the most charming possible way, would I ever find the prize that I was seeking: a Buddha that really said something; or, a Buddha that really said nothing— and said it loudly enough for me to hear.
>
> —Jeff Greenwald, *Shopping for Buddhas*

Authenticity is the ultimate prize sought by tourists in pursuit of an undiscovered Other. But it is also the ultimate prize sought by anthropologists and other Westerners going to the Himalayas in order to encounter Sherpas. When faced with the realization that the identity of the Other or the Other's symbolically potent artifacts is in part a reflection of the observer's desires, then authenticity becomes problematic for all sorts of people. If the Sherpa who is presented to us is a reflection of our desires, then is there a more authentic Sherpa who lies just beyond these desires? Or is that Sherpa, too, because already *constructed* as more authentic, also already transformed into the inauthentic by our scripted desires? Sherpa identities are constructed in a heterotopic space where imagined or utopian realities infiltrate and reconfigure the spaces assumed to be real. Authenticity persistently slips away, and what remains is a placeholder—a sign called Sherpa. But Sherpa, the sign, is deeply attached to its referents in Sherpa people, many of whom have vested interests in maintaining the linkage between their name, its potent significations, and their beings. Within the transnational interplay of the "imagined" and the "authentic" are multiple interests dedicated to establishing the authenticity of Sherpa identities. Where, then, is authenticity located? And for whom is it generated in both anthropology and in the Khumbu, Nepal? In this section I discuss the desire for authenticities of Otherness in cultural anthropology as a general problem, and then turn to the ways in which authenticity has been dealt with in some of the Himalayanist literature and in literature on the anthropology of tourism. I begin with the problem of reading effects of modernization as "de-authentification," wherein authenticity is taken to be that which is not produced for or from the observer's desires.[46]

Examining the success of the modernizing apparatuses delivered by Westerners to Sherpas leads one to the gaze of Westerners, and particularly to Western desires to locate in Sherpas both sameness and difference. In doing so, however, one has to avoid the problem of denying these Sherpas the ability to be "modern" in any way other than that which arises from the West. In the first instance, Sherpas are denied the ability to be anything but different from the West—they are traditional, exotic, Other. In the second instance, Sherpa Others who are seen as "modern" are simply deemed mimics of Westerners. In both cases, Sherpas are defined by the West. Not only do both perspectives erase the presence of other non-Westerners in Sherpa lives, but both also point to the agency of Westerners and the lack of agency of Sherpas in the construction of their own identities. This problem, I believe, is related to the more general difficulty cultural anthropology has today with representations of cultural difference at a time when power is recognized as itself deeply bound up in the act of "representing" and capturing Otherness. One needs to locate Sherpa "agency" without, I suggest, making that which is located a more "authentic" site for Sherpa identity, essential and enduring regardless of the desires of those who gaze on and write about it. This means recognizing what is at stake in the notion of authenticity. I suggest that authenticity becomes the logic by which a discourse of difference persistently recuperates and invests itself with value.

An impasse is reached when one recognizes the irreconcilable gap between Othering, as implicit in the process of identifying cultural difference in those people ethnographers write about, and reflexive attempts to avoid Othering by exploring how representations of cultural difference can always be traced to the desires of, and power invested in, those who author them. Either the differences are taken to be real (and "out there") or they are taken to be products of Western desires and needs for difference (and "in ourselves"), but not both. Rey Chow (1993) posed part of this question, not as a problem inherent in cultural anthropology today, but as a peculiar problem faced by post-Orientalist scholars. "What kind of cultural politics is in play," she asks in a discussion of possible readings of Orientalism, "when a professor from Harvard University accuses the men and women from the 'third world' of selling out to the West"[47] because they are not Chinese (and "different") in the way that a Western professor would have them be? On the one hand, this reveals both a persistent desire to find in the Oriental something entirely different from the West and a critique of Orientalism (contending that Western scholars have gotten Orientals all wrong) that opens up a space wherein more "authentic" versions of cultural difference are to be found, which again perpetuates neocolonial Orientalism. Either way, the Oriental has to be different. The West authors these differences; they are nothing more than a product of the Western gaze.

On the other hand, attempts to recognize sameness in the modernity of those who get called "Orientals" place one in the same potent position of domination as that Orientalism that seeks only cultural difference. To acknowledge the role of modernizing forces emanating from the West in places like China and Nepal forces one to recognize the success of both mimesis and hegemony—in which the West often dominates. Certainly, to claim that modernity is somehow *not* a result of Western intervention and unequal distributions of wealth and power is to erase (or as Gayatri Chakravorty Spivak argued [1988], to render transparent) the privileged position from which Western scholars write. The problem pertains to ethnographic writing. The ability of the Western ethnographer to catalog "sameness" in traits deemed "Western" forces a recognition of the powerful impact of his or her presence and the presence of those from his or her culture preceding that encounter. Here again, the West reigns and "sameness" is attributed to actual, not imagined or desired, displays of the Other and his or her relationships with the West.

In the first instance, difference reflects back upon the desires of the Western Orientalist scholar. In the second, sameness is attributed to actual relationships of domination with the West, including with Western anthropology. One could also find the reverse: a situation wherein sameness reflects the desires of the author, but differences are actually taken to be real, regardless of the author's desires. In both cases, sameness and difference are seen as real and "out there" in the Other, or they are seen as reflections of the gaze of the Western author upon them, but not both. An impasse is reached in the struggle between positing unconstructed, essential difference and the attempts to avoid this approach by locating all cultural difference and sameness in the producers of such characteristics. Both extremes seem untenable. One posits an "authentic" Other who can come accurately into view regardless of the particular gaze of the ethnographer (as if the ethnographer could be transparent), while the other suggests that all cultural differences are the products of the ethnographer's imagination and desire—that all are entirely and solely contingent on the particular experiences of the author. This is the first difficulty of the discourse of authenticity: where is authenticity located between observer and observed?

Working through the material I collected about Sherpas led me to the realization that the notions of cultural difference with which I work are in fact the sites for the production of both a "modern" and a distinctively Other (and this means traditional) Sherpa. Sherpas do not engage in a mimesis with the West so much as in a mimesis of that which the West desires in an uncannily similar and exotically distinctive Sherpa—a Sherpa who is recognizably different from and yet capable of being the same as, if not better than, the West, at those things the West admires. This mimesis both reproduces and collapses cultural differences between Sherpas and Westerners into a mirroring of identity in which being Other also means being "modern" and remaining different from Westerners at the same time, but in ways that are in constant conversation with Western interests. As a Westerner and an anthropologist, my ability to talk about Sherpas as modern always also evokes the requirement of speaking about Sherpas as Other and traditional. Working through this problem led me to realize that one of my goals might be to find a way to write about Sherpas as modern, and as culturally exotic Others for the "moderns" who gaze upon them, without reempowering the West, by using a method not defined by the West and thus informed by something "Sherpa."

A second problem of authenticity thus arises: what would a methodology not defined by the West look like, especially if all versions of difference (from which an "Other" method might arise) are reflections of the author who seeks this difference? One possible way out of this problem of "scripted" authenticity is to engage in a type of writing about Sherpas that aims to deconstruct the idea that there is a singular authentic Sherpa at every point at which representations of them offer such authenticity. If theorizing and essentialist representations can only work as domination, then perhaps deconstructing the various versions of Sherpas would empower Sherpas by exposing the creators of such authenticity. Or, better still, perhaps noting how various versions of Sherpa identity are themselves contested among different Sherpas and different Sherpa interest groups would contribute to a disempowering of the ethnographer who writes about them by refusing the essentialism of the subjects studied. But these approaches would still leave open the possibility of there always being a "more true" or "more authentic" way of being Sherpa that lies just beyond the gaze of the West, or just beyond the essentialist versions promoted by specific Sherpa interest groups. The first approach would lead to the restored authorship and agency of those Westerners claiming to be able to produce this "more true" Sherpa, which goes beyond the essentialist versions. The second approach, which attempts to "let Sherpas speak for themselves" in all their contested narratives, also suggests a notion of "greater authenticity" that, in turn, not only leads back to Western desires (for nonessentialism), but also disempowers all those Sherpas with whom I came in contact.

This strategy of denying any essential authenticity becomes problematic for the Sherpas about whom I write, for they have vested interests in the outcomes of such a discussion. An attempt entirely to deconstruct their "essentialized" identity, no matter how revealing and disempowering of

Western interests this might be, also disempowers the Sherpas. Representations from the West, especially those that offer homogenized versions of "Sherpa-ness," and all of the demands involved in living up to them, are reflected in the ways Sherpas live and make a living today by being a culture Others seek. As subjects actively negotiating for more attention and more opportunities in transnational markets, Sherpas are aware that not only economic, but also cultural, capital is a source of profit. They, more than I perhaps, are aware of the way that authenticity is a site through which power and notions of value circulate. Undermining authenticity by removing its demands for homogeneity or essentialism is problematic. Fragmented versions of Sherpa identity (traced back to authors' desires and nonessentialist writing strategies) are problematic given the particular relationship that informs my writing about them. This is not to say that all Sherpas participate in such exchanges in exactly the same way. Clearly, some Sherpas have more involvement than others with Westerners, and multiple, often conflicting notions of the best way to become involved with Westerners can be found among Sherpas. But I do not want to deconstruct entirely the essentialist identity configurations—the sites for authenticity—with which Sherpas and I work. It would cost too much for them and therefore for me, for it is precisely during encounters with Westerners that the issues of authenticity and homogeneity, essentialism and authority, become important for Sherpas. Rather, I seek a method that realizes essentialized authenticity in its perpetually mimetic form with those who desire on both sides of the encounter: authenticity is that through which we and they become "more real than real."

Who are these Sherpas, then, who seem to be "out there" now in my text? How do I do justice to their presence in my text, and to the ways they informed me of their desires about their representations? I suggest that the concept of a virtual Sherpa poses a way of dealing with essentialized authenticity itself as an outcome of mimesis, not simply of projection, on the one hand, or of unmediated reality, on the other. Whatever utility it offers, this concept has to operate methodologically the same way it operates ethnographically. What, then, is this notion of authenticity that it transgresses?

I discuss authenticity throughout this text in ways that reveal its problematic nature for an ethnography about Sherpas. Authenticity is about the process of the ethnographic production of truth. Up to now, I have talked about it as a problem of distinguishing between observers' desires and observed realities in ethnographic writing: What is only contingency? What is real? The problem of authenticity is also related to a problem of imputed intentions on the part of those who are being observed. Authenticity debates emerge from a discourse that always attempts to juxtapose "staged" with "real" behaviors, "onstage" with "backstage" actions, some sort of deliberately "faked" identity with "genuine" identity, and, finally, the idea of "incorrect" versions of the Other (incorrect because located in the author's imagination of desires and subjective experiences) with "accurate" and "reproducible" (because "objective") ones. This is directly related to the problem of ethnographic authority because each demands a location for authenticity in contrast to an inauthentic site. In a general sense, I believe this notion of authenticity has been an implicit part of anthropology since the work of Malinowski, where it appeared in the form of desires for scientific, accurate, and objective renditions of the "native's point of view," which were pursued only by excluding the voices and presence of the West (including preconceptions of the "native" held by the ethnographer) (cf. Clifford and Marcus 1986). This view was reinforced and set forth in relation to notions of the inauthentic (at least in the Himalayanist literature) with the adoption of Erving Goffman's idea of "symbolic interactionism" (Berreman 1972, Fisher 1986b).[48] My understanding of Goffman's contribution here is that beyond the concept of accentuating aspects of one's identity that give to others one sort of impression over another (and this is perhaps the most widely accepted meaning of "impression management") lies the less common use of this theory to pose the idea that a "staged" or "pretended" way of behaving exists that can always be juxtaposed to one's "true" or "sincere" identity. The task of anthropology, in Berreman, is to penetrate the stage and discover the truth about the natives by being accepted backstage.[49] This penetrative ability on the part of the anthropologist was what distinguished him or her from the tourist; the tourist might not even know there was (or is) a stage. This idea was only thinkable, however, alongside the similarly compelling idea, promoted in the anthropology of tourism literature, that "touristed" people, like Sherpas, are able to engage in "staged" presentations of themselves and their cultures in response to tourist desires.

Dean MacCannell (1973) suggested that tourist experiences are a product of "staged authenticity" because those who become the objects of a tourist gaze reserve intimate and private places of authenticity for themselves, akin to Goffman's "backstage." MacCannell (1973) and David Greenwood (1977) predicted the inevitable commercialization of those aspects of cultural life sought out by tourists, and concluded that the selling of one's culture (and presentation of self) for profit becomes divorced from "authentic" social life.[50]

My problem with these theories is that all presuppose a hidden authentic (or more "real") culture that could be revealed by piercing the patterns of interaction created by commercial tourism. I suggest that vis-à-vis Sherpas, a place more authentic than that which tourists see does not exist.

The deeper one delves into nontourist Sherpa life, the more obvious it becomes that the strategies for self-presentation observed there parallel those found in tourism, and, in fact, that the tourist gaze has penetrated those "backstage" places with Sherpa consent. Here, Eric Cohen (1988), Malcolm Crick (1985), and John Urry (1990) offer useful insights into authenticity, from suggestions that all cultures, not just those visited by tourists, are "staged," and all are therefore inauthentic in some sense, to the reverse notion that even "staged" behaviors can be authentic aspects of an Other's contemporary way of life. It is this latter theory that seems appropriate to the Sherpa case, for portrayals of "Sherpa culture" reflecting Western "desires for authenticity" are as real a part of most Sherpas' lives today as any existing outside the arena of Sherpa relationships with Westerners.[51]

Tourists enter into seductive relationships with Sherpas. These relationships are held together by an implicit mutual agreement to preserve desirable images of Sherpa identities. Like many Sherpas, many Westerners do not look for a type of Sherpa more authentic than that presented to them as a "staged" by-product of their touristic encounters. It does seem, however, that much of the Western pursuit of Sherpas in Nepal today falls within Urry's definition of "modern tourism," wherein tourists search for the truly authentic, which is believed to exist in a singular, essential identity not manufactured for Western Others. Anthropologists who are engaged in a pursuit of authenticity when they distinguish themselves from tourists by claiming access to a "backstage" and more "true" set of identities behind those believed to be offered to all tourists only raise the stakes of the authenticity discourse, making it seem as if (1) the "true" Sherpas are obtainable, (2) just what that "true" Sherpa is needs constantly to be rediscovered, and (3) anthropologists who know there is a "backstage" to identity, culture, and behaviors are the people most suited to this task of discovery. Anthropologists engage in this pursuit when claiming the authority to reveal essential versions of truth about those who are studied—truths that even they (the "natives") cannot see. Anthropologists too seek a more authentic Sherpa when they hope to find a "false consciousness" among Sherpas who claim they love their work on Everest, or when they seek to explain Sherpa seductions of foreigners as belied by a more "honest" yet undisclosed sense of universal contempt for Western visitors, or when the seductions are seen as "staged." What is authenticity if not a version of essential, and therefore commodifiable, truth about the Other, a truth always demanding to be "original"?

MacCannell (1992) offers a slightly different perspective. He sums up the problem of the penetration of the tourist gaze in his chapter "Cannibalism Today" as a problem of the penetration of capitalism in which anthropology also participates:

The term "primitive" is increasingly only a response to a mythic necessity to keep the idea of the primitive alive in the modern world and consciousness. And it will stay alive because there are several empires built on the necessity of the "primitive": included among these are anthropology's official versions of itself, an increasing segment of the tourist industry, the economic base of ex-primitives who continue to play the part of primitives-for-moderns, now documentary film-making, and soon music, art, drama, and literature. . . . I am arguing that at the level of economic relations, aesthetic exchange, and the sociology of inter-action, there is no real difference between moderns and those who act the part of primitives in the universal drama of modernity.[52]

MacCannell observes a disappearance of all primitives and the rise of nothing but performative or "ex-primitives" in their place. "Ex-primitives" are nothing more than moderns who manipulate for profit their aesthetic presentations of self to the world. In posing this theory, he adopts a dual perspective. First, he acknowledges, as I try to in this book, the inanity of invoking a notion of an "authentic" or "primitive" Other. On the other hand, in the text overall he reinvokes the idea of an authentic "primitive" who must have at one time existed prior to the rise of tourism and whose loss, since the penetration of capitalism, he sees as unrecoverable.

Many Westerners (including tourists), in Nepal, hope to find an authentic Sherpa beyond what they see as a "touristic" display. Manufactured identity, like Greenwood's "culture" that can be sold "by the pound," is presumed to be culture commodified by the commercial development of cultural tourism. Modern tourists looking for authenticity become participants in an exchange of meanings about Sherpa authenticity. They deem certain types of behaviors "authentic" and void an Other whom they see as anything that is modified by their presence. But the "authentic" they seek behind the "commodified culture" is also an inevitable by-product of their presence among Sherpas. The signs that indicate authenticity circulate between Sherpas and Others, furiously sustaining the potential for commodification yet undoing its potential effects.[53] I suggest that, following MacCannell's first position above, rather than posit some split between primitive and "ex-primitive" (substitutable for authentic and inauthentic primitives or Sherpas, now or earlier), we look for a way to move beyond the discourse of authenticity, of primitiveness, and that we look instead for a discourse through which cultural differences are always reflective of desires of the purchasing observer—through which all authenticity reveals its producers—and are taken to be, in some sense, noncontingently real.

Should one assume that because Western observers make such distinctions regarding commodification and authenticity, those observed are doing the same (pace Cohen 1988)? And, if they are not doing so actively or consciously, would they not, through mimesis with Western interests, at least be reflecting this distinction? How, in this sense, would we know what is authentic and what is not? Jonathan Freidman (1990) provides a useful analysis of the relationship between commodification and authenticity in noting how particular strategies of self-identification or self-authentication are not just locally situated, but are also contingent on historic global relationships of economy and polity.[54] In the process, he also demonstrates that authenticity need not be methodologically tied to commodification and modernization.

Freidman demonstrates that the commodification of culture can offer authentication in ways not previously provided for by the rhetoric of "capitalism," that most overused metanarrative of modernity, and that authenticity is always shaped by historical and cultural circumstances (though not, per se, specific sorts of desiring Others). The transnational positioning of Sherpas has enabled many of them to become owners of the productive resources of their economy, most commonly in partnership with Western investor-owners (see chapter 5). Consequently, producing their tradition is not something they perceive, in Freidman's terms, as an externalizing activity. On the contrary, their *production of tradition* as the mimesis of a simulated identity is an act that confirms, rather than denies, Sherpa presence. Moreover, their *consumption of modernity* is an act that enables them to continue authenticating their identity in a social universe—one in which the recruitment of sponsors, like the fostering of friendships with various spirits, can be highly profitable. The idea that mimesis undermines the "authentic" Sherpa is thus untenable. Even when Sherpas claim to produce objects and behaviors that are "authentically" Sherpa, one must recognize such discourse as a response to Western demands for this sort of authenticity. Nevertheless, it would be a mistake to conclude from this that such a discourse makes Sherpa "self-presentations" to Western Others "staged," when Sherpas themselves claim that these very same versions of "Sherpaness" are authentic.

What an analysis of the Sherpas in particular reveals is that authenticity is located in that space where the tourists' need for an exotic Other collides with the equally persistent Sherpa need for versions of themselves-as-Others to be appealing. The idea that there is an authentic Sherpa fuels, and is fueled by, the idea that there is a Sherpa identity that has been modified by the West.[55] In order for Sherpas to remain authentic, they have to produce, reproduce, and simulate an authenticity that is forever and inescapably mobile. Sherpas are as much produced in relation to simulations desired by the West as they are referential of a set of characteristics Sherpas possess. Authenticity shifts within social relationships and is reflected in representations of them that are historically and culturally produced, not only by Westerners but by their own cultural history as well. The search for authenticity ultimately leads to the question of authorship, and to an examination of the intended market for such authenticity. I locate cultural authenticity in the virtual space (which is sometimes textual) created between Sherpas and their observers.

The problem of authenticity in this literature is related to the problem of identifying boundaries between cultures. Frederic Barth (1969) noted long ago from his own work in the neighboring Himalayan region that culture was more clearly enunciated at the boundary regions between groups than within the nameable features of culture exhibited by the groups themselves. However, Barth held onto the idea that culture, exposed in negotiations of identity assertion when and where ethnic identity became problematic, still belonged inherently to one group or another. Among Sherpas and Westerners, an elaborate play of reality is enacted, at once revealing and seducing both observer and observed in what looks like a Goffmanesque play of mimicry. But here one can see a slippage of cultural boundaries, opening a space for reciprocal experience, not mimicry but mimesis, and enchantment, not mythical and mysterious but real. It is a space where culture does not belong to one group or another but rather is mobile and shared between the two. Like Melanesians participating in cargo cults, the Sherpas desire to obtain the privileges held by Western Others; this is often a goal of their mimesis. But radically unlike cargo-cult behavior, Sherpa mimesis reflects not simply what the Western Other is and does, but also what the Western Other seems to want and desire in the form of cultural differences between Westerners and Sherpas. And the reasons are not immediately clear at the outset, despite the truism that Sherpas seek perceived power and wealth and perhaps leisure from the Westerners who visit them. Surely this mimesis *is* also a "local" practice emergent from Sherpa history and culture. Whose culture is this that inhabits the mirrored space of mimesis? Sherpas do not just become like the West or that which the West desires; the West becomes part of them as Sherpas find their place as persons and icons in the Western imagination. In this book, as in the works of Barth and Goffman, culture is intimately linked with identity construction, but it is also linked with power in ways that make an impression-management analysis of the production of Otherness inadequate. I hope my text moves beyond a straightforward analysis of the instrumentality of impression management to a culturally relative analysis of transnational power and seduction, culturally relative because it is told from a perspective born of my relationship with Sherpas.

Culture is the site for power in this book, circulating truths about Sherpa authenticity through utterances and images of Sherpas and Westerners engaged in Himalayan encounters. The notion of "Sherpa," in other words, is taken to be a site where power is circulated as various interest groups make use of it to engage others in seduction. Sherpas' displays of desirability are exhibited in techniques of seduction that draw Others into a space of shared meaning and complicity, just as Westerners seduce Sherpas into the desire to become "modern" by climbing mountains—a complicitous endeavor. Here, seduction is not about being tricked or violated, but rather a mechanism of mimesis. It is about the recognition of one's self via the Other, as when one feels one's self through the caress of another—"and with her hands I feel my skin" goes the line from a popular song. In this space of seduction, among many Sherpas and Westerners one finds a conviviality of power—where both seducer and seduced agree to the obligations of reciprocal exchange, however temporary, because they share the meanings exchanged in signs and images. It is the economy of Sherpas writ large as an economy of meanings in the West, and it requires a rewriting of an approach to writing about people like the Sherpas.

So, whereas impression management has been, especially in Himalayanist literature, about simply becoming like the Other to impress him or her (as status emulation or as "staged" authenticity of Otherness),[56] seduction is about becoming that which the other sees as "different" or "the same" in you in order to allow the Other to find himself or herself in you; seduction is about the power of defining Otherness, and the "productive" effects that definition has on its objects. Moreover, whereas impression management relies on assumptions about the sites from which culture originates and is "owned," seduction acknowledges the impossibility of locating such sites of ownership, for culture moves back and forth in mirroring displays of desire and desirability between, in this case, Sherpas and Others. Whereas some uses of impression management would treat some behaviors as "staged" and somehow inauthentic (preserving the backstage as a secret domain of nonperformance behaviors—the domain sought by the ethnographer), this analysis hopes to show that the idea of "authenticity" is itself problematic; there is no more "authentic" place of identity in a "backstage" region, no identity that is hidden from even the most casual Western observer. There are only virtual identities that bridge the distance between observer and observed, in which all those involved in relationships with Sherpas participate. Finally, whereas impression-management approaches have often been about unveiling ethnographic subjects who negotiate interactions instrumentally, this book hopes to show that ethnography is itself involved in the veiling processes, claiming to reveal how both subject and observer are engaged in seductions of the "real" and the Other, but inescapably revealing this as yet another veil waiting to be lifted in order to reveal yet another authentic Sherpa. The objective is to move beyond the idea of an onstage and a backstage identity to one of an intertextual subject whose very existence persistently and ineluctably draws our attention to the observer.

In the remainder of this book, I analyze ways in which one might move beyond the idea of a singular authentic Sherpa, first by looking at how authenticity is sought in what is taken as a traditional Sherpa uncorrupted by modernization or tourism but is, in fact, produced by modernization itself and by the anthropological concern with an "authentic" subject who can be studied. Ethnographic concerns with authenticity, like those of tourists, mountaineers, and development workers, inform Sherpas' concerns with being authentic and "traditional" in Sherpa ways. Then I look at how authenticity is sought, specifically in those traditions that are then called "authentically Sherpa" in Buddhism and shamanism. Each chapter examines a specific apparatus that has produced Sherpa authenticity. Exploring the sites from which a more authentic Sherpa might issue ends in my positing the existence of many virtual Sherpas whose constructions and "essences" are inextricably linked to the desires of those observing and trying to locate Otherness.

Dear Vincanne,

Namaste. Hope you're having a great time back in the States. It seems like yesterday that we had that wild + crazy dinner at the Amber.

Doma wrote you a letter about the death of her brother in the big storm. (It was big!) Apparently, she was very composed at first; then had some problems. Sherpa friends asked me to come help + after a couple of days I got her to go with me to the psychiatric dept. at Teaching Hospital. The doctor there was really nice + she's much better. She's had this kind of problem twice before - it seems to be biological in large part. I don't know. It was a sad situation, because people were trying to help her - but she completely rejected (hitting, biting) them. I guess that everything will work out OK.

As you can guess from the letter, I've been on the road much of the time since you left.

Write soon,

Take care,

love,

Mary

7. Letter sent to me by my friend Mary soon after I left the field, informing me about our friend Doma.

CHAPTER TWO

Making Modern Sherpas

EMANCIPATION

Upon receiving this letter from my friend Mary, I tried to piece together exactly what was happening in my friend Doma's life. Doma later helped explain it herself when she visited me in New Jersey in 1993. It occurred to me then that Doma's story was somewhat allegorical of one part of that larger set of relationships between Westerners and Sherpas with whom I worked.

In 1987, Doma and her one-year-old daughter lived in a three-room apartment with a shared bath in one of Kathmandu's more expensive tourist districts. It was a convenient location for Doma, whose many foreign friends were easily able to find her when they arrived in the city. Unfortunately, it was also across the street from an empty lot that doubled as a makeshift garbage dump. Horrific odors occasionally wafted through her windows, making her wince and roll her eyes in a gesture of both embarrassment and resignation. This home, which was ideal in so many ways yet imperfect in so many others, epitomized Doma's life. Since childhood, she had experienced fortunate yet bittersweet gains—incredible luck, always coupled with great loss.

Doma was born into an affluent family in Khunde village in the Khumbu region of Nepal, which she always considered her "great good luck." But after her father died when she was an adolescent, her family lost much of its wealth. When Doma was only eight years old, her leg was crushed in an unexpected rock slide that came down on her while she was walking on a mountain trail. She viewed the accident and its consequent injury as her "fate" (*sonam*), and she would have died from the resultant infections had she not had the "good fortune" to have access to the first Western doctor sent to Khunde village by a charitable development organization set up by Sir Edmund Hillary (later called the Himalayan Trust). "Dr. John," as he was called, tried to save her leg, but could not set the bones and stop the infection. Gangrene began to set in, and he ultimately had to amputate her leg just below the knee.

Thereafter, Doma became one of the hospital's special cases because of the dramatic circumstances surrounding her accident and because such a disability had befallen one so young and helpless. The attention the doctors offered her arose from more deep-seated concerns: How could she live in the unpaved and roadless Khumbu if she could not walk? Indeed, how could she be fully Sherpa, like the other villagers, if she could not climb in the mountains? For years, the hospital raised money to provide her with prosthetic legs, which, as a child, she periodically outgrew. Dr. John also made a special point of sending gifts to Doma from New Zealand long after he left the Khumbu.

As Doma grew older, the Trust's charitable efforts on her behalf began to wane. She had learned English from the Khumbu schools run by the Himalayan Trust, though, and began to cultivate friendships with Western mountaineers and tourists who were able to talk with her about Sherpa culture at tea shops and community festivals. Many foreigners found her beautiful, and her insights about Sherpa life and her hospitality were abundant. She was a "typical" Sherpa of the sort they expected to meet in the Himalayas, even if she was not typical in that she could not work on treks or expeditions. Some of her foreign friends became so fond of her that they sent her money and gifts, and occasionally sponsored her to visit them in their home countries. "She has many sponsors," other Sherpas often told me. "That is how she can afford such an expensive apartment in Kathmandu." On her own, with no job, Doma would never have been able to support her lifestyle without regular sponsorship, or so others said. Doma's most important sponsor was an American man who had designated himself her godfather when she was a child. He had gone to the Khumbu on several Everest expeditions and befriended Doma when he visited her family's tea shop and lodge, which were in high-altitude villages en route to the Everest base camp. So even though Doma had lost a leg, she retained a sort of phantom limb in the form of her initial dependence on the hospital and the Himalayan Trust, and her vigilant and successful contacts later with foreign friends.

Nevertheless, Doma herself felt that her foreign sponsors were unreliable resources, sometimes visiting Kathmandu bearing gifts, other times not visiting or writing at all. She once showed me photo albums with pictures of her tour in the United States with another American sponsor, a woman. There was Doma in front of the sponsor's home, atop the Empire State Building, by the ocean in New York, and so forth. That same sponsor, however, had not written in six months, nor had any money been sent. On the other hand, two of Doma's other friends from the United States had visited recently—a wealthy filmmaker and a billionaire whose hobby was mountaineering. Both were in town for climbs and each of them, independently, gave her money, trying in the only way they knew how to take care of her.

Doma's sponsors liked to visit her because she had become their friend. She told them the latest news concerning expeditions and discussed Sherpa life and Buddhist events going on in town. She invited her foreign friends to participate in Sherpa rituals, making them feel somehow more privileged than others by affording them the opportunity to observe aspects of "authentic" Sherpa culture not often experienced by tourists. They felt they were "on the inside," and spoke of her incredible hospitality, her tragic accident, and their desire to help her. Doma always said that her sponsors knew "her whole life situation," which was why they sponsored her. One of her Western friends told me once, apropos of his relationship with Doma: "I am connected by enduring friendships to the Sherpas."

By 1993, Doma would be a successful entrepreneur who owned several companies and traveled often to the United States, but in 1987, she still had little money and no regular, reliable sponsors. She lived from one day to the next, hand to mouth most of the time, gaining income wherever and whenever she could, doling out any extra money to those she knew would help support her when she eventually exhausted her own supply. A year and a half earlier, Doma had become reacquainted with a Tamang man who had been her lover when they were both teenagers in the village where she grew up and where he had temporarily been employed long ago. Doma had given birth to their first child back then, unbeknownst to her lover, who had left for Kathmandu before this son was born. The child died within his first year. When Doma met her Tamang lover years later in Kathmandu, she was in her late twenties—well beyond the age of marriage typical for most Sherpanis—but she fell in love all over again. She and her lover stayed together for several years, during which he promised her marriage and a life together. Doma gave birth to their second child a year later, before a formal marriage, as is customary among Sherpas. But her companion did not live up to his word. He left her in the spring of 1986, soon after that second child, a girl, was born.

Doma then found herself in a desperate situation. She had no husband and no steady source of income, for she could not climb mountains for a living, nor were her family members able to send her money. Finally, she decided to give some money to a Manangi friend for investment in one of the notorious trade ventures for which Manangis (another Himalayan ethnic group) were famous at that time. She thought she might be able to turn a profit quickly, but her friend was arrested in Hong Kong, and Doma never saw her money again. She was devastated.

Doma's closest friend was her mother. Her mother understood and appreciated why Doma had had a child, knowing that Doma would need someone to take care of her later in life, just as she herself had relied on Doma for a certain amount of care. And her mother was her closest link to a generation that knew her family as wealthy—a link that helped keep her connected to elite Sherpa social circles despite her frequent lack of money. Doma's mother often stayed with her during the winters, which meant that Doma's social life was much more exciting than otherwise during those periods because her mother was so popular among affluent Sherpa families. But in the fall of 1988, the same year Doma lost so much money to the Manangi, yet another tragedy struck—her mother died. Faced with this loss and her ongoing financial worries, Doma started sinking into a depression. She wrote letters asking me to help her pay for the funeral. She wondered what she would do now, with no money and no husband to help her survive. She often said that if it had not been for her leg, she would not have these problems. She would have a husband, she insisted. But now she could not lead treks and expeditions. She could not even live in the Khumbu and run a lodge. The absence of her leg prevented her from doing nearly everything Sherpas did to earn a living, for it hurt her to walk. Now, she asked, how would she live without even her mother's help?

Doma's last resort was her younger brother, who had already been able to help her financially in some small measure. He earned a meager income as an assistant guide for a prominent trekking company run by wealthier Sherpas, and was hoping to be promoted some day to the position of sardar, which would increase his income dramatically. Doma's hope was that eventually he would be able to help support her, even if he married, and so she always treated him with special favor. She introduced him to her foreign friends and thereby furthered his career. When he came to Kathmandu, she always insisted that he stay with her, never asking for any remuneration for the extra expense of his food and lodging. "Normal" filial affection was for her cut from the same cloth as self-interest in her own survival.

Then, in the winter of 1989, her brother was working as a high-altitude expedition sherpa on Everest when a terrible blizzard struck. Doma's brother was one of many on the expedition who died in the storm. A few weeks later, I heard from other Sherpas that she had had a "breakdown." Finally, I received a letter from our mutual Canadian friend, Mary (see fig. 7), explaining that Doma was so distraught on hearing of her brother's death that she went mad (*nyombu*). His death was apparently the last straw for her. She was shouting obscenities, her friends said, crying uncontrollably, hysterical, biting and hitting everyone who tried to help her. After several weeks they called Mary and asked her to take Doma to a hospital for help. The doctors there offered psychotropic drugs to calm her down. Doma's Sherpa friends all agreed that her problem was "biological."

At first it seemed strange that, given the social circumstances precipitating Doma's breakdown, her Sherpa friends would so readily deem her problem biological. It seemed obvious that the deaths of family members and her financial insecurity precipitated her outbursts. Surely, calling her problem biological would not help her get the social support she seemed to need. Rather, she was provided with drug therapy. Why had she not used traditional healers, I wondered—lamas or shamans? Surely they would generate the social solutions she seemed to need. When she went to the doctors, she was put on psychotropics and told she would probably need to use them whenever she got depressed, for her problems were the sort to which she was innately predisposed. Two years later, a Sherpa from Kathmandu who had a new job in New York City spoke to me, and he brought up Doma's "biological" problem, which he said could "recur any-time" and for which "she needs to take drugs." But four years later, Doma herself told me that she had gone "crazy" then, not in any permanent sense, but as a temporary reaction to being so extremely sad and worried. She said her personal *lha* (god) had become too upset. She said she was afflicted as a result of her anguish and anger. She was at her wits' end, and she had a mental collapse.

Given Doma's own explanation of her experience with being "crazy," I had to wonder how it benefited others to call her condition biological, or how it benefited her to go to the hospital. But the answer was in some measure obvious. Like her phantom limb, the Western resources Doma had grown up with had become an internalized part of her identity and even the identities of other Sherpas, and her and their reliance on a bio-medical approach and solution to her condition was in this sense predict-able. In many ways, the biological label placed on her condition revealed a great deal about Sherpas' relationships with Westerners, relationships that were mediated through medicine. Doma's biological condition not only reveals the Sherpas' appreciation of Western medical services, but epito-mizes the seduction of Sherpas by a particularly Western view of their problems. It also discloses much about a Western image of Sherpas—about a set of Western desires for a specific type of Sherpa—that Sherpas have aspired to and become.

On the one hand, Doma was identified as having an organic problem. For many physicians and, eventually, Sherpas as well, such a diagnosis did more to mask the social dilemmas of an invalid Sherpa than to enunciate them. Drug therapy made it possible for Doma to forget and perhaps even to cope with her hardships, but did not alleviate the social conditions that made her life difficult. Rather, a focus on biological causes and solutions deemphasized those conditions. By adopting this particular biomedical view of her problem, Sherpas and Westerners alike allowed her social and familial needs to be obscured in favor of a diagnosis that would label her an inherently flawed Sherpa. On the other hand, diagnosing Doma as biolog-ically flawed reconstituted her in a new *social* guise—a guise drawn from her relationship with Westerners as an invalid yet ideal Sherpa. For West-erners, her perfection as both a typical and an atypical Sherpa made her a vehicle for demonstrations of Western benevolence that rearticulated a way of being Sherpa defined by the West. Doma was unable to do many of those things the West deemed essential to "Sherpa-ness," and so she was perceived as flawed in an irreversible, natural way, just as her "craziness" was perceived as biological. Yet her hyperconsciousness of being Sherpa, of the identity through which she had gained sponsorship from an early age, was equally present. Doma was, in this sense, truly ideal, in fulfilling a Western desire for a Sherpa Other by her very dependence on the West. This was an Other through whom the perceived generosity of Westerners became visible to me and other foreigners, and to Sherpas. Doma was truly a modern Sherpa. Beyond this, Doma presented Western doctors and Westernized Sherpas with a more comfortable way of viewing an invalid Sherpa that fit everyone's view of what the ideal modern Sherpa represented. Surely Doma already represented this by being crippled, outfitted with a prosthesis, and dependent on the Western agencies that had helped her. Her new medical crisis could not help but be interpreted and processed in a way that affirmed the identity already constructed for her by the history of Western involvement with Sherpas.

As an allegory introducing the theme of this chapter, Doma's particular relationships with Westerners exemplify Sherpas' relationships with the West in general. What, then, does it mean for Sherpas to be "modern"? What at first appears to be evidence of a Sherpa who is no longer truly or traditionally Sherpa in her reflection of Western interests is ultimately evidence of a modern Sherpa whose authenticity is indisputably caught up in relationships with Western interests. The grafting of Western modernity onto Sherpas like Doma has been accomplished in a number of ways. Modernization among Sherpas has involved engaging with Westerners in both mountaineering and trekking tourism and in development programs, in ways that render Sherpas both similar to and different from Westerners. In this chapter, I explore how Western modernity in Sherpas' lives has been advanced by biomedical resources and activities, first through physicians and medical researchers on mountain expeditions and later through hospitals and clinics in Sherpa villages. Although there have been other significant arenas in which Sherpas have been modernized (for example, through schools; see Fisher 1990), I focus here on medical activities.

Biomedical programs were important because they offered new ways for Sherpas to experience identity through biomedical conceptions of their bodies, and because they redefined the notion of the social for Sherpas so that it correlated with disease categories. Altogether, this meant reconfiguring Sherpa subjectivity.[1] As it did elsewhere in Nepal, the particular construction of subjectivity resulting from Western programs played a critical role in sustaining Western development programs in the area.[2] To understand these activities requires an understanding of the attraction Sherpas hold for Westerners—an attraction that made Sherpas seem both worthy of attention and desperate for intervention from the West. It also requires looking at the specific mechanisms of modernization at work in the

Khumbu, through which modern Sherpas were created and maintained. Finally, it requires an examination of how projects of modernization have been successful and have thereby been able to create virtual Sherpas: in order for Sherpas to remain worthy of aid, they have had to remain traditional in all the ways the West desired. Modernity is reflected back onto Westerners in ways that mirror Western desires, but this mirroring entails a mimesis that, because it demands that Sherpas be "traditional," is also embedded in ways of being Sherpa not entirely encompassed by Western modernity. The West cannot be erased from Sherpas, but neither is it totalizing.

OF MOUNTAINS AND MEDICINE

Early Himalayan expedition accounts are replete with stories about the rigors of the mountain climb and the important role played by expedition physicians in helping make such adventures less daunting and more profitable, in more ways than one.

> George Band has to distribute rations to the acclimatization parties. A sheep has been purchased and the Sherpas, as good Buddhists, will not kill it, so George Lowe has offered his experience as a butcher.
> The arrival of an expedition invariably attracts the halt and the maimed [from the local communities], and Mike Ward [the expedition physician] has many cases to examine. There are teeth to be pulled, sore eyes, ulcers, fevers and obscure stomach pains to be cured. Nor must I overlook Griff Pugh, who is setting up shop in his physiological tent and is anxious to weigh us on the big scales used for assessing our loads, puncture us with needles and drive us down the hill to a starting point for his Maximum Work test.
> This afternoon, we paid our first official visit to the Monastery at the invitation of the monks.[3]

Wedged between descriptions of time-honored expedition exotica such as the slaughtering of sheep and visits with Buddhist monks, one hears in the passage above the echoes of a familiar modern spirit—that which pursues the unknown in order to name and then control it. In that endeavor among Westerners and Sherpas in the Khumbu, the biomedical physician and researcher have figured prominently.

In the diary entries of Western mountaineers, one reads of the sleeping pills doctors prescribed to help climbers rest before their difficult assaults, and about the treatments they offered for both major and minor ailments suffered en route.[4] Usually, expedition groups included medical researchers, whose project funding often helped offset costs, and whose studies were aimed at enhancing climbers' performance and gathering data for use on future expeditions or elsewhere in science. Griff Pugh, for example, went along on the Hunt expedition, a British expedition, in 1953. While the mountaineers explored the limits of their human potential in climbing, Pugh explored the limits of human potential in other ways. He tested climbers to ascertain the limits of the body subjected to stress at high altitude, and what medical interventions might be of use in surpassing those limits.

On one Hillary expedition in the early 1960s, Dr. Thomas Nevison of the United States Air Force was brought along to perfect monitoring equipment for spacecraft.

> "Here at 19,000 feet we are subject to a number of adverse environmental factors, much as an astronaut will face in space. We want to know how the space environment will affect the astronaut's heartbeat, respiration, and brain activity. We must have lightweight, fool-proof electronic devices that will monitor his condition and radio the information back to earth, and this is an ideal testing ground." And so we [members of the expedition team] found ourselves serving as stand-ins for a spaceman in Tom's experiments. "This won't hurt at all," he would say, and before I could think of a good excuse he had shaved small areas of my scalp and slipped needle electrodes under the skin. Wires from these needles led to a strange device we nicknamed "Frankenstein" that recorded brain waves as well as our pulse, respiration, and temperature. We like to think that our experiences with Tom's fiendish device were of some help to Astronauts John Glenn and Scott Carpenter on their orbital flights months later.[5]

The efforts of such biomedical researchers and physicians added to the body of Western scientific knowledge and extended its reach throughout the world. In the process, Sherpas also became willing and compliant subjects. Not only did they receive biomedical care while on expeditions; they were recruited as guinea pigs for the experimental work of the physicians. From the account of the 1954 British expedition, we learn that

> an experiment of a different but no less important nature was at that time taking place in the Icefall [a rough portion of the Khumbu glacier]. We were keen to do everything possible to ensure that the stores required to support the two Assaults, on which the whole plan depended, should reach their destination. Michael Ward had in his medical chest some Benzedrine, a drug used successfully in the war to maintain the endurance of troops during periods of prolonged fighting. Its particular property was that of suppressing a desire to sleep. Michael considered that it might be risky to make the initial tests with this on the Lhotse Face itself, so it was administered to two volunteer Sherpas working in the Icefall.[6]

The assault on the Himalayas was undertaken by the British with the same fanfare as a military attack on an enemy, where the enemy was both the mountain outside the men and, in a more subtle presence, within them, in both a physical, biological sense and a more ephemeral, spiritual one.

Medical aid helped the climbers in their quest to conquer both outward and inward regions, and Sherpas were at their sides throughout, as aides in the actual ascent and as subjects in the ancillary medical research. But while Sherpas participated as subjects with the same enthusiasm as the Western climbers had, they perhaps apprehended the whole endeavor differently. One must surmise that the rendering of modernity among Sherpas (to the extent that it was exemplified by taking unfamiliar Western drugs and becoming willing subjects of research) was at least partially oblique, upon learning in the above example that, after receiving the Benzedrine, an amphetamine, the Sherpas responded thus: "One said: 'Splendid! it has cured my cough.' The other had a different but no more helpful experience: 'Fine! it helped me to sleep.'"[7]

This ability to contribute to the expedition with all the gusto shown by foreign participants and yet experience it somewhat differently than those foreigners epitomizes Sherpas' response to Western modernity. Sherpa participation has been full and complete, yet *different by design*. Under the gaze of the West, Sherpas were supposed to become modern in all the ways imagined beneficial, yet remain traditional and attractive as cultural Others in all the ways imagined desirable.

When Tenzing Norgay allowed Yves Malartic and James Ullman to recount, in their two separate books, the tale of his successful ascent of Everest alongside Edmund Hillary, this dual sensibility came through in the description. I begin with Norgay's relationship with the expedition physicians. The physicians examined all the Sherpas selected for high-altitude work, and sent home several Sherpas diagnosed with heart murmurs, telling them they were unfit for the difficult climbing ahead. Norgay was troubled by this, but not because the physicians had usurped his role, as sardar (leader), as the gatekeeper for the Sherpas—Norgay himself believed in the physicians' diagnostic abilities. Rather, he was troubled because the doctors had waited until the Sherpas affected had gone all the way to base camp to turn them away, making it seem as though Norgay had misled these Sherpas, who had worked so hard up to that point, into thinking they might have a chance to reach the summit. Here, it was not the modern diagnoses that were a problem for Norgay, but rather the triage decisions that prevented some from becoming fully modern.

Physicians actually introduced modernization's most seductive resources to Sherpas like Norgay and often were the prime authorities on becoming what was perceived as modern. On the day before Tenzing Norgay's ascent to the summit, the person he turned to for reassurance was one of the expedition physicians, a surgeon:

> Exhausted by the climb, Dr. Evans slid into his sleeping bag. Worn out also by a terrific day—the climb up to the South Col and two trips to and from the camp and the snow-covered couloir—Tenzing stretched himself out near the doctor.

"Tell me everything, Dr. Evans, I beg of you. Is it possible [to reach the summit]? Can it be done?" "I tell you, Tenzing, you won't have to come back to Everest ever again—for this year you are going to succeed—if the weather is right," was Dr. Evans' reply.[8]

With the help of physicians and biomedical research, Sherpas were brought face-to-face with Westerners and a universalized desire for global visibility. Armed with the right medicines and scientific knowledge, these Westerners were able to scale the world's highest mountains and meet what they deemed its greatest challenges. Sherpas were inserted into this globalizing apparatus. News of Hillary's and Norgay's successful ascent of Everest was withheld from the media for two days so that it could be more dramatically announced on the day of the coronation of the queen of England and the Commonwealth, Elizabeth II—the first coronation ever to be televised. Later, Norgay and Hillary were flown to London so that the queen herself could confer knighthood on Hillary and the George Medal on Norgay, who was not a British subject.[9] The Sherpas were brought into an international spotlight as accessories to British glory and recipients of the attention that would later be focused on larger, postcolonial programs of modernization inspired by and directed from the West.

A modern Sherpa emerged—one of the many perpetually new modern Sherpas to come—when Norgay proved he was as desirous and capable of reaching Everest's summit as the Westerners. However, this modern Sherpa was more complicated and multidimensional than that. When Norgay finally neared the summit of Everest, with "authorization" from his consulting physician, it was to Chomolongmo, the goddess of Everest, that he turned for final authorization. "I offer everything, my very life, to Chomolungma—she will preserve me,"[10] he said before reaching the top.

How did this modern Sherpa come into existence, and why was the idea of there still being something "different" about that Sherpa so attractive to Westerners? Sherpa involvement with the West via expedition work involved both receiving care from biomedical doctors and achieving success under terms and conditions set down by foreigners. Biomedicine played an important role in creating modern Sherpas whose own measures of success revealed mimesis with those represented by Westerners. It also made Sherpas the recipients of Western benevolence and, as such, the means by which Westerners defined themselves in relation to a cultural Otherness to which they could, ironically, aspire. The very modernization of Sherpas, which held the potential for an ethnographic erasure of Sherpa subjectivity in a regime *not* of colonialism, but of tourism and development (the seductive apparatuses of modernity), had to ensure that Sherpas would remain ethnographically present by way of their "cultural difference."

A VIEW FROM THE HIMALAYAN TRUST: CULTURAL GUARDIAN AND AGENT OF CULTURAL CHANGE

> It is the fear of collapse, the sense of dissolution, which contaminates the Western image of all diseases. . . . But the fear we have of our own collapse does not remain internalized. Rather, we project this fear onto the world in order to localize it and, indeed, to domesticate it. For once we locate it, the fear of our own dissolution is removed. Then it is not we who totter on the brink of collapse but rather the Other.
>
> —Sander Gilman, *Disease and Representation*

In 1966, the Khunde Hospital opened its doors to the three thousand or so mostly Sherpa villagers of the Khumbu, in the highlands of northeastern Nepal. The opening was the culmination of several years of raising funds, collecting supplies, and then transporting metal roofing, timber, cement, nails, and windows by foot from lowland Nepal. Dr. John McKinnon, a New Zealander, was the first to staff the eight-bed hospital equipped with a generator-powered X-ray machine, simple blood- and urine-staining equipment, pharmaceuticals donated by international organizations and passing mountaineers, BCG vaccines, depot iodine injection supplies, and minor surgical instruments.[11]

The hospital was the crown jewel of several projects begun in 1961 by Sir Edmund Hillary. During a 1975 expedition, Hillary's wife and one of his two daughters were going to join him. On their flight into the Khumbu, the small plane crashed and both his wife and daughter were killed. Some say Hillary thereafter found solace in pouring all of his energies into his Sherpa development charity. They say this tragedy brought Hillary closer to his Sherpa friends, as he became part of their extended families while he promoted Western-style development in the areas of education, health, and infrastructure. He maintained a small apartment adjoining his Sherpa sardar's home, and after the loss of his loved ones he lived there with his "Sherpa family" for part of each year.

The hospital was the ninth of many development projects funded by Hillary's trust, designed specifically for aiding the Khumbu's inhabitants.[12] The projects preceding the building of the hospital included the construction of six schoolhouses and an airstrip, and the laying of water pipes for centralized water supplies in each village. The hospital itself was centrally located in the Khumbu and its services were provided free of charge. Its goals were to provide regular medical care to as many Sherpas as possible and to improve the overall condition of their health. It was restaffed every two years by foreign physicians, sometimes in pairs. Scholarships were provided to promising students in the Hillary-built schools and a few of the best performers were sent for medical education outside the country. In 1993, the hospital was still staffed by foreign physicians.

All of the trust's projects were carried out on expeditions that attracted economic support from Western volunteers because of their dual orientation. The volunteers aimed to help the Sherpas through programs creating the type of infrastructure described above. They also intended to climb and "conquer" mountains. The latter became construed as yet another way to help Sherpas by giving them lucrative employment and lessons in servility, making use of their "innate talents" and "essential cultural traits," as noted by Hillary:

> The Sherpas have given much to Himalayan mountaineering and the mountains have given much to them in return. Not only have expeditions supplied a valuable source of income for the villages, but they have given the young men a chance to produce their finest qualities of courage and fortitude. Small aid projects such as mine have grown out of comradeship developed on the mountains. For these reasons as well as my own personal affection for the great peaks, I will always try to include an unclimbed summit in any expedition I may organize.[13]

A desire to seek unexplored challenges and then master them was shared by all the members of Hillary's expedition teams. He described his first expedition to build a schoolhouse as "an expedition with a difference. We planned to assault two great unclimbed peaks, members of the party were mountaineers of wide repute, yet our major program involved much more than this. We intended to repay in some measure the debt we owed to the Sherpas who live in the shadow of Mount Everest: we would build schools for them, pipe fresh water, and treat their diseases."[14]

For the Westerners who went to help Sherpas, "conquering" those aspects of Sherpa life that were seen as dirty, impoverished, or underprivileged—different from Western life in ways most Westerners deplored and pitied yet often needed for their own self-realization and confirmation—became as important as conquering those unclimbed peaks. This was a tradition rooted in the colonial period, when surmounting the great peaks was equated with hunting the great tigers. And like the tigers hunted or the mountains climbed, the Sherpas had to measure up to those who would be their conquerors or saviors. In order for the Sherpas to be "improved," they had to be both worthy and needy of help. Thus, Sherpas were seen as endowed with many virtues Westerners admired, yet burdened by what were seen as "nasty" impediments of life in the "primitive world." "Saving" the Sherpas would require making them "like" foreigners in all the ways in which Westerners thought themselves privileged, yet preserving them as culturally distinct. This approach would also guarantee the continued fulfillment of Western desires for exotic Otherness, which would flourish with the growing tourist economy ensured by the trust's construction of a high-altitude airstrip at the base of the Khumbu region.

Foreigners' earliest descriptions of Sherpas are filled with adjectives of praise. A physician on one of Hillary's "School House Expeditions" wrote that Sherpas were "grave resourceful people, with great charm and sense of humour. Their hospitality is rightly renowned; they strive to please and help, yet do so with quiet pride and dignity without a trace of servility so that it is easy to accept them as equals."[15] In another account we are told that

> five Sherpas, led by the indomitable veteran Dawa Thondup, who had graduated to the select South Col team after setting an outstanding example in the Icefall and the Western Cwm, came down the slopes to Camp V as we of the first Assault party arrived there that evening. Some apparently almost fresh—Dawa was one of these—others staggering with fatigue, they passed straight on towards Advance Base. Each smiled as he went by; more than one boasted of having only a mug of tea since seven o-clock that morning.[16]

These people, with whom Westerners had dealt for more than fifty years, were admired for numerous qualities. The Sherpas, who had for nearly half a century already guided Westerners on expeditions, shared their food, danced and sang with them, transported loads for them, and died on the glaciers alongside them,[17] were heroically stoic, convivial, devoted to their employers, and, in addition, somehow able to forge a living in the desolate high Himalayas. Hillary himself commended the Sherpas for "their hardiness and cheerfulness, their vigor and loyalty, and their freedom from our civilized curse of self pity"—all qualities that justified his desire to help them.[18]

Westerners found among Sherpas a type of noble native who was not exactly savage, but who could certainly be improved upon with the proper Western guidance. Against a backdrop of praise and admiration, Westerners found among Sherpas a great many problems, which served as opportunities for Westerners conveniently to insert themselves into the Sherpa landscape. Thus, even though physicians on the early expeditions and those who first staffed the Khunde Hospital conceded that overall the Sherpas enjoyed "a rather high standard of living," that "their general health was good,"[19] that there was no obvious malnutrition among them like that which so plagued people of the lower elevations, and that there were no tropical diseases, unlike in other regions of Nepal, they still noted important medical needs that Westerners could satisfy. Sherpas had no access to dietary iodine, leaving a majority of the adult population disfigured with swollen necks from goiter, and resulting in cretinism in some children. Many Sherpas had visible skin lesions and impetigo due to "lack of hygiene." Gastrointestinal diseases were common. There was a high incidence of gastritis and ulcers. Some 25 percent of the children had respiratory infections or irritations, and added to this was the nascent presence of tuberculosis. Scattered reports from mothers who disclosed the number of times they had given birth indicated that perhaps one-quarter to one-half of the children born to Sherpa mothers died before the age of thirteen from infectious diseases or accidents. Beyond this, reports noted that the bulk of the population was illiterate and poverty was widespread—so widespread that Hillary told of children who were forced to wear the clothing of siblings who had died of smallpox.[20]

Clearly, there was room for medical and educational improvement among Sherpas. The hospital had no problem attracting patients. In addition to many Sherpas' exposure to biomedical care on expeditions, Sherpas in the villages of the Khumbu had also had a chance to learn something about biomedicine before the hospital arrived through earlier smallpox and tuberculosis vaccination programs carried out by Hillary and the trust, and then from a massive effort to introduce iodine into villagers' diets to eliminate goiters and the cretinous offspring resulting from hypothyroidism. For the purposes of medical science, all villagers—except the inhabitants of one entire village, set aside as a "control"—were given the iodine.

One obvious issue for the trust was how, given its explicit goal of not "changing Sherpa culture," to avoid altering those aspects of Sherpa culture seen as desirable while modifying those seen as undesirable. The difficulty of striking this balance was illustrated by Hillary's attempts to avoid inadvertently creating welfarism among Sherpas. Although Hillary had founded the Himalayan Trust on the premise that Sherpas were owed a return favor for having helped him reach the summit of Everest, he had formulated a different idea by the time the trust's projects were actually under way. He insisted, for example, that even when villagers were not uniformly supportive of his development efforts, they contribute an equal share of labor alongside foreigners engaged in the construction of schools. When they did not (because they claimed they felt ill, having recently been immunized for smallpox), Hillary publicly admonished nonparticipating Sherpas for their "laziness." "In a fine old fury I gave an ultimatum—tomorrow there'd be a man from each house carrying timber and the children would enroll or we'd pick up our building material and put a school at Phorche [a different village] instead. I stomped off, leaving them in a stunned silence, and Desmond, Tom and Phil [other members] only waited to deliver a few more well-chosen words before departing as well."[21] Hillary was careful, though, to reward those Sherpas who were particularly loyal and hardworking (qualities he felt should be cultivated in Sherpas) on his expeditions by giving them or their families scholarship money and special assistance from the trust. But any effort to "improve" Sherpas had to be carefully directed to avoid "spoiling" them.

Similar concerns regarding welfarism arose over the years at the Khunde Hospital. Its services had always been offered free of charge to Sherpas, and yet in 1982, the physicians implemented a one-rupee fee, which they felt would help stem a rising "welfare mentality." Their aim was to rekindle, with respect to health care, the Sherpas' sense of resourcefulness and responsibility—ironically, the same qualities already imputed to Sherpas by admiring foreigners. The American doctor at the Khunde Hospital in 1987 told me that

> the best part of working here is the people. They seem grateful and they are good to me. It is more rewarding to work in a place where we get reactions from people. I also like being in a culture where I don't have to battle freeway traffic. I also like Sherpa values. They have a simple culture. I like the way they raise their children. Most children are put to work early and they have a sense of responsibility. Most seem to respect that hard work is a part of life and they have a strong work ethic. There are spoiled ones, but most are not. I like the fact that there are so few material things which distract them.

The physician wife of this doctor also admired Sherpa resourcefulness, but additionally voiced a concern over the rise of welfarism. "It irritates me," she said, "when a young Sherpani from Namche Bazaar comes into the clinic asking for baby bottles which she can get from us for only one rupee. It is obvious that she can get them herself from Kathmandu. Her husband is a sardar and earns a good living. He could easily bring them to her." She continued by reminding me of the trust's mandate: "The Himalayan Trust does not want to remake Sherpa culture."

The paradox inherent in the notion of Sherpas who somehow remain unchanged by modernization programs designed fundamentally to alter their daily lives is like that noted by Baudrillard for the anthropologist: "the simulated sacrifice of its own object in order to preserve its reality principle."[22] The lament over the loss of an untouched Sherpa reveals the West's need to preserve the very illusion of such a Sherpa—an illusion that is as central to the Western construction of self as it is to the Western modification of Sherpas.

Western images of Sherpas owe as much to what the West desires as to what is actually there. Fisher, paralleling Hillary's own comments, observed that "the reason Westerners are so enchanted with Sherpas is that the qualities the Sherpas are thought to possess are not only those Westerners admire; they are also precisely those they feel they should have but conspicuously lack or do not adequately measure up to. So Sherpa society, or the Western image of it, represents a dramatic realization of what Westerners would like to be themselves, hence the frequently breathless enthusiasm of the former for the latter."[23]

The process of creating a Sherpa who fulfilled Western needs and desires was certainly advanced by the biomedical programs of the Himalayan Trust. The physicians' desire to modify Sherpa life without undermining Sherpas' "natural" attractiveness led to contradictions in care giving, since the doctors involved, like mountaineers and tourists today, related certain "traditional" practices and habits to poor health, yet hoped to leave intact those "traditions" that made Sherpas exotically desirable. Even with its contradictions, modernization was successful.

A VIEW FROM THE CLINIC: MECHANISMS OF MODERNIZATION

The industries of development have been particularly potent in producing an ambivalent discourse of the Sherpa Other, while managing to skirt accusations of cultural domination leveled at colonials, even though the mechanisms of power at work in development agencies are often similar to those employed by colonialist regimes. Under the guise of benevolence and political and economic interest, development agencies engage in a contradictory mission: both to preserve cultural distinctiveness and to produce cultural sameness. The following letter written by the president of a nonprofit computer foundation devoted to Himalayan charity illustrates the duality at work:

ANOTHER GOOD PC CAUSE

After reading [the] May column, with its mention of donating used [personal computers] to worthy causes, I thought I'd write about the nonprofit Himalayan Computer Foundation. Our mission is to preserve Himalayan culture, promote education, establish progressive health care, and to protect the region's environment. For our first project, I'm writing a custom Paradox application to improve patient tracking for eye hospitals in Nepal, and Borland's Philippe Kahn has donated three PCs to help. Computer technology is an electronic bridge across the chasms of a divided world.[24]

The irony inherent in attempts to preserve culture while changing it goes unnoticed and unaddressed in most development programs, including those provided for Sherpas. In a multicultural, religiously heterogeneous, caste- and class-stratified society like Nepal, to disregard the obvious questions of whose system of education, whose version of health, for whom would the environment be protected, and to whom is it of use to track eye patients is naive at best, hypocritical at worst. The production of sameness by Western programs aimed at modernization is actually promulgated through the rhetoric of preservation of cultural difference. Most programs like the one described above are at least partially successful, if success is measured by the overwhelming desire among the region's inhabitants for computers, more sophisticated software, and biomedical health care.

Hillary's expedition-and-development teams were successful partly because they promoted "progress" in heroic fashion. Eventually, they fostered a deep-seated sense of foreign benevolence and privilege that Sherpas, thus seduced, felt they needed. At the time of the first "School House Expedition," for example, the foreign doctors were confronted with an outbreak of smallpox, which prompted a quick and effective immunization effort. They immunized seven thousand people before the virus could infect them. Only twenty-five Sherpas died in the epidemic (although more were scarred), and the villagers responded with an elaborate display of gratitude. "'You have saved our lives,' said the four village headmen of Khumjung when they came with *chang* and [felicity] scarves to express their thanks," wrote Hillary in 1964. "'But for you, we would all now be dead. You are undoubtedly the father and mother of our village!'"[25] (The attribution of kin titles to Westerners is significant, as I show later.)

Dr. John McKinnon, the first doctor in Khunde, made a special effort to provide Sherpas with interventions that would positively dispose them toward Western notions of health and hygiene in the future, since he saw them at the outset as a largely "medically unsophisticated people."[26] He offered eye surgery for cataracts, amputations for damaged limbs, tooth extractions, and fast and effective treatments for diarrhea and respiratory ailments during his many years in the Khumbu. By the end of the first fourteen months of operation of the Khunde Hospital, Dr. John reported that although most villagers still placed their faith in spirit mediums, lama medicine, and prayer, he was seeing from twenty to thirty patients each day either at the hospital or in outlying villages. By the end of the second year, the Khunde doctors had seen a total of 2,888 outpatients per year (in a population of roughly 3,000), and had inserted twenty-seven IUDs, treated 21 patients at the eight-bed hospital, and seen more than 722 patients per year as outpatients for tuberculosis, respiratory problems, conjunctivitis, skin lesions and lacerations, diarrhea from parasites, arthritis, gastritis, antenatal care, and ear infections. By 1985, slightly less than twenty years later, the number of outpatients per year (including those treated at outlying clinics where Sherpas sought treatment for the same problems) would double. One hundred sixty women were using contraception (including seventy using intrauterine devices and eighty using Depo-Provera), twenty-six babies were delivered to Sherpanis in two years, and the hospital's tuberculosis patient-treatment rate was still on the rise.[27]

Like expedition physicians, who were ultimately viewed by Sherpas as gatekeepers to success on the mountain, the Khunde doctors came to be seen as gatekeepers for Sherpas who aspired to achieving optimum health—the type of health defined and embodied by Westerners themselves. To promote this goal, physicians had to instill in Sherpas a way of thinking about their health and hygiene that required being at least partially observant and critical of their own culture, and wholly dependent on the West. The representations of diseases afflicting Sherpas made by expedition physicians and Khunde doctors drew causal links between culture and health—between tradition and tragedy. It was because Sherpas preferred the flavor and symbolic uses of Tibetan salt rather than Indian salt, for example, that they lacked iodine in their diets. It was their traditional lack of concern for hygiene, coupled with the habit of rubbing oils into hair and skin, that explained their skin lesions and gastrointestinal disorders. It was their smoke-filled homes that caused their eye and lung irritations. It was their small living quarters with no walls to divide living spaces that exacerbated the spread of tuberculosis. And it was their addiction to strong tea, alcohol, and hot chilies, coupled with otherwise bland meals of potatoes, barley and buckwheat flour, butter, and only seasonal milk, that gave them ulcers. In 1987, physicians also began to attribute ulcers to overwork on expeditions by Sherpas who did not handle stress well (in other words, in some sense, by Sherpas who were not good at being the "Sherpas" the West found so attractive).

Many of the qualities of being "different" that made Sherpas so attractive to foreigners also came to be seen as pathogenic. Being healthy, in the Western view, meant modifying Sherpa lifestyles so that they more closely resembled those of Westerners—but it was still important to remain culturally non-Westernized. One trekking sardar from the Khumbu articulated the first part of this mandate when I asked him to describe his visits to the hospital. He said, "We learn that we could be doctors ourselves; we should be doctors ourselves." Above all, this meant adopting the hygienic and health-conscious habits practiced by physicians at clinics and at the local school, where they taught health classes on a daily basis. It also entailed making use of Western doctors for Western-defined health needs on a regular basis. At the hospital, I observed numerous cases in which doctors reminded Sherpas of their own responsibility for their health, particularly for treating themselves with medicines and making regular disclosures of their state of health at the clinic.

Ang Lhakpa

The doctor, with his back to the Sherpani Ang Lhakpa, leaned over his record book and in the Sherpa language, smiling, asked her name: "Kherang ming la khang sii?" He then asked how old she was, what type of sickness she thought she had, and how long she had had it. Ang Lhakpa told him she had a sore throat and a sore, aching body. The doctor lifted his instruments from the counter, examined her eyes, throat, and ears, and finally placed his stethoscope on her chest, asking her to take deep breaths. He then felt her neck to check for hidden swollen glands beneath her skin. He asked whether or not she had taken anything for her sickness. She said no. He asked why she had not come to the hospital sooner, and she did not answer. He then turned away and began to record his diagnosis on a three-by-five-inch card that held her name, and in the large book that listed all the patients seen that season, one per line. Ang Lhakpa sat quietly, looking at the walls, then at the doctor, then at me. He collected some medicines, which he placed in a small, empty bottle for her. He kept one pill out, which he gave to her with a cup of water, telling her to take this pill today, and then to take three each day until she was finished with all of the pills. She reached into her dress and pulled out the one-rupee note undoubtedly placed there for the doctor's visit. She gave it to the doctor, who stuffed it into the money-payment jar sitting on the counter, saying "tuchey, tuchey" (thank you, thank you). She returned his thanks: "tuchey, lassay, tuchey" (thank you, okay, thank you), and left at 11:45.

KENCHI

A Sherpani named Kenchi came in complaining of a cold and asking for another birth-control shot (Depo-Provera). The doctor told her to sit on the table. Mingma (the Sherpa assistant) asked her name and then wrote it in the record book. Dr. D. scolded Kenchi, telling her she was one month early for her shot. She explained in the Sherpa language that the previous time she had come to get her birth control shot one month late and the doctor had reprimanded her, so this month she came early. The doctor did not respond directly to this information, but told her that her cold was not very bad and that she should go home and return one month later for the shot.

PASANG

Pasang was diagnosed with tuberculosis. He came in and a second American doctor (the wife of Dr. D.) told the translator and assistant, Mingma, to have him sit on the stool near the diagnosis table. The doctor recognized Pasang and recorded his name and age without asking. Obviously familiar with the routine, Pasang began to cough up some phlegm within the doctor's hearing. He then walked toward the door, where he would have been able to spit his phlegm outside. Foreseeing the potential loss of a specimen, the doctor, also as if on cue, quickly grabbed a sputum pan and gave it to Pasang, reminding him that she would like to look at the sputum. He cooperated by expectorating into the pan. The doctor then returned to her records and left the room to consult with her husband about this man's case (noting that Pasang was long overdue for his antibiotic drug refill, and therefore now a defaulter).

Both doctors subsequently returned to the room and began to look over the patient's record. They discussed the fact that he had received medication before but had defaulted on three different treatment programs. The doctors sighed several times, shaking their heads and debating what to try next. They considered at least ten medicines and finally decided to use a new combination of those drugs they had, to date, used the least. One of the doctors eventually explained to the patient (through the translator) that he was still suffering from tuberculosis because he started taking many medicines but then stopped before he was really cured. The doctors left the room again. The patient meanwhile sat silently looking at the wall, with all its medicine, and then at me. We smiled and then the doctors returned. Dr. D. told Pasang that they had two more medicines he could try that might work in combination, but if he defaulted with these there would be no more. "Tell him it is like slitting his own throat when he stops taking the medicines," the doctor said, graphically running his finger across his throat. The patient was quiet, simply nodding in response to the doctor's warning, issued via the translator.

The two doctors then turned back to the counter to determine how much medicine to give Pasang, and had the translator fill an old pepper jar with the drugs. The patient then conversed in Nepali with the translator and the female doctor. He explained that he had recently lost a child. The translator told this to the doctor. The doctor said that she had heard that a baby had died, but she had not known it was his baby. She looked pained as she turned back to the medicines. She explained that he should take the pills, along with some other vitamins (which the doctor also supplied), each day. The patient asked if he could eat any and all foods. The doctors said yes and then discussed whether they should travel back with the patient to his home, to see if his wife had also contracted tuberculosis. They agreed that one of them would make a visit to Pasang's home while doing rounds at the outpatient clinic in that village. Finally, the patient gave one rupee to the translator, who stuffed it in the payment jar, and the patient left, smiling and repeating "tuchey, tuchey."

Lhamo

The doctor was angry about the arrival of yet another patient (Lhamo) who was a tuberculosis case defaulter. The doctor came in with Mingma (the health assistant), who explained that the doctor was upset that no one had been bringing Lhamo in for her treatments. "No one is taking responsibility for her," the doctor said. Mingma translated her response: "She says she has been very busy." The doctor responded, "Don't they realize they saw her almost die before?" When Mingma translated this, Lhamo remained silent. The doctor said "Okay," agreeing to give her another five months' worth of treatments. The doctor then left, while Mingma stayed behind to count out the pills. Upon the doctor's return, Mingma told the patient again that she must take the medications every day and return for a checkup each month—saying that it was *her responsibility* to come in.[28]

One of the outcomes of the doctors' work in the Khumbu was a situation in which Sherpas knew that they should visit the hospital or its clinics for most of their health problems, even if they did not follow all of the doctors' advice.

The educational and clinical efforts of the hospital presented Sherpas with a new, and Western, way of viewing themselves physically. The biomedical version of the body as reified and compartmentalized, organ by organ, system by system, was internalized by many Sherpas, so that when they now spoke about the optimum care available from physicians, they frequently referred to specialists and the need to isolate the body's components to take advantage of localized cures. I accompanied a sardar from Kathmandu named Mingma Tshiring to the hospital there, and he explained how confusing it was for him at first because it had one area for blood tests (phlebotomy), one for eye disorders (ophthalmology), one for one organ malady and one for another, another for bone problems, and yet another (which he called the X-ray ward) for "coughing in the lungs" or tuberculosis. For Mingma, the hospital fragmented the body into various parts, as if it had exploded into its constituent components and was then reconfigured in the spatial layout of hospital wards. And this was what made treatment there so desirable. "If we can afford to go to specialists, then we always go there. . . . They are best medicine because they know all about that part of the body . . . eyes, bones, like that," he said. The specialization of doctors in general made them more likely to be sought after by Sherpas, whether they worked in the hospital or not. Private-practice specialists were the optimal choice for those who could afford them. But even the hospital in Kathmandu had more specialists than the clinic in the Khumbu. This was one reason seriously ill patients were often sent to Kathmandu when they could not be effectively treated in the Khumbu, Mingma explained—the Khunde doctors were not "specialist enough" and some patients needed more-expert care than they could offer. The difference between this view of the body and that offered by the Sherpas' traditional healers (lamas and shamans) is great.

Many Sherpas with whom I spoke characterized their diseases in terms introduced by Western physicians, and made an effort to reveal these internal "truths" about their bodies to specialists in Kathmandu, believing that these specialists' narrow focus enhanced the Sherpas' chances for successful diagnosis and improved health. "My friend told me there is a German doctor who has very good equipment," explained another Kathmandu sardar, Phurba, to his friend Tsamgi, who had a knee problem. "He has a computer with the X-ray [possibly a sonogram]. You can see inside . . . your internal parts, on the computer screen. This would be good for your knee." Ang Tshiring, the owner of a trekking agency, also revealed this bias when he told me he might take his sister, who was suffering from something that Western physicians said looked like multiple sclerosis, to New Delhi because they had a CAT scanner there. They would be able to "see if she had a problem in her brain," he said, and launched into a diatribe against the Kathmandu hospitals, which he felt were poorly equipped in the area of diagnostic technology.

Phurba Tarkey Sherpa lived with his wife in Kathmandu, where he ran a trekking-supply shop. On one of my visits to their home, both told me excitedly about their recent appointment with a specialist in Kathmandu for treatment of the wife's gallstones. "We could see the little stones on the screen there, in her stomach. You could count them." A few months later, they had made another trip for a second "video" of her "stomach," which showed that the stones had disappeared. When his wife became sick again soon thereafter, Phurba was confident that it was not due to the stones, since they had been able to see in the "video" that they were gone. Rather, he attributed his wife's latter illness to the recent death of her mother, which had caused her to worry and become sick—an idiomatic expression of a type of "traditional" medical conception that equates emotional states with physiological conditions.

The biomedical "truths" described above were apprehended by many Sherpas by way of technologies aimed at isolating and objectifying body parts. As the Sherpas became increasingly familiar with such techniques and as they placed their faith in them, they also started to adopt the positions from which Western critiques of biomedicine emerge. Mingma Tenzing Sherpa, for instance, told me a few days after his return from a hospital visit that if Western doctors are the measure, "your stool is more important than you are," because they seem to diagnose all disorders on the basis of stool samples. Later, he talked about the same issue in reference to blood. Elaborating on his view of a biomedical approach to the body, he observed that "they [the Western doctors] treat the body as a mechanical thing . . . like a machine, that is all." Mingma seemed acutely aware of the precedence given diagnostic techniques that focused on the analysis of body parts rather than on subjective experience. Nevertheless, he still wanted to go to the hospital, to see if there was something "defective" in his blood, when he felt sick. "Two times, I gave blood as a donor during a blood drive run by French doctors. They told me it was good to have blood taken because after your body makes new, fresh blood. Now I don't think I have enough blood for a test. I need to give more urine and stool tests also." We walked to the clinic that afternoon. The lab technician presided over a room that was packed with jars, test tubes, rubber tubes, a microscope, slides, and a refrigerator. He told Mingma that he couldn't just "do" a blood test because there were "over fifty things to check in the blood," and he would need a doctor's prescription to know what to check for. "You have to go to the doctor first, and get a prescription for a specific test. You have to go back to the doctor after the test anyway, so you might as well go now." Mingma decided that he should go to the doctor that evening. He was anxious to find out, he said, "what in my blood is causing my problem." Conscious of the Western critique of a nonholistic biomedical approach to health care, Mingma's comments suggested that the biomedical method in which he was placing his faith was also one he sensed was incomplete. Mingma scheduled an appointment that evening with someone he called "a specialist" (in fact, a general practitioner) and returned to the streetside clinic for blood tests the next day, only to find that ultimately, his malaise could not be diagnosed.

For Sherpas, once the body's isolated components could be pinpointed as the sites of various afflictions, a commodification of the body (as the object of biomedical care) commenced, in terms typical of a Western economy. Accompanying Sherpas' views of the material and internal loci of their diseases was their commonly held belief that a cure required specific types of treatments, valued primarily according to their quantity and cost. Through sickness, Mingma's body became part of a market system of exchange where health, and just as importantly, the perception of health, could be bought as a commodity. In the Western view of health care internalized by Sherpas, social relations were rarely directly implicated in health and sickness, and the money expended and the quantity of "things" purchased for cure became the index for the severity of a disease and the effectiveness of treatment. This was particularly true regarding childbirth. Sherpanis often indicated that the cost of going to a particular hospital was directly related to the potential for a "successful" delivery, despite there being no evidence of lower success rates for births at free hospitals or at home.

In another example, Sherpas with whom I spoke often gauged the severity of their ailments by the number of glucose bags they were given during hospital stays. It was not the therapeutic qualities of glucose but rather the quantity required that impressed them. When Mingma Doma's sister was hospitalized for diarrhea in the middle of a pregnancy, her sister summed up her condition not by discussing the sickness itself and what had caused it, but rather by noting that "they gave her ten bags of glucose!" Similarly, when Kenchi from Khunde village told me that her husband's mother had been in the hospital for a week and I asked what the problem was, she replied first that she had been given "sixteen bags of glucose!" and stuck out her tongue as she shook her head in disbelief. How could anyone need that many bags of glucose? He or she would have to be very seriously ill. Glucose, I soon learned, was not just the index my Sherpa friends used for gauging the seriousness of their diseases, it was often a label for the disease itself. Ang Temba, who was in Kathmandu for only a few weeks while waiting for the trekking season to begin, had been in the hospital overnight for diarrhea. When I asked him what illness he had had, he said "Three bags of glucose sick . . . not too bad."

For Sherpas, and no doubt for others in Nepal, the embrace of biomedical technology and an internalized biomedical view of the body, objectified by organ systems and "things" used for treatment, was associated with being modern (like foreigners) and emblematic of the profitability of a modern lifestyle. To take advantage of these resources was to be part of a system that promised both cultural and financial benefits. Availing oneself of technologies such as intravenous drips, sonograms, and CAT scans indicated both the internalization of a Western sense of the objectivity of one's body parts and a recognition of the powerful resources that Westerners offered. Westerners provided access to further opportunities for modernization, and, implicitly, they were seen as providers and producers of knowledge about the self.[29]

The idea that the body could be improved upon with the use of technologies from the West was not the only new idea biomedicine offered. Conflict-laden social events were traditionally noted as the leading cause of health disorders in diagnoses offered by Sherpa healers (particularly shamans), but, to Western-trained doctors, the realm of the social was only significant insofar as it related to pathogens identified under a biomedical approach. Such pathogens were then related to internal systems of the body, which were, in turn, linked to those "things" appropriate for treatments. Social conflicts were not an issue for Western physicians, but social relationships that might be disease vectors were, because they were seen as potentially pathogenic—external conditions that could create internal disorders. Thus, sexual relations were addressed by Khunde doctors when they organized fertility and sex-education programs at both the hospital and local schools for Sherpa children. The hospital walls were lined with posters outlining the biomedical explanation of human fertility and contraception. Sexually transmitted diseases were discussed in school programs, and treatments for venereal diseases were offered at the clinics in exchange for information about sexual partners. Sherpa students with whom I spoke about classes taught by hospital doctors repeatedly said that the most important thing they learned was (in English) "everything about human reproduction," "all about family planning" and the "health of the body."

Even parents learned from their children the significance of certain medical interventions regarding sex. At the Fangnyi (annual picnic celebration) in 1987 in Kathmandu, for example, contraception was a big theme. Typically, Sherpas get together during Fangnyi with close friends (often of the same age group) and each contributes money to buy food and drinks for a picnic. It is also traditional for participants to play jokes on one another. For example, they stuff small items (gold, charcoal, wool, wood, etc.) into their dumplings, and when someone bites into one it is taken as a humorous prediction of the character of the person who receives it (thus, the one who bites into gold will be rich; the one who eats the charcoal speaks with a black mouth—that is, tells lies; the one who receives the wool is shy, and so forth). Other favorite pastimes at Fangnyi are cross-dressing and role playing. At the 1987 Fangnyi, which gathered several hundred Khumbu Sherpas at their Kathmandu monastery, young people arrived cross-dressed in wedding clothes. After the mothers and fathers in the parents' group took up pots and pans in a mock display of musicianship and Sherpa dancing, the young bride (the *nama*, or daughter-in-law—in this case, a boy dressed as a girl) demanded her dowry. Thinking quickly, one of the young mothers ran out to the corner pharmacy while the other women and men delayed the young "bride," taunting him with sexual jokes about the handsome groom (the *makpa*, or son-in-law—a girl dressed in men's clothes). Within minutes, the mother returned from the pharmacy and offered her "huge" dowry to the daughter-in-law—she opened a brown bag and showered the couple with condoms.

Given that sexual relationships between Sherpas and Westerners are one of the important ways in which modernization has entered Sherpa lives, the hospital's focus on specific kinds of sex (safe, nonreproductive) is not surprising. Even Sir Edmund Hillary was not excluded from conventional wisdom about such relationships. The joke told by Sherpa men was a simple question: "Hillary first?" This referred not simply to his successful ascent of Everest with Tenzing Norgay (there was a question about who had actually reached the summit first), but also to his live-in relationship with the family of his sardar, whose wife, it was suggested, was "offered" to Hillary first. Sexuality was one area in which social interactions were scrutinized and reconfigured for Sherpas by way of biomedicine. Biomedicine redesigned Sherpa social life so that medical intervention was now a requirement for sexual relations that had reproductive, or "population-level," consequences.

Similar concerns arose in the care of tuberculosis patients. Western doctors treated patients as social entities whose potential to spread disease was their most important characteristic. Doctors routinely asked their tuberculosis patients who else in their homes had symptoms, how long it would be before these others could come in for an examination, and how far away they lived in case the need for a home visit for diagnosis arose. They demanded this knowledge about social conditions from their patients. And the doctors claimed that their Sherpa patients were far better at providing both medical histories and narratives of contagion and infection than were the first-year medical students they encountered during residency back home. The doctors also stressed how important it was for certain individuals to stay at the hospital as inpatients, in order to ensure regular treatment and reduce exposure to the patients' family members. The idea of the medically relevant "social" aspects of life became, for many Sherpas, as associated with the presence of pathogens as with the presence of doctors.

Pinzo Sherpa was a young sardar who had moved temporarily to Kathmandu to obtain trekking work with his cousin's agency. Pinzo had suffered from tuberculosis for a long time before recognizing it as such during a trip to the doctor. When he had finally lost so much weight and was coughing so badly that he was having trouble trekking, he visited a

Western clinic in Kathmandu. He was given antibiotics in pill form and told to take them daily and return for checkups every two weeks. Because he often was away on treks for one to two months at a time, though, Pinzo was unable to return regularly to the clinic. He ran out of pills, and thought he had already improved enough to forgo further treatment. A few months later, he became so sick that he went to a second clinic for help. This time, after informing the nurses there that he had previously taken pills for tuberculosis, he was put on injectable antibiotics. After a month of these treatments, he was at his wits' end. He could no longer work because he had to go to the clinic every day. Without work, he had no money. Without money, he had no way to pay his rent or buy food. Ultimately, when a nurse gave him an injection that went through the back of his arm, narrowly missing a sore and painful bone and spewing antibiotic all over the floor, Pinzo jumped up and yelled that he would no longer stand for the treatments. Since most of the symptoms of his disease had disappeared, he left the clinic and did not return.

The next time I saw him, Pinzo appeared close to death. His cousin, Tshiring, told me that he had tuberculosis again and could not afford treatment because he needed to continue earning money. What could he do? Tshiring asked me. He could not employ Pinzo, who had become too weak to work. Tshiring had been giving him money each week to help pay for his rent and food, but now Pinzo was dying. I asked why Pinzo was not put in the hospital and was told he had refused because he was afraid to lose his home and position in the trekking company. I decided to try to help him myself. When Pinzo agreed to go with me to a clinic for another diagnosis, the doctor there told us that, as a two-time defaulter on antibiotic regimens, Pinzo might not be eligible for treatment a third time. Public-health policy in Nepal mandated that tuberculosis patients receive treatment only three times before actually being considered a menace to society as carriers of bacillus strains that would not respond to any available drugs. Pinzo was perilously close to being judged such a threat.

Analyzing the series of events that had taken place in Pinzo's life led me to recognize certain techniques of what Foucault called "biopower" deployed in this place far from the West. At the clinic, Pinzo was his biological condition—a body diseased with tuberculosis belonging to an individual who had been judged irresponsible concerning his health. At the social level, he was a population concern—a potential biological menace to the rest of society as someone with a disease beyond the scope of potentially successful medical interventions. Thus, the clinical, biomedical view of his condition pinpointed the biological systems of the body as the logical site for interventionist strategies that would effect control at the individual and population levels. But Pinzo was nearing death not simply because of his biological condition; he was also dying, albeit indirectly, because of the social and medical circumstances that made it impossible for him to work.

Pinzo did survive, in part because a nurse-practitioner friend and I, as the neocolonial heirs to Hillary, found a missionary support home that provided him with room and board so long as he stayed "under twenty-four-hour-a-day surveillance" there through an entire course of treatment, until he was given a clean bill of health. Six months later, newly disciplined not only in clinical but also in Christian confession, Pinzo had recovered. And he had become convinced by me of the efficacy of biomedicine and Western sponsorship, both of which he credited with saving his life.

One of the consequences of biomedicine's attentiveness to particular areas of social relations seen as relevant to tuberculosis pathogenesis in the village was the Sherpas' effort to redesign the insides of their homes spatially, to reduce the potential spread of respiratory ailments therein. Sherpas explained that the new, or remodeled, homes looked more like that of the Khunde doctors, with the kitchen separated from the sleeping rooms and the library. Sherpas intertwined wanting to create more healthy living environments with a desire for what came to be perceived as a more prestigious spatial arrangement for their residences than that found in traditional homes. The traditional Sherpa home typically had two levels, with animals and tools occupying the entry level, which had dirt floors, and family living space on the second level, which had wood floors. The living space was made up of one main room, with a mud and stone wood-burning stove built up from the floor at one end, and (if the family could afford it) a separate room at the opposite end that was reserved for the gods, known as the *lhang* or *lha khang* (god residence). One side of the home had windows that opened out onto the center of the village, and the walls on this side were lined with benches where family members slept, ate, and entertained. The back walls, which faced the mountains, were usually windowless and lined with tall, wall-to-wall shelves containing most of the family's possessions, including large copper water pots, mountaineering equipment, and trunks of clothes, valuables, photos, and ritual paraphernalia. Modern Sherpa homes were built with the same windowed and shelved wall arrangement, but also had a wall dividing the kitchen from the remainder of the residential space and, rather than a separate room for the *lhang* (except in the wealthiest homes), there was usually a shrine (*chusam*) that took up the entire far end of the living room. In a few of these houses, one could also find a metal stove imported from Kathmandu (again following the example of the Khunde Hospital), custom-designed not only to cook food but also simultaneously to pipe smoke to a chimney, heating a reservoir of water.

The adoption of Western views about more-hygienic spatial arrangements for Sherpa homes illustrates both the advance of the biomedical presence and its off-target reception by some Sherpas, who at times seemed more attuned to the form than to the substance of the designs recommended and embraced by foreigners. Although modern Sherpa residences were ostensibly divided so as to create a more healthy environment in the main living room, the effect of the separated rooms was to crowd families into the smaller space of the kitchen, where it was warm for most of the day, leaving the remainder of the house and its "fresh" air empty. Despite this unforeseen (and medically undesirable) outcome, the new design continued to flourish. Thus, it was not just the Sherpas' desire to avoid smoke and crowded (unhealthy) daily living that prompted the home remodeling undertaken in the Khumbu. It was also their desire to have homes like those of foreigners, or at least like those that foreigners wanted for them, even if hygiene was not always maximized therein.

The desire to adopt Western-style habitats was further revealed in the comments of Pemba Tshiring, a successful Khum Jung sardar, who told me how he had designed his new home to be more like the home of the doctors. He said he found that style very comfortable. He also felt "it would be attractive to Westerners who might come to stay with [him] when they finished their treks or expeditions," and hoped to install a private shower as well. This too would be appealing to foreigners, and to him, he added. At the same time, he said it was important that his shrine be in the front, or living, room, so that the expensive Buddhist books (for example, a *domang*, one of the sūtra texts) he planned to purchase would be kept, with their shiny silk covers, in that main area. I was well aware that this arrangement called for placing the shrine in a more public spot than usual—in plain view of Pemba's family, friends, and foreign visitors.

Beyond prompting a new approach on the part of Sherpas to the design of their living quarters, there were numerous other mechanisms of modernization set in motion by the hospital. Many of them involved the same process of cultural reification found in tourism—one that led Sherpas to view their culture as capable of being modified to imitate creatively that of Westerners and to retain the presence of such Westerners in the Khumbu. To some extent, this required the adoption of a biomedical perspective about certain life processes and states hitherto not considered medical by Sherpas—again, to become the type of Sherpas desired by the West. Childbirth among Sherpas, for example, had always been considered a risky event, not so much for mothers as for infants. Newborns were considered vulnerable because they had had no time to build up their spiritual protection (*rlung rta*, discussed in the next chapter), and thus were particularly vulnerable to attacks by envious ghosts, witches, and other angry demons and deities. A biomedical approach that persuaded as many mothers as possible to deliver in the hospital redefined childbirth for Sherpas; the mother now was deemed as much at risk as the infant, and the presence of the physician was thus considered more of a necessity.

Historically, few Sherpanis called on professionals of any sort for assistance during childbirth, preferring to deliver in their own or their mothers' homes with only the help of one or more close female relatives.[30] Infants were usually small, and labor, based on women's accounts, generally did not last long.[31] I could find no older Sherpanis who were aware of women who had died in childbirth (which by no means indicates that it did not occur, but rather that it was likely quite rare compared to other regions of Nepal). By 1987, however, the majority of Khum Jung and Kathmandu Sherpanis delivering infants did so in hospitals, or at their own homes with the aid of a Khunde doctor. When asked why it had become so important for Sherpanis to deliver at the hospital, they most often replied that, at the hospital, the doctors were able to make "the cut" (the episiotomy) and sew it up. Few women, however, knew whether or not it was actually common for Sherpanis to tear the perineum during their deliveries. In fact, it was not common for women in most of rural Nepal, due to their squatting positions during childbirth and the small size of newborns. Whatever the history of actual tearing (about which we know little for Sherpas), it was clear that contemporary Sherpanis considered an episiotomy a necessary part of a normal delivery.

Finally, routine antenatal checkups were fast becoming the norm for Khumbu Sherpanis. In addition, Sherpanis were encouraged by doctors to have regular "well-baby" checkups after delivering. Tashi Sherpani of Khum Jung had a one-year-old son, and she told me it was important to bring him to the doctors to make sure he was growing at the "correct" rate—a rate the physicians told her was appropriate. Tashi was very proud of her son, who, she often reminded me, was large for his age, but still on the charts, according to the doctors at the Khunde Hospital. She attributed his size not to her breast-feeding but to the massive supplements of infant formula she fed him.

Another arena in which biomedical views of well-being were adopted by Sherpas was that of mental health. Sherpas distinguish between cretins (*kuwa* or *kuma*), mad (*nyombu*) people, and depressed people (who suffer from a condition called *pang*). Whereas people who are *nyombu* or victims of *pang* are often seen as suffering temporarily, *kuwa* and *kuma* are viewed as permanently in that state (but not necessarily so in their past or next lives). *Nyombu* victims are characterized as disoriented and illogical. *Pang* victims are frequently women who have recently given birth or who are related to someone who has recently given birth, although I was told by a few people that men are also susceptible to *pang*. According to Sherpas, the *pang* sufferer cannot go outside in the sun, cannot have her clothes placed

8. Nima Gelden (left) and Ang Tashi, Khum Jung village, Nepal, 1987.

in the sun, and cannot eat any foods that are exposed to the sun. In addition, she cannot socialize without becoming more ill. In one case I found, both a new mother and her mother had been suffering from *pang* for more than six months.

Medical treatments for these conditions are sought from a variety of healers. Only biomedical physicians, though, place these conditions in the same category of disorder—mental disability. Notably, whereas *kuwa* and *kuma* are not considered by shamans or lamas to be "sick" as a result of their condition alone and are, on the contrary, treated as normal Sherpas who can fall ill for the same reasons as any other Sherpas (including by inadvertently offending demons or deities, becoming the object of a witch's wrath, getting an imbalance of humors, or contracting one of a variety of biomedical pathogens), the condition of cretinism, in and of itself, constitutes an "abnormality" and therefore a disorder in the view of biomedical physicians. Biomedical forms of treatment locate all three conditions on a continuum of mental disease, with cretinism usually being the most severe and depression generally being the least permanently debilitating. One of the reasons all these ailments are treated categorically as similar is that all of them are viewed as brain disorders that, for the most part, can be addressed with biomedical intervention. Cretinism in and of itself cannot be cured, but the condition that causes it—lack of iodine and hypothyroidism among mothers—can be, and was among Sherpas.

Pang and episodes of "craziness" (labeled mania, psychosis, and schizophrenia) were treated by physicians at the Khunde Hospital with psychotropic drugs.

Physicians in the Khumbu advertised their ability to treat psychiatric diseases with drug therapy, and offered patients "cured" of these ailments as the most compelling evidence of the benefits of biomedical care. When a woman from the village of Khunde committed suicide in 1985 by hanging herself in her own home, the Khunde doctors were distraught not only because their treatment of this woman had been unable to prevent her death, but also because other Sherpas with mental disorders might hear of this episode and conclude that the treatment was worthless.

Modernity asked Sherpas not only to think of their culture as adaptable to the extent of encompassing the hygienic regimens of the hospital (tooth brushing, washing with soap, boiling water, and so forth) and generally more health-conscious lifestyles (including not drinking *raksi*—distilled *chang* or liquor—remodeling their homes, eating iodized salt, and the like). It also asked Sherpas to think of their very bodies and related diseases in new ways—ways that ultimately reinforced their need of Westerners, evidenced by a growing dependence on physicians to address conditions traditionally viewed as nonmedical, such as childbirth and mental disorders. For a number of possible reasons (such as the success of the Khunde Hospital, the "heroic" types of biomedical intervention offered there, the outside funding that supported these interventions, the financial and social opportunities symbolized by the doctors and their practices, the hospital surveillance and education programs), becoming modern in the Khumbu eventually came to mean, for Sherpas, reproducing the conditions of need on which foreign agencies depended for the perpetuation of their own presence in the region. This meant becoming the ideal, yet flawed, Sherpas that Westerners wanted to see, and remaining the "typical" traditional Sherpas that Westerners also wanted to see.

Internalized Otherness and Mimesis

Sherpas came to think highly of Westerners, to praise their programs, and even to ask for more care. Such requests arose first with respect to the establishment of more schools in the Khumbu. According to Hillary, when he asked whether there was one thing that he could do for a particular village, an individual named Urkien Sherpa responded, "With all respect, Sahib, we know you have little to teach us in strength and toughness. We do not envy you your restless spirits. Perhaps we are happier and more content than you are? But, knowledge for our children—that we would like to see."[32] In another case, four Sherpas implored Hillary for a schoolhouse in the following letter:

Sir, respected bara Sahib
Sir Edmund Hillary,

We the local people, the Sherpas of Thami, Khumbu, came to know that your honour, helping us in all respects, is going to open some more schools in Khumbu. We Thami people are requesting your honour to open a school at Thami just like Khumjung. Though our children have eyes, but still they are blind! So all we Sherpas of Thami are praying your honour to make our children just like those of Khumjung. We hope your honour may consider our prayer.

Yours,
Chewang Rimpi Sherpa, Thak Noory Sherpa,
Kinken Kung Sherpa, Khunjo Chumbi Sherpa[33]

Although schools were high on the Sherpas' priority lists, it is clear that biomedical services were just as integral to the process of modernization, if not more so. This was in part because the hospital's techniques (when not heroic) were more subtle, and in their own way more demanding, in that they presented to Sherpas fundamentally new ways of viewing themselves as corporeal beings.[34] By the late 1970s Sherpas who were exceptional in school were occasionally sent to medical school in India. Requests for more clinics in regional areas followed soon after the hospital arrived. In 1986, one could find numerous indications of Sherpas' adoption of the potent imagery of medical need for the sake of foreigners. There was a sign posted at one of the Sherpa hotels in Lukla, the village at the airstrip serving as the gateway to the Khumbu region. It was one among many found throughout the region. Hung on the wall above the dining room, placed there deliberately to catch the eye of any tourist entering Sherpa country, the sign read: "Donation of medicines and currency from any trekkers, mountaineers and other willingness people for Lukla Health Post [not run by the Himalayan Trust] will be highly accepted. It will be very helpful to the local people as well as the trekkers.—In charge, Himalayan Lodge."

In the postcolonial era, the perpetuation of a set of needs among the colonized has served to reestablish the power and presence of the West. Such needs arguably have the potential to foster an even more subtle form of domination than colonialism itself. The processes through which Sherpa needs have been created have not originated in the context of political domination, but rather in the context of tourism and charitable development aid. This has resulted in job opportunities, educational programs, scholarships, sponsorships, and the availability of biomedical care. Needs have been created among Sherpas that have subsequently allowed them to position themselves as potential recipients within an entire discourse of need—itself embedded in a larger discourse of desirability issuing from the West. By being needy, Sherpas become desirable. But, again, this all occurs not in a postcolonial setting (where difference is articulated in terms of resistance and racism) but rather in one of tourism and development (where difference is articulated through desirability). Sherpas have had to remain attractive enough (in positive ways) to be saved, and yet needy enough (in negative ways) to legitimize both the foreign use of Sherpas on expeditions and the ongoing foreign presence that can enhance the condition of Sherpas through Western intervention. The goal is to keep the West around, not to be rid of it. This is the first "seduction" of Sherpas discussed in this book—a term deliberately ambiguous with regard to who is doing the seducing and who is being seduced.

A sense of self-discipline among Sherpas, stressed in biomedical approaches to health and promoted through hospitals, now coexists with the Sherpas' need for ever greater cash incomes. This need is also fostered by biomedical conceptions of health as a commodity. Together, these perspectives have helped reinforce the Sherpas' awareness of their dependence on Westerners for work.[35] But laboring on the mountains is itself only assured for Sherpas as long as they can maintain healthy bodies and a monopoly on the resource of labor supplied for high-altitude treks and expeditions. For Sherpas, this has meant becoming fundamentally involved not only in the bodily form of ideal "Sherpa-ness" but also in the production of such cultural images of themselves. This has also inevitably meant being able to engage in a mimesis with Westerners by becoming whatever Westerners desire in order to keep them enamored of Sherpas. The tourist market reflects the Sherpas' dependence on the West, highlighting their difference from and similarity to Westerners—differences and similarities already etched on Sherpa bodies by the biomedical world. It is also possible to read this as a form of cultural seduction that goes beyond the idea of absolute winners and losers and replaces it with mutual exploitation and mutual gain—a seduction in which both parties agree to uphold the virtual images of Sherpas that they have generated. Sherpas are seduced by a Western Othering of themselves. But Sherpas also seduce Westerners by capitalizing on their itinerary of desires for difference and vulnerability. Sherpas do so for their own benefit—they become mirrors that reflect Western interests and positive images of themselves. This expenditure of cultural and behavioral capital turns profitable in the ongoing presence of Westerners, who can offer Sherpas the modernization they seek.

HETEROTOPIAS AND MODERNITY

Most foreigners who have visited the Khumbu since 1951 have been rich, not only by Nepalese standards but also by the standards of other Westerners. These mountaineers are often well-educated, urban professionals who seem able to indulge their every whim for adventure and cultural titillation. Exposed to such foreigners, Sherpas have started to reassess their own social mobility. Most of the Khumbu villagers hired by mountaineers in the early days of Himalayan exploration were from the least wealthy families in their area. The wealthy considered this work beneath them. Many were newly arrived Tibetan immigrants who did not own land and thus had to perform wage work for wealthy Sherpa families in order to support themselves. By undertaking the risky business of portering for foreigners on high-altitude expeditions, poor Khumbu villagers were able to accumulate wealth in short periods of time. With the cash they earned, these villagers returned to the Everest region and acquired land, livestock, and prestige by sponsoring communal festivals and religious events at monasteries and in their homes.

After decades of involvement in mountaineering and trekking tourism, the Sherpas of the Khumbu were in 1987 less divided by economic disparity than they were before the onset of trekking. My Sherpani friend Ang Tashi, commenting on wealth in the Khumbu, said "We Sherpas are all the same. All Khumbu's people are not rich, not poor." Her remarks obscured the presence of Sherpas who lived dangerously close to the poverty line, and others who were wealthier than many foreigners who went to Nepal. But overall, Ang Tashi's perception of a general equality was shared by many Sherpas, despite their preoccupation with who, at any given time, had more money than they personally did.[36]

Many Sherpas continued to visualize their own social mobility following a trajectory laid down by Westerners, because the images of foreign-aided development were images of improved status.[37] In Nepal, people who were modern, educated, and healthy, as Pigg (1992) notes, did not "carry loads." Like the elites of the Sherpa community at one time, foreigners did not carry loads. And now neither did the Khumbu Sherpas who had become wealthy as a result of sponsorship or education from the West. Young Sherpa boys aspiring to be sardars were loath to carry other people's loads unless they were high-altitude porters, and when doing that work they were careful to use Western-style backpacks rather than baskets and woven straps held across the tops of their heads, the consummate symbol of low-paid labor.

My friend Norbu, for example, had placed himself in the awkward position of having agreed to help a family move rocks for the foundation of its new home because he was in love with the family's resident niece. He watched the older day-laborers carry the loads in baskets held from their heads, but he himself refused to place the strap there and instead draped it below his neck across each collarbone and uncomfortably suspended the stones from there. Although this resulted in an aching back and shoulders the following day, Norbu was more worried about people thinking him pitiful if they saw him carrying a burden with the strap on his head, particularly in light of his having come from a poor family. Norbu had recently dropped out of high school before his final year, primarily because of low grades, but he had already learned a lot of English there. With this, he hoped quickly to secure a position in a trekking agency, but was afraid that if he was seen carrying loads like a common porter, he would not be chosen by a village sardar to work as a sherpa guide. He also insisted on "dressing for success." He felt that wearing the clothes of a sardar, such as high-quality trekking boots or tennis shoes and a good down parka, would better situate him within the industry. Finally, he thought he should "know all about Western things, like English language, like the doctors and [their] medicines, so that we can become like the doctors." For Norbu, this desire to pattern himself after foreign physicians was somewhat misguided, since he had opted for a trekking career rather than for furthering his education. It occurred to me that it was the doctors' lifestyle that Norbu aspired to more than their actual occupation. Moreover, Norbu hoped to recruit me as a sponsor; he sent me letters attesting to his ongoing needs over the years. These letters always began with an indication of how life was progressing in the Khumbu, followed by some stories of major religious or cultural events. They then explained how hard life had become financially for him and discussed his aspirations—purchasing a home and (years later) educating his children.

Pigg noted that for most Nepalese, it was important to identify with the "deliverers" of development rather than with its "targets," but in Norbu's case and those of most other Sherpas, the two were ironically intertwined. Although he wanted to live like the doctors, he recognized that he needed to remain a "target" in order to achieve this goal. The merger of a globalizing discourse that touted the benefits of modernization with local notions of social status had widespread effects in the Khumbu, making even the poorest villagers feel that attracting foreign development programs by being more Western, and by being more needy in ways Westerners defined, would translate into upward mobility.

Becoming modern and continuing to receive the benefits of such modernization were contingent on remaining worthy of aid. For Sherpas, this meant remaining needy and also "traditional" in all the ways designated by the West. The mimesis that this required demonstrated how Sherpas could become like, and embrace the same desires as, Westerners. But it also revealed the ultimate impossibility of Sherpas becoming Westerners that was inherent in the Western discourse itself. In order for mimesis to work, Sherpas had to remain *different* from their foreign friends by being needy and subordinate in ways Westerners could "fix," and by being admirable laborers in all the ways Westerners wished they themselves were, or by being exotically, culturally different. With the Sherpas' recognition of their need to sustain the presence of a foreign Other who could fulfill specific Sherpa desires, mimesis was complete, and the process of modernization was effectively pushed forward. It is this last quality of mimesis that is the most interesting, and that best illustrates the polysemic character of modernity. Look again, for example, at the letters requesting support from Hillary sent by local elites and consider that they were not simply the result of a desire for modernization, but rather were sent by persons who hoped to bolster their own prestige in village politics by securing such valuable gifts.

Modernization and local politics became entwined in a way that promoted the former and perpetuated, within the latter, a strategy on the part of the village elite aimed at obtaining external patronage.[38] Kunzo Chumbi, an elderly Sherpa from Khum Jung, reminded me nearly every time I visited him of his great support of the Western presence. He spoke often about his 1960 tour of the United States. He had convinced Hillary, Marlon Perkins (of Mutual of Omaha's *Wild Kingdom*), and Desmond Doig, a journalist who participated in the first Hillary "School House Expedition," to take him abroad with a scalp of a yeti (abominable snowman), which the Westerners wanted to borrow for scientific scrutiny at home. In the United States, Kunzo Chumbi met with the media and mentioned that in addition to the yeti scalp he had specifically brought a gift from the Khumbu for President Eisenhower. He was unable to present the gift in person, but was assured by his travel companions that it would reach its destination and be warmly received. Kunzo Chumbi then returned to the Khumbu with a great deal more prestige than when he had left. He was already a village leader, but now, by the logic of reciprocity to which he and other Sherpas ascribed, he had foreign sponsors as well.

Kunzo Chumbi and one other *mi che* (big person) Sherpa, Ongchu, who vied with him for political leadership in Khum Jung village, played Hillary's generous offers off one another. One took credit for obtaining Hillary's financial support for the construction of schools. The other took credit for obtaining funding for centralized village water systems. One claimed it was his "work" throughout the United States that had garnered worldwide recognition for the Sherpa name. The other claimed it was his hospitality to the anthropologist Furer-Haimendorf that led to the Sherpas' introduction to the West. The competition went on and on.

Here, the goal of political self-aggrandizement for Sherpa elites was realized by linking themselves to, and making use of, the processes of modernization. In the case of less wealthy Sherpas, the particular strategies employed varied—as Doma's history, related at the beginning of this chapter, illustrates. What all these Sherpas, whether rich or poor, shared was their recognition of the need to adopt and internalize a view of themselves

From the top of the
world's tallest building
EMPIRE STATE
I was photographed in
LIFE Color 1472 feet
above the street and
looking out over the
most fabulous skyline
of the world.

9. Memento of Kunzo Chumbi's tour of the United States.

that reflected what Westerners wanted to see. An "ideal" Sherpa had already been configured by the West. Even the "secret" of the yeti had captured the Western imagination long before Kunzo Chumbi's arrival in the United States. By making himself an exotic representative of Shangri-la, Kunzo Chumbi could appear on television and display his famous yeti scalp as evidence of the reality of one of the great mysteries of the world—a mystery as spectacular as Everest or Shangri-la itself— kept alive by the Sherpas. Kunzo Chumbi embodied for Westerners the image of Sherpas as keepers of exotic Himalayan culture, artifact, and fantasy; it is no wonder he graced the cover of Furer-Haimendorf's 1964 ethnography. At the same time, the shared strategy of Kunzo Chumbi and Ongchu employed mechanisms of modernization to create a heterotopia through reverse seduction, in which Westerners were also being used to satisfy certain Sherpa needs and desires.[39] Why did Kunzo Chumbi care so much about his gift for President Eisenhower? Why were Kunzo Chumbi and Ongchu both interested in making sure I knew they had been instrumental in bringing fame to the Sherpas?

I was having lunch in Khum Jung village one day with Kargen Sherpa, who had worked as an expedition guide for fifteen years. I had asked him if he used the Khunde Hospital often, and before responding, he leaned over and opened a drawer under his small kitchen stool. He pulled out an oversized plastic bag filled with packaged pharmaceutical drugs. He told me he had salvaged the drugs after his last Everest expedition with the Japanese. "The expedition doctor was going to throw them [out]," he said, "but I can bring them to the hospital and they will use them. They know better how to treat us, and then all Sherpa people get to use them. It is better than throwing them [out]," he added. A truly medically modern Sherpa, I thought, who had learned both to desire these drugs and to depend on the continued presence of foreigners to prescribe them for his use. Health was achieved through a clinically and socially articulated self-discipline synonymous with modernity. I asked him if the doctors would be able to read the Japanese labels on them and he replied, "Maybe not, but they would like to get them anyway. It's better if we give these to the hospital, because Western medicines are very strong, and we cannot take them ourselves. . . . Anyway, they will appreciate the gift."

I later realized that the gesture probably stemmed from more than Kargen Sherpa's schooling in the techniques of a modern medical apparatus. His characterization of this offer as a gift carried the same sort of weight as comments made by Tenzing Norgay in his Everest accounts—requests to the goddess of Everest, Chomolongmo, made with felicity scarves and her favorite foods and fragrances, to authorize his climb and ensure its success. It is the same idiom heard in Kunzo Chumbi's account of his visit to the West, and in Doma's and Norbu's attempts to recruit me as a sponsor. In using the language of reciprocity, so typical of shamanism, a form of healing largely overlooked by biomedical physicians in the Khumbu early on, these Sherpas all revealed the subtle way in which it has been possible for Sherpas both to become modern in ways patterned after Westerners and to remain different in ways desired by the same Westerners, who also knew about gift exchanges in their own way, forging an inherently heterotopic participation in modernity.

I met the Sherpas' first Western-trained physician, Dr. Mingma, when he visited the Khumbu in 1987. I asked what he found challenging about practicing medicine among Sherpas, and he told me that some of the most difficult situations emerged when patients tried to give him gifts. "A patient's family will come to visit me with *yangdze* [a luck-bearing gift] and *kata*s [felicity scarves] when their family member, like their child, is sick. You know, they are asking me to save their child by offering me something I will like, as if I could change the outcome of the patient's health if I am pleased. I always do the best I can for my patients, but some things I cannot control." Dr. Mingma explained how hard it was to deal with patients who viewed his services like those of the shaman. The characteristic mode of operation for a shaman is one in which reciprocal exchanges are used seductively to obligate supernatural agents believed to be causing disorders. Such acts reflect a code of social reciprocity among the living as well. This type of gift giving frustrated the Sherpa doctor, for whom "good practice" was uncontaminated by obligatory bonds of reciprocity, and for whom seduction was unrelated to "scientific" practice. Even if he had the chance, he said, he could not cure all the diseases because they were too numerous, often too far advanced, and occasionally too complicated for his sparsely equipped clinic. His assumption was that patients offered gifts in order to procure, by the logic of reciprocal obligation, a fortuitous outcome.

The Khunde Hospital doctors were also frequently given gifts by Sherpas under their care. "People from the Pharak [just south of the Khumbu]," one doctor told me, "are particularly nice to bring foods because they know we don't have fruits and vegetables. They bring apples from Pharak, *rigi*s [potatoes] from Khumbu." He explained that he always felt better when the gifts did not come from a patient or his or her family during treatment but at some point long after it was completed, as if the gesture was more freely made then. In that case there would be no expectation of a return favor from the doctor, since his work was already done. He appreciated it that villagers brought the foods later, because, as he said, it showed their appreciation of the hospital. He also felt these cultural anomalies made his work in a foreign land more attractive. He spent a great deal of time learning the dances and songs of the Sherpas (which greatly impressed them), and once told me that he loved working there as a doctor because "to work in a place like this is an anthropological experience." Other Khunde physicians shared this view, and encouraged those patients who asked to bring lamas and shamans into their hospital rooms for special healing ceremonies.

The giving of gifts to doctors was important to Sherpas since it enabled them to establish a relationship of reciprocity that they felt might be useful in times of medical need, despite obvious indications that many of these same Sherpas, contrarily, viewed their health purely as a commodity. In Kathmandu, Sherpas went out of their way to establish friendships with their physicians, assuming that, as Pinzo Sherpa once told me, "if we get to know our doctor, then he will treat us better. If we are friends with the doctor, then he can help us." This entailed, among other things, paying more to visit doctors at their private clinics than to see them at their public hospital posts. In fact, establishing reciprocal ties with physicians did often enable these Sherpas to be seen before others at private clinics, and to receive what many Sherpas believed was better medical care.

I also heard many stories about Dr. John, the first Khunde doctor. Among Sherpa villagers he was one of the most respected and well-remembered physicians, because, as they said, "he was a really good doctor."

But I learned that this was not only because he offered dramatic cures through surgery and cataract operations. His reputation for being a good doctor owed at least as much to his having made so many house calls, and having even become a ritual brother (*trowo*) to many villagers. The worst physicians, villagers insisted, had been the husband-and-wife team who were at Khunde for two years in the early 1980s—they had refused to make house calls and had instituted the one-rupee fee. No one remembered these doctors forging any ritual brotherhood or sisterhood ties.

Thus, alongside an index of efficacy that gave top priority to specialization, cost, and objectification of the body was another index used to evaluate the physicians themselves. It was not based on cure rates, knowledge, or expertise, but rather on criteria measuring the physicians' social interaction with the village. Biomedical operation in the Khumbu was not merely a replica of that found in a Western context, and this was not simply because it dealt with a traditional culture modified by modern, hygienic, and medically safe practices. The reach of the clinic in the Khumbu was much more expansive, extending outward from the hospital into Sherpas' homes and inward within the hospital into Sherpas' bodies in ways that resulted in an objectification of their persons—as Sherpas configured by Westerners. To be a modern Sherpa meant to forsake the traditional in some ways, by altering diet, house structure, and even desires to approximate more closely those of Westerners. But being modern also involved remaining traditional in other ways that were perpetually attractive to the foreign Other, in their justification of the foreigners' continued presence in the region. This included becoming dependent by never achieving modern perfection, and becoming idealized as an exotic Other who was attractive enough to sustain foreign interest. It also meant emphasizing ways of being Sherpa—such as thinking of visits to doctors in terms of reciprocity—that reminded foreign doctors that they were, in fact, in a foreign culture.

Biomedical practices were aimed at producing a mimetic effect, and thus were effective in creating a set of behaviors among Sherpas that satisfied desires for Sherpas who were both like and unlike Westerners themselves. Within the vast orbit of the clinic and its modernizing agendas, a heterotopia arose. This, for many Sherpas, was the space in which they mirrored Western desires while simultaneously seducing foreigners to slip "through the looking glass" and enter into an "authentic" relationship with them. Being a traditional Sherpa and becoming a modern Sherpa at the same time blurred the boundaries between the notion of a fixed, authentic Sherpa and a mobile, intertextual one. The space within which a singular identity might have been constituted by the West was disrupted by a hybrid set of interests and a willingness and desire to keep all these "traditional ways of being Sherpa" alive. Was there a more "authentic" way of being Sherpa that was not "determined" in any way by the Western gaze in these relationships—namely those seen in Buddhism and shamanism? Or was that, too, built into the discourse of modernization that Sherpas and foreigners came to use? In the next chapter, I explore another way in which authenticity is constituted for Sherpas by looking at the institutions of Buddhism, and at how Buddhism configures a Sherpa of its own, but one that is also configured by Western interests in Sherpa spirituality.

10. Trekkers at Tengboche.

CHAPTER THREE

Buddhist Sherpas as Others

TRANSNATIONAL BUDDHISM

In October 1988, the daily newspaper of Colorado University carried a news article about and photograph of visiting lecturer Phurba Sonam, the Sherpa monk mentioned in the introduction, from Nepal's Tengboche Monastery. He was holding up the masks used in Mani Rimdu celebrations (see Kohn 1988) that he had made in the 1988 course he taught at Colorado called "Masks, Mandalas, and Mountains."[1] The article read:

> As part of the course, Sherpa [Phurba Sonam] made a sand *mandala*, a geometric representation of the cosmos, in a room in the Honors Department, as well as traditional Buddhist dance masks. But someone got into the locked room and the *mandala* was mysteriously dismantled last weekend. Sherpa said, "I have no idea who did it. It wasn't simply destroyed, but the sand was swept neatly into the corner, and not a single grain was spilled." . . . [Phurba Sonam explained to me later that the loss of the mandala was not serious, for it would have been destroyed anyway; that was its purpose, to teach detachment.] [A student named] George learned [from this] that "Buddhists don't believe that attachment to anything is good. . . . It is better to be giving." Sherpa said the main idea he hoped to impart to students is that "we are all the same, we are all brothers and sisters," whether Hindu, Christian or Buddhist.

He further said of his experience teaching this class, "I was very excited by the class, and enjoyed it very much. This kind of class allows people to 'get inside' each other, and increases understanding."

Phurba Sonam had been educated at Tengboche, the Khumbu region's premier monastery. He was one of the Sherpa monks who was invited to travel to Japan for a performance at the Japanese Little Museum of the World. Japanese investors in this museum had proposed creating small replicas of cultural and architectural wonders of the world, and a Sherpa monastery was one of their stellar exhibits. They imported rock cutters, artists, and wood-carvers from Solu-Khumbu for the detailed crafting and decorating of doors and windows. As a final stamp of authenticity, the investors invited the monks from Tengboche Monastery to Japan for the opening ceremonies. The monks performed several of their famous Mani Rimdu dances, known to both Sherpas and tourists from around the world thanks to several books on Sherpas (including ethnographies). Phurba danced with the others, and commented that the Japanese people there were so much like Sherpas, and the *gomba* so much like the one it was modeled after in Solu, that he felt "at home." He talked about returning to visit his Japanese friends as soon as he could.

Phurba had caught the "travel bug" while first visiting the United States several years before, crossing the country in a mobile home with an American sponsor interested in Buddhism whom he had befriended in Kathmandu. The circumstances that brought Phurba to Colorado University several years later, however, were somewhat different. As he was crossing a main intersection in Kathmandu, some lottery-ticket salespeople beckoned to him to buy a ticket. At the same time, two Sherpani friends standing across the street egged him on—clearly in jest, for monks were not supposed to desire worldly goods such as the rewards of the lottery. Later, when he passed that station again, another friend called out to him, "Today is your lucky day, *thawa* [monk], why don't you buy a ticket?" Thinking it auspicious that three people had encouraged him thus in the same day, he did buy a ticket—just one, his first and last. Later, when the drawing took place, he found he had won! His first prize was a new car worth three lakh rupees, the equivalent of fifteen thousand dollars.

Phurba did not know how to drive, and knew he could not use a car in the roadless Khumbu. So he had his American friend teach him to drive one block on an empty road in downtown Kathmandu and then sold the car for cash. Next, he said, he had to deal with the problem of having all that money. He invested part in an educational trust fund to provide scholarships to eight students for their entire course of education at the new Tengboche Monastery School (built in 1986–87). He considered this an offering to the *gomba* that would help generate Buddhist knowledge and more monks, he said. He used some of the money to return to the United States, where he was invited by the Naropa Institute in Colorado to teach a course on Buddhism. He was also invited by Kim Malville, former head of the Honors Department at Colorado University, to teach a course on Buddhism through mask making. Masks, he told me, are an important aid for Buddhist practice. They are not used to conceal reality, he said; they are used to learn more about it. Malville had met Phurba Sonam while on a trek in Nepal and they had stayed in touch through letters.

After his visit to Colorado, Phurba returned to Kathmandu, where he invested the remainder of his money in an organization he called the Tengboche Trust, consisting of the Tengboche Rinpoche (the abbot), Phurba's American friend, and Phurba himself. One of its projects, he said, was producing small gift cards to sell to tourists to raise money for the new monastery school.

Where does the circuitous path that traces the life of Phurba Sonam take us? Toward an understanding of the transnational character of Buddhism. It is epitomized at least in some measure by Phurba Sonam Sherpa himself.

He is a messenger of history—a history told by Buddhism, tied to a sense of progress defined not simply by lamas and monks, but also by Western interests. A genuine Buddhist scholar, on the path toward becoming a bodhisattva, does not attain enlightenment or enter nirvana until all sentient beings have attained enlightenment. In Phurba Sonam's case, following this path seemed to lead to his further engagement with the West, and toward an understanding that could be universal—that would enable him to see all foreigners as potential Buddhists and himself as a translator for them. Moreover, his was a path that seemed to be unfolding of its own accord before him rather than as he intentionally planned it, and on that path he was able to see resonances of "sameness" between himself and his culture, on the one hand, and the Others with whom he came into contact, on the other.

For Phurba, the world is divided into the *chiwa* (outside one), the *nangwa* (inside one), and the *sangwa* (secret one)—those outside the monastery, those inside, and those initiated into the secret, inner level of practice, respectively. He explained the distinctions this way: "You can compare it to the White House and the whole country of the U.S. as the *chiwa*, then the president himself, [at that time] Ronald Reagan, is the *nangwa*, and the *sangwa* is the 'real' story of being president that we never see." Buddhist empowerment (*oung*) at the first, outermost level simply means being a good Buddhist and practicing religion in order to gain religious knowledge. The most significant of the vows taken at this level is that of becoming a celibate monk. Vows at the next level are undertaken with greater understanding and commitment to such things as religious practice *within* the monastery. The highest-level vows propel one toward a secret level of practice that "cannot be reversed." The final stage of this level, *sangwa*, was described by Phurba as "lightning" or "electricity" being added to wires previously "dead" (this from a young man who had grown up in a region that had no electricity). He added that the person can achieve *chi oung* by becoming a monk, *nang oung* through mental commitment and understanding, and then *sang oung*, which "means he is granted a wife, *yum*, the female principle." *Yum* is the opposite of *yab*, the male principle, and together they symbolize the joining of wisdom and compassion. With compassion, one could become fully committed to helping others so that they too could be better Buddhists, offering them the gifts of the "triple gem" (the Buddha, his dharma [teachings or religion], and his community)—the gift of enlightenment through the teachings of Buddha—with detachment and no expectation of return.

Phurba viewed the *chiwa* population—the potentially converted— as infinite. This made his job all the more critical. Still, Phurba did not think he was on a mission to save the world; he told me he only wanted to learn more about how to be a good Buddhist, how to convey his knowledge to others, and how to be more compassionate in the process. To this end, "one did what one could," or what *sonam* determined one could. This was his attitude. He ventured abroad to teach, made sure that within the Khumbu more *chiwa* Sherpas would have a chance to enter the monastery, and tried to become a better Buddhist through efforts that often involved the "seduction" of foreigners. In this last respect, Phurba's quest was not wholly unlike certain interventionist strategies of the West being played out in Nepal. One of Phurba's main concerns when I first met him in 1982, for example, was learning better English so that he could communicate more about Buddhism to the many Westerners on spiritual quests of their own whom he encountered. Frequently he was asked to give tours of the monastery to wealthy foreigners trekking through the region. His excellent *thangkas* (religious paintings) also attracted foreigners. In the early 1980s, he was commissioned by Westerners to paint several large *thangkas*. Thereafter, many who had heard of him requested these paintings when they went through the Khumbu. I was pleased to receive his Christmas card in 1990, bearing the illustration reproduced on the cover of this book.

One of the wealthy Western friends purchasing *thangkas* was a San Francisco businessperson who, according to Phurba Sonam, had already learned a lot from him about Buddhism. I was told that this, along with his love of mountaineering and trekking in the Himalayas, led this man to set up a charitable organization of his own, the Himalayan Foundation. Over the years, the foundation sponsored several important projects at the Sherpa monastery and throughout the region, including some small hydroelectric programs and a cultural museum founded by Sherpas. Not surprisingly, when the monastery burned down in 1989 from a fire resulting from the electrical system financed by the foundation, it was the foundation (among others) that contributed a great deal of money for its reconstruction.

Phurba explained this American's relationship with the monastery. "He is a *jindak*, not only for the monastery but for Sherpa people. He is like Hillary" (whose organization also contributed to the reconstruction of the monastery). I asked him if the monastery was particularly attentive to thanking this *jindak* for all his contributions, noting that I had seen him seated next to the *rinpoche* at the Mani Rimdu festival the year before, with a long *kata* around his neck. "Oh no," he laughed, "that is not thanks. There is no thanks for being a *jindak* to the *gomba*. If you give money to the *gomba*, your thanks is you get merit. *You* get the benefit, not the *gomba*. Why should the *gomba* thank? That would be double thanks for the donor," he said, and laughed again.

Phurba explained that the *chiwa* are viewed by the *nangwa* as, at best, potential initiates, and at least as persons who support their religion by being good Buddhists and becoming *jindak*s. The latter are a source either of monetary and other material contributions or of sons and daughters who, in later becoming monks and nuns, could help disseminate spiritual knowledge. The *jindak* is like an alms giver in that he or she enters into a relationship with the monastery, which, as the recipient of the individual's contribution, is then the conduit through which the donor gains merit.[2] Merit is achieved through acts of compassion, particularly "unattached" compassion—that given freely without expectation of return. The *jindak* is seen as the one who benefits from the giving, because he or she is given the opportunity to attain a "higher awareness" through a gesture of detachment. The monastery thus makes it possible for the *jindak* to gain spiritual merit, and the sponsor can expect no other return for a contribution. The mere presence of the monastery is the sponsor's recompense. Although the idealized form of unattached giving is undermined in practice by desires for reciprocity, the ideal continues to play an important role in Sherpas' relationships with Westerners—in fact defining one idiom through which mimesis with Western interests occurs. Unattached giving is replicated in relations between foreign sponsors (also called *jindaks*) and Sherpas. Although these relationships are typically construed as reciprocal, Sherpas repay their sponsors only in the sense that they continue to be the Sherpas their sponsors desire.

Phurba Sonam helped me understand the transnational nature of Sherpa Buddhism in a number of ways. First, it is emergent in Sherpas seeing themselves today as Buddhists through the eyes of foreign Others who go to the Himalayas in search of Buddhist experiences as well as Himalayan adventures. This transnationalism is as real for monks and lamas as it is for many lay Sherpas. Sherpa Buddhism can also be examined from a historical perspective, with particular attention to its gradual expansion, arriving in the Khumbu with Sherpas from Tibet and then exported to foreign shores via Sherpa monks like Phurba Sonam. But how can one explore this last form of transnationalism without falling back into a discourse that credits Buddhism with more "authenticity" among Sherpas than is imputed to biomedicine or other modern influences, or that treats Buddhism as somehow outside the gaze of the West? Sherpas become modern in becoming the "Buddhist" Sherpas desired by the West. But in doing so, they also become more Buddhist in ways defined by that religion's principles.

Foreigners hoping to find an authentic Buddhism in Sherpas enter into a world of mimetic representations wherein Sherpas offer foreigners the Buddhism that foreigners want to see. It is a Buddhism marked by novice levels and novice interpretations—*chiwa* practice—and therefore it is also defined by Buddhism's own desires for a "virtuous" Sherpa. Buddhist monks and lamas hope to teach Sherpas and foreigners alike to transcend subjectivity, just as my text aims to transcend notions of authenticity. That goal is counterpoised with its opposite by Sherpa or foreign Buddhists in the first case and by ethnographers in the second, because of their recurring desires for a fixed subject (and for reciprocal bonds), or for authenticity (enabling ethnographies to fix Otherness in a form that is permanent and commodifiable as cultural difference, particularly in writing), respectively. Whether we look to Buddhist philosophy or to the ethnographer's nemesis in representations, what we are left with is something in between; we are left with the idea of a virtual subject. Becoming virtual Buddhists for Westerners does not mean becoming less "authentic" Buddhists in the eyes of the West or of the Sherpas themselves. On the contrary, it entails taking Buddhist lessons more seriously and drawing closer to the transcendence of a fixed or essential subjectivity.[3]

Buddhism in the Khumbu

Not long after their emigration from eastern Tibet, Sherpas called on the married lamas practicing Buddhist Tantrism in their small hermitages on the high slopes of the Khumbu's northeastern mountains. According to the Tengboche Rinpoche, the Khumbu's first hermitages were purportedly founded about 370 years ago by three sons of the lama Buddha Chendin. Chendin was a grandson of Pazjin, the first Sherpa believed to have settled in the Khumbu upon arrival from Tibet.[4] Chendin's famous son was the lama Sangwa Dorje. He studied in Tibet and then returned to the Khumbu, where he helped found three mountain hermitages and the area's first real *gomba* in the northeastern village of Pangboche. The village layout supposedly resembled the shape of the lama's holy-water container (*phembu*), and so the first *gomba* was situated in its center. Chendin's other sons, Rolwa Dorje and Kemba Dorje, founded hermitages. One was in Kerok, where the reincarnated Kerok lama-*amchi* (doctor) still resided as of 1987, east of the village of Thame at the base of the main Sherpa mountain pass to Tibet (the Nangpa-la). The other one was in Gomgila, at the southern tip of the Khumbu triangle, where the reincarnated Gomgila lama-*amchi* lived. The last Gomgila lama died in 1985, but in 1989 his reincarnation was discovered in a Sherpa family from Pangboche.

Although religious services were performed by the Khumbu's lamas for a long time, Sherpas had no place to send their sons for celibate education (aside from the small and understaffed Pangboche Monastery) except Tibet's Rongphu Monastery, which was on the other side of the Nepalese border in the shadow of Everest. With the increase in their wealth around the turn of the century, however, Sherpas of the Khumbu began building their own larger celibate monastery at Tengboche in 1916—a project set in motion by Lama Gelu and his mentor and teacher at Rongphu, Zatul Rinpoche (Ortner 1989; Tengboche Rinpoche 1987). Lama Gelu was a

Sherpa villager who became a religious man following the deaths of his wife and four of his five children. The parallels between his life and Hillary's go beyond even the personal tragedies they suffered. Each in his own way was a major contributor to the configuration of Sherpa identities in the twentieth century. Each of these persons launched projects that would have long-lasting effects on Sherpas' self-identity, and both of these projects were intensified after their founders' own kindred were lost to them.[5]

Lama Gelu went to study at Rongphu. When he returned to the Khumbu he lived in retreat in a cave on the slopes of Khumbila (Khumbu'i yul lha, the Khumbu's patron-deity mountain) for three years, three months, and three days.[6] While receiving his education at Rongphu, Lama Gelu had been told by the abbot there, Ngawang Tenzing Norbu, to establish a celibate monastery in the Khumbu. In response to his anxiety about raising the money necessary for such an undertaking, the rinpoche assured him, "When you were Lama Buddha Chendin in a previous life, I was your son Lama Sangwa Dorje. So, because of this close relationship, you won't have any problems building the monastery and the future will be very good."[7] This reassurance was significant because Zatul Rinpoche was himself the living reincarnation of Lama Sangwa Dorje; it was as if Lama Gelu's son was urging him to undertake this project. After sufficient funds were collected from villagers and other sponsors to pay for supplies and three years of labor, the monastery in the Khumbu was completed. It was called Tengboche (also spelled Tyangboche, Tyangpoche, and Thyangboche). The monastery's first abbot, Chetang Chotar Rinpoche (also known as Lama Gelu), was installed.

After several years, the monastery was populated with monks from both inside and outside the Khumbu community. Then, only eighteen years after its founding, tragedy struck. The monastery toppled to the ground during an earthquake, and on that same night the Tengboche Rinpoche died. Funds for reconstruction were sent from Rongphu, and eventually the *gomba* was rebuilt, this time even larger and better than before. A carpenter specializing in the construction of monasteries and an artist expert in painting religious frescoes were brought in from Tibet. In the end, the reconstructed monastery far surpassed the initial edifice. By 1935, the reincarnation of Lama Gelu was found in the young son of a Tibetan immigrant and his Sherpa wife living in Namche Bazaar. Pasang Tenzing, also known as the Tengboche Rinpoche, and as *tsawi* lama (special or "root" lama) to Sherpas, was still the abbot of Tengboche in the mid-1990s.

Soon after Tengboche was built, a second monastery was constructed in the Thame valley to serve the growing number of families in that region who wanted to give their sons a monastic education. Later, two nunneries were also founded in the Tibetan tradition of *serkyim*, a self-supporting community of religious scholars associated with a monastery on (in Tibet)

11. *Thangka* of Tengboche monastery, painted for the Tengboche Trust by Phurba Sonam Sherpa.

tax-free lands (Aziz 1978). In 1987, the villages of the Khumbu supported a retinue of religious professionals—scholars, monks, nuns, doctors, and a plethora of village lamas (monks who had broken their vows)—who made up approximately one-tenth of the area's entire population. Three lama-*amchi*s resided in the Khumbu: one in Pangboche, one in Kerok, and one in Gomgila, who was still very young in 1987.

By the late 1970s, another facet of Buddhism had become visible in the Khumbu. A monastery called Laudo Gomba was built on the western face of Khumbila Mountain. It was sponsored by foreign Buddhists, in conjunction with a popular monastery in Kathmandu devoted almost entirely to the service of Western Buddhists who went to Nepal seeking retreat and an intensive education in Tibetan Buddhism. As more tourists visited the Khumbu, more foreigners interested in Buddhism also arrived. They could be found at monastic events, in retreats, undergoing religious training, interviewing monks, living at monasteries, filming, videotaping, and writing books and news articles about the Buddhist religion.

The Sherpas' Buddhism was thus introduced by foreigners and by Sherpas into transnational arenas much more vast than those existing before the turn of the century. This expansion drew on portrayals of a forbidden and remote Shangri-la found in Western accounts. Along with thousands of Tibetans living in Kathmandu as refugees since the late 1950s, Sherpas became for tourists (and others) some of the most accessible living representatives of the Tibetan Buddhist culture. Aware of the attraction they held for Westerners seeking both adventure and spiritual epiphany in the Himalayas, many Sherpas, including monks like Phurba Sonam, applauded the suggestion of the Tengboche Rinpoche that more monks begin to learn English as part of their religious training, so that they could then teach foreigners about Buddhism. One Sherpa from Kathmandu pointed out that a lama of even higher standing, the Khentse Rinpoche from Bhutan, had "emphasized learning and teaching English so they could teach everyone about Buddhism. We need to teach others about virtue," he said. "So, now, even the head lama [of Tengboche] is supporting English. Before, he was not supportive, but since his trip to Japan, he now sees a need for teaching English." Who better than the Sherpas, for so long viewed as possessing those positive attributes believed to be in short supply among Westerners, to teach others about virtue? The presence of Western spiritualist interests in the Khumbu quickly became part of its history.

In 1989, as noted, Tengboche Monastery again experienced disaster. A hydroelectric system had been installed to reduce the monks' need for firewood. After only a few months of operation, a space heater was left plugged in one night under a mattress and caught fire. Nearly all the monks were away at the time—many at the funeral of a *rinpoche* in Kathmandu, and others at the funeral of an important Namche villager. When the smoke finally cleared, villagers who had run miles to reach the *gomba* and then worked for hours to try to save it could see that the entire structure had burned to the ground.

As if reliving his past life, the Tengboche Rinpoche flew up to the monastery from Kathmandu via helicopter and surveyed the damage amid the still-smoldering pieces of wood and ash-filled air. One flat stone displaying a fresco of Guru Rinpoche, Padmasambhava, one seventh-century adept credited with bringing Buddhism to Tibet, was visible at the base of the rubble, undamaged—the guru's eyes blazing and his scepter raised. The scene, along with the Tengboche Rinpoche's obvious distress, was caught on a videotape made by the American partner in the Tengboche Trust. He had accompanied the *rinpoche* on the helicopter and put himself at the monk's service in helping address the disaster.

At first, there was a movement among the Sherpas to pay for the reconstruction entirely by themselves, with no money from foreigners. The *rinpoche* also began promoting the idea that the loss of the monastery was not to be lamented. Monasteries, after all, were like mandalas—the "blue-prints" for monasteries. Their destruction was, in fact, a sort of creation, in the sense that it taught one about detachment. He thereby turned the unfortunate event into a lesson and additionally touted the monastery's reconstruction as an opportunity for villagers and others to earn merit. He reminded villagers that the chance to rebuild was fortuitous. Their new *gomba* would be even better than the old one. Soon the American's videotape was circulated among foreign sponsors and friends of the monastery, arousing sympathy and financial aid. By the time the reconstruction started, Sherpas had recruited support from many foreigners and foreign groups, including the Himalayan Trust, the Himalayan Foundation, and a host of private donors, in order to meet the total projected cost of three hundred thousand dollars. The Himalayan Foundation, founded by the friend of the monk Phurba Sonam Sherpa, for example, ultimately contributed one hundred thousand dollars for basic construction materials.[8]

The intersection of Sherpa and Western laities involved in *chiwa* practice is seen in the role adopted by both as *jindak*s for the monastery. Being a *jindak* in this case meant being able to overcome one's attachment to wealth by giving it to the monastery. During the celebration of Bumtsho, a festival reinvented by Sherpas in Kathmandu in the early 1980s and later moved to the Khumbu, Sherpas paid for the famous Khentse Rinpoche to fly by helicopter to Tengboche so he could preside over the services. At the end of the ceremony, he spoke from his windowsill perch on the third floor of the *gomba*. It was a lecture that Sherpas taped and later listened to over and over again in their homes. One Sherpani explained to me that because she had not given money to sponsor the event (although her sisters and mother had), listening to the *rinpoche*'s words was the next best way for her to derive benefit from Bumtsho, for it taught her about being a good Buddhist. Khentse Rinpoche's speech included these poignant passages on wealth and the dharma (translated by a monk from Tengboche; the full text is found in Appendix A):

> Birth means death. As soon as one is born, then death is inevitable. When death comes, even if you are wealthy, you cannot stop death. Your money cannot buy life. Even if you are beautiful, your death cannot be stopped. Your beauty makes no difference when you are dead. You cannot change death. You cannot buy your life, nor can you take your money with you. It can be used for this life, but you cannot buy life.
>
> Religion is a virtuous thing, bringing patience and compassion. Virtue and the practice of meditation follows with you after death. Your money and your car, you can't take with you. Wealth is no protection. It is like a rope around your

neck. It will hang you. Do not die with wealth. Some people become drug smugglers, but many people die from drugs. Those who get the profits are single
persons, but these people end up with a hell life [in their next life]. They only
look in one direction—toward that of wealth. But wealth is useless. The only
virtue is the mind. The mind is useful. You should pray. You should respect
educated people, those who know religion. Do not die with your wealth. You
cannot take it with you. When you have that money now in your hand, while
living, let's share with other human beings. Give alms. Help poor people. You
give one time and, after, you get more compassion and you can give more and
more. Your compassion gets stronger and then you don't mind giving away your
wealth. Don't waste wealth, don't save wealth. Realize between right and wrong.
You should pray.

The next section of this chapter explores some of the strategies of Buddhism aimed at teaching Sherpas and others a transcendence of attachments, and the ideal realization of an inner "primordial truth" (or body of
primordial wisdom—*ye shes lus*) not obscured by notions of fixed subjectivity or attachment that evolve from it. Those attempting to locate an "authentic" Sherpa subject that lies beyond the Western gaze often begin by
looking at Buddhism among Sherpas, which is the contemporary heir to
the Buddhism initially introduced to Tibet centuries ago. Lamas and
monks lecture Sherpas on these tenets of Buddhism regularly. One would
want to analyze, then, how successful these Buddhist teachers are at achieving Sherpas who fit their own ideal image of them, and whether such "constructed" Sherpas are any more or less "authentic" than those encountered
in the Western imagination. Finally, one would want to explore the impact
of Buddhism on Westerners, for whom, in a sort of implosion, becoming
Buddhist means acquiring the qualities Westerners presume to be essential
and inherent in Sherpa culture, even when such qualities are those that
deny fixed and essential subjectivity.

BUDDHISM IN EARLY TIBET: THE CIVILIZING PROJECT EMERGES IN THE KHUMBU

Buddhist legend has it that many centuries before Padmasambhava, two
Buddhist doctors petitioned the goddess Tara as follows:

"Great Goddess, by your leave, Tibet is a country of wild men who have faces
like *raksha*s [ogres], abounding with demons harming people, and the people are
more foolish than cattle and do not acquire merit. They do not know what
should be done and what should not be done. Whatever is said to them, they
understand the opposite of it. They requite good with evil and they do not know
the teachings of medicine. They are committing sins. That is not a country

where the teachings of medicine can be furthered. Please give us leave not to go." [And] Tara explained: "It has been prophesied by the Buddha about the country of Tibet, and all the Buddhas have discoursed on Tibet and Avalokitesvara was made the special protector of Tibet. Avalokitesvara is the chief protector and I am helping him. When you go to Tibet you will teach the people medicine, in the way the Buddha comes with his teaching. There is no doubt of success."[9]

The Buddhism practiced in the Khumbu is *rnying ma pa*, the first Buddhist practices to emerge in Tibet after the arrival of such Indian pundits as Santaraksita and Padmasambhava. This Buddhism, like every form of Sherpa Tibetan Buddhism today, is a direct outgrowth of the teachings of Nagarjuna, an Indian philosopher from the first or second century B.C., who revived Mahayana teachings at a time when they were in decline in India. Nagarjuna founded the Mādhyamika school of tenets and taught emptiness based on Buddha's Prajnaparamita teachings, the *Perfection of Wisdom Sutras*.[10] Nagarjuna's philosophy was that of the Middle Path—a philosophy that might be understood in terms of both practice (it falls between asceticism and indulgence) and conceptualization. Conceptually, the Middle Path emerges from a realization of emptiness, of the absence of fixed self-nature in anything; for example, by posing the possibility of one extreme (an assertion), one is always capable of posing an equally compelling case for its opposite. The impossibility of identifying a fixed essentialism or of proving any single assertion leads one to realize that such claims (and self-natures) are illusions. What is real, then, is impermanence. The Mādhyamikas, the Dalai Lama writes, "assert a selflessness of phenomena that is an emptiness of inherent existence."[11] If the inherent qualities attributed to a thing or person are always potentially counterpoised by assertions of the opposite (e.g., Sherpas love to climb mountains *and* Sherpas hate to climb mountains even if they love the money they earn doing so),[12] then Sherpa becomes an empty category—a place where emptiness is revealed to those who want to essentialize these people.

When early Buddhist adepts arrived in Tibet centuries ago in order to teach such philosophies to the populations there, they found people who were receptive to their teachings but deeply steeped themselves in traditions that were in many ways contrary to esoteric Buddhist philosophy. Like the two doctors who petitioned the goddess, Buddhist translators who took their religion from India to Tibet in the eighth century depicted the new region as a giant female ogre whose limbs had to be pinned down by Buddhist *stupas* (large shrines, symbolizing the mind of the Buddha).[13] The inhabitants, like the land and its spirits, were viewed and portrayed as red faced, untamed, and barbaric—uncivilized in their not-yet-Buddhist ways.[14] Such translator-adepts eventually did convert Tibetans to Buddhism—at first only the elites, but by the eleventh century almost the entire population. This did not come about without a struggle, however, for religious practices among Tibetans at the time of Buddhism's arrival were already well developed; they revolved around local spirits of the earth, celestial ancestors, and shamanic ceremonies aimed at creating long-term, obligatory ties between the people and the demons and deities surrounding them.[15]

One of the first tenets Buddhists no doubt attempted to instill among Tibetans was the principle of emptiness, but doing so required a gradual indoctrination. First, local demons and deities with whom the people were in reciprocal and obligatory relation had to be accommodated rather than dismissed as inherently empty or illusory. Also, Buddhists presumably had to convince converts how to practice detachment, including detachment from spirit entities and others (family, friends) on whom they depended for survival. Prior to the introduction of Buddhism, the main sources of health, well-being, and prosperity among Tibetans were most likely the close bonds of reciprocity they tried to develop with the spirits who controlled the natural and celestial universes. The relationships people had with demons and deities—spirits—in historic Tibet were probably not unlike those Sherpas had with their spirits when I worked with them, or so histories would have it.[16] These histories describe such relationships as being like those that subjects had with kings before the arrival of Buddhism—that is, formatted on unequal dyadic bonds of patronage and exchange, negotiated through shamanic intercessors.[17]

This focus on give-and-take relationships with others—whether human or spiritual—shifted, no doubt, with the gradual rise of Buddhism among Tibetans, and the new focus stayed with Sherpas when they brought Buddhism with them to the Khumbu much later. One of the important accomplishments for Buddhists was probably to create in Tibetans and therefore in Sherpas a sense of their own emptiness, which was only possible if they transcended notions of identity embedded in the group or the collective. Buddhism has thus had continually to posit that rather than the collective, the individual is the center of the universe—that the universe, in fact, radiates from the person. From there, it has had continually to reinforce the idea that rather than being a fixed subject, the individual is a transient and ultimately illusory entity. The Buddhism now practiced among Sherpas has advanced these concepts in a number of ways. Notions of subjectivity, for instance, play a key role in Sherpa Buddhist approaches to demons and deities, as do Buddhist configurations of the body, which indirectly promote among the Sherpa laity notions both of individualism and of an elusive and transient subjectivity.[18]

DEMONS AND DEITIES

Buddhism deals with the problem of engaging demons and deities in obligatory relationships of interdependence by suggesting that such spirits can
be conquered or sent away. Historically, Padmasambhava is believed to
have used his Buddhist knowledge to subdue certain deities and demons
whose presence was confirmed by pre-Buddhist priests. It was, after all,
these pre-Buddhist priests who were able, through possession, to make the
voices of spirits heard and their presence seen. After subduing the demons
and deities, Padmasambhava did not, however, banish them, for such an
act would no doubt have been unacceptable to the majority of the Tibetan
population not yet converted to Buddhism. Instead, he cleverly extracted
a promise from the most important of them to uphold, as guardians, the
Buddhist religion. To this day, the guardian deities form an important part
of Buddhist rituals in the Khumbu.

Like the biomedical doctors in the Khumbu centuries later, early Buddhist lamas and monks aroused support for their cause—the promotion of
their religious beliefs—through heroic efforts to help others conquer demons and better manage local deities. Padmasambhava revealed that he
was more capable than were the local priests of eliminating the nefarious
activities of demons and deities. Thus began the long and complicated
relationship between demons and deities in Buddhism—the same demons
and deities to which Tibetans, like Sherpas, were and are attached through
obligation and reciprocity. Rather than befriending the spirits, lamas render them less powerful in a victim's life. This view was apparent in one of
many ceremonies I watched, this one for a Sherpa villager named
Ongchu,[19] who had summoned ten lamas and monks for a healing ceremony, or effigy ritual (*kurim*), specifically called *luzongu* (an exorcism ceremony). This ceremony was based on a text found in the Buddha's Heart
Sutra called *shinying du dok* (*sher snying bdud bzlog*: "turning back of demons
with the Heart Sutra," Lopez forthcoming). In order to explicate this ritual, I have relied on a translation of a version of the ritual graciously provided by Donald S. Lopez, Jr., knowing that it probably contains minor
variations from the ceremony I witnessed (a written copy of which could
not be obtained).[20]

The monks arrived early on the morning of the ceremony, and immediately set to making the *tsampa* dough used in constructing the effigies (*glud*,
or ransom) for the event. They first molded two effigies of humans, one of
the sponsor, Ongchu, and one of his wife, Phuti. These were then dressed
to resemble the couple as closely as possible; clippings of their hair and
snatches of fabric from their clothes were used. (In some cases, sponsors
would even use their own jewelry.) Other effigies were then constructed,
including those of local deities (especially the patron mountain deity) and

those of the demonic entities thought to be involved in the sponsors' afflictions. Rather than making the spirits more real by constructing effigies of them in order to become possessed by them, however, the lamas built effigies of all actors and relied on images of the Buddha as mimetic figures through whom they were meant to overcome afflictions. The completed effigies were set in the center of a table with other offerings such as butter lamps, colored flags, sweets, and incense. These were surrounded by four rows forming an outer square of smaller *torma*s (effigy figurines made of dough) of the *lus* (body) symbolizing various lesser gods and spirits who would be recruited during the ceremony to support the work of the Buddha. Each of them was given an identity by being pressed with a woodblock mold depicting a small, soldierly spirit (one of the protector gods, the guardians of Buddhism). At the center of the square altar, the two effigies of the sponsors were placed facing a small idol of the Buddha, set atop several powdered-milk cans and draped with a white *kata*.[21]

The set table formed a three-dimensional mandala. The remaining conical *torma*s were arranged in a row around each of the four sides of the mandala, with each row painted a different color depending on the direction it faced. Inside the square sat an effigy representing the local mountain deity, Khumbila, an effigy of the Guru Rinpoche (Padmasambhava), and an image of Sakyamuni Buddha, who sat across from the effigies of the sponsors so that they could look upon him. This mandala was significant, for it represented the universe and functioned both as a meditative aid for achieving higher Buddhist awareness and as a model of that mental state. Just as the supplicants in the ceremony were supposed to focus their thoughts on and "become" participants in the ritual via their effigies, I was told, so too were the officiants surrounding the altar supposed to fix their minds on the Buddha who sat facing them, imagining that they were "becoming" Buddha himself. In becoming the being from which the entire universe radiated, the practitioners were believed to be capable of performing great spiritual and mundane feats, including the eradication of ailments.

The monks recited the entire text in unison, beginning with an invocation of the various entities represented by the effigies. Again, this included the guardian demons and deities, who would supposedly help protect the religion. Once all the effigies were consecrated as the particular agents whom they represented, in a process punctuated by cymbal, drum, and horn music, this assembly of supernatural agents was then given a lesson in Buddhism by the monks, who had "become" Sakyamuni Buddha. The agents were instructed about the virtues of compassion and other fundamental Buddhist tenets concerning clearing the self of illusions and other obstacles, as the sponsors (or patrons) were taught to recognize the utility of identifying with or "becoming" the Buddha image, as demonstrated by

12. Ongchu Sherpa.

13. Phuti Sherpa.

14. Effigies of Ongchu Sherpa and Phuti Sherpa.

15. The *kurim* altar set up as a map of the universe, a *mandala*, with Buddha seated at the center and Ongchu and Phuti (in effigy) looking at him.

the officiants. The protector gods were reminded of the importance of Buddhism and of their need to protect the religion.

Lopez's translation of the event is instructive. It begins with several stories of historico-mythical figures repelling demons and undertaking supreme achievements via Buddhism. The instructions for the performance of the rite of exorcism then begin. After all the requisite *torma*s are made and placed on the altar,

> the effigy [of the patron] is then dressed in a garment made from clothing belonging to the patron and is placed in front of the Buddha image with its face turned toward the Buddha and its back toward the officiant. In this position, the effigy stands as both a substitute and protector for the patron, acting as his surrogate before the demons. . . . The officiant then visualizes himself as the Buddha, seated in the midst of the four demons. This is a position of both danger and power, from which the long process of exorcism is executed, with the officiant, as the Buddha, playing the role of first host of the demons, then as the agent who enters into a contract with the demons, and finally as their conqueror. The text instructs the officiant to recite:
>
> *From the nature of emptiness [appears] a cushion of jewels, lotus, and moon [upon which sits] the chief of teachers, the complete and perfect Buddha Sakyamuni. His body is gold, with one face and two arms. His right hand touches the earth, his left is in the gesture of equipoise. On his head is the crown protrusion. He is adorned with the*

thirty-two auspicious marks and eighty auspicious minor marks, such as wheels on the soles of his feet. He emanates boundless light and beams of light. A retinue appears; the pledge and wisdom beings non-dual. He is attended to the right by the noble Avalokiteśvara and to the left by the eight dear bodhisattva sons[22] and the eight supreme śrāvakas,[23] such as Śāriputra. At his heart on a lotus and moon is the great mother surrounded by her sons, the buddhas of the ten directions. At the heart of the great mother is a moon mandala. At its center is the letter āḥ. At the edge appear the letters of the Heart Sūtra. They radiate beams of light together with their own sound, making an offering that delights the conquerors and their children. All the blessings and powers gather and touch those gathered for the rite, as well as all sentient beings, purifying all sins and obstructions and pacifying all sickness, demons and obstacles; the meaning of the eighteen emptinesses is created in your mind.

Here, rather than visualizing the Buddha and the residents of the *maṇḍala* as arrayed before the mediator, . . . the officiant visualizes himself as Śākyamuni Buddha, adorned with the major and minor marks. . . . [T]he visualized pledge beings fuse with the actual wisdom beings. The mediator [visualizes a goddess seated on a moon disc which radiates a visualized Heart Sutra (that is, the actual scripted words)] . . . standing upright around the edge of the moon disc at the goddess' heart, not simply the letters of the mantra, but the entire sūtra, for . . . [T]he entire sūtra functions as a mantra in this ritual. (Lopez 1996)

The ceremony continues as the officiants (as Sakyamuni Buddha) implore various demons (causing disorder) to "abide in their image" or become visible to the officiants, in order that they can be negotiated with.

Assembled army of the demon of the Afflictions, so that the afflictions of sentient beings might be removed, when I, the mantra holder, invite you, I beseech you to come here for just a little while and abide in your image. Jah hum bam hoh.

This is the same mantra that is used to cause the wisdom beings, the actual buddhas and bodhisattvas, to merge with their visualized doubles, the pledge of beings, to bring the beneficent deities into the presence of the mediator. . . . In order for the demons to be placated and turned back, they must be made visible and brought into physical presence. Hence, dough images are made for them, which they are then invited to enter and animate: "the making and existence of the artifact that portrays something gives one power over that which is portrayed."[24] . . . The four demons and their retinues have been turned away [*bzlog*] from the Buddha by the power of the Heart Sūtra so that they now face outward, toward the effigy of the patron. . . . If the rite is being performed in order to destroy an enemy, the officiant is instructed to say, "By the power of the words of truth of the noble three jewels, may our enemy so and so today be summoned, liberated [i.e., killed], and his flesh and blood eaten by the gods and demons of the world. May his consciousness be led into the dharmadhatu." (Lopez 1996)

It is important that the effigies of the patrons are taken as "ransom." In texts I have found that deal with this term, ransom is spelled *glud* ("a thing given as ransom" or "a ransom for life") and is related to the verb *bslu* ("to ransom life" or "to seduce" [Das 1983]). But more takes place here than simple trickery, for this ceremony calls for mimesis. Just as the officiants are meant to "become" the Sakyamuni Buddha, with all his adornments, so too are the patrons meant to "become" the effigies, with all their adornments. The Heart Sutra text reads at one point: "This beautiful effigy of a human I offer today as ransom for the person." But Lopez writes:

> This does not seem to be a case of confusing the demons into thinking that the *ngar mi* [effigy, "powerful human" or "human as I (am)"] is the patron; rather the officiant's task is to convince the demons that the *ngar mi* is more desirable than the patron. The assumption, of course, is that they cannot but agree to the bargain. *As a result, the person represented by the* ngar mi *will eventually come to possess the wealth and beauty of the dough double.*[25]

The ceremony's crescendo occurred as each of the effigies was "converted" to the teachings of the Buddha and they were then removed from the altar, several at a time, and sent out of the house. Finally, after the Buddha and patron deities had been placed on the home shrine of the sponsor, and every person present had exited, the altar centerpiece representing Ongchu and Phuti was removed from the house. A trail of *tsampa*, marking the effigies' path out of the house, was swept up by the monk following the removal of the last effigy, which itself was carried out backwards so as to make sure all of the participants were out ahead of it. At a place outside the village, far from Ongchu's home, the effigies were placed under old dried baskets and hay, and, after some final recitations with musical accompaniment, were set ablaze.

For the lama and monks, the meanings of the *kurim* were multiple.[26] To accommodate different levels of understanding, the monks explained, ceremonies were tailored to different levels of knowledge and awareness. At a minimum, performances were supposed to educate the sponsor about the importance of practicing Buddhism, but most of the laity relied on elaborate symbolic paraphernalia, which expressed the meaning of the ritual in lay terms. In fact, this ceremony, like most *kurim*s, was not understood in its most esoteric and literal sense by the lay Sherpas present. They comprehended it only in the broadest, most conceptual terms.

One older monk remarked, "We do the *kurim* to obliterate obstructions and send them out. The *torma* is a thing, but really it is an idea in our mind. If we get sick, bad things happen, or if people say bad things about us—gossip—this is to send these obstructions away. The *torma* is for visualization of what is in the mind—the obstacles." I asked him about the presence of demons. He said, "Demons? There are no demons. What are these? It is our imagination that creates demons." Nevertheless, Buddhist texts themselves refer to demons and spirits as if they were "real" entities. According to monks and lamas, then, the *kurim* is aimed at teaching Sherpas about becoming more like the Buddha, on whom, as their effigies demonstrate, they are supposed to meditate. Becoming like the Buddha means becoming detached from those notions of reality that lead to attachments—attachments to various material things such as the body, the notion of demons (or the reality of them), and ultimately the concept of the self as being fixed or having a singular self-nature. The burning of the effigies during the final stage of the ceremony signifies, for the monks, that all people will die, that the body is impermanent. Demons and deities are recruited to help the sponsor recognize this.

For most of the Sherpa laity, however, the *kurim* is more than a way of overcoming dependence on demons and deities through a higher level of individual awareness and transcendence of subjectivity. It is most often seen as a chance to outsmart the spirits. Ongchu, for example, who had had some religious training at the monastery, viewed his *luzongu* as more than an educational event wherein he actually read the ceremony text with monks and meditated upon "becoming" the Buddha on the altar. He also saw it as a means of tricking the demons into consuming the effigies of him and his wife, rather than the couple themselves. The demons were first lured by being fed, which tricked the demons into becoming obligated to entities that they, in essence, were invoked to embody during the event.

Lopez notes that both interpretations are at work. Although the officiant is told to recite "I have no attachment to him [and offer him freely]" as he gives the *glud* to the demons, in the end, "in effect, the demons and the patron (with the officiant acting as his agent) enter into a contract [by accepting the *glud*]. The demons are to understand that any breach of this contract carries with it a penalty; should they not keep their part of the bargain, the officiant, through his surrogate, the Buddha, will . . . visit them with punishment" (Lopez 1996).

For Ongchu and many others, the idea that the demons were lured with butter lamps and food offerings and were then cast out via the Buddhist ceremony was central. In the end they were destroyed along with the demons, by fire. Especially key to the ceremony was not simply the sending away of the demons but the initial realization of their presence; in the same way that the patrons truly became their effigies, the demons were made to have a presence in this world of material essence. The pedagogical message brought together these worlds by showing that demons, or deities for that matter, were quite real in the sense that anything observed in the world is "real." For the lamas and monks, the message was thus also about the potential transcendence of the world where spirits (*shrindi*) were accepted as real and consequential in this way.

Through the efforts of the Buddhist monks and the sponsor, the spirits were supposedly rendered less potent, the first step toward recognizing them as illusory. This differed greatly from shamanistic ceremonies, wherein spirits were exalted and glorified so the sponsors could involve them in long-term relationships. Sherpas often summarized the difference between the shaman's practice and the lama's practice by noting that shamans "invite the demons and deities into one's home and make them friends" and lamas "send them out and banish them." Also significant in the ceremony were the mechanisms involved in their subordination, because they were those of mimesis; the officiants had to "become" the Buddha figure at the center, just as the patrons had to "become" the effigies placed between the Buddha and the demon figures. This mimesis is related to the problem of impermanence, and requires a further exploration of the problem of the reality or unreality of spirit entities.

The problem of dealing with demons is demonstrated by close scrutiny of one category of demons referred to by Sherpas as *gek*. *Gek* are, literally, "obstructions" or "obstacles," and Sherpas often speak of those *gek* years, *gek* weeks, and *gek* days, determined astrologically by birth date, that are considered inauspicious for them. Sherpas never engaged in dangerous or critical activities during *gek* times. This meant that events ranging from getting married to working as an expedition climber on an Everest ascent were undertaken only after soliciting the advice of a Buddhist lama, who could determine if the event would coincide with *gek* times.

Gek in a general sense signified psychological disorder, but also denoted a class of demons found in Tibetan literature, revealing the breadth of the category and its untranslatability as a single Western construct.[27] To overcome *gek*, one had to overcome inner turmoil stemming from greed, anger, or ignorance. Tibetan Buddhism broadly defined all demons, *gdon*, as "powers that bring about illness." They were, according to translations by one Western scholar,

> no more than the embodiment of disturbances of psychic and bodily disequilibrium, primarily caused by the influence either of the planets, of the *'byung po* [demons and elements] in the world above, between heaven and earth, or of the *gnyan* [spirits] in the underworld. . . . [But] in describing the *gdon* it should also be mentioned that they appear in three groups, outer, inner, and secret (*phyi, nang, gsang*). The outer *gdon* appear in material form as demons, planets, etc.; the inner *gdon* are released as powers of destruction through the commission of evil, sin and defilement; the secret *gdon* arise from a faulty control of the vital breath of respiration (*rlung*) during the process of yoga.[28]

Thus, it is not that demons or deities do not exist, but that for some Buddhists the outer *gdon* are the most prevalent, while for others the inner demons are central.

Practices aimed at confronting *gek* or the *gdon* at any level are equally significant, although those practices undertaken at one level may result in faster progress toward enlightenment. I was told by monks that instructing Sherpas and other laypersons requires an extensive use of symbolism about the way demons are understood and about the connections between levels of practice. One monk explained the problem this way: "If you tell someone the pot is really white when it is covered with black soot, who will believe you? If you clean it, then show how white it is, then they will believe you." Consequently, the monks use a variety of techniques to demonstrate that demons and deities are important, not because they can be enlisted to provide satisfaction and comfort, health and well-being, but rather because they reveal a type of inner truth about the person that can be "tamed" and made aware of impermanence.

At the most sophisticated level of Buddhist practice, the issue of the "reality" of demons and deities is no more problematic than that of the "reality" of anything else.[29] No longer are deities and demons viewed simply as external sources of protection or wrath, or representatives of the community through some association with a specific lineage, clan, village, kingdom, or mountain. They are now viewed as just one part of the universe created out of the self. More importantly, these demons and deities, like the universe itself, are just illusions. For the advanced Buddhist, all reality is transitory and illusory, and so too are such spiritual beings. In this sense, the self is illusory and impermanent and the failure to realize this is the basis of all suffering. In practice, however, the "fact" that the self is as illusory as anything else is less apparent to the Sherpa laity than the "fact" that demons and deities are as *real* as anything else. Laypersons typically treat demons and deities as more real, in a fixed and permanent sense, than do the adepts. This is true even though impermanence is recognized as an inevitable aspect of life.

Lamas are considered gifted not simply because they can mediate between spirits and humans but because they set an example as individuals capable of subordinating the "reality" of the spirits to the will of the practitioner, or, to put it differently, of cutting through the illusion of the "reality" of the spirits. In one sense, this means that the lamas are more capable of engaging in mimesis in which the boundaries between themselves and the deity Sakyamuni are eliminated. Lay Sherpas are aware of the potential demonstrated by the lamas and monks and in some sense aspire to it. They know that the mechanism on which their well-being depends is that which is demonstrated by the monks as mimesis. To the extent that they are aware of the necessity that they "become" the effigies depicted, the laypersons accomplish the same practice as that of the officiants, albeit on a slightly less overtly proficient level. The notion that one can "become" the imagined entity is thus central to the practice of being

Buddhist, for it instantiates a lesson in impermanence. For the laity, belief in impermanence does not necessarily hinge on the reality or unreality of the demons; rather, impermanence exists whether or not demons are part of the world—demons too are subject to the "truth" of impermanence. Thus, they note, it is worth trying to achieve what *kurim*s tell them they should strive for in this form of mimesis, or to become that which is imagined for them in the ceremony, for it may well work to teach demons about impermanence in the same way it teaches them.

The presence or "reality" of the demons and deities in *kurim*s is particularly troublesome for those who do not follow the logic of Buddhist perspectives. Because this logic forms a fundamental basis of tantric Buddhist practice and resembles idiomatically the way in which lay people conceive of Buddhist tenets, it is worth pursuing this problem a bit further. F. D. Lessing notes this in his translation of a *bla bslu* ceremony (written by an eighteenth-century lama), which he refers to as "Calling the Soul" (and Samten Karmay retranslates as "The Restoration of Precious Life: Ritual for Recalling Life and the Soul"),[30] and which contains uses of effigies similar to the ones in the *kurim* described here. Lessing notes that although the eighteenth-century Tibetan lama documenting this ceremony says "people unable to see the ultimate truth hold, of course, the superstitious view that ghosts and demons working mischief bring outside powers into action, and it is for this reason that they can be repelled," he still, Lessing notes, believes in the fruitfulness of "interference with the life process by some outside power."[31] Lessing continues with an explanation of his own: "Learned lamas, it is true, adhere personally to more philosophical theories, but at the same time they compromise with the needs of the populace. This attitude of theirs finds support in the Scriptures which say that the Buddha himself adjusted his methods to the conceptual amplitude of his audience."[32]

The problem of demons, with whom one must engage in reciprocal bonds, is related to the problem of deities, with whom one is ideally meant to engage in mimesis. In fact, it is the presence of the deities and the relationship the practitioner is meant to form with them that defines the category tantra (Samuel 1993). This relationship is one in which the practitioner is supposed to transform himself or herself into entities that we in the West usually think of as having no material form, such as divine beings. One scholar explains the problem of the reality of deities in view of this quality of Tibetan Buddhist practice this way:

> It is enough to call attention to the fact that tantra presupposes a belief in their [the deities'] existence and that tantric practice involves identification with a divine or ideal being, whether that being is conceived of as objectively existing or as representing the eventual state of buddhahood of the practitioner. (The

acceptability of either or both interpretations is taken by Buddhists as an indication of the skillfulness of the Buddha, who is said to have taught in such a way that one teaching can be validly interpreted in many ways, depending on the intelligence of the listener.)[33]

The recognition that demons and deities are no more real than the self leads to the realization that at some level they are *interchangeable* with the self. On the metaphysical side of this equation, one is confronted with the proposition that if none of the foregoing is real, then neither are such things as tables and chairs. The flip side of this notion is that demons and deities are in fact as real as anything else in the physical world, making them frighteningly concrete.[34] Recognizing the inseparability of spirit entities from anything in the material world, for Sherpa monks, is an important step toward the transcendence of subjectivity, and this is why mimesis becomes instructive.

Stephan Beyer offers insight into the tantric practices of Buddhism, revealing the requirement of thinking of reality in a manner unfamiliar to most Westerners. He recognizes the kinship between impermanence and "non-reality."[35] *Kurim*s typically make use of effigies by investing them with life—having the effigies actually "become" the entities, rather than just symbols thereof. This same principle is applied to more-specific meditative practices of Buddhist practitioners in which one transforms oneself into a deity. Describing a ritual of this sort (in honor of the goddess Tara), Beyer notes that effigies are used as simulacra:

> The "effigies" and the "substitutes" of the Tibetan protective rituals are magical simulacra, and the vivid appearance of the visualized image is a simulacrum for both public reality and the deity himself: to control the image is to control the object. In Tantric soteriology the divine body is a simulacrum for the cosmos; mind, breath, and semen are homologized to one another and to the forces that create and destroy the universe.... Just as a Western astrologer mediates the influence of the planets through manipulation of their corresponding colors, minerals, and plants, the Tantric seeks in the world and in himself as many interconnections as he can find, and the yogin's body is the magical simulacrum not only of the deity he has become but also of truth, bliss, freedom, creation, and dissolution.... The aim of all contemplative manipulation is the power to control the mind, the breath, the universe. Power is the key, and the source of power is the deity; just as the yogin may use his vivid visualization as a simulacrum for events, he uses it as a simulacrum for knowledge. To create and become the deity is to "own" the deity in one's person, to be master even of the deity's enlightenment.[36]

The relationship between becoming an "ideal" form of deity and transcending attachments resulting from desire is one that emerges over and over again in ritual texts from which the Sherpas' *rnying ma pa* Buddhism derives today. Geoffrey Samuel (1993) offers another example of this sort of ritual practice in a case that elucidates the critical processes of detachment (overcoming desire). In a discovered text (*gter-ma*), a mythical figure named Kuntu Sangpo—a deity whose texts were "discovered" in the fourteenth century—speaks about the dangers of attachment while discussing desire:

> A dualising mind breeds doubt, hesitancy and insecurity,
> And with the development of subtle craving (in compensation),
> Overt compulsive karmic propensities gradually crystallize.
> Food, wealth and clothing, home and friends,
> The five stimuli of sensual pleasure, and loving companions—
> Obsessive desires beget torments of frustration;
> Compulsive desires are but worthy of delusion,
> And the karma of an ego craving objects is never exhausted.
> When the fruit of craving ripens,
> Born as the hungry ghost tormented by frustrated desire,
> Oh, the misery of hunger and thirst!
> Through this my prayer, the Buddha's aspiration,
> All sentient beings possessed by compulsive craving,
> Neither setting aside and rejecting the pangs of frustrated desire
> Nor accepting and identifying with compulsive craving,
> Should release the stress inherent in dualistic perception
> So that Knowledge may resume its natural primacy—
> Let all beings attain All-discriminating Awareness.

> Practitioners are intended to treat Kuntu Sangpo as an image of what they themselves can be. In reciting the prayer and in doing the meditation they are conceiving of themselves as Kuntu Sangpo, modeling themselves on Kuntu Sangpo, and through this analogical shift taking on his qualities. . . . An analogic shift of this kind, conceptualized as taking on the identity of one or another deity, is the central act of all Vajrayana rituals.[37]

Embedded in the Buddhist practices of Sherpas—that is, *rnying ma pa* practices—is an assumption that the self is transitory and is thus capable of becoming a simulation, like the deities that adepts themselves become.[38] Detachment from the idea of singular self-nature, like detachment from external things such as demons, enables one to become more like Buddha (or in the case of the effigy, become that which is depicted as one's ideal self)—in this sense, a sort of virtual being. Thus, when Ongchu informed me that he both identified with the effigy of himself (in the sense that he was supposed to "become" that entity) and recognized its ability to be destroyed by fire, along with the demons who afflicted him, he was informing me about the potential for things like demons to become less significant as one's phenomenal existence in the material world became less significant.

As one became less attached to one's body, so too one became less attached to a notion of the fixity or permanence of the subject. Ultimately, the meaning of the relationship to deity figures has important implications for understanding the processes of mimesis with desirable, constructed images of the self. Despite the mixed reading and interpretation Sherpa laypersons have of these rituals, the procedure of mimesis with such images is recurrent in other aspects of Sherpas' lives and becomes particularly important in view of the relationships Sherpas have with Westerners carrying strong desires about who Sherpas ought to be. Even though not all Sherpas are as adept at the practice of Buddhism as lamas and monks are, and even though they do not always interpret the world in the same esoteric ways as the lamas and monks do, Sherpa lives are in general saturated with reminders of impermanence and opportunities for the sort of "analogical shift" or mimetic engagement with simulacra, both via lamas and monks and via Western Others.

BECOMING BETTER BUDDHISTS

Clearly, lamas and monks had a particular interest in turning Sherpas into better practitioners of Buddhism, and were aware, as lay Sherpas were, of the Western gazes on them. But what exactly did being a "good" Buddhist mean for the Sherpa laity? Sherpas spoke with me about what it meant to be a good Buddhist in various inconsistent, and sometimes even contradictory, ways. "After we read the *kurim*s, we learn how to be better persons," Mingma Tenzing said. He had been taught how to read religious texts (*peca*s) as a child, while briefly enrolled in the monastery. But since he had dropped out when he was a young man, he only read a little, and often only during his own *kurim* ceremonies. "I understand some of it; for example, I learned that if I don't believe in jealousy, then it cannot hurt me." He noted that most Sherpas do not actually understand much of the religion they support, that "some people don't even know the real meaning of *om mani padme hum*" (hail to the one who holds the jewel and the lotus).[39] And yet a younger Sherpa who worked as a storekeeper for one of the large trekking agencies remarked: "The lamas teach by example. They don't actually teach lessons like a schoolteacher. Only the older monks who are educated do this. The *gyeshe*s [Buddhist monk scholars with the equivalent of a Ph.D.] are very important because they are teachers. But the lamas don't teach. Only by their example, they show us what is good and what is not good. That is why it is best to be a *gyeshe*, because they are very educated."

He went on to say that when he donated money to the monastery, he felt it important to give to monks individually because "when [one] give[s] to the lama, he does not necessarily give it to the whole monastery. But if [one] give[s] to individual monks, then even the lama gets some of that money indirectly." Contributing to monasteries and sponsoring *kurim*s remained principal strategies employed by wealthy villagers to garner prestige and obligate fellow villagers (which was not the motivation of monks and lamas). The owners of Sherpa trekking agencies, for example, frequently contributed to monastic events because they realized that in doing so, they engendered loyalty from Sherpa employees who would then, in the hope of obtaining sponsorship, feel obligated to perform well for the owners.

For Sherpas striving to become better Buddhists, and for those locating Sherpa identity in their religious practices, one of the most salient features of Tibetan Buddhism is its attempt to deal with the tension between a concrete individualism and interdependence and an ability to recognize the transient nature of all persons and things, a recognition that mandates a lack of attachments. An appreciation of the concept of impermanence is necessary before one can transcend subjectivity, yet this notion stands in opposition to the idea of a fixed self that underlies the reciprocal interactions that make up everyday life and bind villager to villager, or foreigner to Sherpa. A similar, and related, tension exists between the importance Buddhism places on compassion—exercised toward others, with their well-being in mind—and its equally strong emphasis on detachment and independence from others. Acts of compassion might easily be interpreted as offerings within a logic of reciprocity, where the compassionate giver would expect some return for his or her actions. This may be why, in some schools of Tibetan Buddhism, true compassion only becomes possible with a *bodhicitta* mind—a mind of altruistic motivation—which recognizes the liberation of humanity as of far greater importance than the liberation of the individual, and which recognizes that the latter is contingent on the former. At any rate, in all schools of Tibetan Buddhism there is a widespread sense that the individual, the being from which the universe radiates, is alone responsible for his or her actions, and yet that a notion of individual or fixed subjectivity must be overcome, because from a fixed self springs attachment to self and others. Below I examine how Sherpas reconcile these competing demands. I then turn to the question of how this particular articulation of Buddhism is informed by Western interests in finding "authentic" religious Sherpas, and what role it plays in the formation of sponsorship relationships between such Sherpas and foreigners.

Ideas about being good (or better) Buddhists were often intertwined with the concept of fate or karma—a principle of causation or consequentiality that cannot be altered. But achieving Buddhist enlightenment also involved techniques of personal improvement associated with merit (*payin*), demerit (*dikpa*), and spiritual protection or knowledge (*rlung rta*, a folk idea, "wind horse," referring to prayer flags offered to bring one spiritual knowledge or protection). In order to enhance one's life, one was required to do everything possible to gain merit (through acts of compassion, such as saving lives or becoming a *jindak*) and avoid obtaining demerits (by avoiding activities such as drug smuggling). But such efforts brought one face-to-face with demands for reciprocal engagement and attachment. And lamas and monks regularly conveyed to the Sherpa laity the importance of becoming detached from family and friends, because from attachment springs suffering. However, with *rlung rta*—acquired spiritual knowledge or protection—notions of individualism were reconciled with detachment. In obtaining *rlung rta*, one could be compassionate without attachment; one could engage in "unattached" compassion.

Sherpas often told me that, after a *kurim*, the lama presiding would warn them against visiting with friends. For example, Doma reported after her most recent *kurim*, "I went to Devu Rinpoche [the *amchi*] and to *tsawi* lama [the Tengboche Rinpoche], and they both told me 'don't go visiting at other people's houses. You get *theep* [pollution].' It is also a big danger for [my daughter] if she watches any bad things, like killing or red meat [which is associated with death]." In another case, Tshiring Lhamu, who lived in a small house at the edge of Khum Jung village, said that she had visited the lama just a week earlier in order to receive a blessing for her newborn son. She told me her story: "After I had my baby, when he was very young, he got sick and I took him to *tsawi* lama. He said don't eat food in other people's homes. But what can I do? Everyone calls to me to come eat with them." It was a monk named Ngawang Gazu who finally explained to me why lamas and monks frequently advised against too much socializing. He said, "Lamas teach us that we cannot rely on other people. We must rely on our own religious knowledge." Following the lama's instructions meant avoiding involvement in reciprocal village relationships, for these generally gave rise to attachment.

Many Sherpas with whom I spoke said they thought one's level of religious achievement was reflected in one's health—the greater the spiritual awareness one attained, the less likely one was to get sick. Thus, I often heard Sherpas comment that "the lamas never get sick." If attachment is seen as the ultimate source of suffering, which includes poor health, then those who are least attached (i.e., lamas) are believed to be least likely to suffer. This view was made apparent in the comments of a Sherpani from Khum Jung village, who told me, "Of course the lama does not get sick, because he has so much *rlung rta*." The more *rlung rta* people have, the less significant their bodies become, until they gain so much religious awareness that, according to Tsamgi of Phortse village, "they can make their bodies fly!" This feat, frequently attributed to the Khumbu region's high lamas, was deemed a consequence of their ability to make their physical beings entirely subordinate to their transcendent consciousness. In the end, Sherpas felt the best way to ensure good health was to become more like the lamas.

The dance story of Tolden, performed yearly at Mani Rimdu festivals, was often cited as an example of how the lama teaches Sherpas to emulate him in other ways. Tolden is sometimes depicted as a man who does not engage in religious activities. He marries and has children and, when sickness befalls his family, spends all his money on a shaman to cure them. Nevertheless, his wife and child die. In another version of the tale, Tolden is a porter too ignorant to become a sardar. He simply carries loads, spends no money on religious ceremonies, and never learns to pray. He is plagued by a cough that seems to get worse until he can no longer work. (The parallels with Pinzo, who had tuberculosis, are striking.) He is portrayed as pitifully unschooled in spiritual and economic matters. Finally, at his death, he is left with nothing—not even religious knowledge. One eighty-year-old Sherpani explained to me the significance of Tolden's story: "He means we should be like the *thawa*, otherwise we will be like Tolden. [The story] is like *chellup* [a holy substance offered by lamas, believed to be medicinal], like vitamins, like a blessing. It shows our life situation if we don't follow the lama."[40]

In addition, the monk Phurba Sonam explained to me that Tolden's story teaches observers about the importance of detachment and impermanence:

> When you are born, you must die. Everyone gets sick, but this shows one the physical body. It will get sick, diseased, and die. The main idea is that you must meditate. Otherwise, you are wasting your time. [The story of] Tolden says the lama, the *lhawa* [god one, or shaman], and doctor—none can save your life. They will care for sick people, but we are all mortal—*jiktenba*, destructible bodies. At that time of death, nobody can save you. Not even your relatives can help you then. You must leave your body behind. Then, you must walk by yourself.

One of the most interesting ways in which lamas intervene in Sherpa lives, indirectly promoting both individualism and detachment, is through the successful persuasion of young villagers deemed to have the ability to become shamans (which is indicated by their frequently being possessed) to become monks instead. One such convert, who had just entered the monastery in 1987, told me that he had become a monk because he was convinced that lamas could better teach him how to handle spirits. He explained:

> About seven years ago, some men came here asking me for *mogyo* ["hunting" or divination] because I was able to do it for Chumbi's son [whose body he located after the boy had died in an accident seven years earlier]. I can do *mogyo*, but then people come here all the time and the monks will get angry. It was a

big problem at my home. When I came here I learned about that from the lama. Too many people coming to my home all the time, and too much gossip. Now I understand it is the lama who separates nicely the spirits from the sick people, not the shaman.

Lamas' purported ability to separate spirits from persons was in some sense representative of their related ability to teach villagers to separate, or detach, themselves from other people. Attachments to either people or spirits presented the same potential threat (that of being materialistic and greedy) and offered the same potential benefit (that arising from reciprocal exchanges).

While most Sherpas considered their practice of Buddhism to be an important component of their ethnic identity, it seems apparent that esoteric Buddhist insights on the nature of impermanence were, for the laity, deeply intertwined with the presence of demons and deities and the demands of these entities for reciprocity and a type of permanence. Many Buddhist *kurim*s were interpreted, in fact, not merely as lessons in obtaining a higher consciousness that would transcend the body and its attachments, but also, as Ching Nuru, a young man of Khum Jung, told me, as "more expensive versions of what the shaman does. If you are rich you call the lama; if poor, you call the *lhawa*."

The following story provides another example of the blurring of conceptual ideals between shamanism and lamaist Buddhism. When I departed from Kathmandu in late 1987 to return to the Khumbu, I left behind a circle of Sherpa friends who socialized together on special occasions. This group included Doma, who was often strapped for money and who lived with her daughter in a rented apartment. The family of Nima Chottar also formed part of our circle. Nima, with his wife and five children, was quite wealthy. He had earned a living as a sardar for many years, had become an owner of a trekking agency, and had now invested in other businesses as well. These families were the best of friends when I left for the Khumbu that winter. When I returned to Kathmandu from the Khumbu the following summer, however, they were not speaking to one another. Doma was teary-eyed as she first described the rumors that Nima's wife, Phuti, was supposedly spreading about her. She claimed Phuti had been telling other Sherpas that she, Doma, had smuggled drugs into the United States, and this was why she was rich. "I am not rich," she pleaded, "and it was not me who did black business [smuggling]. It was Nima. He is very rich from the black business." When I asked her why she thought Phuti had spread rumors, Doma replied that Phuti was "jealous because her daughter has a lot of education, but she cannot find a job. I am starting a trek agency, and I don't even have SLC [a school-leaving certificate]."

Five days later, Doma was in her bed, recovering from an illness that had sent her to the hospital. Her daughter, too, had become sick the day after my last visit. They had both suffered bouts of vomiting and diarrhea for two days. Then, with the help of a friend named Angchi, they went to the Teaching Hospital, where they were put on glucose drips. Angchi took care of them, bringing them food she had cooked at home and paying for their taxi rides to and from the hospital. When I went to see her, Doma said she needed to see the *jhankri*, a Nepali shaman, because there were no Sherpa shamans (*lhawas*) then available in Kathmandu. Aware of my own interest in and familiarity with local healing practices, Doma called me to help her go to the *jhankri* after calling her Sherpani friend to help her go to the hospital—an irony we were both able to appreciate.

We waited until dusk and then, with a fifty-rupee note and some rice in hand, we ventured down the street to an alley jammed with people in a dusty part of the city not visited by tourists. We waited our turn and eventually advanced to the front of the crowd. There, sitting before us as we hunched over on our knees, was the *jhankri*. He wore ordinary clothes and had little in the way of ritual paraphernalia. He had Doma pour the rice, now moist from being held so long in her palm, onto a brass plate. After fingering the grains and observing us both, he spoke with Doma for a few minutes. Doma handed over the fifty rupees and we left. (At the time I was sure this was a moment of authenticity.) Back at her house, I asked what had been said. She told me that a *boksi* (witch) was responsible for her problem, and we had to offer her some butter, rice, and incense later that night, at the crossroads, between her home and that of the *boksi*. I probed further:

"Where is the *boksi* from?" I asked.

"From the east side of my house," she said, a remark I noted with interest because that was where Phuti's house was located.

"Is it someone you know?" I continued.

"How can we know?" she said. "Only we know that the *boksi* was jealous."

"Do you think it is a Sherpani?" I asked, guessing that she suspected Phuti was the culprit but knowing she would never identify a witch to me outright, or to anyone else if possible.

"Yes, it is a Sherpani from the east side," she confided, "but who can say who it is?"

Only one Sherpa family lived anywhere in the area to Doma's east, which strengthened my suspicions. Later in the day, when we walked to a place in the road directly en route to Phuti's home, where Doma had left the offering for the *boksi*, Doma explained that the gift would serve to obligate the witch and force her to reconcile her differences with Doma, revoking her wrath and enabling Doma and her daughter to recover.

A day later, I visited Nima Chottar's home, where Phuti and her daughters were all preparing for a different ceremony, a *kurim*. *Thorgyap*, as this particular *kurim* was called, would cost Nima's family Rs. 5,000. One lama and two monks with advanced education were required to perform over the course of three full days. Aside from meals and payment for the services of the lama and the monks, the family had to provide an abundance of cookies, candies, butter for sculptures, *tormas*, endless supplies of tea for all involved, flags, altars, and a treasure to be hidden beneath the floor of the home.

Thorgyap was an exorcism *kurim*, intended to "eliminate the obstacles in Nima Chottar's life," explained one of the monks. The family with whom I sat throughout the ceremony, however, informed me that the *kurim* was being held to rid Nima's house of bad influences, which had led to a number of minor maladies. Nima's daughter and wife had staphylococcus infections, and he and his wife both had diarrhea. His son was not feeling well either. The *kurim*, he said, would eliminate the source of these afflictions from his home.

The ceremony was elaborate. The monks recited and performed *mudras* (ritual hand gestures) to invoke Guru Rinpoche (Padmasambhava) and lesser personages, who were accorded places on a table near the main effigy. The central effigy in this case was not a model of the victims, but rather a five-foot-high conical *torma* with two flags emerging from its sides, each painted with flames of yellow, blue, pink, orange, and red. It was capped by a small representation of a human skull, which I was told signified impermanence. This was perched atop an image of Guru Rinpoche, which was painted on a small piece of paper and draped with a gauze cover. That, in turn, was placed over an image of a white wheel, symbolizing the "wheel of life." The large *torma* itself rested on a mass of crisscrossed thorny twigs painted half black and half red, which served as a *rawa* (fence to keep the *torma* bounded). The whole structure was contained in a large cooking pan, similar to a wok, set on a frame surrounded by small butter lamps (meant as offerings) and smaller effigies (symbolizing lesser figures recruited to help "convince" the spirit represented by the central effigy of the merits of Buddhism).

After invoking the various entities who would participate in the drama, a symbolic three-day battle took place between the Buddhist practitioners and the obstacles represented by the *torma*. Afterwards, the *torma* was removed from the house to the crossroads between Nima's and Doma's homes. In fact, it was set ablaze on the same spot where Doma had made her offering to the witch only a few days earlier, for it was from this direction that the spirit obstacles in Nima's home were believed to have emanated. Back at Nima's house, the monks fixed four prayer flags, also called *rlung rta*, at the four corners of the roof. Inside, they had broken the cement floor just inside the front door and deposited, in a hole in the earth below, a secret treasure (which I was not allowed to see) that, when covered up again, would prevent the harmful entities from entering.

Phuti told me that the ceremony was supposed to rid her house of *drultzi*—spirits riding into the home on the backs of visitors. I asked if there were any particular spirits that might have caused her family's problems, to which she responded: "You never know which spirits exactly, but we think maybe *pem* [a witch] brought *shrindi* into our house when she came to visit. Usually, *pem* makes the person sick directly. If she sees something or someone she doesn't like, she can make [that person] sick. But sometimes she comes into [our] house with others, like her *sems nagpo* [her "black mind," filled with bad thoughts], and brings *shrindi* with her. If that *pem* comes into our house, she will bring *shrindi* with her." I asked about the sources of *pem*. "Anyone can be *pem*. Your *gyaptak* [a spirit attached to oneself] pushes you to be *pem*. If your *gyaptak* loves too much someone else or the things they have, then you become *pem*," she said. (*Gyaptak* are personal spirits that come to one at death, often because they have caused one's death in a previous life, and are carried over into one's next reincarnation attached to the *sems*.) "Or," she continued, "if your *gyaptak* makes you angry with someone else, you can become *pem*. The lama will not say if it is *pem* [causing your disorder], since he does not believe in *pem*."

Nima himself spoke about obstacles in an abstract way that was more like the understanding held by the monks. "Obstacles," he said, "can be anything . . . from our past life, from this life . . . in our minds. . . . We read the texts to learn about these things." He had been educated in a monastery, but left to lead a secular life soon after learning to read.

It seemed clear to me that Doma and Nima's family were engaged in a symbolic battle with one another stemming from Doma's and Phuti's initial argument. In keeping with their wealth and status, Nima and his family performed an elaborate *kurim* ceremony to rid their home of the spirits that they believed caused their family's illnesses. Indirectly, they were clearing away the obstacle of their relationship with Doma, but the ceremony had the effect of clearing up obstacles *in* their relationship. With her more meager resources, Doma went to the hospital and to the shaman. The latter helped her make an offering to the *boksi* involved, resulting in the creation of the potential for a reciprocal bond with Phuti on which she could rely for good health. A parallel can be drawn between her need to engage this spirit in an ongoing relationship and her need to remain close to Nima Chottar and his family. The outcome of all the proceedings detailed was that Nima's family and Doma began to speak again, after each had ostensibly eliminated the problems associated with the presence of the other's angry spirit. By the time I returned to Kathmandu in 1989, the two parties were again the best of friends.

What message does this story convey? At the least it leads one to conclude that *kurim*s are not only about Buddhist lessons in the transcendence of subjective reality. According to many Sherpa sponsors, they are as much (or even, for some, more) about chasing away supernatural interlopers after luring them in with the trappings of some sort of deal. In the end, Nima Chottar's wife's interpretation of a *kurim* has a great deal in common with the shamanistic rituals sought out by Doma, in the account above, than it does with the practices of literate Buddhists. On the other hand, Nima Chottar himself explained at some length to me that, based on his own years of education at the monastery (before he broke his vows and began to work in the trekking industry), the most important part of the ceremony was the reading of the texts. In the texts themselves, he noted, it was written how to become unattached to these obstacles. This was about "enlightenment," he said.

The different levels of interpretation revolve around a difference, some Buddhists say, between relative truth—truth that obscures (*kun rdzob bden pa*), such as, as I understand it, that which obtains in a notion of a "self" that is useful but not real—and absolute truth or holy meaning (*don dam bden pa*). The former assumes the reality of the subject and the inviolate ability of the subject to affect the world. (This is important if one wants to envision the individual as the center of the universe in allowing for the individual's ability to affect that universe.) The latter, on the other hand, stresses that the very concept of subjectivity on which individualism might rest is relative. In absolute terms, the subject, or self, is no less illusory than demons and deities—than the world we see around us, which is actually transient and quite illusory. Sherpa interpretations of Buddhism are situated somewhere between the notion that the self is fixed and permanent, making long-term relationships with others feasible and necessary, and the esoteric notion of an elusive and transient self.

AN EXPANSIVE AND EXTENSIVE BUDDHIST BEING AND *RLUNG RTA*

One way in which Sherpas' concepts of the self are mediated by Buddhism is through conceptions of the body. These conceptions are largely influenced by their use of Tibetan *amchi*s practicing *rgyud bshi*, the root tantra Buddhist medicine, developed over the last millennium on the Tibetan plateau.[41] The view subscribed to by *amchi*s (of whom there were three in the Khumbu) is that the body consists of three main humors: wind (*rlung*), bile (*tiwa*), and phlegm (*pagin*). An imbalance among these elements is thought to lead to any of 108 types of disorders. Astrological conditions at birth, physiological conditions linked to karma, miscellaneous external conditions, and demons are all believed to play a part in various illnesses. *Amchi* medicine also configures the body within broader discourses of

Buddhism engaged in by all lamas and monks, as follows: The material body, *rag pa'i lus* (body of touch, sense), supports an inner innate or peculiar body, the *ngyug ma'i lus*, consisting of two components—*rlung* (a vibratory power, as well as the wind humor) and *sems* (the sentient mind or consciousness, also called mind-light). In objectifying the world around us, the *sems* is responsible for creating *samsara* (the endless cycle of rebirth), since it makes the idea of the "permanence of the world" more real. But *sems* can ultimately be a means of tapping into *ye shes lus* (the body of primordial wisdom), which is innate in all beings and which is capable of going beyond a duality of existence, that is, a subject-object universe (existence—nonexistence, I—not-I).[42] Meditation and discipline enable one to transcend the *sems'* objectifying tendencies and achieve one's transcendent consciousness or primordial wisdom. Objectification only obscures primordial wisdom. Continuing to objectify the physical body as the sole locus of the self, for example, or to treat it as fixed in the form of an object in a permanent ego, only serves to obscure wisdom about the illusory nature of the self.

The *sems* is similar in nature to the *yid lus* (mental body), which is the seat of the dichotomizing faculty and other inner weaknesses. *Yid lus* is attached to one's physical being (distinguishing between I and not-I) and is vulnerable to karmic inheritance (*leka*, or work), arising from a sense of fixed self, and from attachment. This can be overcome by *ye shes lus*, which is free from worldly contamination and therefore without material form. *Ye shes lus* is the seat of *bodhicitta*, and therefore enables one to give without attachment, so that compassion becomes an act of independence and transcendence rather than interdependence. It follows that the more one exists in one's transcendent body, the less the body of touch (the body afflicted by humoral imbalances) will be affected by the material universe.

Amchi medicine deals effectively with both the material and the transcendental qualities of the person. A close examination of the difference between the material body and its relationship to the universe that it is thought to produce as a transcendent body, however, reveals that the line between the material body and its transcendence is actually quite indistinct. One way to understand the relationship between that body and the transcendent nature it is thought to contain is through an exploration of *rlung*. The Tibetan medical view of the body posits it as coextensive with the universe. *Rlung* is defined as both internal and external; the wind of the body, like breath, is seen as coextensive with the winds or airs of the natural world. This same wind, on which the *sems* is believed to ride in enlightenment, is also tied to one's emotions. Anger, grief, and prolonged stress can produce diseases of *rlung*.

Here we see how Tibetan notions of the body differ from those held by most Westerners. The body is not treated by Tibetans as separate from the mind (as in the mind-body dualism found in Western philosophy and epistemology). Rather, the body is one manifestation of consciousness; transcending the body is only possible by becoming totally embedded in the body, and then realizing its illusory nature. (Recall that Oungde and Phuti were meant to "become" their effigies before watching them burn up.) Demons here are not psychological but real.

Aside from treatment with pharmaceuticals to improve the function of the *rlung*, one of the folk Sherpa ways to strengthen one's wind humor is to gain *rlung rta*. *Rlung rta* are, again, the prayer flags placed on a windy hillside to disseminate one's prayers throughout the universe in one's absence, but the phrase also denotes a quality one can achieve or possess. Placing prayer flags on hillsides, practicing meditation, making donations to a monastery, reading Buddhist texts, performing *kurims*—all contribute to one's store of *rlung rta*. In this sense, *rlung rta* refers to religious knowledge or awareness; thus, people who anger too easily are viewed as having *rlung* imbalances. The more *rlung rta* one possesses, the less likely it is that one will get sick. And for lay Sherpas, the more *rlung rta* one accumulates, the less likely it is that one will be prey to offenses from supernatural entities. A more generalized esoteric interpretation is that the less attached one is to the physical body, the less likely it is that one will be afflicted by other essences believed to affect the physical world (such as spirits). This concept of the body found in Tibetan medicine, in which a move away from objectification is seen as positive and desirable, is rather different from the view held by the Western doctors with whom Sherpas also come into contact, notably because the former maintain that the subject *is* the object (and together they are able to raise consciousness), whereas the latter maintain that the body (as object) can be treated effectively as separated from the mind (locus of the subject).

Theories of *rlung rta* exemplify a Buddhist approach to the individual as being expansive and coextensive with the universe, and this conception is held by most Sherpas. Ideally, in Buddhism, there are no boundaries between the internal being and the rest of the universe. This ultimately enables one to recognize the impermanence of the material world and to transcend it. And that means transcending notions of individuals, as well as one's attachment to material entities (such as physical bodies, relationships to others on whom one depends for sexual intimacy, shelter, food, and so forth). This notion of the person as coextensive with all things can be found among lay Sherpas in other contexts as well, and many Sherpas indicate that they function mostly in the material universe. Nevertheless, attachments do not undermine one's ability to recognize the importance of transcending them. The mimesis approach employed at the highest levels of Buddhism and espoused in the Sherpas' Buddhism at all levels, in which practitioners meditate on "becoming" various deities or demons as a form of detachment, is often reworked by lay Sherpas in ways that actually promote attachments to others, even while their own subjectivity might seem flexible. For this reason, it is useful to examine where Sherpas' expansive notions of the body are demonstrated.

In walking the mountain trails in and around villages of the Khumbu one is struck by an unusual sight: discarded clothing hanging from the tops of trees and bushes. I was told that these used and no-longer-wanted items would be safe there from the dirty heels of passersby. But if the clothes happened to fall to the ground and were stepped on, their owners would suffer ill effects. In this sense, the clothing belonging to a person had clearly come to be considered as much a part of that person as his or her skin, even after the clothes had been discarded by the owner. In another example, small protective strings, *tsung di*, are given by lamas to Sherpas to wear around their necks, along with protective amulets called *shunga*, for months, and sometimes years, at a time. When they are finally disposed of, Sherpas take pains to deposit them in a clean place in the hills that people seldom visit, or else near a sacred place that will always be clean and unspoiled by pollution of any sort. The hair left in one's brush is treated with the same care, and is placed far from any place people are likely to visit. "Our *sems*," Doma explained to me, "is still in that *tsung di* or hair, and if people walk on it then we will lose our way at death [during the *bardo*, the intermediate state before rebirth] and won't find *devachen* [heaven]." People's belongings are thought to continue to affect them long after being separated from their physical beings. For most of the laity, as long as one has any physical presence or possessions, one's *sems* is coextensive with them, as it is with the rest of the universe.

Another typical example of this belief was that many Sherpas I met avoided sharing drinks with anyone with whom they did not want to be associated intimately. A man's and a woman's use of the same cup signified a close personal relationship. I learned this, much to my embarrassment, when I offered some *chang* I could not drink to a married man, whose wife became enraged because he took it. Additionally, the sharing of cups with those of *khamendewa* (mouth-not-sharing) status was believed to operate in the same way "pollution" (*jutho*) does in the case of Nepalese Hindus. This should not be confused with the Buddhist notion of pollution called *theep*; here, the high-status (*khadewa*, or mouth-sharing) drinker would only temporarily become low status. The shared beverage was viewed as somehow connected to the initial imbiber even after it crossed beyond the actual boundaries of that person's physical being.

A person's wealth is also deemed part of his or her physical being, and the acquisition of wealth is even viewed as a way of ensuring health. *Yang*, for example, is a Sherpa term denoting both luck and wealth. It refers to a principle of augmentation, which is often applied to money. The more *yang* one has, the more *yang* one can continue to attain; the less *yang* one has, the less one can acquire. The accumulation of *yang* in the form of wealth is seen as highly desirable. Sherpas who feel they have lost *yang* (because they have suffered a great or sudden loss of wealth, or some other misfortune) hire lamas to perform *yang gyou* ceremonies in order to "call the *yang* back." This daylong ritual requires that families collect their most valuable possessions in a single pot. Effigies are constructed of the home of the afflicted, along with various *torma*s representing gods of the region. Recitations are aimed at calling back the *yang* and at recruiting the various gods represented to watch over it. The pot containing the existing wealth is symbolically placed inside the effigy home, and at the end of the ceremony is stored on a shelf in the real home, where it is not touched for an entire year.

Yang is not simply something appended to one's being, however; it is considered an intrinsic part of one's person. Thus, it is common to find Sherpas with gold-capped teeth who feel that the presence of *yang* in their mouths will not only guarantee nutrition for the body, but will also eliminate any possibility of swallowing poison (*thuk*). Pieces of turquoise, coral, amber, *zee* stones (valuable striped agate beads), and pearls are also thought, as *yang*, to improve one's health by their presence, and to draw out unwanted bodily substances through secretion. Things worn on the outer person are seen as directly related to things on the inside. The idea of the wealth of the things (*nor*) one possesses as somehow synonymous with the wealth of the body is illustrated by *zungshii*, which, it was explained to me, is the internal essence of the person. When one has a small Buddha figurine blessed, it is not considered complete until it is filled with items of great value (turquoise, coral, pearls, gold, money, rice, silver) and sealed at its base. Then the figure is painted to render it more lifelike. The filling of the Buddha statue is a way of giving it an internal essence, "like a heart (*snying*)," I was told.

Even one's thoughts are believed to produce effects outside oneself, in effect making one's perceptions reality. The potential for altering reality in this manner ranges from the profound, especially when undertaken by lamas, to the mundane, when undertaken by less proficient Buddhists. Lamas claim to be able to affect and even avert catastrophic situations, such as the flood of 1986, which, I was told by one lama, "would never have happened if [he] had known about it ahead of time." He said that he would have diverted the water that overflowed from a broken glacial lake, and thereby prevented the destruction and death it caused. Less dramatic illustrations of this belief in extensive mental power include many Sherpas' view that they can make themselves sick by thoughts (*namdok*) alone. Thus, if one is certain a glass is dirty and drinks from it anyway, one will inevitably get sick—even if the glass is clean. The idea that what is in one's mind can directly create external reality is best expressed in an aphorism re-peated by Ching Nuru from Khum Jung, as he tried to console me one frustrating afternoon:

Da dokpu lemu chung sii, tsambuling lemu.
Da dokpu gokpu sii, tsambuling gokpu.

(If I am good [in a good mood], then the whole world is good.
If I am bad [in a bad mood], then the whole world is bad.)

Another good example of this notion of the inseparability of physical from mental being, as well as the expansive quality of the individual body in the material universe, is the widely accepted explanation of diseases of *rlung* as those brought on by excessive anger, or "thinking too many angry thoughts," as one Sherpani noted. Just worrying about someone else's anger can allegedly make one sick. Similarly, another's anger actually di-rected toward oneself is also believed to cause illness.

In a manner that replicates *kurim* mimesis, even photographs are deemed to have an effect similar to one's thoughts, in that, by fixing some-one in time in a representation, they can supposedly turn that particular depiction of a person into an ongoing reality. Consequently, Sherpas were often reluctant to let me photograph them in less than their finest clothes. The act of being photographed dressed as affluent individuals was seen as having a beneficial effect on their wealth, making them wealthier, whereas being photographed in old, dirty, or torn clothes that made them look poor was thought actually to make them poorer. Moreover, I was told of their anxiety that photographs of them might be discarded later and end up in places that were dirty, like the garbage, and this would surely bring bad luck to them. The idea that photographs are capable of producing the subject depicted as a reality replicates the relationships Sherpas have with Buddhas and deities pictured in mandalas, since these are also thought to become "real" through the Buddhist practices of those who own them.

Photographs are accorded a status similar to that of dreams, which are also believed to have some bearing on future events. But with dreams, the opposite principles sometimes apply. Dreams of lamas sitting in one's home or of oneself dressed in finery allegedly foretell death, since such scenes are typical of funerals. Conversely, dreams about crossing rivers are considered lucky, for they signal the accomplishment of one's goals. One's prescient knowledge is deemed effective not simply in foretelling the fu-ture but in creating it.

The concept of sentient rebirth also exemplifies the Sherpa belief in an extensive being, although in this case it is the conscious mind that suppos-edly moves from one body to the next. In this view, rebirth results from dharmic action, or religious work, in this life, which work takes its future shape in a physical body. Here, beauty, wealth, and the human form are thought to be the result of past mental or physical exertions. Purported *trulkus*, or sentient rebirths (*trulku* means, literally, "emanation body"), were not common in the Khumbu, but there were several well-known people (other than lamas) who had been reborn in this fashion. One toddler, believed to be the reincarnation of a Sherpa in his sixties who had recently died, began to talk about visiting "his home" and meeting with "his friends" in a household that belonged not to his family but rather to the deceased man. The deceased's relatives offered this child gifts and economic support, after "confirming" that he was, in all likelihood, the reincarnation of their dead grandfather.[43] In 1987, another two-year-old began to talk about visiting "his tea shop" at the base of the village, even though the daughter of the man who had owned the tea shop until his death four years earlier was now the proprietor of that business. The deceased man's family was waiting to see if there were other signs of this child's being a *trulku* when I left the region in 1987. By 1993, they had decided he was, in fact, the reincarnation of their relative, and frequently gave him gifts.

This concept of transmigration across lifetimes further demonstrates an expansive notion of self. Lamas are called when a Sherpa dies, and one of their tasks is to create a small mandala-shaped image with a figure at the center representing the deceased. Sherpas call this print a *kenney* picture; it is believed to hold the *sems* of the person who has died. To release the *sems*, monks or lamas first remove it from the lifeless body by taking a few hairs from the top of the head. The holes remaining in the scalp ostensibly enable the *sems* to escape from the physical corpse. The *sems* is then believed to be captured in the picture used during the ceremonies of recitation performed when the deceased is in *bardo*, to prepare him or her for the journey through that intermediate state. Later, when the body is burned, so is the *kenney*, which releases the *sems* for rebirth.[44]

Coexisting with this belief in the travel of the *sems* to one's next life are other important notions of transmigration across lifetimes. Karma, the principle that "fitting results issue from the moral quality of all actions,"[45] works across lifetimes. This is thought by lay Sherpas to mean that actions that are not meritorious, or sins (*dikpa*) in one's life may result in an unfortunate rebirth in one's next life. The moral quality of one's behavior is transformed into the actual circumstances of one's future lives. Lay Sherpas also apply this notion of karma to nonmoral things such as money. Accumulated wealth is thought to be transferable to one's next life, providing one has earned enough merit. Many Sherpas state that they can inherit half of all their wealth upon rebirth if they gain sufficient merit in this life—which is why it is so important to earn a lot of money now. One must give away a lot of money to a monastery in order to achieve merit, and to be wealthy with only half of this life's earnings in one's future life.

Ideas concerning an extensive and expansive body are frequently expressed by Sherpas, and seem to be clearly tied to representations of the individual found in Buddhist practices, including *amchi* medicine. Lamas explain that the interconnection of person and universe reveals the self as the center from which the universe radiates, but this self is not moored by a fixed or permanent self-nature. Buddhist notions of the body as coextensive with the universe allow for the creation of an "ideal" Sherpa in the image of the Buddha—as Beyer observes, revealing a simulacrum strategy in which one can take on whatever form one envisions, but only through abandoning one's sense of a fixed identity. A version of this transcendence of subjectivity is that it constitutes emptiness, and, as emptiness, is all-encompassing. But despite this notion of being a good Buddhist, many Sherpas think "interconnectedness" means that the self is *not*, in fact, empty, but rather replete with attachments to all other elements of the universe—an interpretation one would expect lamas to find troubling because of its link to incessant desires. In practice, however, the Sherpas' attachments to others actually confirm and promote their Buddhist indoctrination in a rather oblique and arguably unconscious way; these same attachments demand that Sherpas become transitory subjects—subjects who are not fixed and essential and who are able persistently to become that which is desired by those who observe them, including Westerners.

BUDDHIST MODERNITIES

Tibetan monks had been imported to the DeYoung Asian Art Museum in San Francisco in order to construct a sand mandala of the Buddha's Kalachakra teachings for the exhibit "Wisdom and Compassion: The Sacred Art of Tibet" in 1991. The exhibit was sponsored by Tibet House and the museum, organized with the help of local politicians and the actor Richard Gere, and blessed by a special visit from the Dalai Lama. The monks undertook the painstaking exercise by filtering brightly colored sands through metal cones rubbed with wooden dowels—just enough so that fine lines and nearly singular grains filled up the design of the mandala, which was detailed beyond belief. Their construction of the mandala was itself a sort of live performance, viewed by museum-goers day in and day out, until one day a mentally ill woman crossed over the thick felt rope that kept viewers from those on display and stomped all over it, destroying the patterns beyond recognition. Newspapers noted that the curators considered the event a disaster, but the monks commented only that "the mandala was not yet finished." They scooped up the sands and cast them into the ocean and began again. For them, the mandala had already served some of its purpose, for it was in its construction that the artists grew, not necessarily in its completion. It was intended to be destroyed, and this woman had

"The Religion of the future will be a cosmic religion. It will transcend a personal God and avoid dogma and theology. Covering both the natural and spiritual, it should be based on a religious sense arising from the experience of all things natural and spiritual as a meaningful unity. Buddhism answers this description. If there is any religion that would cope with modern scientific needs, it would be Buddhism."
ALBERT EINSTEIN

16. Flyer distributed at the Tibet Shop by Tibetan immigrants in San Francisco, California, in 1983.

only hastened the inevitable. For me, the whole episode, uncannily like the one Phurba Sonam experienced at the University of Colorado, raised questions about what, or who, exactly, was on display.

Tibetan Buddhism occupies a prominent place in the Western imagination, which in part has fueled the interest of tourists in the Sherpas of Nepal. How, then, is the Western gaze incorporated into Sherpa identity when it demands an "authentically Buddhist" Sherpa? Does the Buddhist emphasis on impermanence and an unfixed Sherpa subject undermine Western interests in authenticity, or does it actually help provide Westerners with exactly what they seek, especially when tied to Sherpas' use of impermanence to create reciprocal attachments? Buddhism for Sherpas has, in some sense, been like modernity for Westerners, in that each epistemology employs a well-developed self-disciplinary apparatus aimed at creating a public desire for personal improvement. Although enormous differences exist between Western modernity and Buddhism, there are other similarities of form between the two as well. Thus it did not surprise me to learn that Einstein wrote that, if there were a "religion that would cope with modern scientific needs, it would be Buddhism." Perhaps he saw in Buddhist principles a sort of kindred spirit, similar to that underlying Einstein's relativity theory, which Gaston Bachelard, in 1934, described as "a level of abstraction that required a dematerialization of materialism."[46]

Among Westerners, however, one senses a desire to locate in Buddhism something entirely unlike their own experiences of modernity, and, at the same time, something closely resembling those experiences so as to make Buddhism all the more accessible. In Buddhist Sherpas, foreigners find a reflection of what they themselves desire via *simulations*—imaginings of something both different from and similar to their own Western experiences. On the other hand, foreigners' experiences of Buddhism go beyond this because Buddhism is not solely configured by the gaze of the West; it has its own "civilizing" agendas, which promote wholly different views of subjectivity and self-discipline than those found in the West.

One of the first ways in which Buddhism is encountered by the outsider is as part of the tourist industry. Many Westerners imagine virtually all Sherpas to be exemplary Buddhists and holders of privileged spiritual knowledge, just as they are one and all envisioned as "Tigers of the snow." Many trekkers go to the Himalayas in search of Buddhist experiences, which they often believe they have found in Sherpa religious festivals, encounters with reincarnated lamas, and the homes of Sherpas themselves. This quest among tourists for "the Buddhist experience" leads many Sherpas to invest the money they earn through trekking and mountaineering back into their religious practice in even greater amounts than they might already have because, as they say, they are Buddhists by "culture." This ensures an ongoing dialogue and exchange of symbolic and monetary capital among themselves, Westerners, and monasteries. The Sherpas' desire for this continued reciprocity between themselves and Westerners also results in their efforts to be more accessible and adept as Buddhists for Western students of dharma.

When I entered the trekking agency belonging to a Sherpa friend in 1987, I noticed that the walls were plastered with high-gloss, enlarged photos of spectacular mountaineering feats. Western climbers and Sherpas were pictured atop major Himalayan mountains with the sun reflecting in sharp glare off glacier glasses and national flags held by climbers, all set against deep blue skies and crystalline white peaks. When I returned in 1993, the company had relocated and, in the process, had redecorated. Instead of enthralling expedition vistas, they now had Buddhist *thangkas* gracing their walls. Behind my Sherpa friend's desk was an oversized photo of the Dalai Lama, beneath which was a hand-carved box containing a Buddhist text (*peca*)—even though my friend could not read the Tibetan script in which it was written.

Buddhist images, steeped in exotic mystery, are eagerly reproduced by Sherpas; this fulfills Western desires to locate difference within Sherpa identity. Sherpas and Tibetan refugees now travel abroad in great numbers, and Sherpa monks and lamas like Phurba Sonam come to the West as teachers, offering lessons in Buddhist reality and the route to fulfillment. Is this only a staged presentation of self, performed for Western observers and therefore meaningless in terms of finding a truly authentic Sherpa that exists outside and beyond the Western gaze? Who, in fact, would that Sherpa be, and where would we find him or her? The Sherpa who is truly authentic, by the logic of "authenticity" itself, keeps slipping from our gaze. Buddhist lessons offered to Westerners by Sherpas are viewed as different enough to be educational, yet similar enough to merge with the simulated versions of Buddhism already prevalent in the West. What Buddhist teachers offer might be an illusion of difference that is itself constructed by Western fancy. And yet one would think that foreigners experiencing Buddhism through Sherpas are given more than a simulation of their own making, more than that which Sherpas simply mirror back to them through mimesis. But the form of Buddhism believed to lie outside the Western imagination is just another site for the positing of a Buddhism in which esoteric notions of subjectivity reflect the religion's own desire to create ideal Buddhists. The gaze of foreigners on Buddhist Sherpas becomes entangled with Sherpas' views of themselves in the same way that Westerners often become entangled with Buddhist versions of reality.

Jindak is used by Sherpas to describe both a person who contributes to monasteries and one (usually a Westerner) who becomes a personal sponsor for individual Sherpas. The role of the *jindak*, like most Buddhist concepts, is polysemic for most Sherpas. On the one hand, a *jindak* is supposed to demonstrate a mastery of Buddhist techniques of detachment. Ultimately, this means recognizing that there is nothing permanent about the world of material consequence, especially not money; this recognition liberates one from attachment to any fixed notion of the universe or an iden-

17. Stopping for tea with the monks while trekking through Tengboche.

tity. This is the first step toward transcendence, and is alms giving at its best, for it reveals a high state of awareness. At the same time, being a *jindak* enables one to exploit an association with a monastery for personal gain, such as increased status, honor, political clout, or even merit for one's next life. Acts that are supposed to demonstrate detachment thus often end up creating greater opportunities for attachment—for winning back some benefit in the form of reciprocity as the result of one's gifts.

When foreigners go to the Khumbu seeking a Buddhist Other, they are often drawn into relationships with Sherpas through Buddhist idioms that transform them into *jindak*s. When Sherpas or Westerners give money to monasteries, it is interpreted by Sherpas as a means of gaining both religious merit and local prestige. Likewise, when foreigners give money to Sherpas, it is viewed by Sherpas as a way for foreigners to achieve merit (through acts of compassion) and form local friendships of a reciprocal nature. The Sherpas in this equation adopt the role of the monastery (as recipients of foreign generosity), and at the same time become partners in enduring relationships based on what are thought to be obligatory exchanges (by becoming socially intimate with their foreign sponsors). Sherpas become vehicles for foreigners' aspirations, and in this sense they resemble monasteries simply by remaining Sherpa. Sherpas become better Buddhists while simultaneously promoting the reciprocal attachments that Buddhism defines as problematic (unless—and this is important—

such sponsorship is engaged in with disinterested, detached compassion). Because becoming what the Other desires through mimesis and seduction reiterates a principle of impermanence and establishes a sort of "unfixed" identity, Sherpas reveal yet another way in which they adhere to Buddhist principles aimed at transcendence. Becoming "authentic" in ways that are desired by the West means, ironically, becoming both more essential (in terms of a Western view of "Sherpa-ness") and more "simulational" (in a Buddhist sense). One of the interesting consequences of the Sherpas' Buddhism as seen in the gaze of Westerners is that Sherpas offering this form of cultural practice for tourists simultaneously develop a deeper commitment to the configuration of identity promoted in Buddhism—a commitment evidenced by more than just the money they invest in their religion. Is this not Buddhism at work? Or is it just the playing out of some Western vision of Buddhism that Sherpas willingly demonstrate? What is the difference between them today? Here again I suggest that the notion of a virtual Sherpa is useful, for virtual identity collapses the distance between a projected image and the real thing when it comes to Buddhist Sherpas.

During the final months of the preparation of this manuscript, I was sent a packet of articles on Buddhism and the computer age from the magazine *Tricycle: The Buddhist Review* by a Western dharma student. Long after I had decided on a title for this book, I learned from these articles about the efforts of Western Buddhists to use virtual reality to generate mandalas as visual aids for practitioners of the dharma. I also discovered that a New York diamond merchant and Buddhist monk named Michael Roach had begun a project to transfer the entire corpus of hundreds of Buddhist texts from the new Tibetan Sera Monastery in southern India onto CD-ROMs (computer disks) in Tibetan script, transliteration, and eventually English translation. Roach helps fund his literary project by sending broken diamond chips to an Indian factory (which was donated by Roach to the monastery), where he has taught the monks to recut the stones so they can be sold. Roach began his serious study of Buddhism with an immigrant Kalmuk *rinpoche* from Mongolia who had immigrated to New Jersey. In 1994 Roach was close to obtaining his *gyeshe* degree, after sixteen years of study and several more of renunciation.[47] He already has a large following of Western Buddhist students.

Not surprisingly, given the logic of unattached reciprocity found among Sherpas, Roach was invited to participate as the only Westerner in the annual Winter Debate at the Sera Monastery in 1994. As both a monk and a *jindak*, Roach does not see any conflict of interest between his roles as a diamond dealer (in materialistic pursuit) and a Buddhist adept (aiming to transcend materialism but aware of his phenomenal existence in a material world). The diamond is itself an important symbol in Tibetan Buddhism, denoting both clarity of vision and an ability to cut through illusion. The diamond is the *vajra*, or thunderbolt, a reference to both the double-orbed scepter used by lamas in all ritual enactments and the purported power of the diamond thunderbolt itself to guide one through illusion to the absolute truth of emptiness.[48] Roach's treatise on the diamond, available on CD-ROM, is instructive:

> It is interesting to note that the word "diamond" occurs nowhere in the *Diamond-Cutter Sutra* except for the title. And yet the title itself contains perhaps the most profound message of Asian philosophy, which is fitting for the oldest book in the world. Diamond is the closest thing to an absolute in the natural world: nothing in the universe is harder than diamond; nothing can scratch a diamond. Diamond is absolutely clear: if a diamond wall were built around us we would not be able to see it, even if it were many feet thick. In these senses diamond is close to what Buddhist philosophy terms "absolute truth," or emptiness. . . . Subsequent to seeing absolute truth directly, we understand that reality as we normally experience it, though valid, is something less than absolute. All objects possess a quality of absolute truth, or emptiness: all objects *are void of any self-nature which does not depend on our projections*. In this sense we are surrounded by absolute truth, but have never been able to see it: it is as if this level of reality were like a wall of clear diamond. (Tonkinson 1994, 66; emphasis added)

Later, Roach presents his version of the nature of "emptiness" in a way that is particularly applicable to the problems of relationships between Sherpas and Westerners and attempts to define their identity as essential or as an expression of self-nature:

> The person at work who is trying to get the boss to think I'm bad is truly hurting me. It's nonsense to say it's just empty or that it's not happening. But his wife loves him, and people will swear he's a great guy. You cannot be good and bad at the same time. It's impossible; therefore he's empty. If he were self-existently bad, his wife would hate his guts. If he were self-existently good, I would love him. That's proof in a few sentences that he has no nature. So where is it coming from? It's my perception. (Tonkinson 1994, 68)

In a long line stretching from Nagarjuna, the principal exponent of Mādhyamika teachings (making use of the Perfection of Wisdom [Prajnaparamita] sutras from which these "deconstructionist" Buddhist teachings emanate), Michael Roach joins the ranks of avid Western Buddhists who have begun to take the idea of impermanence seriously. Impermanence and emptiness are central to any discussion of an essential Other—they may, in fact, be its absolute truth. But what a challenging truth that is, for it tells us that the authentic and essential Sherpa we seek, who is different from and yet similar to us in all the ways we desire, may be impossible to grasp as a singular and enduring set of qualities.

I have suggested that one possible outcome of Sherpas' engagement with agencies of modernization, from trekking tourism to anthropological projects, is the obliteration of a sense of fixed subjectivity, in which the notion that Sherpa voices could speak for themselves seems to get lost in Western configurations of their identity. I have posited that one way to find an authentic subject is to examine how those configurations belie an "authentic" Sherpa subject not constituted by the West. That led me to an exploration of how Buddhism constitutes Sherpas in its own way, but this also is ultimately a conversation with the West. Even in the context of Buddhism, Westerners and Sherpas become engaged in simulations of the desirable Other: the Sherpas become virtual for Westerners, and Westerners become desirable to Sherpas as *jindak*s. This unfixed play of identities could be viewed as one consequence of a history of Sherpa involvement with the West, or it could be viewed as one consequence of a generalized incorporation of a fundamental tenet of emptiness among the Sherpa laity. Ironically, whereas esoteric notions of emptiness lead one away from practices of reciprocity and long-term obligations, among Sherpas and Westerners such emptiness also leads to their cultivation. Relationships with foreigners require that Sherpas keep in step with Western interests. Thus, these relationships are unstable from their inception—they have a built-in transience; they are impermanent, despite their construction within essentialist desires from the West and despite their resulting in reciprocal attachments.

When Sherpas' interpretations of esoteric Buddhist concepts are brought face-to-face with Western desires for Buddhist authenticity, an interesting mimetic slippage occurs wherein we are able to see through the mirror of the Sherpas' mimesis of Western desires but never entirely eliminate it. Sherpas mirror back to Westerners an exotic Buddhism already constructed in the Western gaze, especially at public Buddhist events designed for the *chiwa*, where tourists are welcomed and where their donations are deposited as "compassionate" offerings. But Sherpas' becoming what the West desires seems to dovetail almost unintentionally with their becoming what the lamas desire of them. A monk practitioner's ability to "become" a deity exemplifies his mastery of some element of Buddhist practice. A Sherpa's ability to become the "ideal Buddhist," or an expert "Tiger of the snow," exemplifies his or her proficiency at being both "exotic" and "modern" in the eyes of Westerners, and, at the same time, a practitioner of what looks like a Buddhist practice revealing emptiness—revealing himself or herself as an empty (or perhaps virtual) category.

The difference between Western desires and Sherpa practices is obscured for Sherpas themselves when they offer their versions of Buddhism to foreigners as versions of authentic "Sherpa-ness." The word "Sherpa" comes to signify "Buddhist." At the same time, when Sherpas use Buddhism to establish *jindak* relationships with foreigners, they deploy concepts of detachment most clearly articulated in the sponsorship relationships they have with monasteries, but also concepts of attachment that usually accompany gift giving. Impermanence is itself exemplified in the desire for authenticity—in the desire for fixed identities, which become the resting places for truth. In its own way, then, the heterogeneous nature of Buddhism as practiced by Sherpas interrupts the ethnographic process of constituting and locating an authentic Sherpa subject. To put it differently, the Buddhism of Sherpas informs us that writing an ethnographic text about Buddhist Sherpas requires modifying our notion of the authentic and perhaps substituting for it something else consistent with Buddhist versions of reality—perhaps a notion of virtual identities—and that an ethnography would itself have to be something of an exercise in Buddhist practice. This makes it impossible to decide that one of the following propositions could be true to the exclusion of the other: (1) impermanence and emptiness are the sites of authenticity of Sherpa Others, and (2) impermanence and emptiness make it impossible to locate essential or authentic Sherpas. Where is the adamantine (diamondlike) truth about this difference that is so desired by the ethnographer that the desire itself becomes entangled with those who are represented? Does this illustrate an implosion of ethnographic difference into sameness?

Sherpas' relationships with foreigners make visible the principles of emptiness so sought after by Buddhist Westerners arriving in Nepal on quests for spiritual epiphanies. At the same time, such relationships reveal the expansive qualities of the self in a Sherpa universe—a universe in which the self at the center radiates out and is connected to all else within that universe. The interconnections between people, like those between people and things in the universe, enable Sherpas to gain foreign sponsors who are consequently treated like lifelong partners and friends, and thereby engage them in a sort of attached yet unattached giving through acts of "compassion" (sponsorship). Where, one might ask, would one find the geographic and cultural boundaries around this "authentic Sherpa"? They are, I suggest, the same as those envisioned by Buddhists in practice who, by recognizing emptiness, also recognize that boundaries between the self and the Other are always shifting and inherently impermanent because what they enclose at any one time is an empty category. Certainly, one end point of this boundary movement is the spread of Buddhist awareness throughout the world, as suggested in the article about the diamond merchant, Michael Roach: "The image of the *Dharma* being spread throughout the world through the medium of disks emerges consistently in the words of the monks [who are entering the Buddhist texts onto CD-ROM and 'cutting diamonds in the rough']. It is reminiscent of a Tibetan ceremony in which prayers are written on thousands of pieces of paper, and the papers are released into the wind as a metaphor for [or enactment of] spreading the teaching."[49]

Like the wind, *rlung*, the effects of this ceremony are upon us.

CHAPTER FOUR

The Intimacy of Shamanic Sherpas

I RETURN to *The Snow Leopard*, the book in which Peter Matthiessen describes a personal journey toward greater self-awareness advanced by his exploration of Himalayan shamanism. He writes:

> Shambala is a symbol for the Aryan cultures that emerged in that vast region between 6000 and 5000 B.C.—the apparent source of esoteric mystery-cults throughout Eurasia, which have echoes to this day in the Tantric Buddhism of Tibet. According to one Tibetan lama, these mysteries "are the faint echoes of teaching that existed from time immemorial in Central and North Asia." Another believes that "no people since the beginning . . . has ever been without some fragment of this secret lore." This view is supported by ethnologists, who find the same pattern of shamanistic practice not only in Asia and the Americas but in Africa, Australia, Oceania, and Europe. The historical diffusion of such teachings—and perhaps the prehistorical as well—is supported by striking consistencies in the practice of what Westerners, having lost the secrets, refer to with mixed fascination and contempt as "mysticism" or "the occult" but which for the less alienated cultures, past and present, is only another aspect of reality.[1]

By the end of the story, we have come to understand that Matthiessen's experience of this ancient "mysticism" is contingent on his relationship with a particular Sherpa, the trusted porter Tukten, whom Matthiessen views as follows:

> Tukten has elf's ears and a thin neck, a yellow face, and the wide wise eyes of a *naljorpa*, or Tibetan yogi. He radiates that inner quiet which is often associated with spiritual attainment, but perhaps his attainment is a dark one. The other Sherpas are uneasy with him, they mutter that he drinks too much, uses foul language, is not to be trusted. Apparently he has demeaned himself by taking this job as a porter [as opposed to a guide]. Yet they defer to him as if he possessed some sort of magic, and sometimes I think I feel his power, too. This disreputable fellow is somehow known to me, like a dim figure from another life. Tukten himself seems aware that we are in some sort of relation, which he accepts in a way that I cannot; that he is not here by accident is, for me, a restless instinct, whereas he takes our peculiar bond for granted. More often than I like, I feel that gaze of his, as if he were here to watch over me, as if it were he who had made me cut that stick [which Matthiessen used to fend off an attacking dog]: the gaze is open, calm, benign, without judgment of any kind, and yet,

confronted with it, as with a mirror, I am aware of all that is hollow in myself, all that is greedy, angry, and unwise.[2]

The notion of Sherpas as a wellspring of deeper knowledge about the Western self is a common theme in writings about them. Such representations often take shamanism as the most authentic site of "Sherpa-ness." What sort of authenticity is imputed to Sherpas who are able to become guides to the ancient wisdom of shamanism, and why is this access assumed to be available only through intimate bonds with Sherpas themselves? In this chapter, I explore a popular site for authenticity produced both by touristic Western gazes and in ethnographic encounters such as my own. Here, one finds something like the intimacy sometimes sought by Westerners in sexual relationships with Sherpas. However, the intimacy sought in shamanic episodes eventually turns Westerners into those who engage in mimesis with that which is truly Sherpa, or that which is taken to be truly Sherpa.

Here, still, in this reversed mimesis, at this purportedly most historic and ethnographically authentic site for "Sherpa-ness"—where one might hope to discover a Sherpa beyond intertextual constructions—one again finds only seduction and impermanence. In shamanism, we once again discover a "nonessential" Sherpa who merely reflects the social relationships between Westerners and Sherpas out of which his or her image arises. The desire to locate an authentic Sherpa is thus treated in this chapter as one of the central problems of ethnography, raising issues similar to that of a Buddhist impermanence—issues that make singular and extreme versions of truth unsustainable. Like others before me, I contend that the mode of power at work in ethnographic studies seeks a permanent authenticity not found in the dynamic social relationships among Sherpas (or among others, for that matter). To address authenticity, I return to Nagarjuna, who recognized that "reality defies the very possibility of theoretical characterization in terms of any of the extremes, like 'it is' and 'it is not.'"[3] Each rendering of an authoritative or authentic "truth" contains the seeds of its own contradiction. Thus, between the extremes of the observing and desirous ethnographer who "creates" his or her subject and the real Other who is seemingly unaffected by the ethnographer's gaze are virtual Sherpas, who continually and unavoidably refer back to those social relationships giving rise to "authentic" Sherpas.

A graduate student introduced me to yet another Western dharma student who had just returned from Nepal. He had been trekking in Sherpa country and he asked if I had met a particular Sherpa—a deaf man from Namche Bazaar. That man and his family owned a hotel there, and they had initiated a cultural program for tourists—a visual tour of Sherpa culture through still photographs and a slide show. It was shown to visitors whether or not they had somehow failed to notice they were experiencing Sherpa culture already. I had seen the show in its early and formative stages in 1987, and had noted its comprehensive quality then; it offered a smattering of mountaineering, religion, history, and ritual—something for everyone. When I told the dharma student that I had enjoyed the show, he responded with a look of disbelief. "But that was not Sherpa culture!" he objected, aghast at my approval. "It was so sterile and performed! That is not real Sherpa culture!"

Now it was I who was aghast. He continued to offer his insights: "I went trekking and my guide was a Sherpa. We became *close friends*—he borrowed my flashlight but never returned it. I know that is where real Sherpa culture is . . . in this type of relationship. I even met his family. [It is] not in the 'museumified,' packaged culture offered in the lodge at Namche Bazaar!" For many visitors to Sherpa country, the experience of close bonds with Sherpas is perceived to be the key to "knowing" Sherpa culture. For many, this sort of experience is perceived to be available through shamanism because shamanism, in some important sense, is about social relationships; it is about what Sherpas call *thurmu* (togetherness or closeness), and it is about crossing the boundaries between the self and the Other, Sherpas and their Others, through *thurmu*. The idea of virtual identities has for me become a handy way of approaching the question of which Sherpas count as "real" in the eyes of Westerners, and the sentiment of *thurmu* is built into all these versions from the start. To explore the utility of the virtual concept, I begin with the following question: What does it mean to be involved in intimate relationships with Sherpa Others?

SHIFTING BOUNDARIES, TRANSCENDENCE, AND CLOSENESS

"Our Sherpa culture has everything in threes," Nima Sherpa said on our flight from Kathmandu to Lukla, where the airstrip for the Khumbu region was located. Nima, who ran a hotel in Lukla when not working for a Sherpa-owned trekking agency, elaborated as follows:

Like, we are all happy, sad, and in between. Everything is in threes: the rich, middle, and poor. We say *khonjok sum* [the three jewels: Buddha, dharma, community].[4] We also have three worlds. The past was a singing world and when people met they sang to each other. This world is a laughing world. When people meet, they laugh. The future world is a crying world and people will get tears when they meet. In *domang* it tells about a third eye, how we can think of a place and look with our third eye, and then be there. Many years ago, everyone could do this; they could just touch another person who was sick and they were made well. It says in *domang* that after all our changing is done we will go back to that kind of world. We are slowly going back to that now.[5]

Like most of the Sherpas who came to know me, Nima was aware of my interest in Sherpa conceptions of the individual and the body, and tailored his comments accordingly. His remarks here were made in response to a question I had posed: "What is the meaning of *chi nang sang sum?*" As in many conversations I had with Sherpas, my query prompted an explanation that answered other questions I did not yet know how to ask, but did not address this one. (At least I did not know he was addressing it.) I persisted. I had first heard about *chi nang sang sum* in relation to levels of Buddhist practice. *Chi* meant outside, *nang*, inside, and *sang*, secret. And I was, after all, seeking the "secret Sherpas," those not yet revealed by anthropologists or others. So I asked again, hoping he would offer something that looked familiar to the response I had gotten from monks. He was more explicit: "*Chi* is outside," he said, "*nang* is inside, and *sang* is secrets; *sum* is for all three. Outside can mean outside our home, outside our community. Inside can mean inside our home, inside our community. Secrets means there are outside and inside secrets that we must keep. This means some things we share with other people, some things we keep secret to ourselves, and some things we keep secret even from our own [personal] gods [*lha*]."

Once again, I was confounded. Here we were discussing social relationships, not Buddhism. But Nima's words echoed those of Kenchi Sherpani, a married woman from Kathmandu, who had spoken with me weeks earlier:

> Some secret things even husband and wife do not tell each other. Other things, we only tell close relatives. This is *chi nang*—when you have a big problem or secret, and you just tell close relatives like a sister, who I can tell all my life situations to. That means I can tell [nearly] everything but not all. Some things I keep to myself—[for example, if] I have a great problem [and I want to tell someone] but [realize] no one else can solve my problem; if I tell a friend, even he or she cannot help me. If I tell a *close* relative, maybe he or she can help me. [But,] if we say to other people [that is, if we tell them about this problem], then they all talk about me, but no one can help [me]. They all say, "Oh, she is poor, no money to eat," like that. Or, if I say bad things about my sister because she does not help me even though she has money, then people say I have no *chi nang*.

For Kenchi, *chi nang* applied to various situations in which the need for a boundary was perceived. "Boundaries" were, after all, what Nima and Kenchi were talking about—boundaries between social domains, and within a person. Nima continued his explanation of these divisions in reference to a Sherpa penchant for "threes." "It is like *chongo trung sum*, the three offerings for the shrine. We give *khonjok sum la chu pa pul*, meaning this is for the gods," he said.[6]

We give offerings to Buddha with body, speech, mind. Like when we drink *chang*, you have seen one finger goes in the glass and sprinkles a little outside for the gods. We give with body, that is more personal—what I do—I offer some *chang*. Then with speech, that is when we say *gu sung thu la chu pa pul*.[7] Then, I give with mind, that is, secret level, no one knows what is in my mind. That mind can know secrets even our [personal] gods don't know. Like if the lama gives a secret name [to us] at birth and we use a different name, then those gods don't know our *dikpa* [actions that are not virtuous] or *payin* [meritorious actions]."

Nima and Kenchi were describing the shifting boundaries within which they situated themselves in social relationships. The boundaries between the self and close relatives and others, the ones between mind and body and speech, and those between worlds divided by time (past and present and future) and social character (singing and laughing and crying) were those boundaries where *chi nang*—the general sense of "inside/outside"—came into play.[8]

Chi nang, as I came to understand it, was not the boundary of any particular space, but that of any possible space Sherpas might occupy. One who lost *chi nang* had lost a sense of the line dividing inner secrets from outer sharing, or dividing one's own mind from the qualities of the individual shared with others in one's family, or lineage, or village—collectively, one's personal gods. Typically, Sherpas talked of a loss of *chi nang* when people lost their sense of the demarcation between their persons and others with whom they had relationships.

The tension between the individual, perceived as a self-contained unit, and the group to which one belonged through a network of reciprocal exchange generated endless discussions regarding *chi nang*. These revealed a shifting sense of identity in which personal independence was always undermined by calls for reciprocity, and in which reciprocal exchanges constantly reconfigured the sociocentric being. The expansive self radiating from the individual in a Buddhist cosmology was suddenly, in this context, turned into one that was articulated through a series of shifting boundaries within that universe. Was the tension between individual and group, like that between inner self and outer self, the sort of quality "real" Sherpas would exhibit? Had I begun to find a Sherpa who was "authentic"? Was this "secret" Sherpa one who exhibited a dynamic tension between *chi nang* (which involved a recognition of boundaries) and that state of being totally connected to others in a way that denied boundaries, most clearly expressed in the Sherpa word *thurmu*? In fact, it was clear that *thurmu* was experienced by foreign visitors who, embracing Sherpa Otherness, came to feel there were no boundaries—no *chi nang*—between themselves and those the Sherpas they emulated. Consider Tukten Sherpa, the person chosen by Peter Matthiessen as a departure point for his own journey toward self-realization by way of intimacy with the Other:

> Tukten is our sole remaining porter, and he will be paid henceforth as a sherpa, as he is much too valuable to lose. The decision to keep Tukten on was mine, as despite his ambiguous reputation I find him the most intelligent and helpful of our men; also, I feel that in some way he brings me luck. He will go on with me. . . . [Later in the journey, during an evening of relaxation, Matthiessen writes]: Jang-bu is playing his harmonica, and Dawa and Gyaltsen laugh indiscriminately at all they see, but the only one of the Shey party who will dance is Tukten—Tukten Sherpa, cook and porter, alleged thief, bad drunk, old Gurkha, is a dancer, too, and dancing, he smiles and smiles. . . . I sit here as peaceful as a Buddha, and from across the fire, Tukten smiles as if I had held up the lotus. The dancing is over, and now this humble *trulku* [Tukten] of Kasapa is seated thigh to thigh with the ancient [an old woman], delighting her with Tukten jokes while soothing the sleepy infant girl, who has crawled into his lap. There are no boundaries to this man, he loves us all.[9]

Matthiessen has become a Buddha and Tukten, his mirror, has become his muse and his teacher. It was Ama Pasang, the mother of my friend Doma, who taught me about *thurmu* and the transcending and management of boundaries. Ama Pasang walked with me from Lukla to Khum Jung village after a flight we had taken from Kathmandu, returning from a cold city winter to an icy-cold mountain Khumbu. Doma had asked me to escort her mother home to Khunde. Ama Pasang moved slowly along the steep trail we would follow for two days, and with each step another prayer issued from her lips and another prayer bead was turned on a long strand of 108 that she had held in her hand since takeoff. She halted every hundred yards or so to catch her breath, apologizing each time for slowing us down. I kept assuring her that I myself could not walk any faster, and finally put my arm through hers so that we could traverse the next few hundred yards together, not saying a word until we stopped to rest. We made it home the second night before sundown, where I delivered her to her youngest son in Khunde village (the son who was to die on an expedition a few years later).

The next day, I walked over to my traveling companion's home to make sure she had recovered from the long trek. Arriving at her door, I yelled up, "Oh, Ama Pasang! Oh, Ama Passo," dropping the last consonants for an "o," which would show endearment. When she peered out the window and saw me smiling below, she implored, "Solcha shey [drink tea]." I entered to find her sitting near the kitchen fire with her son. She was again reciting prayers, the strand of beads making endless rounds through her thumb and forefinger, accompanied by her chant "*om mani padme hum.*" (Her prayers were her single most important job at this stage of her life, she often said.) I asked how she was feeling following our journey, and she remarked on how tired and sore her feet were. I told her that mine were also bad, and we smiled sympathetically at one another over our unabashed complaints about this inevitable aspect of life in the Khumbu. Ama Pasang finally asked me if I needed anything, or if there was some special reason for my visit. I told her no special reason other than to see if she was all right.

She spotted a *Time* magazine from Kathmandu in my backpack. It was opened to a page featuring an old World War II photograph of Hitler being paraded in his motorcade. He stood with his hand raised in the characteristic salute of the Third Reich. Ama Pasang pointed to the photo, indicating that she grasped the significance of what he was doing—and once again, the vagaries of fieldwork conspired to confound my expectation of neat and tidy insights into Sherpa lives. "Namaste!" she said, as she placed her palms together at her chest, offering a greeting wholly and purposely antithetical to that symbolized by the raised salute of the Nazi regime. She had thought that the hand raised by Hitler was the equivalent of her "Namaste," and she offered a gesture that would suitably respond to the photo, indicating that *she* understood the subtleties of cross-cultural translation. That moment of misaligned cosmopolitanism seemed hilarious to me,[10] despite the gravity of the particular person in question. I had no idea that my laughter in response to her gesture would lead to a discussion of *thurmu*, but it did. Without understanding what I found so humorous, she was delighted that I could laugh so unabashedly in front of her, and told me that I "knew" *thurmu*. When I raised my eyebrows and furrowed my brow to signify that I did not know what the term meant, she said "*Thurmu* is when you helped me on the trail yesterday, when you laughed just now—so close." Her son joined in the conversation and clarified: "It is closeness. *Thurmu* is when you don't have to worry because your friends will take care of you," she said. "If you are in the village, even if you are starving, people will say, 'Come in for *shakpa* [potato stew]' and you eat together. It is no problem, because you are friends. If people come and ask me to eat, drink, but I am shy and say 'No, no,' then they push me to come, to drink with them and eat and talk. Then, after I go, then I ask them to my home for the same. That is *thurmu*."

Thurmu is the sense of connectedness Sherpas have with one another; it is what Westerners hope to experience when they enter "Sherpa country." It was the feeling sought by Doma's foreign friends when they went to Kathmandu and took her out to dinner, or tried to take care of her with financial support. It is what Westerners seek in sexual relations with Sherpas; it is what they seek when they undertake treks and become *jindak*s. It is in many ways the very thing ethnographers like myself have always

18. Gaga Phuti (left) and Ama Pasang, close friends who know the meaning of *thurmu*.

hoped to achieve by inserting ourselves into that part of Sherpa life believed to be "backstage" and essential to Sherpa culture, supposedly rarely visible to the casual tourist visiting the Khumbu. It is perhaps what Walter Benjamin identified as the auratic,[11] and Taussig as a reenchantment.[12] What is this *thurmu* that Westerners do not know to ask for by name, but pursue all the same? And is it characteristic of yet another virtual Sherpa, authentic despite its constructed quality?

I better understood *thurmu* after learning about its opposing principle from a different friend, the monk Phurba Sonam. He told me that the opposite of *thurmu* was *khondup*, "not talking." Communication enabled people to draw together and become friends. Having lots of *thurmu* meant having lots of people to talk to and to turn to in times of need. But *thurmu* was problematic, he said, in that too much of it was as troublesome as too little. "In the U.S. you have no *thurmu*. We [Sherpas] know all about one another and so of course, sometimes we fight. If you like someone too much, it is as bad as if you do not like someone enough. You can like too much . . . you can overlike. You can also dislike, or get angry or hate, and this is also bad," he said. "People get *pem* because they overlike or underlike; also *norpa* [ghost] comes from this." Supposedly, witches were not always aware that they were actually causing illness, since their *gyaptak*s could compel them to "overlike" certain people or their possessions without themselves being aware of those desires.[13] Witches were thought to arise in either this way, via *gyaptak*s, or through deliberate acts of hostility and anger—that is, by "underliking."

Most *pem* who caused sickness to others were not entirely aware of their instrumentality. This was not thought to be the case, however, with the most heinous perpetrators of *pem* activity—women who believed that if they poisoned 108 people, they would eventually receive all of their wealth. "A woman buys the *thuk* from someone, like a *rongba* [a Nepalese from the southern region]," Kandro from Khum Jung explained to me on the way to the Saturday market. "If she prepares it then, as she gets close to the time she is supposed to give it to her victim, it will call out to her 'Kshk, kshk.' Then, if she fails to give it [to her intended victim], it will still call out to her and she will have to eat it herself and then quickly take medicine [an antidote believed to grow next to the *thuk* plant]." Pemba Tenzing, the owner of a trekking agency in Kathmandu, once showed me how he carried a little piece of that antidote in his wallet at all times. He even had it there when he visited the United States.

I was told that a *norpa* could also arrive because of too much or too little *thurmu*. The deceased were thought to become ghosts if they failed to find their way through the *bardo*, the space between death and rebirth. Unfortunates stuck in the *bardo* were doomed to wander invisibly through the human world. Because the living were unaware of their presence, these spirits went without meals or the affection of their families. Ultimately, such ghosts became offended, resulting in sickness for those with whom they lived. One supposedly became a ghost as a consequence of "failing to gain enough religious knowledge." This left one unable to concentrate on one's spiritual knowledge while in the *bardo*, when confronted with various demons and deities in a test of one's ability to overcome them. The monks hired by one's family to recite the *Bardo Thodol* (*Tibetan Book of the Dead*) at one's death were there primarily to guide the sentient consciousness of the deceased through this intermediate, and dangerous, place.

Sometimes the deceased were thought to be unable to concentrate while in the *bardo* because their relatives' affections, like magnets, deflected their attention. If the person who had died and his or her family were too attached (that is, if they demonstrated too much *thurmu*), and the family thus cried incessantly following the death, it was believed to distract the *sems* of the deceased from focusing on religious matters, such as dealing with the spirits of the afterworld while in the *bardo*. This allegedly caused the deceased to lose his or her way and become a ghost. On the other hand, if the family failed to perform an appropriate funeral ceremony, which included hiring monks to read the *Bardo Thodol* and offering massive amounts of food and money to all villagers in an elaborate display of hospitality (that is, if they failed to demonstrate enough *thurmu*), then the deceased might likewise lose his or her way and become a ghost.

Regulating *thurmu* through the exchange of food, goods, services, labor, and favors was a major preoccupation for most of the Sherpas I met and, ultimately, for me during the time I spent with them. One key to a successful social life, it seemed, was not simply to develop as many reciprocal ties with others as possible, but to manage them so as not to become overly dependent on or too independent of others. Sherpas had to oversee carefully the boundaries between themselves and others. In the end, I too began to have difficulty maintaining my closeness to and distance from so many Sherpas. This personal experience of the Other seemed to me a step toward locating an "essential" Sherpa identity. It seemed to present me with that experience of something so different, and so comforting. Surely this was going to be my access to an inner truth about Sherpas, and my point of departure to say something original about Sherpa life. I dug for more evidence.

If diagnoses of psychosocial disorders underscore the rules for "normal" social interaction by noting the failure of that interaction in one labeled "crazy," then analyzing episodes of *nyombu* within Sherpa culture, I thought, might unearth deeply embedded Sherpa notions of normality—and identity—not visible to the everyday trekker in the Khumbu. One of the first things I learned about cases of *nyombu* among Sherpas was that they, too, were viewed as the consequence of having too much or too little *thurmu*.

During the summer of 1987, three people were afflicted with *nyombu*, each following some demonstration of either an abundance or deficit of "closeness." One man, Pemba Tsong, had been living outside the Khunde–Khum Jung areas for the better part of several years, working at his restaurant lodge in a village higher up on the Everest route. He was a wealthy villager of high status, but during the annual Dumje festival (marking the anniversary of the death of Lama Sangwa Dorje, and celebrating membership in the Sherpa community via sponsorship responsibilities), Pemba Tsong was not invited to join the circle of older, affluent residents inside the *gomba*. In fact, he dressed in his best finery for the event, and his presence outside the monastery, where the women, children, and less wealthy village men (including recent immigrants) typically sat, was noted by everyone there. The following day, Pemba Tsong began to say things no one understood, and started to talk of killing himself. He was taken to the Khunde Hospital and given sedatives.

In another case, a young Sherpa named Norbu began walking all over the hills and near cliffs, alternately speaking nonsense or not speaking at all. He was unable to focus on anyone who looked at him, despite his empty stare into others' eyes. His *nyombu* began the night after his mother and wife had had a raging argument. The tensions between mother-in-law and daughter-in-law could be fairly severe in the Khumbu and were called *iwi-nama* (mother-in-law—daughter-in-law) problems. These problems often arose when an eldest son married and tried to set up a separate nuclear household for his new family, drawing income and attention away from his mother and her home. In this case, when Norbu's mother began to beat his wife, he apparently "started screaming at them and just couldn't stop." He tried to kill himself with a knife, I was told. Then he ran out of the house and was not found until the next day, walking dangerously close to a precipice. For weeks, he stumbled through the village with someone by his side to protect him at all times. When his family called the shaman to find out what had happened to Norbu, they were informed that the family god, a *gyurpa lha* (the patrilineage god), had been offended. Appeasing him would require offering expensive food, drink, and flags in his favorite colors; he might then be convinced to retract his wrath. His anger had hit Norbu and not others, apparently, because Norbu had the least *rlung rta* in the household. Underliking coupled with a lack of *rlung rta* had produced his madness. The shaman (*lhawa*) helped cure him.

In the third case, a young woman named Tsamgi started to "go crazy" following several weeks of Dumje parties hosted by her family. Each household owning property in the Khumbu sponsored Dumje on a rotating basis. Her family had been a Dumje sponsor that year, and, since the family members had collected far more rice than they could use for one festival,[14] they were throwing several smaller parties every few nights. Tsamgi's house was filled with visitors for weeks on end, and she was expected to offer them endless hospitality with undying *thurmu*. Her episode of *nyombu* commenced when she began to call out the names of people who were not present and hit with a spoon people who were. She was, I was told, "barking, barking like a dog, not making any sense." After everyone left her house, she became depressed and continued to talk nonsense. Her family called the shaman and learned that she had been put under a "love spell" by a Nepalese policeman stationed in the Khumbu. He had put this spell (*mohani*) on her by feeding her candy laced with a potion to make her fall in love with him. The man had not actually been at Tsamgi's home, but he had seen her at the market several weeks before and had fallen in love with her there. The shaman's ceremony was aimed at engaging the man's spirit in negotiations, wherein he was offered his favorite foods, drinks, and other gifts to dissuade him from pursuing Tsamgi. Thus, the problems attributed to being overloved were as troublesome as those stemming from being socially disconnected, or underloved.

Now I felt I was on the right track. Surely a closer study of such phenomena held the key to a "native's point of view"—to a Sherpa vision of an authentic Sherpa world. I further explored the meanings of *thurmu* and *nyombu*, and found that *nyombu* was not the only condition resulting from problems with boundaries between the person and the group—

boundaries often defined in the context of shared meals and hospitality.[15] Another example, *pang*, was a disease that afflicted certain postpartum women and sometimes spread to their close relatives as well. *Pang* victims could not bear to let sunlight touch their bodies or clothes, for if it did, they became nauseated. They were called "depressed" by members of the hospital staff. They had no appetite and could neither venture outside nor socialize inside.

Lhamo Sherpani had had *pang* for six months when I met her. Her mother had also come down with this condition while taking care of her. When I spoke to Lhamo, she did not know what might have caused her problem. One *lhawa* said it was due to some trouble with her clan god. A lama had told her it was *rlung* and gave her medicines, which had not helped. She had not yet gone to the hospital. When I asked her friends what they thought, one woman, Kanti, described the circumstances of Lhamo's life before the *pang* began:

> It was right after the baby was born. Her mother made her marry [a man named] Kami because she said, "He is a rich man." Lhamo did not want to marry him, but her mother said she must. Then the daughter [Lhamo] said, "He is not a rich man. He has no parties, nothing. He never calls anyone to his house." When they had a son, her [Lhamo's] husband brought only two *mana*s [roughly two cups] of rice, a few potatoes, and two or three *tiple*s [pitchers] of *chang* to the naming ceremony [for the child]. Lhamo got very angry and she fought with her mother and then got *pang*. Thereafter, her mother was fighting too. She said she didn't like [the] husband either.

Kanti added, "His face is black like a monkey—like a yeti—because he is always with his yaks. He says, 'I am a rich man. I have lots of money.' But he has no good food. He never even buys sugar at the market. He has three *zopkyok*, one *zum* [yak-cow crossbreeds, male and female, respectively], and he takes them trekking." Kami, it seems, was stingy and Kanti thought this too was related to his wife's *pang*. I suspected it was not stinginess per se, but the lack of social connections this led to (a matter of underliking), that caused Lhamo's problems.

What all these cases suggested to me was that regulating *thurmu* was a boundary issue; it involved being sufficiently connected to others while also maintaining a certain independence. Boundaries between the individual and others through social networks of *thurmu* were mobile, not only in the sense that they shifted as people become closer or more distant within relationships, but also in that they were applied in a variety of social contexts and sites. Homes, for example, were seen as troublesome if not spaced far enough apart, as in the case of households divided by only a single wall to accommodate two brothers who, inevitably, would fight because they were "too close." At the other extreme, houses outside the village were considered undesirable because they were too far from others and there-fore "cold and inhospitable." Yet the perception of a person's home as nearby or distant was also dictated by whose residence it was. Similarly, people who invested beyond their means in relationships of exchange in order to gain friends were seen as foolish. That was how people viewed one struggling Sherpani who was trying desperately to hawk one of her few fields in order to donate a large sum of money in honor of an extremely well-respected, distant relative who had just died, and whose funeral was being paid for by her immediate kin. At the same time, being without friends or connections was also considered laughable, as in the case of one older Sherpa also named Kami. Always seen walking alone to or from the market, he was consequently given the derogatory nickname Kami Cher, "Kami Alone." But even these indictments were open to revision. The young woman's attempt to gain friends did result in her closer association with more-obligated relatives and villagers, despite their ostracism and warnings that her efforts would backfire. And Kami Cher, despite his nick-name, ultimately became a major festival sponsor and won the support, friendship, and praise of many.

In the end, the more I tried to get a fix on these boundary issues, watch-ing Sherpas and trying to find the middle ground between overliking and underliking that avoided extremes, the more I realized that the "unfixabil-ity" of these boundaries was their essence. Nagarjuna drifted back into my imagination. Perhaps his realization of the "middle path" had something to do with these problems of everyday social life, which produced a great deal of attachment and of inevitable suffering. The mobile quality of social rela-tionships forced one to establish a sense of boundaries between the self and the Other, and at the same time to treat such boundaries as mobile and permeable. I had (many years before reading Matthiessen's book) begun to delight in the idea that I, like Matthiessen, had penetrated some boundary between myself and my Sherpa Others. But for me it was this penetration that made me realize the difficulty of finding a truly singular, "authentic" Sherpa Other.

Thurmu, in adequate supply, was what I sought, like all those trekkers who went to the Khumbu hoping to experience Otherness through the mountains and the even more remote (and therefore more "authentic") practices of the shaman. What did the shamans themselves have to say about this desire for properly regulated *thurmu*? Their logic was clear: one became sick when one lost one's *chi nang*, one's ability to remain between those extremes that formed a boundary around the person. Afflictions arose if one allowed oneself to become too close to, or too distant from, others. But shamanic events aimed at regulating *thurmu* ended up provid-ing one with a less clear notion of an essential Sherpa than I had expected, for shamanic events revolved around two notions: (1) the ultimate transience and impermanence of social relationships, and (2) the profitability of engaging in seduction and mirroring of the desires of those with whom one had relationships in order to create bonds of reciprocity. Shamans allowed boundary relationships to be renegotiated via the mechanisms of seduction and mimesis. Foreigners hoping to "find themselves" by establishing intimate relationships with Sherpas slipped through the boundaries that separated them from their Others ("authentic" Sherpas) and in the process revealed the logic of mimesis within mobile Sherpa identities.

DIALOGUES WITH MIRRORED OTHERS

Once again, Matthiessen's prose serves as the takeoff point for an ethnographic journey into the more exotic and mystical arenas of Sherpa culture and identity. Matthiessen becomes our "Sherpa" guide:

> Tukten, the only man among us who has been there [Dolpo]: one senses that, in one life or another, he has been everywhere on earth. Of his wide experience, Tukten tells tales in that soft voice, and so the other Sherpas listen, but he is not one of them [because he is a porter]. . . . He is helpful and ingenious, and his mesmerizing voice, coming and going on the wind and rain, seems to fascinate the younger Sherpas, although they are wary of him, and keep their distance. One feels they are afraid of him—not of his violence, though they say he fights when drunk, but of his power. Whatever this man is—wanderer or evil monk, or saint or sorcerer—he seems touched by what Tibetans call the "crazy wisdom": he is free.[16]

The power Matthiessen imputes to his trusted friend Tukten is strikingly similar to that sought by many Westerners and ethnographers in shamanic healing, interpreted here as a power of seduction wherein an unstated logic reigns; one becomes the "same" as the Other and as what the Other desires as a source of profit and well-being. What happens when cures are sought from Sherpa shamans? What emerges in the intimate bonds Sherpas supposedly forge between themselves and spirits, and themselves and Western Others, via shamanic episodes?

A-Tshiring was one of the Khumbu region's most prominent shamans.[17] Some said shamans could get sick, unlike lamas, because they were, as they put it, "anti" to the lama and their very practices could put a patron's *rlung rta* at risk. When I met him in 1982, A-Tshiring was famous for his possession cures. When I returned in 1986, he hardly had any patients left because he was dying. At the time of my second visit, he had been sick for six months with a serious stomachache, backache, and persistent cough.

A-Tshiring's wife said another shaman, Lhawa Pembu, had told them that A-Tshiring's problem was caused by a witch to the east of their home. A woman had recently visited their home without eating any food or taking any drink. Although she had been hungry and thirsty, she did not admit this and refused everything they offered. Because she had left hungry, she had unwittingly become a *pem* and was now causing A-Tshiring's sickness. The family tried to satisfy the *pem* by offering her more food and her favorite drinks, but still he did not improve.

A-Tshiring's eldest son, Norbu, lived in Kathmandu with his fiancée, Tashi, and their two children. A-Tshiring and his wife had visited them regularly during the winter in past years. Norbu and Tashi had not yet married because her family had rejected A-Tshiring's son as a suitor from the beginning of their romance. For Sherpas, A-Tshiring was a low-status Khamba (Tibetan immigrant from Kham), as was his son. Tashi, on the other hand, was from a very old, established Sherpa clan, and her family had been among the most wealthy of the village. Her father died when she was young, though, and the family had lost much of its fortune by the time Tashi was an adult. Ultimately, Norbu and Tashi eloped to Kathmandu, where they set up house and had two children whom they supported by themselves. Norbu held a job as a salaried sardar for a trekking agency, and Tashi knit hats, scarves, and gloves for sale in to local tourist shops.

When Norbu learned that his father was very ill, he decided that he and Tashi should return to the Khumbu to be with him and to attempt to be formally married. Through relatives, he began negotiating with his fiancée's family for a wedding date, working around A-Tshiring's illness. With Norbu and his wife and children back in the village, the family renewed its efforts to diagnose A-Tshiring's illness and prevent his death. Norbu and his cousin, Pemba, visited a lama named Gushu Mongten, who lived a day and a half away (by foot), to obtain a divination (*sungdok*) about whether or not A-Tshiring's health would return. They went equipped with A-Tshiring's birth date, a plate of rice adorned with a *kata*, a piece of Tibetan rock salt, and a monetary contribution. Pemba later told me that they had also been trying to ascertain, indirectly, if it would be auspicious for Norbu to marry at this time.

The young men were advised by the lama that A-Tshiring would get a little bit worse and then recover. He was suffering from a *pagin*, or "phlegm humor," disease, but this would clear and he would live eleven more years. On this basis, the cousins decided there was no need to forgo the expense of a wedding now, since there would be no funeral costs that year. Lama Gushu Mongten suggested that they sponsor a *kurim* for the father. They left an appropriate sum for the lama to ensure that a *kurim* would be performed on A-Tshiring's behalf in their absence. Now they had only to determine a suitable wedding date and obtain an agreement from Tashi's family to allow the marriage and help sponsor the event.

Back at his home, A-Tshiring's health was not improving, which the lama had in fact predicted. But now he seemed to be declining even faster than when Norbu and his family had first arrived from Kathmandu. Becoming more and more worried, Norbu discussed the matter with his mother and they agreed to call a famous shaman, Lhawa Palden, for yet another curing ceremony, a *lhabeo* (god descending) ceremony. This event began only after darkness fell, with twelve family members and friends gathered in the home of A-Tshiring.

Lhawa Palden first set up an altar on two shelves under a window to his right. On his left was his drum. His large headdress-crown, each face of which was adorned with a Buddha figure and each side of which was draped with many strips of colored cloth, was placed behind him, reserved for that point in the ritual when he was possessed. On the altar sat a row of brass bowls filled with rice grains, *tsampa*, butter, and incense, all meant to attract the spirits to this place and to the shaman. A lama's *phembu*, *dorje* (a small brass *vajra*, or thunderbolt scepter), and a bell were also placed on the altar. These ritual items would become important later in the ceremony, when the shaman would become possessed by a tutelary lama who would provide A-Tshiring with a prescription for various *kurims*. On the shelf above were more bowls of offerings intended to lure spirits to the event, and, most important, a large brass plate polished to serve as a mirror. In that mirror, Lhawa Palden would see himself reflected, but more significantly, he would see himself as the spirits who possessed him. Many spirits would enter into that mirror throughout the night, and each would see the people in the room, on the other side of the mirror, looking hopefully to the spirits for a cure for their affliction.

Lhawa Palden went into a trance after first making offerings to the gods of the four geographic directions (north, south, east, west) with the Buddhist chant *gu sung thu la chu pa pul* as he scattered bits of his *tsampa* and rice to them. He began his drumming, which was monotonous and slow at first but became more rapid and animated as the spirits neared him. He sang a repetitive chant in a language of the spirits, which no one could translate, not even the *lhawa*, who could not remember what was said during his trances because he was possessed. (His assistant, Phutendu, translated everything else that was spoken by the spirits.)[18] The chant began in a low tonal range and then moved higher, and was meant to invoke the spirits who were present because of their desire to be near A-Tshiring, his family, or the *lhawa* himself.

The *lhawa* was first visited by his tutelary deity, and now the spirits' languages could be translated by Phutendu, a local *minung* (one capable of divination but not possession). Lhawa Palden was then possessed by a ghost, or *norpa*. A-Tshiring's wife and Phutendu then began to ask him questions: "Where do you live? Who are you?" The *norpa* asked for *chang*, tea, and *raksi*. Spitting out this last beverage, he demanded that it be warmed, for he did not like cold *raksi*! Taunting his audience, he refused to tell us who he was until after he had had enough to drink. Finally, we learned that he was Tashi's deceased father, Temba Sherpa. He had died of stomach problems, the symptoms of which were identical to those from which A-Tshiring suffered. The *norpa* Temba ultimately explained his own anger with A-Tshiring and the reason he had caused his disease:

> Many times you came in my house, going up and coming down, over and over, and I met you, but you ignored me [because, of course, as a *norpa* he was invisible to A-Tshiring]. You did lots of things [for other spirit], like *shashu* [offerings of food, incense, and colored flags], *garsu* [butter offering], *lhabeo*, but nothing came to me. Always, you gave these to other people. I met you three or four months ago and you said you went to Yinbola [Kathmandu], and you went to [Khunde] hospital. You took lots of medicine, but still you didn't give anything to me, and that won't work.

Then he asked for rum, eggs, milk, millet *chang*, and porridge with *churpey* (dried hard cheese). The rum was given right away, and other foods were promised for the next day. They would be left on the path near A-Tshiring's house, in the direction of Temba's (former) home. Food exchange was of the utmost importance during the ritual, since it was by accepting this food that the spirits became obligated to the host and hostess. The fact that the spirit had asked for food was a good sign, indicating his willingness to negotiate.[19]

The *lhawa* next became possessed by Temba *norpa*'s *lu*, a water goddess spirit who lived on in the *norpa* as a *gyaptak*. She demanded *garsu*. This *lu* had gone to Temba at the time of his death. She had previously lived in a tree near Temba's *gunsa* fields (winter fields for livestock). Because he had so many of these fields, he had supposedly inherited many *lu* upon his death. The *norpa* Temba continued: "If you didn't do a possession ceremony tonight, from now on you would vomit blood."

The audience members were confused by this because they thought that A-Tshiring suffered from *pagin* disease, which, according to the lama, does not cause vomiting of blood, or *takgyu*. This is usually caused only by a *gyelbo* (king), they explained, the spirit of an old Nepali king who is said to have inhabited the region before the Sherpas. So they asked the *norpa*, Temba, where the *gyelbo* had come from, and found it was now Temba's own god, because he lived in the place once ruled by the king. The *gyelbo* demanded a set of cloth flags in his favorite colors.[20] A-Tshiring's wife went on to ask about A-Tshiring's back pain—why did it hurt him so much? The *lhawa* then became possessed by another *norpa*, this one female. She was apparently shy, however, and upon seeing all the people in the room, refused to identify herself. "Who are you? Where do you live? Are you *pem* or *norpa*?" they asked.

This spirit was revealed to be the first *norpa*'s sister, Tashi's deceased aunt Kenchi. She herself had died as a result of her brother's *norpa*, they learned, and had then become a *norpa* too. While still alive, however, she had been kicked in the back during a fight with a man in the village. Thereafter, she had always suffered back pain, and now caused A-Tshiring the same pain. The family members told her that they had heard she was responsible for this during a prior *lhabeo* and had thus given *shashu* to her before. She said that was good. So why had A-Tshiring not gotten better? The *norpa*, Kenchi, replied, "You did many things for me. That is good. But you didn't do anything for my brother, so you didn't get better. Before, I did lots of *sojung* [worship to remove faults, 'the lama's form of *shashu*'] with Gomgila [a deceased lama], every full moon, fifth day, and eighth day [of the month]. Gomgila said to me I will die this year, and I died." A-Tshiring's wife, expressing concern for Kenchi's welfare, "Why did you become *norpa* if you did so many *sojung*?" "I did lots of *sojung*, but my mind was not ready to do *sojung*, so it didn't help and I became *norpa*."

This *norpa* supposedly also had a *lu* spirit from her house who demanded a *garsu*. She asked for sugar tea or butter tea to drink, either one, and they gave the former to her along with some *tsampa* to put in it. They also promised her more the next day. It seemed that Kenchi had owned a summer field for livestock (*yersa*), from which a *saptak* (earth spirit) had also come to her. This *saptak* demanded white and black cloth flags, which the family promised to leave outside their home for him, hung in the direction of his home. Kenchi's presence at the ceremony was due to Temba, her deceased brother. She brought with her a *lu* goddess and a *saptak* demon, as *gyaptak*s. Temba had himself brought a *lu* and a *gyelbo*. The room was quite busy with spirits coming and going within the same person(s).

Finally, after the other spirits had left, the *lhawa* was possessed by a lama. He sang prayers and chanted as if in a monastery sitting alongside other lamas. They told me this was the *lhawa*'s personal lama, the one who always comes to him at the end of a ceremony. The lama said:

> You have been sick now two or three months, and you are too late to do *shashu*, *garsu*. You must do this early when you get sick. It was hard for you between the fifth and sixth months—you will be again very sick and you must be careful. You need to do the *pharchya lamsum kurim* [removing obstacles from the path, a *kurim* aimed at protecting the sponsor from misfortune through a dangerous or trying time]. You have a little *tiwa* [bile humor] and *pagin* mixed. Then [before] you also had *norpa* but you only went to the doctors and took medicines. This time in our country there are a lot of foreign doctors and you only went to them

but that will not help, you must continue to do *lhabeo* for your own gods. Each year you do *tangdak* [an offering for A-Tshiring's own gods from Tibet], but you did it wrong because you used the wrong place name for your gods. Zaptak is the name of the place in Tibet where your god is from. This [god] is angry.

The audience then asked, "Sometimes we do *sungdok* [with the lama who possesses the *lhawa*] and the lama says to us, 'You have *pem* from the east side.' Is this true or not?" The lama, through the shaman, said, "I don't know, maybe yes maybe no. You have to do *tangdak* every year, right place, right time, right way."

A-Tshiring's wife then took out some incense she had received from another lama, knowing the lama now in the room would appreciate it. Norbu heated it into a smoke with coals and then blew it over the patient and the lama. As the lama was finally "leaving" the shaman, a nephew of A-Tshiring's, who had brought rice and had held it in his hand for the last four hours, gave the rice to the *lhawa* and asked about the health of his own mother. The assumption of all present was that the rice held by this boy could reveal something about his mother, to whom it was connected through him. The lama was nearly gone, however, and the *lhawa* only said that his mother's problem was not serious. After a final round of tea and *chang*, only two or three hours remained until sunrise, and we all went home to bed.

Within several days of her deceased father's and aunt's implication in A-Tshiring's disorder, Tashi's family set a date for her formal wedding to Norbu. This was the same day that they heard about the causes of A-Tshiring's ailment. To help obligate their deceased relatives to A-Tshiring, they sent fresh eggs and butter for the *shashu* to the spirits. The two were married while A-Tshiring was still alive, and Tashi's dowry was secured before the couple returned to Kathmandu. A-Tshiring died later that year after further attempts to cure him were made by other shamans, doctors, and lamas. But his children were taken care of, and Tashi was welcomed back into her family.

Curing was the obvious goal of these shamanic episodes, even if it required explicit reference to class inequality or social bigotry (as revealed in the shamanic reference to so many fields owned by the spirits of Tashi's family, who were preying on the poor). Along the way to cures, a plethora of *thurmu* relationships was often negotiated, amended, and restored, mitigating class and social conflict. The logic of the ceremonies was one of seduction. The patients involved tried to make themselves so engaging that the spirits would feel obliged to abandon their wrath and even protect them—enticed by the same displays of hospitality employed by Sherpas in a wide variety of real-life situations. Such hospitality promoted friendship at the same time it lured one into a relationship of obligation. The suitor of a marriageable girl, for example, sent his best *chang* to her parents when asking to marry her. Contract laborers arrived at the homes of potential employers with *tiple*s filled with their best *chang* and offers of their most sincere compliments. Although *chang* was considered the best way seductively to elicit a sense of obligation, food and gifts were similarly effective. When community arbitrators (*adakches, pradhan panchas*, and so forth) were called upon to settle an argument, the opposing parties either brought their own *chang* or were served large quantities of it in the arbitrator's household, with the expectation that, after being made more comfortable, disputants would be more disposed to reach an agreement. Foreigners are equally seduced by these displays, which frequently result in them becoming *jindak*s. Seductions demand virtual identities

Seduction in shamanic ceremonies involves appeasing the desires of the Other, inasmuch as at least one goal is to make oneself so engaging that the Other embraces one's offer and becomes involved (if only temporarily) in a relationship of exchange.[21] Another example makes this clear. Diki's mother was walking along the path to Khunde many years ago. She was carrying chilies and inadvertently dropped some near a tree alongside the trail. Shortly thereafter, Diki developed a strong pain in her arm. Her mother called the *lhawa*, who went to their home and went into a *mogyo* trance to find out who had caused her discomfort. The family learned that there was a *lu* living in the tree where the mother dropped the chilies. *Lu*s do not like chilies; in fact, they feel polluted by them. Thus, Diki's arm hurt because the *lu* had been offended by Diki's mother. Because Diki was a child and had less *rlung rta* than her mother, it was Diki who got sick as a result of the *lu*'s anger. The *lhawa* told Diki's family that he would have to come back and perform a ceremony to bring that *lu* into their home, where they could thereafter take care of her.

A few days later, the *lhawa* came back at dusk and began to prepare the effigies they would need. He had Diki's family borrow a lamb and had Diki dress up in her finest clothes, even wearing her mother's jewelry. He prepared a small box, decorated with flags and a butter lamp and incense. During the *lhabeo*, when the *lhawa* became possessed, he looked into his mirror and saw himself as the *lu*. The family was then able to speak with her. She was recalcitrant. She was sad because she had been polluted, and angry at being disturbed yet again. After hours of conversation aimed at enticing the *lu*, in which the members of Diki's family said that they would take good care of her, that they were rich, that their home would be very comfortable for her, that there would be no chilies near her, and so forth, she finally agreed to move. A human effigy, Diki sat on the lamb, which served as a make-believe horse. With Diki dressed in her best finery (even though much of it was borrowed), holding the beautiful surrogate home-in-a-box they had created for the *lu* in her arms, they went out to the tree and coaxed the *lu* to go with them. They brought her home that night, set her in a special place in the corner of Diki's house, and promised to take good care of her from that moment on. The next day, Diki's arm was better. When I met her in 1986, Diki was fifty-six years old, her arm was still better, and she still gave that *lu* fresh water and lit a butter lamp for her each and every day.

One did not necessarily want to be rid of spirit entities for good (which would involve dissolving *thurmu*); instead, one wanted to make sure they were never given a reason to become hostile (thus maintaining *thurmu*). Making oneself desirable meant recreating oneself in the image desired by the Other who was both one's oppressor and one's potential liberator. The shaman did this literally by becoming the spirits, visible only in the mirror. Sponsors of the ceremony did this by offering gifts that would demand *thurmu* from the spirit Other. The mimesis that was involved in becoming what the Other sought was aimed at seduction. Seduction did not conceal a hidden, authentic identity. Rather, it concealed the impermanent qualities of identity by making gestures toward enduring friendships and reciprocity. It actually obscured the idea that relationships were inherently unstable, and that making them last required a continuous malleability of identity; it required moving in step with the desires of the Other. The goal of the shamanic ritual was to seduce demons and deities into believing that you intended to be their friend for life—that you would always care for them as any obligated friend would. Sometimes these relationships lasted a long time, but the conditions of the relationship were continually changing. Even Diki occasionally had to renew her commitment to her *lu*. Although she provided her with daily offerings of fresh water and butter lamps, Diki did become sick on two occasions during my stay in the Khumbu, because of that *lu*.

In a final case, dramatic displays of mimesis and seduction, and the social relationships of reciprocity and hospitality these displays promote, are once again demonstrated. Phurba was preparing to build a new residence next to his natal home in Khunde, and called a shaman to ascertain whether or not any spirits on the property would be disturbed by his moving there. Phurba and his brother were their mother's only children. The natal home would be inherited by the younger brother, Mingma, so Phurba needed to establish a household of his own. The transition would be difficult since Phurba provided much of the family income, and would additionally be asking for certain items that he would need to take from his mother's home. His income would hereafter be spent on his own wife and home. This presented a problem for the younger son because the mother was blind and largely unable to do domestic chores, leaving them for the younger son, and they all depended on Phurba for money.

The shaman summoned by Phurba went into a trance and, by looking into his brass-plate mirror, saw himself as the *saptak* who lived in the tree Phurba planned to chop down in order to build his home. Rather than jeopardize Phurba's health, the brothers decided to try to move the *saptak* to a new home. The ceremony began in the evening with the assembling of a village lama, the *lhawa*, his wife (who interpreted for him), Phurba, his brother (who was the other sponsor of the event), two friends, and me. We all ate together, and shortly thereafter the lama began constructing a small effigy of the *saptak* that would serve as temporary lodging for the demon during the move. The *lhawa* then went into trance by offering *tsampa*, rice, and *chang* to guardian deities of the four directions, and eventually, through a mantra-like chant that would enable him to see, in a polished brass plate that served as a mirror, himself as one spirit entity and then another. First, he became possessed by his own deity and eventually by the *saptak*.

The *saptak* was upset at being disturbed. "Why do you call me? What do you want?" he demanded. The brothers quickly invited him to come into their home and make himself comfortable. They asked him if he was hungry and he said yes. Would he like food? He said yes. They prepared him a glass of *chang*, which he sipped and quickly spat out onto the floor. It was sour. They offered him *raksi*, to which he had the same reaction, this time demanding that it be made warm the way he liked it. They warmed it for him.

After several hours of polite conversation, during which time he was only addressed as *saptak rinpoche*, he agreed to negotiate his move. First he said he needed to have branches from his old home. The brothers ran out to retrieve them and placed them on the effigy of the *saptak*.

Next, we learned from the *saptak* that he also had a wife, a *lu*, who came into the mirror as the *saptak* left. She wanted to be moved with him. The shaman, who was now the *lu*, spoke with the family for another hour. An effigy of the *lu* was constructed in female form, along with a collection of her favorite colored flags and a small replica of a butter lamp, since *lu*s always required butter offerings. She was also offered her favorite foods and drink, while the brothers told her how much they respected her and needed her help.

After several hours of wooing, and efforts by both brothers to make the spirits and their other guests quite comfortable, the *saptak* agreed to move one to two hours before sunrise. When he finally left the *lhawa*, we decided that we dare not sleep for fear of missing the designated hour, and so prepared another meal, which we ate together until the time came to move him.

The whole ceremony was completed when the *saptak*, having entered the body of the *lhawa*, agreed to transfer himself into the effigy just long enough for the entourage to escort him to his new home. This we did, in

19. The *saptak rinpoche* and his wife, *lu* (left front), with everything she needs (a flag with her favorite colors, red, blue, white, green, and yellow; her favorite fragrance, juniper; and her favorite light, from the butter lamp).

the black of night over rocky terrain, with one flashlight. When we returned to the house, the shaman's trance had not yet ended. He once again became his personal lama, at which point the elder brother took the opportunity to ask him for a divination about his own future and his trekking opportunities. The younger brother inquired about the family's ailing cow and his own stomach pains, which the shaman dismissed as self-limiting, but suggested that they visit the Khunde Hospital for care.

A parallel between the needs of the supplicant and those of the effigy was not uncommon. This makes sense, since one possible interpretation of the ritual is that it is intended to demonstrate how to reestablish bonds of *thurmu* by recruiting the *saptak* and *lu* (in the particular case above) as friends.[22] In this last example, Phurba needed a new residence for himself and his wife, along with certain material possessions from his natal home. This was dramatized by the actions taken for the *saptak* and his wife, including the transplanting of twigs from his old habitat. The acts of hospitality and reciprocity displayed throughout the event can be interpreted as symbolic of how the two young men should establish *thurmu* between themselves. They were also vivid demonstrations of mimesis in which one became that which reflected what the Other desired. The shaman's ability to become the spirit entities demonstrates the basic pattern: he entreats them to come by seducing them to enter his world, and then by a process of seeing himself, as if in a mirror, he becomes those entities that he locates therein. The brothers, by offering favorite foods and drinks to these entities, are both able to seduce these entities to do what they wish. At the same time they take these entities as models for their own lives—in a manner of speaking, living as if they themselves were the spirit entities. At the outcome, they show us how a simulated desirability enables them to transform the demon into an obligated friend. This is the operative mode of seduction, in which a simulated desirability is used to transform the demon into an obligated friend, and of mimesis to make the self a desirable Other.

Unlike Buddhism, which uses the idea of impermanence to promote the concept of an unfixed subjectivity, shamanism's inextricable association with flexible social arrangements scatters identity throughout the network of shifting relations of reciprocal exchange on which Sherpas depend. Impermanence in Buddhism is related to detachment, especially from people and their reliance on you (and your reliance on them). Repeated calls for shamanic intervention reveal shamanism's own version of impermanence by reminding ritual participants that, despite ritual rhetoric that aims to conceal this very idea, all social relationships are transitory. The shamanic episodes described herein used the idiom of long-term reciprocal attachment to create a network of relations, whether or not these relations were, in the end, long-lasting ones. These networks of exchange were also extended to foreigners in ways that satisfied foreign desires for a bonding experience with Sherpas. Such relationships were portrayed as long-term, and they fixed Sherpas with certain qualities of being Other. In practice, however, they are always shifting as the needs of the partners involved change, and as the currency of seduction—the images—undergoes inflation, like spirits requiring different, expansive selves.

TRANSITORY RELATIONS AND THE ATTRACTION OF SHAMANISM

Phurba Tenzing Sherpa was a successful sardar for one of the largest trekking agencies. He had just finished building his new house (in the small field in front of his parents' home), which he rented to me. One day he told me not to let any shamans enter the residence I was occupying because they might bring spirits inside with them via a process called *drultzi*. He suggested that it would be better if I met the *lhawa*s only at their homes.

I was certainly willing to honor his request, but he had piqued my interest about the *lhawa*. I knew he and his family often called *lhawa*s to their home in order to address their own ailments. I therefore wondered why he was now worried about my inviting the *lhawa* into his house. Was it because it was new? Like Phurba, other Sherpas had told me that if a *lhawa* is kept away from the home, spirits are also less likely to enter. But this *lhawa* was Phurba's maternal uncle. Phurba did not often feel the need to call upon anyone to perform healing ceremonies, but a few weeks earlier he had sought the services of a *lhawa* to heal the family cow, and had turned to someone else. Ultimately, the explanation for all this became clear. He said, "Well. You never know. You do good things for a friend and they don't give back, but treat you badly and so you cannot speak to them." As he spoke, the anger in his voice became apparent. Then, with a great deal of anguish, he told me of his severed relationship with his uncle:

> Four or five years ago we borrowed one piece of wood, maybe four inches by four inches—a very long piece of lumber—from him. Later, he borrowed three hundred rupees from me. Later, they asked for the wood to be paid back, and said that the wood borrowed was larger than the one we returned. They also said it was two pieces and not the one that we took. All this time, I never asked for the money back. Then, he [the *lhawa*] started sending out bad stories about my household. To settle the problem, I bought two pieces of wood and gave them to him, but he still did not pay back the money he owed me [which apparently he could not afford to do]. So, now I don't allow that family into my home, and we don't speak.

In the sometimes petty daily goings-on of Sherpa village life, where currency in the form of gossip could be exchanged for material goods such as wood, the one sure thing about relationships of reciprocity was that they, and their underlying terms, were always changing. The *lhawa* and his nephew did not speak during my entire stay in Nepal. Somehow, the boundaries of *chi nang* between them had been transgressed. Unmet obligations led to a sense that one had overgiven and the other had undergiven, resulting in a form of "broken" *thurmu*. But by 1993 they were again the best of friends, and healing ceremonies were performed in Phurba Tenzing's house on a regular basis. Totally immersed in his job as a negotiator and mediator of village relationships, the shaman, Phurba Tenzing's uncle, and Phurba Tenzing himself, as a Sherpa villager, had to reestablish *chi nang* in order to feel connected by mutual obligations, by *thurmu*.

Similarly, from 1986 to 1987, Ang Truley and his brother, Sonam (who both lived in Kathmandu and worked in the trekking and mountaineering business), were engaged in a terrific battle with one another. Ang Truley, the younger of the two, had been working for a trekking agency founded by his older sister's husband and an American. When the sister's husband died unexpectedly in an accident, the sister asked Ang Truley to run the company for her, which he was doing quite successfully. Ang Truley's brother, Sonam, however, was a competitor of his, and throughout the year, each of their families accused the other of causing them endless misfortune and sickness. By 1993, however, their relationship had changed completely. Ang Truley had finally left his sister's company and joined Sonam in business (along with a third brother). Ang Truley and Sonam were now the closest of friends. The sister's trekking agency, meanwhile, had all but folded after Ang Truley departed, taking several employees and clients with him to the new trekking company. This sister was the new source of Ang Truley's current troubles, and his wife continually accused the sister and her family members of witchcraft against her husband.

In this case, small-town bickering, along with the serious business of transnational trekking tourism and industry competition, ensured the fluidity of long-term reciprocal relationships. Such dynamics undermine any attempt to characterize Sherpa identity in terms of single equations of *thurmu*. Desires to have interdependence but not too much of it were not fixed in any one specific way for all Sherpas; these boundaries were always shifting. I am certainly not the first to note that one of the most difficult aspects of doing ethnographic work, aside from dealing with unpredictable and often stressful social relationships formed in the field, is figuring out how to do justice to these shifting social relationships later in the form of an ethnography. Beyond this, however, trying to define *thurmu* in terms of its extremes—too much or too little—risks turning it into another empty formula for essential "Sherpa-ness." A recognition of the constant fluidity of such relationships leads to the realization that any formulation will be entirely contingent on the social bonds that I, the ethnographer, develop with the Sherpas. This is not a novel observation about the limitations of writing and the theorizing and representational power that accompany it. It is an observation about the problem of capturing a notion of "Sherpa-ness" that is not at the same time a notion of my own desires about who the Sherpas ought to be. It leads me back to the problem of locating authenticity within a group of people who have long been engaged in mimesis with Western ethnographic representations of themselves—representations of fixed and essential Others. In Appendix C, I offer suggestions about how this problem of "truth making" is linked to textuality.

Since contact with Western representations fixed Sherpa identities in strategic ways, the problem of authentic "Sherpa-ness" became inseparable from the problems of intertextuality and mimesis. Trying to understand how Sherpas became intertextual required, for me, a rethinking of the significance of the notion of authenticity as a means of constructing truths about Sherpas that would circulate in both of our worlds. Johannes Fabian (1983) and Pierre Bourdieu (1977) noted this problem of ethnography— the first in terms of the temporality of fieldwork and the second in terms of the impossibility of extracting culture from its "practiced" existence. Others (Clifford and Marcus 1976) also noted the inherent ethnographic problem of creating authenticity in essentialist forms. These problems arise, I suggest, from several sources. First, they arise from a peculiarly Western notion of authenticity, which is only thought to exist in relation to that which is inauthentic (starting with Erving Goffman and reified in works on tourism). Second, written versions of truth in Western societies are taken as more authentic than oral versions (Ong 1982, Goody 1977). Where texts exist in certain primarily oral cultures, for example, they can take on significance as possessors of authoritative knowledge, but the authority of these very texts may be vested in their revelation of truths that were originally spoken (Messick 1992); the further they are from spoken truth, the less believable claims are. In many cultures, written truths tend to be taken as fixed and authoritative, shown in analyses that recognize the problems of "theory as power" and "representations as power"; these analyses are always inherently contingent. The issue of writing about Sherpas becomes tricky precisely because of the tendency for Western audiences, and authors like me, to take as fixed and firm truths about everyday life because they are abstracted from lived social experiences. Nowhere is this more aptly demonstrated than in Furer-Haimendorf's representations of Sherpas, for when he described the Sherpas of the 1980s, they differed so completely from the Sherpas of the 1960s that he was compelled to suggest that Sherpa culture was, essentially, disappearing. This textual problem leads eventually, I suggest, to a nontextual version of the same problem a visitor in my university office had with not recognizing the culture offered by our deaf Sherpa curator as authentically Sherpa.

The activities of the shamans reminded me that Sherpas' identities are intertextual. They are partially the product of writings about Sherpas, whether biomedical, Buddhist, anthropological, or touristic. But they are also what is not written or writable, something only experienced in the face-to-face, ephemeral negotiations of social reciprocity, which are inherently transient and characterized by a high degree of mimesis and seduction. Here we encounter implosion. If I try to fix Sherpa identity in textual form, that representation would find its way back into further constructions of Sherpa identity. The Sherpas I seek are the ones I "produce." Reflexivity is surely at work, but so is the "Sherpa" logic by which social interactions turn representations and mirrored images into actual realities.

In that space of fluctuating reciprocal exchange, among Sherpas for whom becoming the image in the mirror is a means of becoming "authentic," there is no essential Sherpa who can be fixed in time or in a text—identified, for example, as one holding a specific *thurmu*-negotiated identity. If anything, Sherpas are moving targets, always traveling between worlds on middle paths and between relationships that configure desires about who they ought to and are thought to be. Nevertheless, I feel compelled to present this very vision as my essential version of Sherpa identities, and in that act must return readers to the social relationships that produce that representation—a relationship compelled to heed informants' concerns and desires for an "essential" Sherpa-ness in this text.

THE SPECTACLE OF SHAMANIC TOURS

> It remains a myth to the modern world that the abstract act of healing known as Shamanism was used as a medicinal technique to trace the daily problems of illness for people of the ancient world. This technology which has been previously unknown to the world is the focus for which "Shamanistic Studies of Nepal" is being organized to teach the students who are seriously committed to acquiring the wisdom of shamanism. This course runs from 3 weeks to 1 month. A longer program ranging from 3 to 4 months orientation and observation time is also offered for students depending on the client's depth of interest in the entire course.
>
> —Shamanistic Studies of Nepal brochure, 1990.

In the fast-paced markets of cultural tourism, the "next big thing" is always that offering the most exotic experience of the Other to consumers. Shamanism has emerged over and over again through the years as a faddish commodity for seekers of the unfamiliar, but Mohan Rai's company, offering shamanistic tours of Nepal, was, so far as I know, the first to focus on shamanism. A highly charged assortment of shamanistic esoterica signaled authenticity to itinerant Western shamans, while revealing some of the mimesis inherent in Rai's role as a cultural broker. According to Rai's brochure, the qualifications of his shamanic teachers were impeccable; they read like something out of a New Age course guide:

Mr. Mohan Lal Rai: Director, assisted his father, Mr. Dil Bahadur Rai, a former Shaman to the courts of Bhutan, for a number of years. He had many experiences in trekking and mountaineering and is fluent in over 20 languages as well as having extensive knowledge of practical shamanism.

Mr. J. B. Bhandari: He has been a Shaman for over 30 years. Trained by his own Guru in the Rai Shamanic tradition, he is experienced in teaching.

Mrs. Maili Lama: She has been a Shaman since childhood. She received most of her training through experiences with the first Shaman "in non-ordinary reality" and practices in the Tamang tradition.

Mohan Rai did not yet have any Sherpa shamans on his payroll, but several from the Khumbu had already been engaged by the roving Western gaze. A-Tshiring often told me of the time several Europeans made

SHAMANISTIC STUDIES OF NEPAL

SHAMANS OF ALL ETHENIC GROUPS OF NEPAL

P.O. Box: 4627 Tel. 416606 Telex: 2322 BLUSTR NP
Fax: 977-1-226820, Kathmandu, Nepal

20. Brochure for Shamanistic Studies of Nepal, sent to me in the
United States by Mohan Rai, director of Shamanistic Tours, Inc.

a film of his possession trance. One of their camera operators had become sick and A-Tshiring was called in. The foreigners asked if they could
film the entire *lhabeo* that then took place, and A-Tshiring agreed, warning them, however, that if the spirits who came to him disputed their presence, they would have to leave. Ultimately, the spirits were friendly, and
the camera operators were able to capture the entire event on film. A-
Tshiring asked if I had ever viewed that film, and if so, could I get a copy
for him, as he had never seen it. He also wanted to know if other Europeans had learned about *lhawa*s from that film, and if so, did they think
him clever?

Lhawa Nima was pleased to have his *lhabeo* photographed by me after I had gotten to know him over the course several months. He asked several times whether I had the right sort of film for the event, and he made sure to wear his most formal clothing. He asked "Is your flash in working order?" and requested that I send him copies of the photos I took. He and his wife told endless stories about the last time they had allowed someone to photograph them—that person had paid several thousand rupees for the privilege. The value of the *lhabeo* as a commodity had undergone rapid inflation in the years since my first visit in 1982, primarily because of the increasing interest exhibited by foreigners in shamanic events. By the time I returned in 1986, shamanic rituals were perceived, by even the shamans themselves, as "big sellers" that attracted curious anthropological visitors like me. Nima's wife cleverly enhanced the exoticism for my benefit on my first visit to her house in 1986. She emphasized how secret and "Other" shamanic practice was by interrupting her husband while he was recounting his initiation into shamanism. He had just told me about his childhood when his wife suddenly burst in and reminded her husband that he should not disclose these things to me. "Remember the last time you told someone these things?" she began. "Your gods became angry for sharing these secrets!" I put down my pen in surprise. Apparently, neither he nor his wife remembered having already told me his life story back in 1982, when it seemed unproblematic to recount such things. Now, however, I could see it had become a marker of "authenticity" for Sherpas, and for that I would have to become intimate friends with him and his family. Only a few minutes later, we moved into his house for tea. There, his wife reiterated the exoticism of her husband's expertise by telling me that Sherpa shamans, unlike some other (*rongba*) Nepalese, were "true" shamans because they could deal so well with the spirits. She continued her introduction by disclosing information about the last anthropologist to have worked with her husband. He brought many gifts to them, including expensive new house paint from Kathmandu. A few weeks later, I too had become part of their reciprocity network, and in exchange for repeated invitations to possession ceremonies, I, too, found myself hunting for special gifts of Tibetan tea, a thermos to replace their broken one, new tennis shoes for their son, and so forth, on my own visits to Kathmandu. How secret and Other the shamanic event was, and how hard it was to acquire an "authentic" version of it. The shaman and his wife read me well, and I consented to this seduction. The mimetic abilities displayed by Sherpas and shamans in making shamanism yet another site for purported authenticity revealed how various Western desires had become intertwined with contemporary ways of being Sherpa that substituted transient social bonds for fixed truths about them.

Gyaltsen Sherpa, a diviner who was blind, told me:

21. Lhawa Nima Tshiring as the *saptak rinpoche*, wearing his loosely tied headdress, which, I was told, would not fall off when he was possessed, no matter how furiously he rocked his head. His wife translates for the *saptak* in the foreground.

One time, I was on expedition, and I did *mogyo* for the whole group. The sardar was Ang Temba, and we were lost in the middle of the forest. There were three roads and Ang Temba did not know which one to take. It was a German group. I did *mogyo*, and then I told them to take the middle road. That was right. Temba at first said, "Don't do *mogyo*." He was shy because if he did not find the right road he would be very embarrassed by the *mogyo*. But then he told me to do it anyway. When I did, all the members took pictures of me doing *mogyo*. Our guide and Colonel Roberts [founder of Mountain Travel Nepal] could not find the road, and then after I did *mogyo* they found the right road. They were giving me congratulations. They were happy; even Temba [was] happy.

In the 1990s, when Westerners learned about shamanism through Shamanistic Studies, a reverse mimesis could be seen, in which becoming like the exotic Other was the only way to confirm that Other's essence, which was embodied in those qualities perceived of as truly different from any found in the West. The spectacle of this mimesis was nowhere more vivid than in the commodification of shamanism as a tourist attraction. On Shamanic Tours, one could study Nepalese shamanism in programs ranging in length from nearly one month to four months. Which tour one chose de-

pended on the extent of one's voyeuristic desires, or on how proficient in
the arts of shamanism one hoped to become. According to the advertisement, these studies were "applicable to anthropologists, mediators, eth-
nologists, psychologists, and for the persons who are keenly interested in
learning shamanism."

More exotic than Buddhism, shamanism is viewed as offering the potential for epiphany, in a place where the restless and insatiable desires of
Westerners can be fulfilled through experiences of intimacy with the
Other. In many ways, this resembled the desire for a "reenchantment" with
life that was demonstrated by foreigners' seeking sexual relationships with
Sherpas or spiritual guidance from Buddhist lamas. Entering into such
relationships, like entering into those intimate relationships presented in
shamanistic rituals and made visible in possession trances, meant entering
into a space of social intimacy that could not be captured in the written
word. These things simply had to be experienced—or so one gathers by
reading the *Shaman's Drum*, the Western New Age magazine of shamanism.[23] The ethnographer who was in Lhawa Nima's house only months
before me was privy to an experience of *thurmu* through the *lhawa's* ceremony and through his friendship. I, too, was made aware of this *thurmu* the
closer I became to Lhawa Nima and his family. One simply could not
represent such relationships without doing violence to them, by placing
them in an arena where Western academic and literary notions of truth
reigned, and where Western notions of authenticity (versus instrumentally
staged) behavior held sway.[24] This does not mean that a purer Sherpa essence lay just beyond the text, but rather that everything that could be
written about Sherpa authenticity was, by definition, already part of the
virtual identity of Sherpas constructed by those who observed them, literally and figuratively.

For Sherpas, being desirable means being authentic in all the fixed
ways desired by Westerners, while at the same time being capable of infinite transformation—capable of becoming whatever is needed to foster
ongoing interaction. The outcome is an interplay of desirability and seduction that renders the boundaries between Sherpas and their Others indistinct. The mimesis involved in Sherpas becoming the type of Others
Westerners (and I) find desirable becomes intertwined with a way of being
Sherpa that originates far beyond the Western gaze in such practices as
shamanistic rituals. But even this latter Sherpa identity can be read as virtual. The shamanistic event requires participants to present themselves
to spirits as desirable—so desirable that the spirits cannot refuse the supplicant's offerings. Demons and deities are thereby seduced into obligation.
But this seduction has nothing to do with falsifying identity or staging it in
ways that belie a more authentic sort of relationship or Sherpa. Rather, it
involves mutual desires and the potent effect of viewing virtual essences as

real. This seduction is about social ties that make that which is experienced through the Other "more real than reality itself," like virtual Sherpas themselves.

At the end of his book, Peter Matthiessen returns to Kathmandu, where he says good-bye to his traveling companion, Tukten Sherpa. Through Tukten, he has achieved that sense of numinousness and self-reflection that tours of the Himalayas, and journeys with Sherpas, always seem to promise:

> "Goodbye, sahib!" But Tukten insists on escorting me to the door of my hotel, and is sorry that I will not let him pay the taxi. He wishes that I meet him three days hence at the great stupa at Bodhinath, four miles away, where he will stay briefly with his father's sister and renew himself as a good Buddhist before returning to Khunde. . . . In the rear window of the cab, Tukten is ghostly; I stare after him as he withdraws into the dusk. It is not so much that this man and I are friends. Rather, there is a thread between us, like the black thread of a live nerve; there is something unfinished, and he knows it, too. Without ever attempting to speak about it, we perceive life in the same way, or rather, I perceive it in the way that Tukten lives it. In his life in the moment, in his freedom from attachments, in the simplicity of his everyday example, Tukten has taught me over and over. He is the teacher that I hoped to find: I used to say this to myself as a kind of instinctive joke, but now I wonder if it is not true. "When you are ready, " Buddhists say, "the teacher will appear."[25]

Shamanism offers numerous illustrations of how Sherpas reproduce themselves for a tourist and anthropological Other. At the same time, it presents a reversal of the mimesis between Sherpa and Westerner, in which the Westerner becomes the one engaging in mimesis and the Sherpa that which the Westerner would become. The blurring of boundaries resulting from the tourist desire to experience, and in fact become, the Other is repeated at the site of shamanism and in the sponsorship roles foreigners often adopt vis-à-vis Sherpas. An epiphany is sought by Western Others in the reciprocal bonds they form with Sherpas—bonds that reveal an absence of fixed identity beyond the reflection of their own desires. In this context, there is no particular way to "be Sherpa" that is more authentic than any other. Thus, the idea that one can become more like an authentic Sherpa slips away through this mirror of intertextual production, in shamanic episodes and in sponsorship relationships between Westerners and Sherpas. Ultimately, these relationships slip away from us as easily as do those elusive authentic Sherpas. In the final pages of his text, Matthiessen ventures to Bodhinath for one final meeting with Tukten: "In one of these houses, Tukten said, he would be staying with his father's sister. Accosting inhabitants, calling his name, I walk my bicycle round and round the square, under the huge painted eyes, the nose like a great question mark, the wind-snapped pennants—Tukten? Tukten? But there is no answer, no one knows of Tukten Sherpa. Under the Bodhi Eye, I get on my bicycle again and return along gray December roads to Kathmandu."[26] That authentic Sherpa once again eludes our grasp, yet his or her essence remains in the mind of Matthiessen, looking out at him from the Buddha's eye.

Authenticity Revisited

In the end, simulations and the identities of virtual Sherpas are found to be as authentic as anything else taken to be "true" or "secret" Sherpa-ness. They are as real as Sherpas' bodies and as those bodies' innumerable connections to other things, from hair that has been shed and prayer flags to friends and spirits of the family, village, or mountain. Even photographs become reality in the sense that they produce their truths in reality—or so the shaman reveals to us in his mirror work, and so the Buddhist endeavors to practice by evoking himself or herself as some glorious, or monstrous, self. A view of the Sherpa body as extensive—as connected to the rest of the universe of which it is a part—contributes to the possibility that our connections to Sherpas are prefigured in a manner designated by them, not by us.

What began as a treatise on Sherpa mimesis with the modern West is now starting to look like a treatise on the Western mimesis with exotic Sherpas. But the perceived authenticity of the Sherpa who is creatively imitated in an ontological becoming can never be fully confirmed by the Westerner, because the very spot from which that proposed authenticity might originate is a place in a mirror—a mirror of their desires. On the other hand, who is to say that this is not precisely where the Sherpas in these mirrors would have us—gazing at them to learn about ourselves? If we are connected to them by bodily relation, then we are not only part of the global network of *thurmu* that expands far and wide from them as individuals to us, their Others. We are, in that thought, reminded of the way "sameness" has a way of already being present in all these desires for "cultural difference." Authentic Sherpas are there in that unfixable boundary space between Others like me, who look at Sherpas in order to become like them (for that is how we, as anthropologists, are taught to "know" them), and the Sherpas themselves, who deflect our gaze by, as we watch them, becoming more and more like us and working ever harder to fulfill our desires.

Mimesis with art (and with textual artistry) was seen as a form of potential liberation for German critical theorists.[27] A spiritual equivalent of this goes on all the time in the Himalayas, when Sherpas encounter Westerners who simultaneously represent, and try to become just like, them by entering into spiritual and social intimacy with them. If mimesis with the text is a route to liberation from the alienating regimes of modernity for Westerners, then was it the same for Sherpas? For Benjamin, mimesis through the onomatopoeic text represents an opportunity for reenchantment—what I have compared to epiphany here. But I suggest that the text can never achieve authenticity of the subject because of the way in which we tend to treat authenticity as essential and "Other" in the West. Would we have to rethink the notion of authenticity of the textual representation in order for it to serve the interests of "liberating" Sherpas? Westerners engage in mimesis with representations of Sherpas in their persistent search for the sublime (a sort of liberation for them). Sherpas, meanwhile, engage in mimesis with these Western representations as a reiteration of the sublime, or of its endless possibility. They become actors in Western dreams of liberation. But they are also acting on Westerners in ways that reiterate, for them, the possibilities of another sort of liberation, articulated through Buddhism, shamanism, and the modernity they seek, and it is the search for engagement with these practices that entices Westerners and Sherpas into endless seductions. In order to read this process as an approximation of the sublime for Sherpas as well, we would, I suggest, have to rethink what we take to be possible kinds of authenticity of the Other. The nontextual experience of shamanism becomes possible via the text only when the representation of Sherpas engaged in mimesis with Western representations of them insistently reflects back on the social relationships that produce such texts. Authenticity here gets caught in the mirrors that reveal multiple, shifting, virtual Sherpas.

CHAPTER FIVE

Seduction and Simulative Power in the Himalayas: Staying Sherpa

> The story goes . . . that little Nepalese boys would stand outside
> the phlebotomist room of Bir Hospital in downtown Kath-
> mandu in order to sell their blood to the hospital for a few hun-
> dred rupees. They were so thin, the fellow explaining the story
> had a hard time imagining how they even found the veins in
> those wretchedly undernourished arms. Worse still, the boys
> would ignore the hospital's rule limiting the frequency of their
> donations, and they would return every few weeks to give more
> blood because their families needed more money.
> —Nepalese student enrolled in a Ph.D. anthropology
> program in the United States

IT SEEMS ironic that when one of the only two Sherpa physicians working
in Nepal finally went to the Khumbu for a month, he went as the medical
advisor to a group of foreign researchers who wanted to draw blood samples from Sherpas working at high altitudes. "Was life at high altitudes
productive of genetic adaptation or merely acclimatization?" the scientists
asked. Who could serve the needs of this research better than Sherpa
mountain guides? And who would be better suited to facilitate this work
than a Sherpa physician? The world was the laboratory, and Sherpas were
the specimens studied. Unlike the boys outside Bir Hospital, who sold
their blood only for money, however, Sherpas offered their blood for
other reasons as well. As the subjects of such research, they could be
"Sherpa" in yet another way that was desired by the West.

Each day, the foreigners recruited willing young Sherpas, and, in the
Khunde home converted into a global lab, performed tests on their bodies.
Dr. Mingma's presence indicated to these boys that their participation
would in some way benefit Sherpas, for Dr. Mingma was a new sort of
role model, successfully achieving modernization in the style envisioned
by Westerners. The equipment used had been flown in by helicopter or
carried in by porters the month before, in the same way supplies and people were brought to Everest for expeditions. Then the young Sherpa men
opened their veins to the syringes of technicians twice a day, between

rigorous exercise performed on treadmills, stationary cycles, and weight machines.

One afternoon, Phurba Tarkya Sherpa sat in an agitated state across the room from me in his cousin's home. Apparently he had just returned from working as a high-altitude sherpa on an Everest expedition when he was approached by Dr. Mingma and asked to participate in the research. Phurba Tarkya told me that the money was tempting, but he was concerned about the blood loss. Several times during the conversation, he noted that his parents believed that once blood was lost, it could never be replaced. That would leave him depleted, he explained, and might lead to an accident on his next expedition the following month. "If they take blood out, it will make me weak, stupid, not strong. We cannot afford to lose blood. Even if some people get a cut on their finger, they will drink the blood so they won't lose it." Thus blood loss was deemed to have a dual consequence: it would affect both his internal state of being and his external participation in mountaineering activities. Nevertheless, Dr. Mingma assured him there was no risk involved in the experiments, and he was not sure whom to believe. The physician had told him that his blood would replace itself. In Phurba, a not-quite-internalized logic of biomedicine is evident. In him, one finds the rhetoric of unlimited exploration and unlimited self-reproduction, so reminiscent of the Western experience of often reckless expansion, joined with the scientific discourse on replenishable blood). But in him it converges with a fully internalized sense of an expansive body, in which the very act of letting bodily fluids move beyond the boundaries of the person was viewed as having tangible and perhaps irreversible consequences on even unrelated aspects of one's life.

Phurba walked around the room, sat down, and then recommenced the discussion of his quandary. He ate a large meal and suggested that if he continued to eat well throughout the experiments, it might counteract the effects of any blood loss and enable him to remain strong on his next climb. He was worried that Dr. Mingma would think he was afraid to participate in the experiment. Additionally, he was impressed because the researchers had chosen only high-altitude Sherpas for study. "They came here just to take Sherpa blood, not blood from foreigners," Phurba noted. At the end of his meal, he thanked his cousin and aunt for lunch and left, still debating what to do. Two days later, I visited the research team. On my tour of their makeshift laboratory, I noticed that Phurba was one of five Sherpas in the equipment room, riding a stationary bicycle with electrodes and small wires attached to his chest and legs.

Sadism, Donna Haraway reminds us, comes in many forms. "Sadism does not lie, at least not originally, in the fact of causing repeated pain to animals [or humans] in the course of experiments. Rather, sadism is the organizer of the narrative plot and part of the material apparatus for the cultural production of meanings; . . . [it is] about the fulfillment of primate [or human] potential, *not* about the agony of research animals [or Sherpas, or, for that matter, scientists and mountaineers]."[1] The universalized narrative of Western biology (as the fulfillment of human potential) could be readily adapted to embrace Sherpas because it was one that merged the idea of unlimited profit with a preexisting cultural and economic configuration of Sherpas as high-altitude climbers—creating, in this case, the ideal research subjects. In this sense, many Sherpas could not help but become the objects of scientific analysis because they had already internalized a version of their own identity dictated by biological sciences, which deemed them valuable for medical exploration.

It is said today that Sherpas began climbing the Himalayas as guides, primarily for the money. They made far-reaching promises and offered gifts to the mountains in exchange for safe passage. After international renown was won for Sherpas by Tenzing Norgay in the early 1950s, expeditions up Mount Everest were no longer engaged in solely for financial gain. It was clear that, by 1987 at least, Sherpas also ascended Everest because they felt they had a reputation to live up to, and the desire for success of this sort had become internalized. Young Sherpa boys could tell me exactly which villagers had already reached the summit of Everest, and how many times each had done so. "Summiting" was a term I often heard used to describe the rite of passage for becoming a Sherpa sardar and an important person, a *mi che* in the village. This was not the only way to attain local prestige, but it was undoubtedly the most common one. Young Sherpas who knew they would not continue their education beyond high school considered it of the utmost importance to join an expedition and then attempt to "summit" Everest. Unlike other Nepalese, Tibetans, or foreigners, Sherpas defined themselves in part as those who climbed Himalayan peaks. Perpetuating this transnational version of Sherpa identity then became a way for them to support themselves in a tourism-driven economy, both financially and culturally.[2] The culmination of this particular mimesis came in 1984, when a group of Sherpas began planning a "Sherpa Everest Expedition" exclusively for Sherpas, to be sponsored by foreigners and by Sherpas themselves. By 1992, one could read in *National Geographic*, that most reliable of pictorial scopes on Sherpa life, about a successful Sherpa expedition the previous year, during which one Sherpa, Sonam Dendu, claimed, "It is our expedition. . . . It is for all the Sherpas." Lobsang Sherpa, one of the organizers of the expedition, "began dreaming of an all-Sherpa Everest climb to pay homage to legendary Sherpa mountaineers. 'We want to take pride as a people apart,' he said."[3] Pertemba, a successful mountain climber who was now a partner in a Sherpa-owned trekking agency, envisioned the future of mountaineering in Nepal as one in which Sherpas would finally enter the limelight as climbing heroes—as sponsored team members rather than just assistants to foreign expeditioners.

In an economy where images are often as important as physical toil, the production and circulation of favorable representations of Sherpas frequently translates into money. But that does not necessarily make financial profit the primary objective. To remain competitive in the tourist market, but more importantly to remain "Sherpa," Sherpas accommodate foreign visions of whom they are supposed to be. The production and reproduction of images have always been intrinsic parts of the job of portering loads up Everest. On the other (receiving) end, the profits earned thereby can be calculated both in money earned and in the cultural capital of images produced or reinforced. The Sherpa economy is an economy not only of cash but of meanings. Its currency is images, images that constitute symbolic capital. Thus, it is worth exploring how Sherpas live up to their "virtual" reputations, and what the consequences are of their occasional failure to do so.

In 1982, Kami Norbu, like many Sherpas, assumed that when given the chance to work as a sherpa guide (or high-altitude porter) on an Everest expedition, he would naturally be up to the challenge. His two older brothers had been afforded that opportunity, and both had succeeded. One had reached the summit long ago, and was then employed as a top-ranked sardar for Mountain Travel, the largest trekking agency in Nepal. (Soon thereafter, however, he was accidentally killed in a fight with Nepalis at a local tea shop.) Kami's other brother had become a prominent sardar for the same trekking agency soon after reaching the summit with an American group. He then "summited" for a second time a few years later, and since then had come to the United States on a visit sponsored by some American climbing friends. He toured the United States and worked for a few months for his sponsor's company. Between gifts and savings, he had returned to the Khumbu quite wealthy in both senses of the term.

Meanwhile, Kami was still waiting for his chance to ascend Everest. In 1986, he was finally given the opportunity to climb with a British group organized by a longtime family friend from England, and he knew this would be the perfect time to try for the summit. But when he reached the second encampment above the base camp, he found he could go no further. Later, back in Khum Jung, we sat talking by a wood stove and I asked him about this experience. He spoke of how terribly difficult the climbing had been because of the weather; sun and snowstorms blinded him, making it impossible for him to continue. He did not tell me that several members of the expedition and other Sherpas had reached the summit anyway. After he left, his British friend from the climb told me that there had been only minor snowstorms during Kami's attempt. He suggested that Kami had been unable to continue to higher elevations because of a combination of altitude sickness, bad lungs from smoking, and a chronic stomachache. One expedition member said, "He's more of the 'city lights' type than the 'mountain climber' type. He's not like other Sherpas." Having failed to reach the top, Kami himself felt he had failed to live up to his own image of being Sherpa. He had no aspirations to follow his "modern" role model in the shape of Dr. Mingma, for he had dropped out of school after class eight. After this climb, he said to me, "What can I do? My brother has a new home, many *jindak*s, he is a famous sardar. What can I do? I am nothing next to him." Kami's comments about his brother were not prompted by a need for similar financial success. He often remarked that he was in a good situation economically, because as the youngest son he had already inherited the family home and much property. He also knew he could always earn an income as a guide on more-pedestrian treks. Nevertheless, he still worried that he might never get a chance to "summit" Everest like all the other *mi che*. Kami's image of being a successful Sherpa revolved around the image he had of his older brother, the accomplished expedition sardar—itself an image arising from a desire to become the "Tigers of the snow" sought by foreigners. Kami became sicker and sicker after his climb. When his stomachache worsened significantly, he finally visited the doctors at Khunde Hospital, who told Kami he had an ulcer. In some sense, at least, being unable to live up to the Sherpa name was killing him.

In 1987, physicians estimated that 10 to 15 percent of the male Khumbu Sherpa population suffered from gastrointestinal ulcers. At first, doctors attributed this to the typical Sherpa diet, which included lots of *raksi* and chilies. But most Sherpas exhibiting such ulcers also felt extreme anxiety while on expeditions, where the pressure to succeed by reaching the summit was exacerbated by the daily risks of ferrying loads from one camp to another, of being at high altitude for many months, of receiving poor food rations, and of dealing with the politics of deciding who would ascend and who would stay behind. It was in fact more common for expedition Sherpas than for others to have ulcers. Nevertheless, young Sherpa men still believed that, while there might be other ways to earn a living that presented fewer risks than expedition work and trekking (e.g., by staying in school long enough to pursue other professions), there was no other way to become so completely and identifiably "Sherpa," and ulcers were, after all, among the least of the problems one encountered in staying Sherpa.

Sherpas were caught up in an inflationary economy, where the cost of living escalated not only in terms of money needed to survive, but also in terms of the effort required to "stay" Sherpa. It became more and more difficult for young men to pass up opportunities to give blood or to climb to the top of Everest. It was not uncommon for Sherpas to carry loads that were half their body weight over the Khumbu glacier icefall, not once but three or four times a day. The chance to earn more money and win more prestige seemed to outweigh the increased risks of falling due to fatigue or being crushed by the glacier's movements as the heat of day warmed the ice. It is no wonder that the writers of expedition accounts even to this day attest to the undying loyalty and devotion of "their" Sherpas, for the Sherpas' diligent labors and heroic acts on behalf of foreigners on the mountain have always been wrapped up in their desire to appear to be better "Sherpas." Nothing short of death-defying feats were expected of them. Their own lives depended on that. However, James Fisher wrote that 101 Sherpas had died on mountaineering expeditions in Nepal between 1950 and 1989.[4] In 1984, Furer-Haimendorf had reported that 116 Sherpas from the Solu-Khumbu region had died on the mountain since 1953. A Sherpa man involved in the Khumbu mountaineering industry since its inception pushed those figures even higher. He told me:

> One hundred thirty-four Sherpas from Khumbu since 1951 have died on expeditions. These Sherpas [are the ones] I know about, but who can say how many more [there were]? More died on the Indian side than in Nepal. The worst [incident] was twenty-nine Sherpas—Solu and Khumbu—[perishing] in one day. This was at Nanga Parbhat Himal, in [the] India Karakoram, with the British Expedition. Shipton was the second leader this time. This was in the 1950s. Only two [Sherpas] were left [alive]. One lives in Darjeeling, near Lhakpa Tendu's house, Dawa Tendu; he was the cook. [The other one] was from Solu—Sallung—Awo Tendu. That time the sardar's name was Nursang—[also] dead. All dead . . . in an avalanche. They gave us insurance money, maybe a hundred rupees each. [At] that time the salary in India was seventy-five paisa for a sherpa and one rupee and ten paisa for a sardar.

Lhakpa Sonam, the husband of Pasang Lhamu, told me in 1993 that her death was one of more than four hundred on Everest alone. He estimated that more than three-quarters of these had been Sherpas.

Phurba Tenzing Sherpa of Khum Jung observed, "When we go on a trek, we know that at worst we might get *chamba* [a cold or flu]. But when we go on expedition, every day we leave in the morning and we don't know whether we will come back to sleep again in our sleeping bag that night." In a somewhat macabre twist of mimesis, claims about the life-threatening aspects of climbing were essential to the building and perpetuation of the Sherpas' reputation as risk-taking, loyal, and death-defying people. Precisely how many Sherpas had died did not matter. What mattered in this economy of images and meanings was that it was useful to claim that a great many people—most of them Sherpas—had lost their lives in service both to the West and to their own fame and glory.

Being Sherpa involved living up to other images as well, like that of being a good Buddhist as defined at least in part by the foreign gaze. Being Sherpa also meant being kindhearted and hospitable. But that same gaze was responsible for a startling void in the space reserved for the Sherpa Other, when Sherpas failed to be "typical" in all the ways expected by Westerners. When Sherpas were not expert climbers or "exemplary" Buddhists (not even all monks were exemplary, according to some accounts), problems were created not only for a disappointed Western population but also for Sherpas themselves. The story of Pasang Kami illustrates this point.

Sherpa "big people" are invariably the most reputable (and consequently, wealthy) climbers or those whose families had moved beyond climbing to ownership of trekking companies, making them even more wealthy. The more affluent these Sherpas became, the more they sought to contribute their wealth to monasteries by becoming *jindak*s. One such *jindak*, Pasang Kami from Namche Bazaar, had made a lot of money as an expedition sardar. He had recruited foreign sponsors and then traveled several times to the West. In 1986, he agreed to contribute Rs. 15,000 (roughly six hundred dollars at that time) to sponsor a Sherpa ceremony called Bumtsho in 1987. This festival had been initiated only a few years earlier by wealthy Kathmandu Sherpas. When Kami died suddenly in an expedition bus accident (while riding with other Sherpas to the head of the trail) just before the Bumtsho celebration, Khumbu Sherpas panicked. The death of one so young, who left behind a wife and several children, was tragic. And in this particular case, it also jeopardized the success of the upcoming festival.

Pasang Kami's wife still contributed part of the sum promised by her husband as a sponsor for the ceremony (depleting much of the dwindling fortune left after her husband's funeral) and other wealthy villagers made up the difference at the last minute. These donations totaled more than three lakhs (more than fifteen thousand dollars). Even though the Bumtsho festival was saved, conversations criticizing Kami continued long after the ceremony itself had concluded. Surprisingly, Kami's premature and totally unexpected death en route to the mountain was not linked to his work as a famous expedition sardar. Rather, it was attributed to his alleged drug smuggling during trips to the United States, a facet of his life hitherto unrevealed to me and my friends. Villagers claimed that he had probably offended the deities of the Khumbu (especially the Khumbu's patron deity, Khumbu'i yul lha), as well as his own *lha*, by earning money by trafficking in narcotics. Though rarely engaged in by Khumbu Sherpas, this type of illegal activity was considered a major source of *dikpa* because "drugs killed people." I also found it significant that people did not feel that Kami's offerings to the monastery in any way "cleansed" his reputation. On the contrary, they believed that his agreement to sponsor the Bumtsho ceremony would prove ineffective in ensuring him a better rebirth.

Pasang Kami's death and the explanation offered for it converged on two issues. First, the view of climbing as risky generally reinforced the Sherpas' reputation as hardy and expert mountaineers. But Pasang had not died on the mountain; he had died in a bus accident on the way there. Thus, the profit was small in terms of image enhancement, to be derived from his misfortune. He had been doing nothing heroic when he died. Moreover, the notion that taking risks was an inherent part of expedition work was most useful for the Sherpas who survived. Sherpas, after all, still had to climb, and climb without fear. Second, by striving to be a "good" Buddhist in giving so much money to the monastery, Pasang Kami had been well on his way to becoming a *mi che* of the sort other Sherpas admired and hoped to emulate—wealthy, successful, pious. But despite all this, Pasang had suffered bad luck. So the Sherpas attributed his death to drug smuggling; of all the possible ways in which they could have explained his death, this was the only plausible explanation for a successful sardar and pious Buddhist being so unfortunate. Interpreting his death in these terms enabled Sherpas to preserve the transnationally accepted principle that earning a living as an expedition sardar, and becoming an exemplary Buddhist in the process, was what "true" Sherpas did. And while "true" Sherpas had good luck, "non-Sherpa" activity could result in bad luck. Drug trafficking was considered bad by Sherpas for reasons that were "traditionally" Sherpa (*dikpa*) yet inseparable from those emerging from Western expectations about whom Sherpas were supposed to be.

A recent article from a United States newspaper was entitled "Temptation Comes to Shangri-La." Written by Gary Abrams, it describes the arrest of a Sherpa in Los Angeles caught transporting bags of heroin into the United States. The article begins with a reference to the Sherpas' typical identity (charming, unassuming, responsible, "fun to be with," possessed of "high altitude stamina," the "perfect guide on spectacular, sometimes risky treks") and ends with the idea of the sad truth about the struggle for incomes in inflation-ridden Nepal today, driving these innocent villagers to this extreme method of earning income. Again, it promotes the idea of "needy" Sherpas while maintaining that a Sherpa greatly admired by the West could be attributed to "true Sherpa-ness" rather than to external factors.[5]

Many Sherpas were aware of the stakes involved in living up to and perpetuating the positive representations of Sherpas generated by the West. Certainly, they were frequently involved in attempts to manage and regulate the use of the Sherpa image. Among these were the growing number of complaints from owners of trekking agencies in Kathmandu about the many tourist publications, from travel brochures to magazine accounts, that indiscriminately attached the label "Sherpa" to individuals photographed carrying loads. "This is a big problem for us," one sardar noted, "because people will think just anyone is a Sherpa even if they are not." The trouble Sherpas had with such misrepresentations was two-fold. First, inaccuracies of this sort might enable non-Sherpas considered to be lower in social status to benefit unfairly from the Sherpa reputation. (Keep in mind that no one had complaints about the use of the term for aides-de-camp at the world summit meeting.) Second, and more important, these publications might render the situations depicted as reality—or so many Sherpas thought by the logic of mimetic effects with photographs. (Representations were considered extensions of the self, not merely abstractions of it.) Mingma Sherpa of Kathmandu had told me that the potential for photos to produce realities worked in two ways: as a mechanism of the representation making truth claims about the individual so represented, and as a mechanism expanding the spirit of the person being photographed into other spheres and yet leaving no control in the hands of that person over how that spirit was treated. "If someone takes our picture and puts it in many books, then we don't know what will happen to that book in the future. Maybe it will end up being thrown on the ground or left in some dirty place, and that will not be good for us," Mingma Sherpa explained.

Sherpas were interested in actively managing ethnographic accounts of them as well. Phurba Sherpa eventually informed me that he had been filling his fellow villagers in on my work. "What are you telling them?" I asked. He said he was explaining that I was going to write a book about Sherpas that many people would read and that would make me very rich. That way, he said, they would happily answer all my questions. I believed that this was the worst thing he could have told them, for I assumed they would feel exploited. But Phurba assured me I was wrong about this—that his remarks would, in fact, have the opposite effect. These Sherpas would feel exploited if I just collected their stories without any intention of using them for gain. This would be foolish given my own goals, and would make their lives worse, too, for it would "render real" a situation in which other people did not want to hear about Sherpas and their lives—an unfortunate turn of events for people dependent on their positive international reputation. I ultimately learned that the positive evaluation of anthropological representations of Sherpas was not simply a matter of producing them "accurately," but rather a matter of representing Sherpas as desirable and eminently attractive to Others as a consequence of taking seriously their seductions of me—of their cultural impact on me.

It seemed to me that definitions of the Sherpa economy should be configured to acknowledge that, along with monetary profits, symbolic capital was accrued as well, based on an exchange of "cultural" currency—positive Sherpa images. Control over those images was consequently important and revealed how productive the images were for all involved in their exchange, and how connected they were to all those who produced them, including Westerners. The demands of tourism became intertwined with a Sherpa view of the self as expansive, resulting in the creation of these envisioned and possible realities. This economy was not based on the idea that cultural forms were always epiphenomenal to material production—rather, it was based on the realization that there was not much difference between the two. The next question to be addressed (although it has already been partially answered) is "What sorts of labor does such an economy of meanings require?"

CULTURE WORK

By the early twentieth century, Sherpas had become omnipresent in the mountaineering and trekking businesses of the Himalayas, first as wage earners carrying loads and later as owners of trekking and mountaineering agencies. Fisher noted that, in 1978, Sherpas had investments in four of the twenty registered trekking agencies in Kathmandu.[6] I found that by 1987, Sherpas owned one-third of those agencies. However, such Sherpa-owned agencies were neither the largest nor the most profitable. Two foreign-owned agencies dominated the scene, employing the greatest number of both temporary and salaried Sherpa workers. The majority of Sherpas in the industry worked as office employees and salaried field staff, although undoubtedly many wished they had agencies of their own. Fifty-four trekking agencies were operating in 1987. I interviewed personnel at thirty-nine of them (including the largest), and found that ethnic Sherpas filled 45 percent of the cook positions, 86 percent of the sherpa positions, and 89 percent of the sardar positions. The remainder of the field-staff positions were filled by Nepalese of different ethnicities. Many Sherpas were also hired as porters and as drivers of the animals used to carry loads in the Khumbu region.[7] Five years later, by 1992, the two largest and most profitable trekking agencies were owned by Sherpas.

A list of jobs held by Sherpas in the tourist industry tells us little, however, about the functioning of the tourist economy. In order fully to comprehend the Sherpas' economic involvement with the West, one first needs to understand how integral relationships of reciprocity and seduction were to Sherpas' lives before tourism. Westerners are drawn into such relationships while trekking in Nepal, and have in some cases come to expect that. Sherpas become that which is desired by the West; one outcome of this mimesis is Sherpas' efforts to make Westerners feel they are becoming part of Sherpa culture. This is achieved through techniques of seduction that employ simulated images about who Sherpas really are. But where else, among Sherpas themselves, are the contemporary labors of seduction and reciprocity found?

Two forms of Sherpa labor were explained to me: wage labor, or *lamii* ("work person" or wage work),[8] and reciprocity, or *ngalok* (self-labor or reciprocity labor). Whereas *lamii* entails immediate payment for a person-day of labor, with no long-term obligation on the part of either employer or employee, *ngalok* entails no payment other than the obligation to provide a return person-day of labor or service in the future, creating the possibility of long-term, reciprocal relationships between partners. Both forms of labor have historical precedent in the Khumbu, and both are frequently initiated in ritualized "asking" ceremonies, wherein those desiring labor make themselves desirable to potential employers by offering gifts and favors or by engaging in similar "buttering-up" strategies (see Ortner 1978b). Elsewhere, I have described the sorts of agricultural, trade, tourism, and ritual activities in which one finds both types of labor (Adams 1992a). Agricultural work in Sherpa villages provides a context for each—household members offer their services to other households as either reciprocal or wage laborers. Reciprocal labor is repaid with an equivalent amount of labor performed by either the original recipient (the employer) or someone from his or her household (including servants). Both types of labor are engaged in other settings as well. There is also a lot of crossover between spheres of labor and the forms of labor undertaken. For example, if a person works for someone else building a home in a reciprocal relationship, he or she may not only be compensated with obligations for an equal amount of labor performed by that employer or his or her family at some future time, but might find himself or herself additionally repaid by being hired as a salaried or wage worker for that employer's trekking agency. (Here the same person does the labor but the second job is considered repayment for the "free" labor given initially.) The reverse is also true. Wage-labor relationships during the trekking season often lead to reciprocal (or further wage-labor) employment between the same persons during the off season.

Sometimes, a relationship originating in wage labor is transformed into something more closely resembling a reciprocal gift exchange of labor; monetary payment for work is sometimes substituted for return labor by the employer or his or her family, or if money is paid it comes with the expectation that a return opportunity for employment will be forthcoming from the recipient. In many ways, patterns of employment in the city attempt to transform distant relationships into close relationships by fashioning the employment as a reciprocal gift exchange rather than as a temporary wage encounter. Ideally, persons find themselves at the center of all sorts of work exchanges (wage and reciprocal); this network functions more like a family or group of close friends with whom reciprocal ties are presumed (albeit sometimes mistakenly). Patterns of reciprocal labor in the village are reproduced in urban Sherpa communities in both trekking businesses and festival activities. Thus, Sherpa trekking-agency employers consistently hire on the basis of family, friendship, and other relationships that inherently include implicit or explicit reciprocal commitments. Moreover, urban Sherpa festivals are designed on the principle of reciprocal exchange and rotating sponsorship. Household labor is exchanged between families, along with family labor, for numerous events from throwing large parties to building homes, constructing fences around barren property, and transporting furniture.

One of the most important features of Sherpa labor is the way in which efforts to make oneself culturally attractive (to potential employers or to work-exchange partners) are built in as strategies for profit. The process of creating symbolic capital is a central component of the economy.[9] Reciprocal exchanges made during ritual events, facilitated by mechanisms of seductive self-presentation (a type of mimesis of what the Other desires), help Sherpas establish bonds that carry over into business transactions. In fact, the distinction between ritual or social events (which give friends the opportunity to establish business contacts) and business events (which give work associates an opportunity to become friends) is blurry. Although working hours in Kathmandu officially begin at ten o'clock and end at three or four o'clock six days a week, most Sherpas in the industry actually engage in business-related transactions—under the guise of social and nonbusiness encounters—long before and after these official hours.

Actually, these official work hours maximized the time left over for conducting business via social interactions outside the office at the beginning and end of each day. Sherpa agency operators (office employees and owners) found they spent an enormous amount of time socializing with ministry officials, airline personnel, booking and travel agents, hotel managers, and other trekking-agency owners. They often took such contacts out for lunch, for drinks before dinner, for dinner at their homes, and to various social events (especially gambling parties), at which they talked business and politics. They also spent considerable amounts of time "wining and dining" tourists, making sure they were having a good time in Nepal and "getting their money's worth." Most Sherpas did this whether or not it was their agency that had booked a particular visitor's tour. These social engagements were the key to business success, whether one was an agency owner or independent sardar, since they ensured that airline flights and hotels would be available, that trekking permits would be processed expeditiously, that permits for expeditions to certain peaks would be granted, that operations would not be hampered by demands for baksheesh by government officials, that tourist organizers would return the following year with their business, and that opportunities for obtaining foreign sponsors would not be missed. Sherpas thus developed extensive networks of reciprocity, not only with other Sherpas but with influential and well-positioned Nepalese and Westerners as well.

Just as villagers exchanged the labor of household members, so too did

Sherpa agency operators in Kathmandu exchange a variety of business-related commodities. The swapping of employees, equipment, services, and other favors occurred most often between agencies of similar size, whose owners were close friends or kin. One such owner explained that his brother-in-law's agency borrowed his sardars, and his agency borrowed his brother-in-law's sardars, when their respective trek schedules could not accommodate all their employees or all their clients.

> When we have too many clients and not enough staff or equipment, we go to our brother-in-law and send our clients there, or we use their staff here for one trek and we pay the staff ourselves. They also send clients to us. It is not [an] exact exchange. We just do it as personal contact [favor], because we are related. It is like money loans. We go to friends. For example, if you start a business and need money investment, you can get an interest loan. [But] first you go to relatives, then good friends, then maybe the bank. . . . Not to the one who is richest, but to good friends. It depends on how much you need. If you need Rs. 20,000, you go to ten friends who each give Rs. 2000. It's easy. If you have a problem, like death in the family, you can always borrow interest-free from friends. It is not [an] exact exchange. . . . We do trade for equipment, but [as] for guides, they get their own salary and [there is] no charge from us. We let the guides go as a favor to other people and companies, and as [a] favor to the guides. This is a type of *ngalok*.

One of the benefits of the exchange of employees came in building a resource pool of friends and allies throughout the business. This helped guarantee one's ability to obtain employees, clients, and political support at meetings of the Trekking Agency Association of Nepal (TAAN, a lobby-cum-union, for trekking agents) or the Nepal Mountaineering Association (NMA). Although the advantages of exchanging services with friends in the business were accompanied by risks, these could be minimized by engaging only in exchanges with agencies of roughly the same size and capability, and with owners who were friends or friendly relatives (that is, people with whom one had already established social prestige or social debt).

Similar considerations governed agency owners' exchanges of clients. Typically, this took place via referral, but again, only to or from agencies owned by friends or friendly relatives. If one agency received clients it could not accommodate, they were sent to a friend's or relative's agency.[10] Owners kept careful accounts of such referrals, which were regarded as gifts to be repaid at some future date. An agency that received a number of these favors over the course of a year could repay them in various ways—by offering space for a friend's client on an airline flight chartered for one's own business; by sharing the right-of-way on mountain-peak ascent routes reserved for their own expeditions, when the reservations for these routes had all been taken; by influencing decision making within various government ministries where one had social connections, on a friend's behalf; or by helping exchange foreign currency at more attractive rates.

Clients were also shuffled about in interagency transactions on the basis of arrival time in Nepal and nationality. Many agencies specialized in serving clients from a particular country, who tended to visit Nepal during specific seasons. The owner of a large trekking agency stated:

> We do exchange employees, if we have [a] shortage of kitchen equipment and guides. We go to all different companies. [Perhaps] a company runs Japanese, Australian, New Zealand groups which come in winter, but [it is] not busy in autumn. So we contact those agencies and in winter we don't have much clients, so [we] send our boys to other companies. . . . We do [this] on [the] basis of friends[hip] . . . [and] sometimes through TAAN on [a] business basis. At meetings we [speak] informally and there we connect with each other.

One agency owner did indicate that he demanded an immediate payment for client referrals, based on a fixed percentage of earnings derived therefrom, or on a fixed amount per client when he exchanged with a neighboring Sherpa-owned business. However, most agencies viewed this sort of exchange as part of a larger network of reciprocal interactions occurring between friends in the business. No immediate formal payback or even informal baksheesh was generally required, although once in a while such requests were made.

In the tourist economy of the Sherpas, obligations arising in the context of relationships of social reciprocity were as valuable as cash rewards. I was told that having a friend in business was as valuable as having "money in the bank." Establishing reciprocal bonds with others could lead to the accrual of an enormous amount of symbolic capital that could be transformed into cash, just as cash could be transformed into symbolic capital. Thus, being able to create such bonds through seductive techniques that rendered one more attractive to Others was the equivalent of employing cultural strategies as productive resources. This is not a staged presentation of self for financial profit, which would be a form of impression management. Rather, it is a form of "culture work" that collapses the difference between money and its symbolic substitutes in imagery and representations and their meanings.

One of the most interesting ways in which Sherpas established reciprocity bonds through seduction was in instituting *jindak* relationships between themselves and foreigners. In an innovative move deeply resonant with historical patterns among Sherpas,[11] Khumbu Sherpas in both urban and rural communities recruited foreign tourists as their own personal sponsors. *Jindak* bonds were originally created between monasteries and large donors, who, somewhat ironically, purportedly became double recipients (since donors gained *sonam* and *rlung rta*) by the very act of giving their money or material possessions away. Monastery *jindak*s were not supposed to expect repayment, but in fact always received it in the form of increased prestige and other intangible cultural rewards. In theory, foreigners who became *jindak*s for individual Sherpas were also persons to whom no obligation was supposed to be felt. Again, this abstract formulation was a far cry from reality.

SEDUCTION AND POWER: IMAGING THE WEST

9th Feb. '92

Dearest Vincanne and John,
Namaste!

Hope you both are well. We are all OK in Khumbu. Nima is still in Khum Jung. I am in Kathmandu with my eldest son. I brought him here in Kathmandu. He was in the Khumjung School for two years and he did not do any progress from there. Therefore he is here for a better study. He is joining a school named Sun Rise Boarding School. Very expensive though. The school fee is Rs. 1800 per month and cost about 3000 rupees including everything like clothing, medical, etc.

We both Nima and I are hardly trying to pay his education allowance. Because my monthly salary is Rupees 2400 a month. We still have two other sons to grow. I don't know how we can give education to them. 2nd one is two years old and time to join school in one more year's time.

Our teashop business doing OK, good for stay alive. Hope you have a nice time and a happy life in the US. I just forgot your baby's name. Do you have more, or just the one?

Please write us sometime. My eldest son is Pemba, Thukten is the 2nd one and Kansa is the 3rd. 3 sons, and not going to have more. Nima's sister is also in Kathmandu, she came here for the winter and her eldest son is studying in Kathmandu as well. Soon she is going back to home. Lhakpa is watching sister's home near the teashop. Will write you again.

Yours,
Ang Tilden

How seductive the requests for reciprocity are when posed by those with whom one envisions intimate closeness, or *thurmu*. Letters like these fill the mailbags flown out of the Khumbu to countries all over the world, arriving eventually in the homes and hearts of the many foreign trekkers who have gone to the Khumbu and experienced, for a moment, the life of

Sherpas. And it is letters like these that have actually produced innumerable sponsorship bonds between Westerners and Sherpas. Acts of sponsorship range from making small gifts, including nominal amounts of cash, over a short period of time to supplying larger amounts of money, miscellaneous valuable items, business partnerships, and trips to the sponsor's home over a period of many years. Foreigners who regularly send money with letters are considered sponsors. In 1986–87, more than one-third of the families of Khum Jung village received some type of foreign sponsorship. So did nearly all urban Sherpa families originally from the Khumbu, particularly those of agency owners. The ideal situation involved building up an entire network of generous sponsors. Typically, a Sherpa had one major and several minor sponsors, most of whom were unaware of each other. Almost all of the more than two hundred Sherpas living in the United States in 1993 were first invited by American sponsors who, to varying degrees, continued to support their Sherpa friends after relocation. Once in the United States, these Sherpas also cultivated new *jindak*s, for whom they often worked. Typically, sponsors were recruited while they were trekking in Nepal.

Perhaps foreigners were compelled to underwrite the Sherpa lifestyle as one they themselves would like, but were unable, to live. Certainly the ritual dynamics of treks and expeditions helped create an environment in which reciprocity was promoted. Himalayan adventures were like "sacred journeys."[12] They demanded physical and emotional endurance in dealing with the rigors of the altitude, food rationing, demands on the body, and culture shock, and they were loaded with expectations of the exotic and actual ritual performances that took them out of the realm of the mundane and into that of the spiritual. This experience made "liminal" (in Victor Turner's sense) left tourists with a sense of unusual achievement at having either met a new personal goal or survived a great physical challenge. Ultimately, a reversal occurred. Suddenly tourists, hoping to follow the footsteps of the "great white explorers" of years past, found themselves entirely dependent on the expertise of Sherpa guides, who now seemed capable of the great heroic acts expected of them. In this way, Sherpas became "authentic."

Sherpas made use of images of their own skillfulness, but also elaborated on the other images cultivated by the West—an easy thing to do considering that Westerners generally perceived a great disparity between their own financial situation and that of most Sherpas. This perception was initially fostered through mountaineering activities and organizations such as the Himalayan Trust, and it generated further monetary and symbolic capital for Sherpas.[13] Trekkers and mountaineers usually descended from the Khumbu with a surfeit of what one observer called "unfulfilled gratitude." They looked for ways to express their thanks, confirm their own authenticity, and bring closure to their climbing experiences while leaving their spiritual epiphanies intact. More often than not, they turned to their pocketbooks, hoping to pay for their satisfaction by leaving cash tips, or, better yet, by becoming regular sponsors. Entering into such social relationships with "real" Sherpas derived from and perpetuated perceptions of "authenticity." The Other became authentic in the act of Westerners authenticating themselves.

Sherpas in these relationships were aware of their clients' need for closure and for epiphanic elongation, and of the benefit to be derived therefrom in the form of an ongoing *jindak* relationship. Often, special dinner parties were held in their homes for those tourists to whom they had become particularly close. Like traditional betrothal rites and the ceremonies initiating *ngalok*, these ritual meals were accompanied by gift exchanges of food, jewelry, trinkets, and promises aimed at establishing long-term bonds between Sherpas and their guests. In such settings, Sherpas did a great deal of culture work. The dinners usually included Sherpa dancing and *chang* drinking. These participatory events were customarily part of the context of deal making, trade arrangements, and marriages; they also set the stage for displays of mimesis with Others' desires. Sherpas emerged clearly as generous and hospitable hosts and skillful and loyal guides, taking visitors through what many visitors considered to be the "backstage" of Sherpa culture, while simultaneously noting for the visitors the Sherpas' ongoing needs, addressed over the course of three decades of development capitalism by organizations like the Himalayan Trust.

Conversations at such dinners usually focused on the host's involvement in expeditions, and on who among the host's neighbors, family, and friends had performed heroically. The significance of being Buddhist and the economic struggle to survive in the Khumbu today were all discussed. "We want to keep our Sherpa culture, but we cannot do this without giving to our religion, and for this we need money," Kandro's husband from Khum Jung, where I lived, remarked at a "sponsorship dinner" given for me. Kandro herself talked about how important it was to send her children to the expensive English-medium school in Kathmandu. The logic was not one deliberately aimed at "requesting" anything from me. Rather, it was a logic that enticed me to become part of a Sherpa way of life by being able to do things as a Buddhist would: become a sponsor and realize that this too was my way of understanding my connection to the larger universe in which both Sherpas and I participated. This logic was expressed in sentiments about fate, underscoring the preordained character of our connections to one another. Kandro's husband reminded me: "What can I do? It is written on my forehead, what is my future, what is my life. That's all." By the end of a long evening, after a lot of eating and dancing, Kandro offered me her necklace to make me her *tromo*, her ritual sister. Knowing her financial situation, I realized this was an expensive gift for her. How Buddhist, as an act of compassion and of detachment, and yet how intimate, to be given this offering of *thurmu* that would bind me to her in a deep attachment for years to come. I felt the epiphany rising. Swept up in this act of authentication, I gave her my bracelet as a return token, making her my *tromo*. "So much *thurmu!*" I wrote in my field notes that night. Again, was this an example of staged "authenticity" posing as a true site for Sherpa identity? If so, does that oxymoronic concept, as MacCannell notes,[14] not merely push authenticity out of reach once again—beyond the gaze of what we can ever see in a Western-inspired or tourist encounter? Or is this seduction as authentic as any other way of being Sherpa, and does it not require suspension, on some level, of my presumption that pure utilitarianism could be separated from those relationships of *thurmu* and friendship?

Foreigners who became major Sherpa sponsors are afforded special attention on their visits to the Khumbu. They are given seats next to the abbot and village elders during community rituals, and fed and feted like visiting lamas. Sherpas feel this hospitality is essential to the maintenance of their relationships with their sponsors, which are further buttressed by the creation of fictive kin titles for them. Sherpas thus refer to Sir Edmund Hillary, Colonel Jimmy Roberts (the founder of Nepal's oldest trekking agency), and Stan Armington and Mike Healy (other Westerners who were among the first to establish expedition companies in Nepal) as the "fathers of Sherpas." Lesser sponsors are called *trowo* and *tromo* (ritual brother and sister), or simply "friends." Back in the United States, scores of foreigners who have gone on treks or expeditions to Nepal wind up sponsoring Sherpas in the Khumbu. At home, these foreigners refer to the Sherpas they help support as their Sherpa sons or daughters, brothers or sisters, or "good friends."

I received a phone call from a woman in northern California about a year after I had returned from the field in 1987. She told me that she was sponsoring a young Sherpa man on a trip to the United States. He had letters for me from my Khumbu friends and wanted to get together. We met at a café in a shopping mall and the young man, Lhakpa Tendu, told me how much he was enjoying this visit with his "American family." The "mother" said she was "thrilled" to be able to bring Lhakpa Tendu here. She told me she had had a wonderful experience trekking in Nepal—"it was like a rebirth experience. . . . It was so different from here," she said. I asked her why she had sponsored Lhakpa Tendu. "It was a way of returning the hospitality they showed us while we were in Nepal," she responded. Her daughter added, "Yeah, Lhakpa Tendu is our Sherpa family member now." Occasionally, such American sponsors became possessive regarding their Sherpa guests, refusing to allow other Americans who had gotten to know these Sherpas in Nepal to visit or even talk to them on the phone.

Did this evidence a desire on the sponsors' part to preserve "authenticity," enabling them to feel their particular relationships with such Sherpas were unique and that such relationships connected them in a special way to "true" Sherpa life—an experience that would be haphazardly commodified if made available to the masses? This was precisely what the Sherpas I knew hoped to achieve through mimesis with Western representations of them. And it required an ongoing presumption on the part of Westerners of the symbolic value of "being Sherpa." How, I wondered, as I set out to write this ethnography, could I reveal the existence of this widespread seduction without rendering it inauthentic or staged—without turning my very analysis into an "exposé" of hidden agendas of Sherpa involvement with Westerners—agendas that elude most Westerners who arrive there and become involved with Sherpas? Although this is what the discourse of authenticity demanded, it simply did not fit what I saw and experienced among Sherpas.

Like other reciprocal bonds established with Sherpas, the relationship I had with them I considered binding, so I sent what money I could to Ang Tilden for the children's education upon receiving his letter (reprinted above). I also sent another gift to my *tromo*, Kandro. Sherpas employed an entire repertoire of symbolic images that specifically appealed to foreign tourists, largely because it was such foreigners who helped identify these images as "authentic." Kandro's use of these techniques, however, did not make her any less Sherpa; she simply appeared to me to be more "virtual."

For themselves, then, Sherpas also needed to sustain images of foreigners as wealthy and generous, always in search of adventure, and intensely interested in becoming involved on a personal level with their exotic hosts. They had to create virtual Westerners who embodied all that Sherpas considered desirable about the West. Although Sherpas always seemed to envision Westerners as rich, it is worth noting that their definition of a poor Westerner was one who was miserly and who put money above friendship. Ang Tshiring Sherpa, who owned a trekking agency, offered an example: "A German climber [and I have heard this about people of other ethnicities as well], [who] no matter how many years he has come to me for business, will go to another agency the minute that he learns he can get a cheaper price from them . . . this is how they think."

Such Westerners are viewed by Sherpas as those engaged in impersonal exchanges, devoid of any social obligations—people who have no friends because business, for them, is "strictly business." Lhakpa Tsamgi returned from a United States tour taken with her husband at the invitation of her husband's American *jindak*, remarking, "People are too busy there. They spend all their time earning money. They have no time for friends." Pemba Sherpa made a similar observation after his six-month stay in the United States, during which he worked in his sponsor's factory. He said he had

had a good time there, that his sponsors had a successful business and lots of money. But he commented that they spent all their time working and had no time for anything else—not even for spending some of what they earned. Turchen, a Sherpa trekking-agency owner in partnership with an American, offered his sentiments about the importance of establishing social bonds in business after he visited the United States as a tourist himself:

> The difference between the States and here is the social thing. Foreigners who visit here never understand that, when they are in difficult situations, if they talk nice and pay less it is better than if they talk rough and pay more. . . . It is very difficult to make them understand. But you cannot blame them because this is how they have grown up. You make your call and in ten minutes you get a Domino's pizza very hot. Here, no way, you have to go there and ask them to measure it and wait there and get it. You have to know them. Plus, if you have a friend there, even if there is someone there before you waiting, you will get your pizza first. The social things are so strong here. We say that friends or relatives or people who are close to us are cash-value documents. Friends are like cash-value documents. If you have so many friends in so many places, even if you are starving you will have no problems. Making a friend is making an investment; an investment means to make money. You give ten thousand, say, and you will expect to get back fifteen thousand at least. So, it's an investment if you spend some money for a friend, to be a friend. . . . Let's say I go to a restaurant and have a couple of beers, [and] spend maybe twenty-five or thirty rupees [on a friend]. . . . Someday he will remember that I bought him that bottle of beer and he might buy me two bottles or he might do something else for me so I can earn some money. So, making friends is [a] much better investment, because they have cash value.

Even foreign agency operators who had worked for many years in Kathmandu recognized that in the trekking industry in Nepal, determining the bottom line in a business deal involved more than simply considering how much money would be generated. It also meant calculating how many social contacts the transaction might generate or facilitate. These connections could lead to further profits, measured in cash earnings and in increased prestige, promotion of one's culture, and the perpetuation of desirable images.

One reason a theory of impressions management, which embraces the notion of a "staged" Sherpa seduction, is so alluring is that its discourse of authenticity leads to opportunities for profit. Western discourses of authenticity provide what Baudrillard (1983) called a "reality principle" for everything from ethnographic writing to tourist experiences. Positing authenticity necessarily means positing inauthenticity as well. It is this dual production of the "real" and the "not-real" that results in the potential for profit, whether in the context of tourism or of academic publications. In the latter, the credibility of scholars hinges on the notion of an inviolable and essential authenticity always contrasted with inauthenticity. Alongside many others, Sherpas compel us to rethink this discourse. How can we now reconfigure the idea of authenticity, given the seamless construction of Sherpa identities and the way in which the Sherpa economy (in which Westerners are obviously involved) makes use of commodities that are at once both shared meanings and cultural images? Perhaps we must rethink the concept of an "economy" itself in a manner that can accommodate virtual identities. Such an economy depends on culture work—the production of self in ways that can generate the self as both sign and symbol, in that as a sign the self can be free-floating and simulational or still attached to the people who are Sherpa in name and action. I suggest, however, that culture work, whether carried out by Sherpas or ethnographers, requires an attentiveness to the profits and potential violence of representations and simulations and their effects. An ethnography in this economy would have to offer itself as an example of that for which it stands; it would have to approach the whole problem of constituting "Sherpa-ness" in ways that implicitly reflect the need for image production as part of its objective—as its profit source—and therefore its need to engage in seduction. It would have to exemplify a "Sherpa" approach to those images that, in textual form, becomes indistinguishable from those desires invested in the Sherpa image conveyed via the Western author's imagination. I have included in Appendix D a cursory attempt to work through the problem of an economy of meanings in a more abstract fashion. Here, however, I return to this problem by exploring the theme of seduction.

THE SEDUCTION OF THEORY

I suggest that seduction is the objective of the ethnographer as much as of the Sherpas about whom I write. It has been the process by which Sherpas have been made into "moderns" even when this has meant remaining "traditional," and by which Sherpas seduce Western others to step through the veil of "difference" in order to become like Sherpas by becoming sponsors for them. I am intrigued by Baudrillard's argument that in those contemporary settings where simulated images and signs are often devoid of referents, we are most likely to arrive at a useful mode of analysis through a theory of seduction rather than production, and through analyses of sign systems as giving rise to economies rather than as being generated by them. For Baudrillard, an analysis of culture mandates a revision in our thinking about economies. Seduction is not aimed at interpretation of the hidden meaning beyond the surface play of signs, for it embraces what it will wholly at the surface—where the sign is, beyond which there is nothing and therefore nothing to interpret. In seduction, signifiers do not stand for underlying signifieds—signifiers can be free-floating, as can the notion of "Sherpa" in the late twentieth century. Again, an attractive use of the name "Sherpa," of which Sherpas are aware, is made at world political summit meetings where heads of nation-states come together for debate. At these meetings, "Sherpas" denotes those charged with responsibilities for writing position papers and carrying out preliminary negotiations. These "Sherpas" are responsible for bringing their nations' leaders to the summit. Clearly, they are not ethnic Sherpas from Nepal.[15] The name and identity of "Sherpa" is used here as a simulated signifier in an economy where the image of dexterity and endurance en route to the summit, produced largely by the West, is related to reaching the "peak" of diplomatic success.

In Baudrillard's treatment of seduction one finds an economy of meanings, rather than things. An economy of meanings makes use of images as currency, whose values are set by shifting social relationships and by tacitly shared and transitory cultural meanings. The images of Sherpas produced transnationally have value as currency in an economy where profits are accrued on the basis of being desirable and on the currency's (here, the image's) ability to seduce others into relations of meaning exchange. Baudrillard suggests that the constantly shifting meanings that circulate in the contemporary setting create an implosion of meaning, wherein no singular meaning is sustained. Whereas modernity is characterized by eternalism and ephemerality, postmodernity is characterized as a movement to one pole of that continuum—the pole where ephemerality is totalizing. The idea that no meanings can be fixed because of the ephemerality of constantly revised truths leads Baudrillard to nihilism over the absence of meaning. I am moved to the opposite conclusion: that the barrage of constantly revised representations and simulations and the meanings they put into circulation does not leave us with an absence of meaning but rather with a panoply of meanings that all have to be sustained at once and taken as in some sense "accurate."[16] This means living with the idea of "contradictory truths," or the idea that multiple versions of reality are always simultaneously operating within the same people.[17] It also means recognizing that such varied versions of reality do not belong to one or another group but are shared by those who are involved in relationships of seduction with one another.

Unlike Baudrillard, I do not believe that simulations and a theory of seduction eliminate the utility of a theory of production, for cultural images are clearly produced (and consumed) by identifiable sources, and sometimes their meaning is still attached to those about whom they are produced. For Baudrillard, seduction operates at the level of the signifier, not the signified. Theories of production always presuppose that referents exist for those (symbolic) representations of them. This is why, Baudrillard suggests, we must go beyond production, because referents often do not exist for the signifiers that circulate as images of persons and things. An approach that starts with seduction is useful because it renders the search for a singular "authentic" Sherpa, like the search for the signified, moot by questioning the basis for a notion of authenticity. A notion of authenticity presupposes that every signifier has a signified—that is, its place of authenticity. But many of the images of Sherpas are simulations. Thus, in this case, authenticity has to give way to the "effects of desires for authenticity" wherein there is no singular, more true version of Sherpa identity than any other. In fact, one can really only speak of an "effect of desires for authenticity,"[18] which always refers back to and exposes the conditions of its production and which puts authenticity at issue. "Sherpas" at summit meetings are in some sense, then, simulations—they are the free-floating desires of Westerners for a certain kind of Sherpa created in the Western imagination. They are like Shangri-la. This image is profitable not only for those appropriating the name—the diplomatic aides-de-camp—but also for ethnic Sherpas who know that the positive use of their name in these contexts will bring them cultural and financial profits and a sense of accomplishment that derives from the visibility of having internalized Western interests. Profits here depend on the shared cultural meanings associated with the name "Sherpa"—on an economy where meanings are exchanged and eventually shared.

However, "Sherpas" at summit meetings are in other ways *not* simulations, but representations—they have referents in real Sherpa guides whose connections to Western Others can be defined in terms of wage-labor relations for mountain expeditions. Representations of Sherpas that portray them as, for example, intrepid climbers or devout Buddhists are created at least in part out of encounters Westerners have had with actual Sherpas who have demonstrated intrepid skill or religious devotion. So this imagery operates at the level of both *representation* of qualities Sherpas actually exhibit and *simulation* of qualities imputed to Sherpas because they are desired by the Other. Sherpas did live in the mountains and traverse them, but they were never inherently expert at climbing their peaks, as Westerners would have us believe. But Sherpas are now believed to be, and believe themselves to be, *innately skilled* at climbing mountain peaks. This Sherpa is attached to its referent. This virtual Sherpa requires attentiveness to production and seduction, for the latter is a technique of the former. Sherpas are produced both by a Western gaze and by Sherpas who are the object of that gaze.

At the crux of the debate over whether Sherpa images are simulated or representational is, again, the question of authenticity, and it is on notions of authenticity that power relationships hinge. What is the ability to define the Other as authentic, other than the ability to make profits by it, or to sell this as a commodified good? Baudrillard argues (1983) that this has been anthropology's "reality principle"—that which makes it possible for anthropologists to define the "value" of their products. What is authenticity except anthropology in its most profitable guise? The need for authenticity is in part a result of the commodification of cultural difference demanded not simply by anthropology but also by capitalism. To analyze the elusive nature of notions of authenticity, then, one needs to treat economies as cultural systems, rather than treating culture as derivative of the economy, as metanarratives of capitalism do.[19] While it is easy to see how Sherpas' cultural practices of mimesis appear "commodified" by the mechanisms of capitalism embedded in tourism, development, and anthropology, I suggest that the metanarrative of capitalism cannot encompass or do justice to the transnationalism of cultural practices. How are Sherpa practices of Buddhism or shamanism, as objects of the tourist gaze, not simply commodified and made into sites for the production of capitalistic power? Why should we not read all Sherpa desires to reach the summit of Everest, like Pasang's, as products of capitalism's inevitable exploitations of the Sherpas? How insidious that claim would be! Rather, we might consider an economy of meanings, and focus on the productive techniques peculiar to the cultural practices therein. This may unseat notions of power that we often take for granted.

Sherpas participate in an economy of meanings, embodying various notions of their authenticity as a type of currency, not only as signs (wearing their images like signifiers) but also as symbols (attached to the spirit of their being). This economy can also exploit, but not simply for the sake of money. In this sense a theory of production is critical to an analysis of economies of meaning, but it should pay attention to the production of cultural images and the work of culture, which renders such things as labor, currencies, and particularly consciousness culturally problematic (so that, at least, one would not read Pasang's death as an inevitable result of mystification). It should also recognize the potential for alternative notions of subjectivity to inform the nature of value.[20] Such an analysis among Sherpas has led me to an exploration of virtual Sherpas, whose ideas about profit do not distinguish between money and reputation. An analysis that hopes to understand the economies within which transnational cultures are deterritorialized (following Appadurai 1990) needs to begin with the perspective that sees cultural flows as, at least in part, economies of meaning wherein the authenticity of the subject is always negotiated through seductions as the "effect of desires for authenticity."

22. Parachuting to the summit of Everest—the newest fad in Himalayan mountaineering.

THE ADVENTURES OF BEING SHERPA

Ang Temba was terribly excited when I ran into him in 1989. He had just returned from Switzerland, where he traveled each year to visit a French mountain climber–sponsor who gave Temba the opportunity to work at his alpine ski resort and solicit clients for his own trekking agency in Nepal. In this latter regard, Temba explained that he typically offered a slide-show presentation of the Himalayas and various trekking events, including beautiful photos of the monasteries and of Sherpa villages, all aimed at drumming up business.

On this last visit, his sponsor had introduced him to a French adventurer named Bruno Govi, who was interested in arranging an expensive and unusual expedition in Nepal. This would be no ordinary climb, and Govi said he would need a Sherpa agent particularly skilled in handling unique tours. Temba said that Govi wanted to skydive from a plane onto the peak of Everest, stop for a photo shoot, and then hang glide all the way down to the base camp. The company sponsoring this feat would be Marlboro cigarettes (the R. J. Reynolds Company). Apparently, the direct advertising of cigarettes was illegal in Europe. To circumvent such restrictions, the Marlboro company shot miles of adventure-video footage, in which those filmed wore outfits boldly imprinted with the Marlboro name. These videos were then shown in stores featuring Marlboro clothes for sale.

The new Marlboro Man advertisements involved Sherpas in an economy of meanings already potent in the West. Temba was nonplussed by the hype surrounding this particular adventure, but was excited about the notoriety this sort of expedition would bring his company in Nepal, Europe, and the rest of the world. A year in advance, he was already making sure that his personal contacts at the Royal Nepal Airline Company were solid enough to gain him permission to use one charter flight for the actual skydive and another for the filming, without paying such enormous fees that the expedition would be bankrupted. Ang Temba would set himself up to be a recipient of sponsorship by R. J. Reynolds, like other Sherpas sponsored by corporations that had funded expeditions over the years. Govi, already a close friend of Ang Temba's, was convinced that only a Sherpa company with Sherpas the likes of Ang Temba could pull this expedition off. When I asked Ang Temba why Govi had chosen his company, he replied that it was because Govi considers Sherpas—in fact Ang Temba himself—to be his expedition peers, qualified by possessing the same spirit of achievement and will to be the best. Sherpas and foreigners were thus brought together in a transnational economy. The resulting signification of identity through labor that was at once representational and simulational, material and ideological, produced virtual Sherpas.

Ang Temba's seduction of foreign expeditioners compelled him to demonstrate that he was up to the task of orchestrating and participating in their outrageous stunts. He never got the government's permission to use a plane enabling his client to skydive onto Everest, but he planned the expedition anyway. Govi went with him to convince another of his close friends, an Indian pilot for Royal Nepal Airlines, to fly one of the small planes they chartered (a Pilatus Porter) anyway. Temba offered the pilot fifteen thousand dollars (a small sum relative to the total expedition costs), after which he agreed to fly against the mandate of the Ministry of Tourism. The night before the jump was set to occur, well after the expedition team that was supposed to meet Govi on top had set up various base camps to provide supplies along the route of Everest, Ang Temba, Govi, and the pilot decided to run a test flight to make sure the plane could reach a high enough altitude (above nine thousand meters). They waited until darkness fell and then took off, soaring over a small hilltop just outside Kathmandu, where Govi jumped. When the plane landed, the police were waiting. Both Ang Temba and the pilot were arrested and jailed for a day. The pilot lost his job, which he apparently did not mind, for he returned to India and got another. Govi, unable to proceed with the adventure as planned, did join the expedition on foot (even though it was now just another ordinary climb, without a skydiving component). He went back to Europe and, to the great dismay of Ang Temba and his family, died a few years later performing a similar stunt in the Alps. However, if there was one Buddhist lesson embraced by Ang Temba, it was that of emphasizing the recognition and acceptance of the inevitability of death. Relationships always changed, as did friends—not infrequently as a result of the risks encountered in mountaineering. Still, Temba looked back on the events with great nostalgia and pride, claiming "I would do it again. It was worth it."

Culture does not simply coexist with capitalism, or even just operate in conjunction with it. Culture itself constitutes a form of capital, and turns the economy into a milieu for the operation and interplay of multiple modes of power, including that generated by representations and simulations—seductive power. Witnessed in the image of Sherpas as intrepid and skilled climbers and guides (promoted by agency operators), and as hospitable and generous of spirit by their Buddhist natures, they become the perfect companions to Westerners in search of an Other who will receive them and reveal their similarity, and yet remain exotically different. Seductive power is visible in the image of Sherpas as the poor, underprivileged, yet deserving peasants of Shangri-la. It is visible in the image of Sherpas as people who are believed to be still "in touch" with a way of life that places more value on reciprocal social bonds than cash denuded of social relationships. In that, they become the perfect candidates for sponsorship by foreign benefactors who seek a means of transcending the "everydayness" of their everyday lives—foreigners inarticulate in the language of social reciprocity yet momentarily made fluent through their bonds with Sherpas. By sponsoring Sherpas as Others, Westerners "reenchant" their lives with something special and believed to be magical, arising out of Shangri-la itself. Seductive power is found in the image of Sherpas as devout Buddhists—compassionate, hospitable, highly spiritual—making them, along with monks and lamas, attractive to both foreign Buddhists and others seeking religious enlightenment. This power is also seen in the image of Sherpas as sexually desirable partners for Westerners searching for a lost intimacy in a faraway land, and it is in the image of Sherpas as risk-taking adventurers and skilled mountain "gatekeepers." In all of these images so saturated with seductive power, one can also find anthropologists gazing and seeking, creating and discovering authentic Sherpas who, as it turns out, are virtual in essence, or virtually nonessential. There are many Sherpas inhabiting the hearts and minds of the West, and there are many Sherpas who find themselves in the gaze of Westerners. The dance of mimesis and seduction, in which Sherpas and Westerners participate as partners, performing the same steps, makes being Sherpa a transnational yet highly personal and specific affair.

Virtual Sherpas in Circulation

ONE OF the 1991 tour packages offered by Mountain Travel/Sobeck, Inc. of Berkeley, California, was a series of tours called "Seminars in Wilderness Medicine." This set of adventures was designed for physicians and other medical personnel looking to receive continuing medical education (CME) credit through Mountain Travel tours. One of its highlights was the "Everest Escapade." On this tour, seminars were given on health conditions and medical points of interest in the Himalayan villages and regions the visitors passed through, by Ph.D.s and M.D.s trained in wilderness and mountain medicine. Physician attendees were not explicitly asked to deliver care to the villagers they would meet, but the brochures did feature a photo of a Western doctor kneeling over a Nepalese woman on the side of a trail, suturing a wound on her knee. Here was medicine that made a difference, in the most literal sense. Mountain Travel thus cleverly linked doctors' acquisition of CME credits with the Nepal having long been a favorite spot for doctors serving the Third World's poor through altruism combined with exploration and adventure. This juxtaposition resulted in a new version of the "soul-searching" journey that many (like Matthiessen) viewed as "healing" in both orientation and effect.[1]

Another interesting type of Nepal tour offered by international travel companies in the early 1990s was the "Cleanup Trek." A worldwide environmentalist movement had made its way into the Khumbu, focusing on ecological degradation as well as the unsightly residue (litter) of foreign tourism. Lhakpa Norbu Sherpa, one of only a few Sherpa Ph.D.s (a Himalayan Trust scholarship recipient) and a second of the region's only Sherpa former park wardens, published his views on such tours and the participants' motivations for going to the Himalayas: "For unscrupulous climbers, mountain clean-ups provide an excuse for fund-raising at a time when sponsorships for climbing expeditions seem to be drying up. And then there are the well-meaning, who devote their own time and money to fly half way around the world to pick up someone else's trash."[2]

Lhakpa does not mention, but one can assume, that one of the reasons these people want to go to the Himalayas in the first place is that it is the home to the highest mountains in the world. Nor does he mention that they go to see and experience Sherpas and their way of life, although that too, I think, can safely be presumed.[3] In the same journal in which Lhakpa Norbu's comments appear is an advertisement from In Wilderness Trekking (P), Ltd. Beneath a photo of five climbers atop Everest, it reads:

LOOK! A BUNCH OF PEOPLE ARE ON TOP OF MT. SAGARMATHA.
WHY ARE THEY THERE?

Botany, Zoology, Meteorology, Geography are all part of every person's daily life. The mountains, deserts, oceans and skies are always there with a smiling challenge for us. Nature does her best to preserve a balance. But does man?

Indeed, Ang Rita Sherpa, the legend (seven-time Mt. Sagarmatha Summitteer without oxygen), and many other adventurers, explorers, and mountaineers have succeeded in conquering the challenges and adversities of our Planet. But one day all these expressions of admiration may become curses for us.

Time is methodically pressing on, and will not wait for us to prevent this beautiful and challenging earth of ours from falling into a state of desolation. Dear friends, let us survive; let us explore; let us make adventure; let us trek, but let us take a step to preserve and protect what we have and to plant for the future.

With this consciousness, yes, we support your holiday and adventure in Nepal.

From as early as the turn of the century, with the commencement of expedition health care offered trailside to Sherpas, until today, with the arrival of full-blown medical tours of the Himalayan countryside and environmental "cleanup" treks, Western images of the Himalayas have been eminently profitable as symbolic currency. So have images of the Sherpas residing therein, with their admirable achievements and boundless needs. The attraction was initially felt by individuals like Sir Edmund Hillary, and has continued and spread to foreign agencies and governments who have taken an active interest in protecting the area in contemporary times:

> Sir Edmund was as keen to assist the Sherpas to better their families' lives. . . .
> Other agencies have also co-operated with his Majesty's Government in providing projects in the Khumbu region. The New Zealand Government's involvement began in 1974 when a joint task force of officials from New Zealand and Nepal made an assessment of the possibilities for development of the national park, and recommended a programme for bilateral cooperation. Over the following six years, New Zealand national park rangers and foresters lived in Khumbu, working with Nepalese to set up the Park and reafforestation programme.[4]

Almost twenty years later, in 1992, when Lhakpa Norbu Sherpa expressed his own concerns for the preservation of the region, his focus was not merely on garbage and the excuse it gave foreigners to obtain funding for expeditions to Nepal, but rather on the more serious problems of ecological degradation (such as deforestation and erosion), which he feared were being overlooked. To address these issues, Lhakpa Norbu called for the improved operation of the park management system. If it could prove itself effective in handling real environmental crises, then surely it would be able to deal with minor problems such as leftover litter from expeditions and treks. He also advocated creating an organization to integrate the mountaineering expertise of local residents with the administrative and legal expertise of the foreign-born national park advisors. Local climbers could be trained as a litter-patrol team, backed up by the national park system. Finally, Lhakpa Norbu specified that "the financial burden of environmental restoration programs would be placed on the groups responsible for generating the problem." That is, the foreigners who polluted would pay for the cleanup.

Spoken by a Sherpa through a discourse invented and manufactured in the West, Lhakpa Norbu's remarks reveal the impossibility of determining the "ownership" of that discourse today. He was himself an agent for social change and modernization among Sherpas. Yet his words were no more Western than the discourse offered by those promoting intimacy through shamanistic practice; they were Sherpa.

In being constructed as exotically "different" yet needy for the same things the West could offer, Sherpas have served as a site for a Western creation of self. Sherpas have had to be "incomplete" to make room for modern interventions. Like the Himalayan "wilderness," perceived to be in need of the services of Ph.D.s in forestry and park management, the Sherpas who live there are perceived to be in need of M.D.s and Western biomedicine. But Sherpas themselves have simultaneously generated a discourse aimed at instructing foreigners on becoming "better Westerners." To be Sherpa, then, is to have become almost better at being modernized than the moderns themselves. This includes the ability to reproduce those needs on which Western intervention has been predicated, by being different in at least some of the ways that Westerners themselves hope to emulate. Lhakpa Norbu seems to have mastered the canon and the strategy, and turned it back on the West in the form of a discourse that reproduces both the rhetoric of intervention that Western philanthropists and environmentalists desire and the rhetoric of authenticity that Western mountaineers and trekkers desire.[5]

Sherpa identities must never become too Western because their ultimate allure is in their difference. Sherpa needs must reflect a desire to be more like the West, yet Sherpas must remain exotic enough to make "Wilderness Tours," "Medical Seminars," and "Cleanup Treks" remain culturally, not simply ethically or ecologically, worthwhile. Certainly the "Medical Seminars" brochure stressed that cultural difference in their advertisement:

Any trek in the Mt. Everest region is a visual feast for mountain lovers.
This region's unique beauty earned it the honor of being made Sagarmatha National Park, the first such park in the Himalaya.

Our nine day hike offers an unmatched mountain panorama from Mt. Everest (29,028′) to Kantega (22,340′), Thamserku (22,208′), and the obelisk of Ama Dablam (22,494′).

In addition to seeing mountain views, we'll experience the Tibetan Buddhist culture that is prevalent throughout the Himalaya, and enjoy the genuine welcome extended by our Sherpa hosts.

Our trekking route takes us to the Sherpa market town of Namche Bazaar (11,300′), the remote monastery at Thame (12,500′), the pretty villages of Khunde and Khumjung, and on to the famed Thyangboche Monastery (12,500′), where the sight of alpenglow on the summit of Mt. Everest and the views of Ama Dablam are memories to be treasured forever.[6]

When Lhakpa Norbu Sherpa advocates modernization within the discourse of environmentalism, and when Mountain Travel offers adventure tours by "selling" the hospitality of Sherpas, both draw on a currency of cultural exoticism. The Himalayas are worth preserving, for ourselves and particularly for Sherpas, who as a culturally unique ethnic group are worth preserving for the world. The desirability of Sherpas resides in their reputation for possessing certain qualities that Westerners admire and hope to achieve or feel they have lost and hope to regain. The Sherpas' habitat, the Himalayas, and their religion, Buddhism, are both thought to offer Westerners new horizons, enabling them to discover their own inner, but "obscured," identities. Foreigners typically seek out experiences with Sherpas in order to become more spiritual and more "real" in their own minds. The relationships they develop bring them closer to something they view as "authentically" Sherpa while paradoxically entangling Sherpa identities even further with Western desires for exotic Others. Who, then, ultimately "owns" this culture occupying the space inhabited by Sherpas and Westerners?

The reflexive nature of the famed Sherpa spirituality was dramatically displayed in 1993. The Sherpas had created a unique institution, called the Himalayan Sherpa Buddhist School, at four thousand meters, near Phungmoche Monastery. It offers classes on Sherpa culture, language, dharma, and moral education for sixty-five indigenous children (three girls and sixty-two boys).[7] Even though it is not a monastery (although it does offer some religious education), it still attracts Western sponsors. The teachers (all Sherpa) at the school want it to be accredited "as an exclusive school that runs both as a Nepali public school and a school for Himalayan Culture"; the Nepal government provides no funding. As a result, Sherpas have collected all the necessary operating funds from three large foreign agencies, one English individual, and trekkers donating smaller sums. The American journal begun and sustained by anthropologists, *Cultural Survival Quarterly*, announced in 1993, and again in 1994, a new focus for its concern about the disappearing cultures of the world—the Sherpas of Khumbu, Nepal.[8] Contributions to support the school, and the culture, were solicited through the journal. Modern seductions are not only *of* Sherpas, they are also *by* Sherpas. However, how am I to read these seductions without falling into the trap of treating the Sherpa engagement with Westerners as nothing more than a clever manipulation of a staged authenticity? I have tried to reveal that such a distinction is irrelevant. I conclude, here, with a summary, which works to reveal not only Sherpa ideas but also those of anthropology itself.

THE EMPTINESS OF SAMENESS AND DIFFERENCE

Attempts to preserve Himalayan Sherpa culture speak to the desires for cultural authenticity and the seductions that such desires arouse. They point to a locus of identity somewhere between "authentic" and "constructed" versions of who the Sherpas are supposed to be, and raise unanswerable questions about the ownership of culture. Tourism in Nepal, and even anthropology, in its own way, are at least partly about the effects of a quest for authenticity. Thus, they are also about the need to find something seductive enough to be labeled authentic—that is, something perceived as "correct," "nonsimulated," and originating outside the Western imagination. But a historically and culturally situated search for an authentic Sherpa is one that is thought necessarily to involve moving through various layers of constructed identity arising from the mimetic relations Sherpas have had with foreigners, particularly with the West. It is also thought to involve moving through a layer of identity configured by Buddhism, not unlike that of Western modernity in some ways, and certainly constructed with some regard to Western interests. Efforts to locate an authentic Sherpa in some identity beyond these discourses, for example in intimate relationships with Sherpas such as those evoked in shamanic rituals, demonstrates that, even there, little of what one would think of as a singular or essential Sherpa outside the gaze of the West exists that could emerge in the ethnographic and written space of a Western readership. Rather, we again discover many reflections of the observer. Often the mountaineer, the cultural tourist, and the anthropologist are all in pursuit of themselves through the Other, and journeys to the mountain—during which one frequently befriends Sherpas—appear to meet this need.

I have observed that the closer I seem to come to an "authentic" Sherpa, the more I am confronted with a mirror of my own desires. In this sense, I am not exempt from the very mimetic processes I explore in this text. I suggest again that the idea of an authentic Sherpa must be revised; there are, instead, only virtual Sherpas. And, even though these images are aimed at differentiating between an observed and an observer, they ultimately

23. Masked dancer representing a messenger at Mani Rimdu celebration, Thame Monastery, 1982.

24. Masked dancer representing a wrathful protector deity at Mani Rimdu celebration, Tengboche Monastery, 1986.

have precisely the opposite effect, for they implode in the space between self and Other, tourist and host, recipient and donor, in an impenetrable mirroring of identity. Once the notion of the authentic succumbs to that of the virtual, so too does a singular version of Sherpas succumb to many coexisting versions, equally "accurate." The deaf Sherpa guide in Namche Bazaar, offering his "cultural tour" to overnight lodgers, might be happy to hear this.

Finally, I posit that virtual Sherpas emerge from and circulate within transnational arrangements of power and cultural exchange. Desires among foreign researchers for a distinctive and essential Sherpa become part of a consumer nostalgia. Meanwhile, the use of "distinctive" Sherpa images by Sherpas themselves, who are often conducting transnational business, involves a mimesis and seduction that bring Westerners still closer to them. When Ramesh Kunwor, a Nepalese scholar who had recently completed his Ph.D. dissertation on Sherpas, told me that the Khumbu was considered by Nepalese scholars the Ph.D.-producing region of Nepal (because so many Western Ph.D.s were generated there), I laughed nervously because his comment made so much sense and because I was part of that industry. Many Sherpas I met were interested in selling Westerners copies of Kunwor's book about them; this only heightened my eventual awareness of being engaged in a seductive arrangement put in place long before my arrival in the Khumbu. In this sense, the concept of a singular authentic Sherpa existing beyond the Western gaze became even more untenable, not only because "essential" versions of Sherpas are too totalizing to be anything but virtual, but because the very strategies used by Sherpas to engage others in relationships reveal their malleable and transnationally constructed identities—virtual identities that reflect images of them embraced by observing and expectant others.

I return to my packet of articles from *Tricycle: The Buddhist Review*, which includes a short editorial piece by the computer wunderkind Jaron Lanier on the possible use of virtual reality to advance Buddhist ideals. Again, having originally had no intention of indirectly referring in my manuscript title to contemporary technologies of virtual reality by using the term "virtual," I was forced to reconsider this, for Lanier's essay on Buddhism and his computer work resonated strangely with my own observations about Sherpas and the problems of writing an ethnography about them:

> One of the interesting things about Buddhism is the notion that certain types of practice, which are on the face of them value neutral, can actually lead to the development of compassion. On a social level, it seems that media technologies, with their McLuhanesque properties, might very well be our collective "practice." . . . Our minds are potentially fully fluid, but we often think of them as not

fluid because our bodies are not. What one would hope is that realizing how truly fluid everyone is would make it a little harder to have firm ideas about one's enemies. The experience of virtual reality forces you to notice your own experience of consciousness. In the physical world there's a fuzzy boundary between the hypothetical objective environment and your way of interpreting it, but in VR [virtual reality] the world that is presented to you is entirely a human artifact. By noticing the sharp-edged boundary of the objective world in VR, you also notice that there is something on the near side of that boundary. Noticing consciousness is not as trivial a task as you might suppose. In fact, many people in computer science would argue that consciousness does not exist. The only reason to ever bring consciousness in as a consideration is because you experience it; it is otherwise superfluous. But once its experienced, you can't throw it out, any more than a physicist could simplify his job by throwing out one of the forces of nature in order to have a unified theory. So in a sense, VR might serve as a prequel to Buddhism, exposing what must be lost.[9]

Implosion, in some sense, turns things inside out. The idea of loss and impermanence is at play both in the Buddhism of Sherpas and in the imagination of the West. A recognition of virtual realities leads to an awareness of consciousness and, finally, to emptiness. It reveals that the only permanence of Sherpas' identities is that found in reflecting the desires of Others. Sherpas are defined by the relationships that produce tangible versions of them, all hoping to find that which must be "lost." Furthermore, an ethnography of Sherpas becomes a study of their impact on the West, not just the reverse. Their effect on those in relationships with them is potent, but its exact nature is hard to pinpoint. Their effect floats somewhere between engaging us, as "generous" Westerners, in intimate long-term relationships and becoming for us that empty Buddhist vessel into which our desires can be deposited—experiences of "consciousness."

Notions of impermanence and virtual identity figure in any attempt to name Sherpas. This is not only my problem, as an ethnographer. All the Sherpas I have ever met abroad claim "Sherpa" as a surname. This is not simply because their Nepalese identity cards denote their ethnicity as Sherpa; it is also because, as the trekking-agency owner Ang Tshiring told me, "Sherpas [vs. Nepalis] are world famous." Mingma, a recent Sherpa immigrant now doing wage work in New York City, told me that it is because "more people know the name Sherpa than know the name of Nepal." I found, however, that the Sherpas I met were difficult to keep track of, because their other names often changed, especially among children. When they experienced a significant stroke of bad luck or recurring bouts of sickness, Sherpas would often have lamas issue them entirely new names. By shedding their existing monikers, they could purportedly shed their current misfortunes as well. This malleability of identity, or of names conferring identity, is probably not unique to Sherpas, but is significant when viewed in relation to the history of Sherpa involvement with mountaineering, tourism, development, and anthropological activities, in all of which contexts identity has been variously constructed for and by Sherpas as relatively fixed and eternal. The perceived weight and solidity of the "Sherpa" surname is thus countered by the complete impermanence of all other names to which any one Sherpa affixes his or her identity.

These explorations, I hope, lead to some sort of interruption of the conventional ways in which we deal with cultural difference and sameness in ethnography. It would appear that transnational cultural "sameness" and the persistence of cultural "difference" (along with the need for its production) are but two faces of a single anthropological hologram projected onto the twenty-first century. They are the result of differentiation and assimilation strategies emerging from such totalizing global systems as colonialism, development, and capitalism, but more importantly from such regionally specific activities as mountaineering, Third World biomedicine, Tibetan Buddhism, charitable nongovernmental Western aid, Himalayan shamanism, cultural and adventure tourism, and more. Each presents a unique formula for cultural production, and each is apprehended differently by Sherpas and their Others.

Arjun Appadurai, who offered suggestions for dealing with transnationalism, commented on the subtlety of hybridity within a world where culture moves quickly and potently from place to place by referring to Pico Ayer's *Video Night in Kathmandu*. He remarked that Ayer's impressions of the arrival of "things Western" in a place like Kathmandu "are testimony to the fact that, if 'a' global cultural system is emerging, it is filled with ironies and resistances, sometimes camouflaged as passivity and a bottomless appetite in the Asian world for things Western."[10] If the ironies and resistances noted by Appadurai translate into his reading of transnational culture as heterogeneous, then my analysis here of the search for authenticity (in a world of impermanence and shifting relationships) points to the acts of seduction and mimesis that arise therefrom, and have similarly led to my positing a heterogeneous transnational culture, in which a plethora of virtual Sherpas reside. The mirroring of identities that seem to me to be "Sherpa" illustrates how a transnationalism might function. It would not confirm who, in all their "authenticity," Sherpas really are, but would instead perpetually interrupt the very construction of authenticity with persistent questions about what types of relationships, in the transnational milieu, *author* particular versions of Sherpa identity as "different" or "the same."

Khentse Rinpoche Lecture, Tengboche 1987

WE ARE now living in a very lucky time. First, we get a human being's life; it is a lucky life. Otherwise, there are six types of life and other lower lives such as animals who do not understand words, right and wrong, or kinds of virtue (like the dharma). In this way, we are lucky. But lucky ones should do virtuous work as much as possible. Don't be jealous, ignorant, angry. If you are, you will start suffering. You will also make other people suffer. You will find no peace in your life (*zopa* - complacency, not changing moods frequently). After all realize this, and after those who become aware of this, all is better. In this world, there is no West, no East, we are all human beings. Everyone has eyes, nose, mouth. So, we should respect all human beings, even our enemies. We should not disrespect just because of country [of origin]. It is now the time to do this because we will all die. Death will come to all. Like Tibet, it is a religious place, but the situation has come to Tibet where it has been destroyed completely. People work, but many do not finish all of their virtuous work before death. Some die young and some die old, and many do not finish their work.

Birth means death. As soon as one is born, then death is inevitable. When death comes, even if you are wealthy, you cannot stop death. Your money cannot buy life. Even if you are beautiful, your death cannot be stopped. Your beauty makes no difference when you are dead. You cannot change death. You cannot buy your life, nor can you take your money with you. It can be used for this life, but you cannot buy life.

Religion is a virtuous thing, bringing patience and compassion. Virtue and the practice of meditation follows with you after death. Your money and your car, you can't take with you. Wealth is no protection. It is like a rope around your neck. It will hang you. Do not die with wealth. Some people become drug smugglers, but many people die from drugs. Those who get the profits are single persons, but these people end up with a hell life [in their next life]. They only look in one direction—toward that of wealth. But wealth is useless. The only virtue is the mind. The mind is useful. You should pray. You should respect educated people, those who know religion. Do not die with your wealth. You cannot take it with you. When you have that money now in your hand, while living, let's share with other human beings. Give alms. Help poor people. You give one time and, after, you get more compassion and you can give more and more. Your compassion gets stronger and then you don't mind giving away your wealth. Don't waste wealth, don't save wealth. Realize between right and wrong. You should pray.

Everybody says there is no God, but first we believe there is God. Nobody can see, but God has escaped from samsara (he is an enlightened one); they [gods] are in nirvana. They look out for us, but we do not see them. For example, the sun is hot, and the grass is dry, but the sun alone cannot make a grass fire. With glass between the sun and the grass, fire will come. Glass is like belief. It is your trust, so you should believe now in the gods, be faithful. There are many ways of being faithful. Some study; finally, they realize their mind and they believe in the gods; some believe quite strongly, they respect much, then that makes the gods real. Your faith in someone else as a god makes that god real. If you get to nirvana, and you promise in your mind to do work for enlightenment, you too can be successful. For example, if a fish is caught by a hook and he cannot get away, he will only have one option and that is to be pulled out of the water. If you make strong belief to reach nirvana, your faith is like the fish and God is the hook. He catches you and pulls you that way and you cannot do anything but follow that pathway toward nirvana.

You get wisdom and nirvana and you have no need to drive hundreds of miles or climb up mountains, like the Himalayas. It is in your hand, in your decision, in your mind. The potential is already there. Guru Rinpoche is the local god. You should pray to his mandala. You pray to god, any god, and say his mantra [he recites the mantra for Guru Rinpoche, Padmasambhava].

The *vajra* guru has twelve worlds. In the beginning we have samsara. It can solve problems in our life. You should concentrate your mind in one direction. There are many levels and meanings of the mantras; the simplest is when you say the mantra, your mind will concentrate on that and not on other ideas. There will be no room for bad ideas. Like locking the door to your room for a little while. At those times, you concentrate on religious work. Your mind is focused on that and bad ideas cannot come. Nirvana means it is accepting it. It is possible for all. You want to go to the East, West, that is always your choice. It is in your hand—the choice for nirvana. If you do mantras, you get more and more peaceful.... [He continues with explanation of the mantra.] When you do more virtuous work, more human beings love you, they like you, and you get no bad diseases, no sickness, more knowledge and more cleverness. You will live a longer life.

All want to become better people, but few do virtuous things. So if you do virtuous things, you will get a better life. You have education and you may speak different languages of science and you may make airplanes. All of this is for this life, but virtuous things are for your next life. If you plant good fruit, you cannot see it when it is first planted, but when the fruit comes from one single seed, you get lots of fruit. It is the same with virtuous deeds. [Then, he gives a teaching for monks who are initiated, which none are permitted to translate for me because I am not initiated.]

It is important to study, you must listen and learn from other people. You must hear what is being said and then realize yourself. Then you must meditate by yourself and then you can teach other people. Don't consider small virtues as useless. If you see water leaking one drop at a time, it eventually makes one big pot of water. One small fire can burn a whole village. If you think small virtues are not important, you are wrong. Small virtues can make large consequences. Just as small things are important, it is the same for small virtues.

Excerpts from "The Stages of Repelling Demons Based on the Heart Sutra, the Summary of the Vast, Intermediate, and Condensed Mothers"

Translated by Donald S. Lopez, Jr.

(All text is recited except instructions to the ritual master, which are given in italics. Portions in [ ] are additions by Donald Lopez. Portions in { } are my additions.)

{The text begins with an offering of respect to the lama, followed by a description of the text, followed by two stories: one about a practitioner who suffered death because he practiced black magic by invoking harmful deities, and the other about dGe-ser, who obtained the method of getting rid of spirits (an auspicious gift).}

From that point on, the harm of the spirit king was pacified and [dGe-ser] was able to use his mind for the dharma. . . . By practicing it he was freed from the harm of the spirit king. In the same way, if one makes an effort at this, whatever you wish for, such as the supreme achievements, will be quickly attained.

{The text explains how to prepare an effigy and place offerings in front of it, how to make the torma with stamped impressions of the various demons and spirits who will take part in the drama, and how to put oneself in the correct state of mind for the event. In front of the effigy altar:}

What is before[?] me is unobservable. Therefore, it becomes emptiness. From the nature of emptiness [appears] a cushion of jewels, lotus and moon [upon which sits] the chief of teachers, the complete and perfect Buddha Sakyamuni.

{The recitation continues with the invocation of honoring passages recited to the various figures that are meant to be visualized by the ritual master.}

O white divine demon and hosts of white demons, abiding in the realm of nothingness, hosts of divine demons and your emanations. When I, the mantra holder, invite you to your excellent form here [on] the seat prepared, I beseech you to come here for just a little while and abide in your form. Jah hum bam ho. They dissolve and are nondual.

Then the Heart Sutra:

In the language of India, Bhagavatiprajnaparamitahrdaya. In Tibetan, Transcendent and Victorious Essence of the Perfection of Wisdom. One Section. Thus did I hear at one time. The Bhagavan was residing at Vulture Peak in Rajagrha with a great assembly of monks and a great assembly of bodhisattvas. At that time, the Bhagavan entered into a samadhi on the categories of phenomena called "perception of the profound." Also at that time, the bodhisattva, the mahasattva, the noble Avalokitesvara observed the practice of the profound perfection of wisdom and saw that those five aggregates also are empty of intrinsic existence. . . . In the same way, no suffering, origin, cessation, path, no wisdom, no attainment, no nonattainment {exist}. Therefore, Sariputra, because bodhisattvas have no attainment, they rely on and abide in the perfection of wisdom; because their minds are without obstruction, they have no fear.

{Ritual mudras accompany the ceremony, including sounding musical instruments, and these are indicated throughout the text.}

Just as in the past the lord of gods, Indra, contemplated the profound meaning of the perfection of wisdom and, through reciting the words, repelled all opposing forces such as the sinful demons, so in the same way, may I also contemplate the profound meaning of the great mother, the perfection of wisdom, and through reciting the words repel all opposing forces such as the sinful demons and (*specifically, if there is a sick person, say the name*) for so-and-so, may those obstructing demons who lead in the disease in the beginning, who took up residence [literally, "build a nest"] in the middle, and who provide no benefit in the end all now be repulsed [clap], destroyed [clap], pacified [clap], and completely pacified by the performance of this repulsion of demons with the Heart Sutra and by the words of truth of the noble three jewels{the triple gem: the Buddha, his community (sangha), and his teachings (dharma)}.

Also, bless the white torma, say the mantras and the four names as before and then say from: I offer this white torma endowed with a hundred flavors and a thousand potencies to the assembled armies of the demon of the aggregates. May it turn into enjoyments, their exhaustion unknown, that agree with their individual thoughts, *etc. to the offering in front of the deity of the aggregates, to the expression of the power of truth and the dedication as before. . . . Then offer the torma in front of the images of the demon of the lord of death and say*: Just as the treasury of the sky has everything (?) so may I act with my own power, lacking the annihilation of resources, without striving, and without being in danger. *Then say the words of truth*, By the power of my thought. . . . *and dedicate it as before.*

{The text continues with like invocations and admonishments for some time. It closes with the following:}

[Through the magic of printing], the forms of hundreds of letters magically appear immediately on the white surface, without tiring the fingers [by copying]. The [text] comes from the cell of those who made the offering for the printing[?], the monk 'Jam-dbyangs-dbang-rgyal, endowed with faith, charity, and wealth, and the monk-official of the Potala Blo-bzang-blo-ldan. Through the merit [of printing the text], may all transmigrators such as ourselves quickly attain omniscience which conquers the four demons and in the meantime may all sickness, demons, and obstacles be quelled. Sarvamangalam.

Musings on Textuality and Truth

SOME OF these problems are pursued in anthropological work on the nature of institutions in modern Western societies. Mary Douglas wrote in her book *How Institutions Think* (1986) that it is possible to apply Durkheim's main thesis concerning primitive classifications to the "moderns" (that is, to modern society), despite his hesitation to do so. She analyzed the way in which institutions do our thinking for us, by, for example, limiting the options for the terms and conditions on which we perceive reality. Institutionally derived categories condition and configure our own categorical thinking (for instance, wine choices are by grape type in California because of the institutional categorization of wines by region in France). Her analysis is contingent on the idea that institutions are able to make use of written forms of language that have the effect of distancing representations of things (or people, or events) from their referents over time, a theoretical area investigated by Jack Goody, and later by Walter Ong. The teleological evolution that can be found in each of the latter's works places them squarely within an ethnocentric and universalizing tradition of modern Western culture, yet within that context, they both offer interesting insights about the significance of written language in our society. Both authors argue that an outcome of written language is its ability to fix "truth" in ways that make singular versions of truth persist over time. We, I think, tend to believe that one can always check a written record for accuracy and this means that regardless of the mnemonic, or any other aide-mémoire, strategies of oral keepers of truth (oral scribes and so forth), written versions will "fix" truths in ways that are at some level more inflexible than those kept orally. This is because we Western literates tend to think of written sources as more authoritative than oral sources. One outcome of this "fixing" of truths about social life is, for Western literates, a first step toward abstracting truth from lived experience.

Written language, especially in modern Western societies, has been used to abstract truth from lived experience in astounding ways. Literary productions come to serve as a representation of reality, fixing (whether through empiricism or not) truth in ways that are not necessarily tied to experienced events or things. Some forms of writings are better at this than others. Bachelard (1984, 13) noted that mathematics, for example, postulates truths on the basis of concepts, not observed experience, and in doing so it creates a world on the basis of these principles. His famous aphorism that "whereas the first project of science was to create reason in the image of the world, modern science has gone on to create the world in the image of reason" sums up the potential for abstraction in representational truths. We "moderns" often take the representation as the starting point for reality rather than the referent. Latour also had this insight when he noted that one of the ways "truth" gets fixed in texts and from there takes on an abstract life of its own, particularly in science, is through the "cascades" of knowledge that become uncontestable. Eventually inscriptions in the form of published truths, scientific equipment, and technologies become "black boxes" that we either cannot afford, or simply do not feel it is necessary, to challenge:

> The cascade of ever simplified inscriptions . . . allows harder facts to be produced at greater cost. . . . Although in principle any interpretation can be opposed to any text and image, in practice this is far from being the case; the cost of dissenting increases with each new collection, each new labeling, each new redrawing. This is especially true if the phenomena we are asked to believe are either invisible to the naked eye; quasars, chromosomes, brain peptides, leptons, gross national products, classes, coastlines, are never seen but through the clothed eye of the inscription devices. (Latour 1986, 17–18)

The fact that ethnographic representations can abstract truth does not, however, preclude the possibility that knowledge *received* from textual sources is not contested and variously polysemic as it gets caught up in what Morris calls the "social processes of work and reproduction." "Truths" made available in textual form are received in a multiplicity of contextually dependent ways, and their meanings are always subject to change. This means that ideally one would be compelled to study the relationships that produce truth, not simply the end products that get called "truths." Then one would have to take "textual" descriptions as, inevitably, incomplete versions of that which they hope to depict.

Nevertheless, "texts" are used as indexes of factuality, and are therefore valued as such in Western epistemology. They are the very basis for a commodification of knowledge and experience, especially in ethnographic writing where "texts" are the currency of tenure and promotions. Although we tend to accept it that not all written sources are intended to produce truths—as Bahktin (1981) pointed out for the case of the novel—even those fictional literatures are sometimes taken as a starting point for "reality" today. In fact, it is precisely the function of the simulacrum, Baudrillard (1983) argues, to preserve the idea that there is a reality, or rather a "reality principle," and thus to conceal that there is no singular truth. The idea of authenticity works in this way, as a simulacrum. This is why, Baudrillard suggests, that in order to apprehend societies in the late twentieth century we need a theory of surface play, of sign and seduction, rather than warmed-over materialist theories of production and consumption that presume an interpretable reality beyond surface images. The idea of a truly authentic Sherpa serves an anthropology that is hegemonic, just as the idea that every sign has a referent serves an economy that commodifies in material form all that is exchanged within it (e.g., capitalism). Anthropology commodifies itself through a discourse of authenticity.

Textual authority makes use of a notion of fixed or absolute truths that are unchanging in part because of their abstracted, and textual, form and presence. These strategies are wholly different from those used by shamans, for whom textual sources are not the source of truths but for whom mobile social relationships are. Moreover, the notion of impermanence embedded in the idea of absolute truth within Buddhism is one that relies on an abstract, conceptual literate practice. This level of abstraction and "truth making" is found throughout Buddhist cultures of the Himalayas, which contain notions that textual inscriptions of truths are inherently capable of providing one with access to spiritual epiphany, or that their appearance in texts, even when spoken, lends them their authority. Many Buddhist communities are not literate, yet they hold fast to the idea that texts are sources of authoritative knowledge. Holmberg found that among Tamangs, texts play an important role in rituals despite their primarily oral use, where they are taken to be binding oaths, because "properly invoked and chanted [the texts] are incontrovertibly powerful and truthful" (Holmberg 1989, 183–86). He cites the Tibet scholar Eckvall to describe this: "By a strange working of the law of association, the written printed letters themselves on any paper, even when the meaning is unknown, are sometimes called *Chos* [religion, law] by the illiterate and accorded worshipful care and treatment by all. A devout Tibetan scholar will reverently touch his head with a Tibetan book, even when he knows it is secular in subject matter, because the letters in themselves retain something of religion" (Holmberg 1989, 185).

Holmberg notes that for the Tamang, the written texts do not take the form of "doctrinal abstraction through reading and meditation" but rather of "ritual practice directed toward immortality" (ibid.). Literate resources embodying truths are used primarily as oral techniques of practice. Nevertheless, even in this case, one of the differences between lamaist practitioners and other religious specialists was the former's unique abilities to use truths that emerged from literate sources.

At the same time, Buddhism's literate abstractions are reembedded in practices that are meant to disperse the sense of permanence through which they work. Absolute truth in the Buddhist sense undermines itself. While Western textuality abstracts truths in order to bring about a sense of the fixed nature of reality and the absolute reliability of the material world, Buddhist textuality abstracts truths to bring one closer to an awareness of the unreliability of the material world. The end point of abstractions in Buddhism—an ephemeral reality—is ironically much like that revealed in shamanic practices, despite the latter's inability to rely on texts and the former's dependence on them. It is the same sort of reality principle that provides us Westerners with a desire to find an "authentic Sherpa" who is found in the social bonds we might have with Sherpas—the same sort of bonds revealed to us by shamans. But the closer we look at shamans, the more mirrors we are forced to see, just as the closer we look to find an authentic Sherpa, the more likely we are to find, beneath the appearance of exotic difference, an overwhelming sense that we are looking into mirrors at ourselves. But only by seeing them as "different"—and only by thinking of shamans as "different"—does either of them fill this role.

Anthropology, which claims to produce ethnographies based on some version of objective "truths" rather than fictions, is unable to avoid producing abstracted representations of experienced life. In recent years, ethnographic writing has come under extreme scrutiny from a persistent questioning about its ability to abstract truths from lived reality. Authoritative ethnographic displays that claim an ability to "represent" objective truths are challenged by those who claim that ethnographic truths are not "discovered" but rather always "produced." What is at stake is not that ethnographies are or are not "truthful" but what anthropologists and their readers take to be authoritative knowledge—what constitutes authoritative truth? The challenges posit, at one extreme, something akin to the idea that "facts" are "manufactured" for the purposes of theory making by ethnographers who, by making themselves transparent, try to convince their readers that their informants happen to be perfectly capable of demonstrating resolutions to the most serious theoretical questions. This sort of ethnography provides the more obvious techniques of abstracting truths—truths of the same sort described by Bachelard and Latour, above, that are abstract theory even if they are fixed to referents. Referents become wedded to theory in this process, not the reverse. At another, more generous, extreme, challengers note that the idea that ethnographic truths are produced can mean that ethnographies are produced from the dialogic relationship between the field-worker and her or his informants. Ethnographies are records of lived experiences, which are then retold and fixed in a particular form that has the ability to speak for the author. Ethnographies of this sort are not fictions, but they come closer to the type of truth production Bahktin noted for the novel—dialogic. Extended narratives are frequently used as a technique of conveying that any particular truth they convey may be simply one version of truth among many produced in dialogue with those studied. But even the most "honest" (in the confessional, theoretical, and historical sense) conversational or narrative accounts of field experiences seldom make claims to being "fictions."

Thus, ethnographies that make claims to offer "truth," that give those they study a highly abstracted, overly theorized character, and that are in fact simulations in the same way in which modern science is a simulation, do not claim the status of fictions. But even ethnographies that claim only singular, situated versions of truths seldom also come to us as fictions. Truth in ethnography is saturated with and defined by the lexicons of authenticity and difference that, together, make "truth." So we need to recognize that it is as untenable to claim that cultural differences come to us only as products of the ethnographer's imagination and desires as it is to claim that real cultural differences exist in the Other in ways that are visible other than through the observational lenses of those who write about them. Here, we are back again at the place where a notion of virtual Sherpas becomes useful. Reconstituting Sherpa subjectivity in a form that is recognizable by Western audiences necessarily makes that representation no more than an abstract simulation or representation—a surface play of images or representational images meant to seduce via various truths. We are not able to "penetrate" Sherpas hidden behind their mimesis of Westerners, or lamas, displaying themselves as desirable enough to gain merit, sponsorship, friendship, and support while preserving a more "authentic" version of "Sherpa-ness" that only "insiders" might see. The surface play of images constituted in and through social relationships is both the starting point and the end point for Sherpa identities in this ethnography. This does not mean that because simulation exists, "real" Sherpas do not; rather, it suggests that simulation and realness are collapsed into one another— both real, both simulations and representations, all the time.

Production/Seduction

Metanarratives of capitalism are promoted by rhetorics of cultural authenticity. In fact, one of the reasons it may be difficult to get beyond such metanarratives is that doing so would require a fresh approach to analyses of culture. Contemporary theorists note that cultural images should themselves be viewed as productive resources, but few recognize the far-reaching implications of such claims.[1] If cultural images and meanings are not simply commodities but are in fact responsible for actually setting the terms and conditions of exchange and the value of the items transferred, then culture itself is the economy, not merely something epiphenomenal to it. The idea that culture is epiphenomenal to the material bases of economies, being occasionally implicated in production but even then only as a collusive resource,[2] may be the dominant cultural simulation on which a Western economy of meanings depends. Marshall Sahlins was headed in this direction in his book *Culture and Practical Reason* (1976), via structuralism. I conceive of this project by a different route. I begin with the observation made by Jonathan Parry in a rereading of Marcel Mauss: "Mauss's real purpose [in *The Gift*] is not to suggest that there is no such thing as a pure gift in any society, but rather to show that for many the issue simply cannot arise since they do not make the kinds of distinctions that we make. So while Mauss is generally represented as telling us how in fact the gift is never free, what I think he is really telling us is how we have acquired a theory that it should be."[3] The notion of gifts is central to a discussion of the difference between utilitarian and free exchange in our society, where the economy is believed capable, in its purest form, of reducing all social relationships to the cash nexus and rendering things like gift exchange epiphenomenal (because wedded to the realm of culture) to material economic production.

Perhaps, as Parry notes for Mauss, we have adopted a theory that posits that culture is epiphenomenal to economies, rather than productive in its own right, because such a theory supports a materialist reading of history. Nowhere is this bias in favor of materialism more evident than in Marxist social theory. A labor theory of value, for example, is based on an internalized recognition of the difference between use value and exchange value. It suggests that, in market economies, things are valued in terms of the cost of the labor required to make them. But the cost of labor, like the cost of objects, is itself socially and culturally relative. Marx noted the possibility for a productive aspect of culture as another characteristic of capitalism, in which a commodity could become fetishized and its value determined by the market forces through which it both came into and passed out of existence (the money-commodity-money transaction). But for Marx, this culturally dictated stage of capitalism emerged only after that stage in which the worth of an object, still invested with its use value, is determined by its intrinsic utility. Taussig noted, in a chapter on the baptism of money in his book *The Devil and Commodity Fetishism in South America*, that Marx drew on Aristotle's distinction between "what are today called use-value and exchange-value." (Also found in Marx's *Capital*.) Taussig cites Aristotle here:

> Every article or property has a double use; both uses are uses of the thing itself, but they are not similar uses; for one is the proper use of the article in question, the other is not. For example, a shoe may be used either to put on your foot or to offer in exchange. Both are uses of the shoe; for even he that gives a shoe to someone who requires a shoe, and receives in exchange cash or food, is making use of the shoe as shoe, but not the use proper to it, for a shoe is not expressly made for exchange purposes. The same is the case with other articles of property.[4]

If the concept of culture as a productive resource were taken seriously, then the very idea of use value would have to be seen as culturally determined. This is because, as others have noted (see Appadurai 1986), it is not only the social utility, but also the cultural signification system, of things that dictates their worth (including their intrinsic value) in any society.

Baudrillard offers some interesting arguments about this. He suggests that the advance of social life through historical epochs to the contemporary should not be measured by a shift in the approach taken to a valuation of commodities—the shift from use to exchange values—as Marx proposed. Marx's theory, he notes, assumes an inherent use value that emerges from the intrinsic qualities of the object. Eventually, the "evolution" of such objects into exchange-value items means that their value is now determined by social (class) relationships (a labor theory of value). Finally, the object comes actually to represent those social relations in a manner abstracted from the labor required to produce the object itself (fetishization), and in the process makes labor itself an economic object—a commodity with exchange value. The use value, in contrast, remains separate and intact, cemented to its intrinsic utility. This founding of his labor theory of value on an intrinsic use-value quality is particularly troublesome when applied to the notion of liberation. What is liberation in the Marxist sense, other than the discovery of the "proper use" (i.e., an intrinsic use) of the "self"? Baudrillard critically asks, as if there was a universal notion of the "proper" or "liberated" use of the self. In asking this question, Baudrillard reveals an extraordinary cultural agenda in Marx reminiscent of the very Enlightenment thinkers he set out to critique.

Baudrillard (whose relationship with Marx itself changed over time) ends up flipping Marx on his head. First, he notes that Marx offered a critique of political economy based on revealing (or unmasking) commodity fetishism—Marx noted that things seen as intrinsically endowed with value (because the labor relations that actually produce them are masked) are in fact invested with a value directly drawn from those hidden relations of production. In critiquing Marx, Baudrillard notes that Marx must himself assume a value of that thing produced which can reveal the social relations underlying its production. But instead of proposing an entirely culturally (or socially) contingent notion of value, Marx invokes an Aristotelian notion of value that makes use of the idea of an object's intrinsic use. Baudrillard thus observes that Marx limits his own critique of capitalism in assuming there is a more "proper" use of things than that which is socially contingent or culturally determined. (This, Baudrillard recognizes, is the key to Marx's claim for false consciousness, since it demands a "true" consciousness that can see proper "uses" of things or the self.) And so Baudrillard offers instead the idea that objects have no intrinsic value (and therefore there is no "hidden consciousness" that can be unmasked). The value of things, like that of labor itself, is always socially contingent (with which Marx would agree for capitalism) and culturally constructed—that is, not "intrinsic to the thing itself" (with which Marx might not agree). This, then, makes capitalism itself a product of signification. Baudrillard states:

> Indeed, just as exchange value is not a substantial aspect of the product, but a form that expresses a social relation, so use value can no longer be viewed as an innate function of the object, but as a social determination (at once of the subject, the object, and their relation). In other words, just as the logic of the commodity indifferently extends itself to people and things and makes people . . . appear only as exchange value [labor to be bought and sold]—[so] the restricted finality of utility imposes itself on people as surely as on the world of objects.[5]

Marx's theory of utility, in other words, extends itself to the world of people as well as objects. Elsewhere, Baudrillard criticizes the concept of "fetishism": "What we are dealing with first is signs: a generalized code of signs, a totally arbitrary code of differences, and that it is on this basis, and not at all on account of their use values or their innate 'virtues,' that objects exercise their fascination."[6]

Baudrillard notes that Marx's whole argument rests on the principle of utility—this is Marxism's, and political economy's, "reality principle." But ironically, it is also Baudrillard's "reality principle," for he views radical historical progression from the past to contemporary eras as based not on a shift from use to exchange values, but rather on fundamental transformations in our relationship to signs, culminating in relationships that cannot escape the utilitarian demands of exchange. He sees a move from an era of counterfeit to one of reproduction, and finally, to one of simulation.[7] Unlike past eras in which signifiers stood for actual things, people, and events (and wherein interpretations could therefore be right or wrong), the contemporary era offers no way of establishing one interpretation as superior to another, for all dissolve in a surface play of images in which signifiers are no longer tied to referents and representations are no longer tied to originals, and simulations reign. For Baudrillard, however, all possible interpretations still *serve* the "reality principle" of utility. There are multiple uses served by multiple interpretations, none of which can be deemed more correct than another. There is only seduction—a convergence of meanings with images—and all meaning exists only at the surface (with no reference points that can validate them as right or wrong). These meanings are caught in endless ebbs and flows of exchange, wherein what is meaningful today is exchanged for a new set of meanings for tomorrow, where truths serving one objective today are conveyed only to be exchanged for truths serving other objectives tomorrow. (Here, his concern about the media as a site for cultural production is important.) No production is possible that might conceal a more true, or a more useful, meaning of signifiers or things, events, labor, etc. For Baudrillard, the only escape from this place where every sign is offered as part of the utilitarian exchange system is death, fatalism, and silence. Only then is it possible to evade the endless absorption of meaning into the surface display of images, because death forecloses any possibility of exchange.

Baudrillard arrives at this conclusion by presuming that in a society before simulation and representation, something like a "free" gift did exist, in the sense that it had symbolic value (tied inextricably to the social relations that produce it). He refers to the gift economy as one in which an object is invested with "symbolic exchange value," being "inseparable from the concrete relation in which it is exchanged" (Baudrillard 1981, 64). This derives from his reading of Marcel Mauss. As objects with symbolic exchange value, these objects are not codifiable as signs; they cannot contain any of the qualities of commodities. They are purely symbolic. The object given, as Mauss also noted, always contains something of the person who gives it. Once removed from the gift economy context, the object obtains significance as a sign. "It assumes its meaning in its differential relation to other signs" (1981, 66), rather than in relation to the relationship between people. Because it is connected to real relationships, Baudrillard seems to argue (if I understand him correctly), the object is not really an object—it has neither use nor exchange value. It simply binds two people (or more) together and symbolically stands for that relationship. What exactly is exchanged (as an object) is not important; rather, what is important is only that something is exchanged. In this situation, Baudrillard seems to feel that the principle of utility does not apply; the absence of the market and its commodification (along with the absence of sign relations of objects) accounts for the absence of the demands of utility in the precommodity setting, and this accounts for a certain freedom. Contemporary Western societies, he seems to presume, have lost this principle of freedom because our sign system only generates signs that are endlessly produced as part of the utilitarian design of the market (at least in later works; see Baudrillard 1988). Meanings are generated in relation to sign systems, only to be imploded by the incessant circulation of new meanings associated with old signs. Here, I venture that Baudrillard has fundamentally misread Mauss, for, as Parry notes above, at least one of Mauss's intentions was to demonstrate that there have never been "free gifts"—it is only we who think there should be. Despite Baudrillard's success at proposing a theory of the contemporary, his teleology ultimately comes unraveled; there is nothing to prevent objects from being both symbolic and functional in a sign system. There may be less distance between the contemporary and the "not-yet-contemporary" than he imagined. Perhaps there is less difference between the "presimulational," "prerepresentational" counterfeit society and the contemporary than Baudrillard would contend. Perhaps he has acquired a theory that the sign should be more different for us than for Others—as Mauss noted with regard to the gift.

This reading of Baudrillard suggests, following Sahlins (1976), that capitalism should perhaps be recast as an entirely cultural construction.[8] It also suggests, on a related note, that the contemporary tourist economy of Sherpas is not one defined by the collusion of a distinctive premodern, or even precapitalist, and postmodern, or late capitalist,[9] economy but rather is an economy of meanings in which both foreigners and Sherpas participate as willing partners in seduction. No doubt Baudrillard would read my analysis as one that succumbs to the problem of "culturalism," perhaps in the same way that Sahlins (1976) might have (by "autonomiz[ing] this field of consumption [that is, of the systematic production of signs] as an object of analysis") (Baudrillard 1981, 114), and I would agree with him, but not the sort of culturalism that subsumes culture (ideological work) under the rubric of superstructure. Rather, mine is one that presupposes certain logics at work in culture—not simply, as I see Baudrillard saying, one that presupposes certain kinds of logic that are free-floating within the system of exchange into which all objects (and the signs scripted on them) are absorbed. In my analysis, the sign systems that govern value and labor, and the culture work involved in generating them, are translatable into social relations. In Baudrillard, these sign systems are no longer attached to, nor reducible to, social relationships.

Notes

INTRODUCTION

1. I received this information from Sherpa informants; I am not certain it is the correct number. I was told that the only other woman ever to receive this honor (awarded posthumously) was Birkuti, the Nepalese princess who was sent to marry the Tibetan king, Srong Bstam Sgam-Po, in the seventh century; she was credited with bringing Buddhism to Tibet. Tenzing Norgay was also a recipient of the Nepal Tara.

2. Lhakpa's comments reminded me of one of my first meetings with a Sherpa in 1986, when I had arrived for a full year of fieldwork. That Sherpa, also from the Khumbu, had said of Edmund Hillary, "He is like a father of Sherpas."

3. Tsing 1993, 214. In fact, Sherpas are involved with foreigners from all over the world (Europe, the United States, Canada, Russia, South America, Australia, Japan, China) and with many different kinds of persons from each of those cultures. Their reception of these visitors reveals both attention to national specificity and generalizing tendencies that gloss all non-Asian, non-African, English-speaking visitors as Westerners.

4. In this sense I have focused on Western representations and histories as opposed to Asian tourist representations (except in one case), even though a great number of Japanese and Korean tourists also engage in sponsorship relationships with Sherpas.

5. Nepal, His Majesty's Government 1986b.

6. Ullman 1955, 52–55.

7. Miller 1965, 245.

8. For example, Malartic 1954, Ullman 1955, Hunt 1955, Morris 1958, and McCallum 1966.

9. I use *Westerners* here, but I could also use the term *colonialists*, whereas elsewhere it becomes more difficult to use *colonialists*.

10. See also Ortner 1978b, 93–95; Ortner refers to the effigy as a scapegoat—an interpretation that was also examined by Karmay and Lessing.

11. Ullman 1955, 57–58. It is noteworthy that this had to be recorded by a Westerner in order for it to appear in print.

12. Hillary 1964, 3. At that time the trust was, I believe, called the Sherpa Trust. It is interesting that this passage has origins in the Bible's New Testament, in reference to comments Christ is said to have made regarding sinners. Later, I provide other examples of this type of request from Sherpas.

13. Mimesis has been discussed by critical theorists (Habermas 1974, Benjamin 1978) as a potential method of liberation from the alienation of modernity. Surrealism, for example, was discussed and attempted as a method in Taussig 1987. I return briefly to this in chapter 4.

14. John Thompson, introduction to Ricoeur 1981, 16.

15. I argue the opposite in the chapter on shamanism; namely, that the text takes

on fixed and essential meanings in the Western context. Nevertheless, as a representational medium, the text circulates back into mimesis with Sherpas in ways that resonate with those explained by Ricoeur.

16. Ricoeur 1981, 180.

17. By "work" he means something specific: "A text is not only something written but is a work, that is a singular totality. As a totality, the literary work cannot be reduced to a sequence of sentences which are individually intelligible; rather it is an architecture of themes and purposes which can be constructed in several ways. The relation of part to whole is ineluctably circular. The presupposition of a certain whole precedes the discernment of a determinate arrangement of parts; and it is by constructing the details that we build up the whole" (ibid., 175).

18. Ibid., 178.

19. Although I have been continually inspired by Taussig's work, I was surprised (and reassured) to find only after drafting this book that in his own book on mimesis he is concerned with many of the same issues that compelled me toward the analysis in my book. For example, he begins with his wonder at a Cuna shaman who engages in mimesis with spirits, only to realize that another mimesis is already embedded in the figure of the shaman himself and his instruments—a mimesis in which he and Western colonialism are implicated.

20. Bhabha 1984, 126; Bhabha says this is an adaptation of Samuel Weber's "formulation of the marginalizing vision of castration."

21. Ibid., 127.

22. See Fisher 1986a for the insight (following Hillary, in Ridgeway 1982) that Sherpas possessed qualities Westerners wished they themselves had.

23. *Webster's New Collegiate Dictionary*, s.v. "virtual."

24. The light, in other words, emanates from elsewhere, typically from somewhere behind the observer.

25. I am aware of the unproblematic linking of Foucault with people like Ricoeur here.

26. Many would also say this is true in colonial relationships.

27. I refer readers to a plethora of ethnographic works on Thakalis (Ted Ricardi, James Fisher, William Fisher), Tamangs (Alexander Macdonald, David Holmberg), and Rais (Lionel Caplan), and to general ethnographies by Christof von Furer-Haimendorf and Dor Bahadur Bista.

28. See, for example, Furer-Haimendorf 1964, 1975, 1984; Sherry Ortner 1978a, 1978b, 1978c, 1989; and Robert Paul 1976a, 1976b, 1979, and 1982.

29. The attraction "Tibet" has held for ethnographers of Sherpas reveals Tibet as a partially imagined place, an attraction Peter Bishop (1989) explored in a book he called *The Myth of Shangri-La: Tibet, Travel Writings, and the Creation of Sacred Landscape*.

30. De Certeau (1989) refers here to Foucault's procedures, not Sherpas', and the emphasis is his.

31. Ridgeway 1982, 720.

32. Pawson, Stanford, and Adams 1984; Pawson, Stanford, Adams, and Norbu 1984; Brower 1991; Stevens 1993.

33. Barbara Aziz (1978) wrote an extremely useful ethnography of frontier Tibetan life, reconstructed from interviews she held with Tibetan immigrants in

the Solu-Khumbu, and I would place her work between these and those of Ortner and Paul vis-à-vis attention to literal concepts.

34. I refer readers especially to Ortner's discussions about the Western view of Sherpas as ideal porters, which contributed to the "small" Sherpas' resistance to "big" Sherpas (160–65). Sherpa "small" people, she argues, were feeling "big" because of the positive attributions associated with "Sherpa-ness" given by foreigners. On the question of Sherpas' response to foreigners, I also refer readers to Adams 1989 and 1992a, where I argued, respectively, that Sherpas' healing practices reveal a mode of production in tourism that engages Westerners in reciprocity relations (rather than proletarianizing Sherpas), and that tourism relations of production are patterned after reciprocity relations that engage foreigners as long-distance, long-term sponsors for themselves. Ortner's insight that this strategy of recruiting outsiders as sponsors is part of a *habitus* is one I wholly agree with and yet one that I believe needs to be carefully discussed in ways that do not reproduce that "logic" as somehow more authentic than others, because it has historical visibility.

35. Allen 1992 discusses Ortner's book, and other scholars have offered these criticisms orally.

36. For a brief overview of the question of Buddhism and literacy in the Solu-Khumbu, see Kapstein 1993.

37. Furer-Haimendorf 1984, xi.

38. As a Himalayanist, I am also influenced by anthropologists working in that region. I believe my work reflects a growing interest among Himalayanists in accomplishing several goals, inspired, I believe, by a more general interest in anthropology in understanding the relationships between discourses and the construction of the person, variously configured as identity or the body. A notable example is found in the work of Ernestine McHugh (1989). In the Himalayanist literature, my book perhaps follows most closely on the heels of Stan Royal Mumford (1989), although I came upon his book well after I had explored many of the same tensions between shamanism and lamaism in my dissertation, *sans* reference to Bahktin. Others, too, have recently offered ethnographies focused on identity and the construction of the person among Himalayan groups. Notable among these others are David Holmberg (1989) and Robert Desjarlais (1992). One of the major distinctions between my ethnography and these other new perspectives in Himalayanist literature is that while the discourse of modernization that penetrates every nook and cranny of the Himalayas today is strikingly absent from their texts, it is a major focus in mine. My attention to the discourses of modernization found in tourism, development, and anthropology is both complemented and inspired by conversations I have had with a colleague, Stacy Leigh Pigg, over the last seven years. Although Pigg's (1992) work is focused on the mixed-ethnic community of Bojpur, in East Nepal, which has experienced little development through tourism, many of her insights about the effects of a successful set of apparatuses for modernization in Nepal on those who are targeted as its recipients are equally applicable to the Sherpa cases I explore.

39. Examples of this approach in anthropology arrive from many corners, but I have been most influenced by John Kelly's 1991 study of representational strategies of the management of gender, labor, and relations of production through a dis-

course about virtue in a colonial regime, and Louisa Schein's 1993 dissertation concerning the mobile identity constructions of ethnic minorities living under what she calls "internal Orientalism" within the Chinese state. Schein implicitly makes the argument that if ethnographies are examined as products of a politics of representation of their own, then it is important to acknowledge the presence of our politics in our own texts.

40. Mitchell 1991; Vaughan 1991.

41. Gupta and Ferguson 1992.

42. I refer to a reenchantment of the sort Taussig speaks of in his reading of Benjamin. Benjamin (1969) refers to an illuminated state of being—an ability to experience the aura—erased by the secularizations of modern life, but which can be reignited through certain forms of art. This is, I think, similar to that which Westerners pursue through intimate relations with Sherpas.

43. Mumford 1989 also explored the dialogic medium of shamanism, but relied for this on a reading of Bahktin with which I disagree.

44. Early attempts include Wolf 1982, Sahlins 1988 (in response to Wolf), and Bourdieu 1977, but more particularly, I follow Sahlins 1976, Kelly 1991 and 1992, and Ong 1991, and I respond to such works by nonanthropologists as Harvey 1989 and Jameson 1991, which fail to take "culture as production" seriously.

Chapter One

1. I am indebted to Bob Desjarlais, who suggested this after reading an earlier draft of the book.

2. Hillary 1964, 61.

3. Ibid., 100–101.

4. E. F. Norton et al., quoted in Miller 1965, 244. Miller also reports several of the rare passages in which Sherpas are portrayed by Westerners either negatively or as if they are not innately gifted as climbers.

5. Hunt 1955, 208 (emphasis added).

6. Doig 1966, 546.

7. Ibid., 554.

8. Ibid., 562. Western researchers have not failed to pronounce that one of the most identifiable features of Sherpas is their physical skill and endurance. A seemingly endless source of fascination has been the question of whether Sherpas are acclimatized or adapted to life at high altitude.

9. I do not have the complete citation for this journal. It was taken from a collection of news memorabilia collected by Pasang Lhamu's husband, who received the article from a French climber. I have translated it from the French.

10. Lama 1993.

11. Shoukang 1984, 10.

12. "Taking the Pain Out" 1986.

13. McCallum 1966, 39.

14. Church 1985, 24.

15. Lamar 1986, 16.

16. Hunt 1955, 80.

17. Hillary 1964, 31.

18. McCallum 1966, 71.

19. Carrier 1992, 84.

20. Matthiessen 1978, 168.

21. Ibid., 158.

22. Bishop 1962, 512. The translation of *om mani padme hum*, according to Yael Bentor and Daniel Martin, Tibetologists from the United States, is "hail to the one who holds the jewel and the lotus"—Avalokiteśvara—rather than "o the jewel in the lotus."

23. Doig 1966, 545.

24. Internet communiqué from July 5, 1994, issued by Paul Butler in Sydney, Australia.

25. Furer-Haimendorf 1984, jacket.

26. Furer-Haimendorf 1964, xiv.

27. The group is named Mecano, and its music is distributed by BMG Music, New York, New York.

28. Ahlgren 1991, 44.

29. Ibid., 46.

30. In 1978, Agehananda Bharati noted that the actual and ideal Himalayas were worlds apart. The Himalayas in representations were often a place more ascriptive than actual—a place of mystery and religious heritage, yet also, as Gerald Berreman noted in 1972, a place that urban sophisticates thought was populated by "hillbillies." In the Nepalese context, Sherpas were also viewed as low caste, because they were Buddhist rather than Hindu, yet they were attractive to tourists in part because of that religious affiliation. Sherpas were perceived as uneducated Nepalis, yet recognized as having privileged access to foreigners, to foreign visas, and to foreign incomes. In Nepal, the perpetuation of ideal perceptions of the Himalayas led to the use of the cultural richness of Sherpa religion and folk customs as tourist attractions, which also allowed for closer scrutiny of Sherpa fiscal and political life. I suggest that the distinction between actual and ideal in regard to Westerners is moot because all the "actual" Sherpas visible to this author contained those ideal qualities ascribed to them by foreign sources. A different book on Sherpas and other Nepalis might come to different conclusions.

31. Nepal, His Majesty's Government, Ministry of Tourism brochure, 1986.

32. Nepal, His Majesty's Government 1986a.

33. Nepal, His Majesty's Government, Ministry of Tourism brochure, 1986.

34. Jeffreys 1985, 178.

35. Lama 1993.

36. Greenwald 1990, 31, 42.

37. Matthiessen 1978, 33–34.

38. Sandrock 1988.

39. Doig 1966, 576.

40. Chevally, cited in Miller 1965, 249.

41. Furer-Haimendorf 1984, 76.

42. The Sherpa whose story is told talked with me one day about that passage. He explained that when that ethnography came out he was furious, so furious that he decided to file a lawsuit against the author. (At last notice, the author had allegedly agreed to settle out of court with Temba, rather than taking it to an interna-

tional court.) But his specific response to the passage and the ethnography as a whole was interesting, for it revealed that his cultural and fiscal interest in "managing" the representations of Sherpas did not entail eliminating the image of Sherpas as desirable to Westerners. Indeed, he was concerned with the opposite problem. He said that the passage was factually incorrect. He had never actually married the Sherpani in question. He had never even done *sodene* (a second marital "asking ceremony") with her parents, let alone a formal wedding (*zendi*). She had borne his first child, but he had not intended to marry her. Because she had his son, it is true that she was then supposed to marry Temba's brother, who died soon thereafter in an accident. But the issue, for Temba, went beyond his particular story, for he felt that the whole presentation of Sherpas involved in relationships with foreign women was overdrawn and unfairly negative. The author had portrayed Sherpa men as somehow corrupted by the West because they were so attractive to foreign women. Not only did it reveal that they were frequently seduced by Western women into leaving their Sherpani wives, but it also revealed that such interethnic marriages were an indication of the collapse of Sherpa culture. It seemed to the Sherpa involved that the author offered this incident as yet one more indication of the "decline" of Sherpa culture. (For me, it is an interesting illustration of the way an ethnographic account of an incident "fixes" it as typical.) The authority of the author in question speaking for or about Sherpas was contested not, I suggest, because the representation made Sherpas seem sexually attractive, but because it portrayed them as losing their culture through their sexual involvements with foreigners, and because it could make Sherpas seem "immoral" in the eyes of foreigners. For the Sherpa involved, the problem was not the idea that Sherpas were attractive, but that such attractions could lead to the decline of their culture. Since the Sherpa was married to a European yet still considered himself fully Sherpa, one can see how this passage might be insulting to him. Finally, it is useful to note that the factuality issue may have represented a means of contesting the negative representation overall. My own pursuit of the "facts" of the case turned up information that supported both "factual" accounts.

43. Trekking Agencies Association of Nepal 1988.

44. Tiger Mountain Treks and Expeditions brochure, Mountain Travel Nepal, 1987. Mountain Travel Nepal is owned by Jimmy Roberts, a Britisher, but administered at its highest levels by Sherpas, who, I was told, help design the brochures. It also advertised as one of its exclusive tours the "Tibetan Safari," but the only things hunted on these camping tours were old cities, pilgrims' bazaars, monasteries, the Potala Palace, and culturally authentic Tibetans.

45. Sherpa Society Trekking Tour brochure, 1987.

46. This implicitly occurs in Geertz (1982), for whom a hermeneutic method is only possible once one is "inside" a culture. By distinguishing a method like "thick description" for anthropologists, he distinguishes anthropologists from others who might enter into cross-cultural encounters. He does not, however, explicitly deal with tourism and may, in fact, concur with my opinion that the difference between anthropologist and tourist is one of degree of involvement, but not one of kind.

47. Chow 1993, 3.

48. There is another way in which I think Goffman's work intersects with anthropological theories about behavior in cross-cultural encounters. Evans-

Pritchard (1947) notes that shifting identity is a feature among those who define themselves in differential segments of their lineage in acephalous political groups. The idea of shifting identity also becomes prominent in the work of Abner Cohen (1969), who argues that the Hausa make use of their ethnic identity *as Hausa* to gain market advantages in an Ibo town of Nigeria. Finally (and I realize I am skipping much here), Larry Rosen (1984) demonstrates the way in which identity is always contingent on the social relations that make it possible to treat some people as holding particular status or not at any given time—identities are negotiated. I see my work as taking a slightly different approach to the problem by including the ethnographic process in the cross-cultural encounter, and by suggesting that the idea of distinctive cultures that might be brought to any encounter (pace Barth 1969) becomes problematic. I also suggest that this makes it difficult to engage in discussions about "authentic" locations of identity in specific behaviors that mark off cultural belonging.

49. Berreman 1972.

50. MacCannell 1992 moves significantly from this perspective.

51. Urry 1990 also explores the issue of authenticity among tourists and suggests that there is such a thing as a post-tourist who "knows that they are [*sic*] a tourist and that tourism is a game, or rather a whole series of games with multiple texts and no single, authentic tourist experience" (100). The post-tourist is a postmodern phenomenon; he or she emerges from the postmodern condition where aesthetic forms are not separated from one another, or, as Urry notes, where distinctions "between culture and life, between high and low culture, between scholarly or auratic art and popular pleasures, and between elite and mass forms of consumption" (86) break down. Along with this there is a breakdown of the distinction between the image and the referent—for the image becomes its own referent and, therefore, lies between representations and reality.

52. MacCannell 1992, 34. I suspect that MacCannell will find my ethnography exemplary of what he considers a fundamental utopian misreading of the touristic encounter, where the "desire for profit without exploitation" compels me to see everyone getting rich together. I do note the violence done to Sherpas in their tourism economy, but aim to move beyond the metanarrative of capitalism, which can only turn "primitives" into slick "ex-primitives" somehow corrupted by the cannibalistic drives of capital and profit.

53. Modern tourists dissatisfied with a "touristic display" are all the more captivated by what they take to be its opposite in "authentic" culture. Thus, both authenticity and inauthenticity are seductive because the latter actually boosts the value of the former. Consequently, any discourse of authenticity (which inevitably posits an inauthenticity) supports a theory of commodification of culture in which culture is viewed as manufactured, bit by bit, for Western Others. The more terrains of inauthenticity arise, the more valuable is the supposed terrain of the "authentic." The commodification of culture that renders some aspects of Sherpa life inauthentic makes all the more highly valued as a commodity the realm of the so-called authentic. (MacCannell notes this irony of commodification. I understand him as saying that this means the tourist pursuit of the "authentic" can never actually be fulfilled. I return to this in chapter 5.) Rather than authenticity being that which is juxtaposed to commodified culture, as some theorists would have it,

authenticity is brought into existence through a theory of commodified culture, and vice versa: a theory of commodification is served by a theory of authenticity. In the same way, again, anthropology commodifies its products at least in part by making claims to authenticity in the form of original and uncommon facts and insights about "Other" cultures.

54. In one case, Freidman (1990) examines Congolese *sapeurs*, drawn from the "ranks of the lumpenproletariat inhabiting Brazzaville and Pointe Noire." The *sapeurs* purchase haute couture from Paris for displays in a *danse des griffes* at home. They wear their designer clothes with the labels on the outside to associate themselves not only with Paris, but with an external "life force" coming from gods and ancestors and from Europe as well. This consumption is not deauthenticating for *sapeurs*, Freidman argues, because they view these symbols of modernity as the essences of self. They enable "a real identification with higher and thus more powerful forms and substances" differentiated by historical fact of origin—but not by character—from other local elements of that life force. The *sapeurs* thus produce their authenticity through a "consumption of modernity." They are not inauthentic because modern; they are all the more authentic as moderns who participate in, from their perspective, a globalizing strategy of self-identification. Contrasting the *sapeurs'* consumption of modernity with the identification strategies of another group, Freidman explores the Ainu of Japan who, having been politically, economically, and socially disenfranchised from their nation, now engage in the "production of tradition." The Ainu have established schools for teaching their language and culture, and traditional villages that produce handcrafted Ainu goods for tourists. "It is in defining themselves for the Japanese, their significant Other, that [the Ainu] establish their specificity," he notes (321). Here again, the Ainu are not deauthenticated by the commodification of their culture, for they remain in control of the production of their "culture-for-others." Finally, Freidman offers the example of the Hawaiians, with their unique history and set of global relationships. Having been completely disenfranchised from political, economic, and social spheres of control in the state and (unlike the Ainu) also disenfranchised from the tourist commercialization of their culture, they view commercial productions of culture as "externalities." Thus, like us, Freidman notes, they neither consume modernity nor produce traditions as acts of self-authentication.

55. Baudrillard 1988, 166. This is an example of a simulacrum—it conceals not the "real" but rather the absence of a singular "real."

56. Berreman 1972, Fisher 1986b.

Chapter Two

1. This chapter is informed by the work of Foucault (1973, 1979, 1980, 1988), which explores the mechanisms of "biopower," productive power, and self-discipline through the clinic and other modernist apparatuses (explored in Adams 1992b).

2. Stacy Pigg (1992) explores this issue more generally for Nepal, noting that modern subjectivity does not need to be created in order to sustain development programs; its absence is justification for initiating or sustaining them.

3. Hunt 1955, 88–89; this is a record of the first successful Everest ascent.

4. In McCallum 1966, there are multiple journal entries attesting to the need or lack of need to take sleeping pills to rest, and in Hunt 1955, one reads, "Thondup, our head cook, is here, which means good meals for all of us. . . . Closing the notebook, I reach for a sleeping-pill, blow out the candle, and snuggle down for the night" (175).

5. Bishop 1962, 528–29.

6. Hunt 1955, 164. One can read in McCallum 1966 (125–26) about a similar activity on the American expedition in 1963: "I'm only taking enough gear and clothes to last 10 days this trip [from base camp]. . . . Will Siri [the physician] continues to use us as human guinea pigs, and he's running radioactive iron through some of the guys today."

7. Hunt 1955, 164.

8. Malartic 1954, 241–42.

9. Norgay actually lived in Darjeeling at the time of his ascent of Everest, so although he was not born a British subject (he was born in Nepal), he was technically an Indian citizen before independence and so he could be called a former subject. Had he been a subject he probably would have received knighthood.

10. Malartic 1954, 212.

11. A point attesting to the uniqueness of the Sherpa case, in comparison with other ethnic groups of rural Nepal, is that this hospital was, in 1966, better equipped and better staffed and funded than almost all the medical services in the rest of Nepal.

12. The Himalayan Trust was funded not only by private donors, but initially by large corporations such as Sears and World Book (the encyclopedia company) (Fisher 1990).

13. Hillary 1964, 8.

14. Ibid., preface.

15. Pearl 1965, 584–85.

16. Hunt 1955, 208.

17. The Gurkhas (Nepalese soldiers in the British army) are also notable in that they too were viewed with special idealism (Des Chene 1991, 1992).

18. Hillary 1964, 1.

19. Pearl 1965, 586.

20. Hillary 1964, Pearl 1965, Lang and Lang 1971, Fisher 1990. Hillary wrote that the poor health conditions of Sherpas were "due to dirty conditions and aggravated by a complete lack of any sort of medical knowledge" (1964, 100).

21. Hillary 1964, 60.

22. Baudrillard 1983, 14, in reference to the Tasaday of the Philippines.

23. Fisher 1986b, 47.

24. Silver 1991.

25. Hillary 1964, 49.

26. "Khunde Hospital Reports," Khunde Hospital.

27. The doctors saw 3,807 outpatients at the Khunde Hospital, and 2,030 patients at the clinics.

28. After the last encounter, I asked the doctor about the problem of defaulters and he explained to me that most of the patients were not defaulters. "That is, we have had a lot of success with tuberculosis, but it is still a problem."

29. Frantz Fanon wrote in *Studies in a Dying Colonialism* (1965) about the resistance Algerians had to colonial medicine, on the grounds that independence would have to entail a rejection of all things colonial. He also pointed out how, even in these conditions, there was a widespread internalization of the idea that Western medicine, because it was colonial, was powerful. In pointing out how unscrupulous colonial medical practices were, he indicated a widespread consensus among recipients. Nevertheless, its use was not uniform.

30. Many Sherpas believe that if other people know of a child being born and are envious, this will cause a protracted labor for the mother and that can result in the transformation of a male child into a female child—perceived as an unfortunate outcome.

31. There were five births during my stay in the Khumbu and I noted short periods of labor for all, although this is mostly based on anecdotal accounts and not on direct observation.

32. Hillary 1964, 2.

33. Ibid., 3.

34. Fisher 1990 explores the impact of schools.

35. Hospital records are important surveillance mechanisms that help produce knowledge about Sherpas' needs. They are similar to the reports usually generated on expeditions regarding the performance of each of the Sherpas who is employed, noting weights carried, heights reached, and noteworthy characteristics. They were retained at the Himalayan Club offices in India, and since Nepal was opened, are kept at trekking agencies in Kathmandu. The records are also reproduced in published accounts of expeditions written by climbers. Sherpa sardars are expected to produce these reports regarding the staff they hire.

36. Ortner (1978b) noted similar opinions.

37. Pigg 1992.

38. The need for external patronage is documented as a historical practice among Sherpas in Ortner 1989 (in that case, for founding monasteries). A Sherpa *habitus*, she suggests, was visible in Sherpa efforts to resolve conflicts (often brother-brother conflicts) by way of recruitment of sponsors from outside the community (which could mean anything from supernatural agents to Rana state administrators). One of the outcomes of such sponsorship was, repeatedly, the founding of monasteries. The idea of a *habitus* is attractive and would suggest that we might be able to insert Westerners into the place of traditional external sponsors in the Sherpa cultural logic of conflict resolution and monastery founding. Surely one could find ample evidence that foreign sponsorship was used by Sherpas to support monasteries. However, this would lead us down the path toward another version of authenticity in the form of a *habitus*. That it is Westerners who are now brought into sponsorship relations with Sherpas changes the nature of that *habitus* in form and content. The Western gaze neither deauthenticates Sherpas (by making them Western constructs) nor gets simply "patched into" an ongoing and logically "pure" *habitus* that also persistently claims the space of authenticity. It is the discourse that demands authenticity that sets up the whole issue of a continuous *habitus* as problematic—either there was an authentic Sherpa who no longer exists, or there is a timeless Sherpa who always exists regardless of the presence of the West.

Neither perspective can solely suffice; obviously things are not the same now that Westerners are embedded in Sherpa lives, but the presence of Westerners does not make Sherpas' "authenticity" disappear either.

39. De Certeau (1984) offers a critique of Foucault in a theory of consumption that notes that consumption practices variously reinforce or subvert discourses.

CHAPTER THREE

1. Sandrock 1988.
2. See also Kleiger 1988.
3. See also Ortner 1989 for a history of monastery foundings in the Solu-Khumbu region.
4. Tengboche Rinpoche 1987. Others argue that Sherpas in the Khumbu actually migrated there as poor settlers from Sherpa communities in the Solu region to the south. There they worked as herders for wealthy Solu families, tending their yak herds during the hot summer months and helping secure trade for Solu merchants. It was not until the Rana government of Nepal gave monopoly privileges for trade with Tibet to Sherpas in the Khumbu region—enabling them to act as exclusive intermediaries—that wealth emerged in the Khumbu proper (see Ortner 1989).
5. Ortner refers to him as Lama Gulu. She also provides a more complete history of the Zatul Rinpoche, founder of the Rongphu Monastery in 1902. (See also Aziz 1978, 209.) Ortner discusses other monastery foundings that followed Tengboche, and the presence of another, competing lama in Namche village, who founded a noncelibate monastery and whose students then enrolled at Tengboche (compelling him to leave the area).
6. Furer-Haimendorf 1964, 130; Tengboche Rinpoche 1987.
7. Tengboche Rinpoche 1987.
8. Thompson 1993, 30. *Shangri-La* is a travel magazine published in Nepal.
9. Attributed to Bi Byi dGah-byed and Be-lha dGah-mdzes-ma, Buddhist healers, in response to Tara (a goddess), who told them to bring their medicine to Tibet. Rechung Rinpoche 1973, 179.
10. Hopkins 1979, 109.
11. Ibid., 53.
12. See the example of Michael Roach below.
13. Macdonald 1984.
14. The gender implications of this subject have been discussed elsewhere by Janet Gyatso.
15. The arrival and rise of Buddhism in Tibet and the creation of Tibetan Buddhism is a long and complicated topic, encompassing changes taking place over thirteen centuries, and it is a topic to which many Buddhist scholars have devoted considerable time. I discuss it in some more detail in Adams 1992b, but refer readers to Snellgrove 1987 and Samuel 1982, among others, for more details.
16. I work from Snellgrove and Richardson 1968; Richardson 1949, 1953, 1963; Lalou 1952; Rona-Tas 1955; Blondeau 1977; Stein 1957a, 1957b; Karmay 1987; and Lessing 1951.

17. If examples from the Khumbu are helpful, then one might imagine that in early Tibet, if a person were sick or if crops did not grow, it was probably thought to be due to some offense against a deity, demon, or fellow villager. Commonly, deities and demons were ostensibly angered by the person disrupting their habitat with noise or pollution, or by outright destruction (cutting down trees, clearing fields, damming rivers, and so forth). In order to regain health or prosperity, the person had to entice these spiritual beings with offerings that would thereafter obligate them to the giver—who was then required to engage in ongoing worship of such demons and deities to keep them involved in reciprocal alliances. Families were careful to plant flags atop high mountain sites on behalf of their lineage gods. Household deities and spirits were offered fresh water, food, and flags on a daily basis to ensure their comfort. The treatment of sickness by shamans required offerings of favorite foods, colors, and enticements meant to foster reciprocal obligations with spirits who could assist the afflicted individual. Karmay (1987) offers one case study of a historic Tibetan ceremony that resembles the ceremonies of Sherpa shamans.

18. On this matter, I am influenced by Ortner 1978c.

19. I have used this example elsewhere (1992b), but with a different spelling. The ideas here continue my exploration of Sherpa Buddhist notions of self or no-self more completely than was possible in that essay. Here, however, the emphasis is on the unfixed, mobile qualities of the "subject." Also, in that essay I argued that a notion of the body and of the individual had to come into existence before it could be treated promblematically—as an unfixed entity.

20. Lopez notes that his version had no date or place of publication, and he found three other versions that contained minor additions to and elaborations on the basic ritual. Based on my observation of the ritual, I would guess that his text is close to the one used by the Khumbu monks. Of the other texts with which he has compared his translated version, one was written by a nineteenth-century scholar.

21. Ortner describes a ceremony similar to this in which, she was told, the altar represented the Buddha's hand, with each of the four rows of spirits placed at each of the Buddha's fingertips (1978b, 95–98). Her drawing of the layout of the altar is somewhat different from the layout on the altar I saw.

22. Mañjuśrī, Vajrapāṇi, Avalokiteśvara, Kṣitigarbha, Sarvanīvaraṇaviskambhin, Ākāśagarbha, Maitreya, and Samantabhadra (Lopez 1996).

23. Śāriputra, Maudgalyāyana, Mahākāśyapa, Ānanda, Rahula, Aniruddha, Subhūti, and Upāli (ibid.).

24. Lopez calls it mimesis, citing Taussig 1993, 13 (ibid).

25. Lopez 1996 (emphasis added).

26. There were many types of *kurim*, including exorcism rituals (*dozonggup*), blessing or empowerment ceremonies (*tshe-oung*), offerings of prayer flags for religious knowledge or protection (*rlung rta*), and luck-calling ceremonies (*yang gyou*). All were thought to have medical as well as other purposes.

27. Beyer 1978, 293–301, explains the categories of spirits.

28. Tucci 1970, 175; see also Tucci 1955.

29. Geoffrey Samuel, Mark Tatz, and Richard Kohn have all discussed this with me, and I am indebted to them for their help. I take full responsibility for the particular rendering of ideas here. Buddhists systematically assimilated the

terminology and cosmology of pre-Buddhist religion (Karmay 1975, Stein 1972). In doing so, they had to continue to allow for some lay, perhaps *chiwa*, practice, which meant both accounting for real demons and making use of a concept of a mind as a useful way of bringing about an internalized sense of responsibility for conscious work.

30. Lessing 1951, Karmay 1987.

31. Ibid., 264.

32. Ibid., 264–65.

33. Robyn Brentano wrote this in an interesting 1993 master's thesis for New York University. She relies on Newman 1987.

34. Mark Tatz formulated it this way for me.

35. Beyer 1978.

36. Ibid., 93–94.

37. Samuel 1993, 15; Samuel quotes Dowman for the passage from Kuntu Sangpo. Vajrayana refers to the thunderbolt or "diamond" practices, which are the particular forms of tantric Buddhism practiced in Tibetan cultures; they emerge from Mādhyamika tenets.

38. Samuel notes that this is not the emphasis in *dge lugs pa* traditions, which consider tantra to be a high level of practice, achieved through gradual and progressive stages. *Rnying ma pa* Buddhists practice a more "shamanistic" form of Buddhism, he argues, which makes greater use of the deities as instruments for personal transcendence at all levels of practice.

39. Again, there is controversy over the translation (see above, page 267n.22); "hail to the jewel in the lotus" would not be a way of hailing Avalokiteśvara.

40. Paul 1982 offers a description of the Tolden character from Mani Rimdu.

41. Meyer 1988, Rechung Rinpoche 1973, Dhonden and Kelsang 1983, Dash 1976.

42. Tucci 1970, 58–63.

43. Furer-Haimendorf 1964 also provides stories of *trulku*.

44. Holmberg 1989 notes a similar practice among Tamangs (210).

45. Taken from Matthew Kapstein, personal communication, October 19, 1994.

46. Bachelard 1984, 69.

47. To date, the only Western *gyeshe* known is George Dreyfus, who studied in Dharamsala and now teaches religion at Williams College.

48. Snellgrove 1987 (131) notes that as "it is the weapon of the Vedic god, Indra, transferred to the yaksa (local divinity) who acts as escort to Sakyamuni in the early Buddhist period, 'thunderbolt' might suggest itself as a convenient translation. Precisely as the wielder of this weapon this chief of yaksas, known as Vajrapani (Thunderbolt-in-Hand), appears as a chief of Bodhisattvas in several tantras, for he has become the holder of the supreme symbol of this whole latter phase of Buddhism ... and with [his name] Vajradhara (Thunderbolt-Holder), becomes the supreme being of tantric traditions. He may also be acclaimed as Vajrasattva (Thunderbolt-Being), but this is more logically understood as a general appellation of the highest state of tantric being, a term formed on the analogy of Bodhisattva (Enlightenment Being)."

49. Tonkinson 1994.

CHAPTER FOUR

1. Matthiessen 1978, 55.

2. Ibid., 52–53.

3. Discussed in Snellgrove 1987 and in the more obscure source from which I take this passage, Chattopadhyaya 1976, 24–25.

4. *Khonjok* is a desired essence. Nima explained to me: "*Khon* [jewel] is difficult to find. Your *pama* [father-mother] give birth but you will never get a second one. You may have money but you cannot hire or buy or find anywhere this *khon*." *Khonjok sum* was described by a monk as *sangye*, *chos*, and *gedun*, meaning the essence of enlightenment (embodied in Sakyamuni), the dharma, and the community of virtuous scholars, or monks and nuns. The analogy the monk made for me was that the three *khonjok* (the center from which radiates the potentially Buddhist universe) include the university, the books, and the professors.

5. The division of the universe into three comes directly from Buddhist discourse, where triads are common. See also Mumford 1989.

6. It actually means "I make an offering to the Triple Gem (*khonjok sum*): the Buddha, his dharma, and his community."

7. By this he meant that he gives with *gu sung*, referring to the three bodies: body, speech, and mind.

8. Desjarlais 1992 (186–91) notes the importance with regard to health of boundaries divided into outside, middle, and inside among Helambu Sherpas.

9. Matthiessen 1978, 270.

10. I take this from Jim Boon's work on "cosmomes" (1992), cosmopolitan moments that have a conjunction of meanings that are not perfectly aligned but are obliquely shared; these are not moments for which hermeneutic closure could be seen in any way.

11. Benjamin 1969. For Benjamin, it is an auratic [aura-like] experience of the sort once provided by ritual and later lost in the age of mechanical reproduction but now potentially reignited through certain types of art, especially film.

12. Taussig 1987. It resembles the "reenchantment" Taussig describes in its macabre form, as that genre of writing that aims to reproduce a "space of death," wherein terror overtakes other narrative forms that might tame it.

13. This differs from what Furer-Haimendorf wrote regarding *pem*, that "no good-natured woman kindly disposed towards her fellow-villagers is in danger of turning into a *pem*"(1964, 263).

14. Dumje required that sponsors provide food and money to the entire village. About five families sponsored Dumje every year, and all families who were householders in the village were expected to sponsor Dumje on a rotating basis.

15. See also Ortner 1978b and 1978c.

16. Matthiessen 1978, 85.

17. There were three full *lhawas* in the Khunde–Khum Jung region while I was living there. Two of them died in the three years after I left, and one, I was told, had moved to Kathmandu. However, since that time, I was also told, two new *lhawas* have emerged in the two villages.

18. Every Sherpa shaman made use of a translator, who made sense of the language used by the spirits who possessed the shaman. I watched many possession

ceremonies and recorded the spirits' (via the translators') dialogues with the audiences.

19. Ortner writes that "not eating means anger, not eating means asceticism, both anger and asceticism mean (from different starting points) social non-cooperation" (1978b, 144). "The Sherpas . . . have a subsistence economy within a system of private property. Thus, there is little practical pressure for exchange of material goods, and at the same time a strong and culturally encouraged sense of possession of one's property. In such a system, we would expect giving and receiving to be particularly uncertain and troublesome, and indeed for the Sherpas they are. There is great cultural elaboration of the notions of generosity, greed, and stinginess. And, while these are all on the side of giving, we find too that there are problems with receiving, for receiving puts one in a position of debt and obligation, and this is considered uncomfortable" (1978b, 65). I think Ortner's comments hold true for Khumbu Sherpas (and certainly her work informs mine), except that it was not clear that being indebted was more troublesome than it was desirable. Being overly indebted and being unable to repay one's debts were undesirable, but both indicated equally common strategies of bringing to a close one's various social relations of exchange.

20. A host of interpretations could be offered here regarding the significance of Tembu's immigrant status and the adoption of a local place god.

21. The format of the shamanic event is not peculiar to Sherpas. Many other Nepalese shamanic events are like those of the Sherpas. Pigg informs me that in Nepali, one of the verbs used to describe shamanic exchanges is *phakaunu*, to seduce, to flatter (as in seducing a woman or "buttering up" someone important). In that it is like *chakari* (Nep.)—the skillful use of flattery to create reciprocity. One is reminded of the Kula described by Malinowski. (Pigg, personal communication.)

22. The idea that shamanism could redress social conflicts or potential social conflicts is not new. Others have worked on this, including those who contributed to the edited volume by John Hitchcock and Rex Jones in 1976 (see also works by Linda Stone, Kathryn March, and Bob Desjarlais), and these are consistent with views put forth by Levi-Strauss and Victor Turner. Moreover, the idea that a sociocentric identity was pervasive among Himalayan groups was explored by Ernestine McHugh (1989).

23. See, for example, Skafte 1990.

24. In some way, this problem required entering into the space of, following Rey Chow's (1993) reading of Lyotard, the *differend*.

25. Matthiessen 1978, 316.

26. Ibid., 321.

27. Jay 1985; see also Benjamin 1978 and Habermas 1974.

CHAPTER FIVE

1. Haraway 1989, 233.

2. I am interested in going beyond the type of Marxist analysis offered by Hochschild (1983), who suggested that capitalism can commodify human emotion and expressive behaviors by studying airline flight attendants.

3. Carrier 1992, 70, 74.

4. Fisher 1990, 189. He notes that between 1920 and 1989, 101 had died, but this includes those from Darjeeling and Nepal. These deaths, I should also state, as he does, often bring insurance payments to families. He notes that 3.2 percent of all climbers above base camp die. The Sherpa death rate is 2.6 percent because, he says, some expeditions use non-Sherpas as well. Many Sherpas die from accidents before they reach the mountain. For example, bus accidents that occur because the buses are loaded down with gear or encounter mud-slides en route to meet the foreign members at the mountain base are common. Fisher also discusses attitudes toward climbing (130).

5. Abrams 1994.

6. Fisher 1990, 115. He also offers contemporary statistics on the trekking industry.

7. Khumbu Sherpas also owned tea shops, lodges, trekking-supply shops, and souvenir shops in both the Khumbu and Kathmandu. Most families that owned land in the Khumbu also produced crops of potatoes, barley, or buckwheat during the short monsoon growing season, and many families reared animals—yaks, *zopkyok*, and *zum*, which were used for trekking, trade, plowing, and local transportation. In the village where I worked, only two men still engaged in full-time trade activities between Nepal and Tibet. The topic of a different ethnography could be the type and nature of the relationships Sherpas had with many of these other Nepalese ethnic groups, as I have noted.

8. I have elsewhere (Adams 1992a) published material on this. I do not know the spelling of the Sherpa word for wage work, and none of the Sherpas with whom I spoke knew how to spell it either. The Sherpa word for work is *leka*.

9. Bourdieu's theory of symbolic capital is principally concerned with the way in which symbolic activities, such as those in reciprocal exchange, can provide an ideological system through which economic exploitation is sustained. He develops his work (1977, 1979) principally around French and German theoretical problematics (e.g., how classes can reproduce themselves), and analyzes classes in the industrialized societies, and nonclass cases such as the Kabylia, as economies that operate on a principle of direct cultural misrepresentation that integrates symbolic with economic exchange. By focusing on the *habitus* that "mediates between social structures [in the structuralist sense] and practical activity" (Brubaker 1985, 758), he offers what I would call a Durkheimian explanation for mystification, or a structuralist explanation of Weberian theory. Because he offers a way of examining structures of thinking within which symbolic capital takes precedence, his work is useful. My own employment of his notion of symbolic capital makes use of a less-developed aspect of his theory that, I would maintain, must be dislodged from Marxian moorings, especially for analysis of "premarket" economies; symbolic capital does not merely serve to misrepresent social reality in such a way as to perpetuate economic division or exploitation (although it can); it can also serve to reproduce symbolic systems in which material economic relations are, or might be, nonexistent. Brubaker elaborates on this: "Self-interest, in this economy, is not reducible to material interest. . . . Just as self-interested calculation extends, tacitly or explicitly, to symbolic as well as material goods, so power exists in the form of symbolic as well as economic capital. . . . Power in the form of symbolic capital is perceived not as power, but as a source of legitimate demands on the services of others." (1985, 756).

10. In addition to group tours booked through overseas agencies, much of the clientele in the trekking business was FIT (Free International Traveler).

11. See Ortner 1989.

12. Graburn 1977.

13. Urry also explores this issue (1990, 66–87), but he reduces the cultural labor in the service sector of tourism to a logic of capitalism, such that profits are only accrued for companies that can exploit that labor.

14. Again, MacCannell 1992 (chapter 1) points out the irony in tourist pursuits of the "authentic" that can never be obtained since once something is produced for "tourists" it is already "inauthentic."

15. For example, see fig. 4; Church 1985; and others mentioned in chapter 4.

16. My movement away from Baudrillard (1981, 1983, 1988) stems from, among other things, my failure to see the need for his teleological movement from the symbolic (in premodern society) to the sign (in postmodern society). As I explain in Appendix D, he maintains (if I have understood him correctly) that objects are in the former still attached to their referents in symbolic ways (the gift economy wherein the thing symbolizes the relationship or the person), and in the latter always potentially unattached to that which they signify. I do not see the relationships between symbolic and sign forms as mutually exclusive. This is particularly important in view of the way that the name "Sherpa," for example, has a sign form (shown below) and a symbolic form in the sense that it still stands for real people whose circulating identity is the foundation of their economy.

17. This is an internalized and mobile hegemony (the term offered by Gramsci with reference to political parties) that posits a multiplicity of political interests that coexist, but always in such a way that singular groups possess singular interests that come into conflict with one another. Hegemony occurs when one version comes to dominate others, which remain in contestation with it because of the formation of blocks of interest when the state is aligned with specific interest groups, but the contestation remains. I suggest that within Sherpas themselves the multiple versions of "who they are supposed to be" come to reside together, even if contested.

18. This phrase was inspired by Luis Vivanco and Eugenia Caw, graduate students in the Department of Anthropology at Princeton University.

19. I discuss this more thoroughly in an article called "The Profitability of Shamans and Lamas: Transnationalism and Power in Himalayan Healing," in progress.

20. This would only point to the dominance of a Western theory of capitalism again. This is not to say that capitalism cannot reveal exploitation, but it is to say that claims to discover a subjectivity that is somehow false for those we study because they cannot see through it seems terrifically ethnocentric.

Conclusion

1. Going to the mountains, for many Westerners, is a geographic and spiritual equivalent for going to the doctor. Pat Pannell alerted me to the lyrics to the song "Closer to Fine" by Emily Saliers of the Indigo Girls. The song's refrain is amazingly resonant with my text, revealing the situatedness of my own Western insights: "I went to the doctor / I went to the mountain / I looked to the children / I drank from the fountain / There is more than one answer to these questions pointing me

in a crooked line, and the less I seek my source for some definitive, the closer I am to fine." Would this be what Western readings of Buddhism indicate also?

2. Sherpa 1992, 28. Lhakpa Norbu's views put him at odds with many of the Sherpa trekking-agency owners, for whom the work of bringing trekkers into the Khumbu was their livelihood. He, like several other Sherpas, had received his education in forestry and park management fields via the Himalayan Trust in New Zealand. They were not fully involved in the trekking and mountaineering businesses. In fact, one agency owner explained his complaints in this way: "These Sherpas who were given education in New Zealand blame all of the garbage problem on trekkers. In fact, our trekking agencies bring in the highest-paying tourists, who buy everything at full price in Nepal, from hotels, to porters, to fees. They are paying thirty-five rupees per day to trek and they sit at Namche Bazaar huddled in their tents with a small kerosene stove to warm themselves because the National Park forbids foreigners from using firewood to stop deforestation. Other trekkers come in and pay no money to tour agency's but go 'on their own' to the Khumbu and stay in Sherpa lodges in Namche Bazaar. Even though they pay only a few rupees per day to stay there, they can warm themselves and dry their clothes in front of a huge fire in the stove of that Sherpa lodge, which is allowed to use cord after cord of firewood in each season." He went on to say that even the Himalayan Trust wardens (like Mingma Norbu, another former warden) own lodges and place no restrictions on their own use of firewood. Even the National Park offices at Jorsale do not use kerosene. "They use more wood just to stay warm than any group of trekkers I have ever brought to Khumbu," he said.

3. As warden of the Sagarmatha National Park, Lhakpa devoted considerable time to the issue of a "living museum," one that attracted tourists not simply for its scenery but also for its human inhabitants.

4. Jeffreys 1985, 178.

5. One cleanup expedition proposal was submitted to the Ministry of Tourism by a Sherpa-owned agency. The agency was outraged at Lhakpa Norbu's accusations of "ulterior" motivations. For the agency owner, it was impossible to distinguish between tours spurred by "sincere" concerns for the Sherpas' environment and other similarly labeled tours. He argued that the reasons behind the environmentalists' efforts were the same as those behind cleanup expedition requests made by mountaineering concerns: both wanted to preserve the environment for Sherpas and the rest of the world, and both wanted to earn a living doing so.

6. Mountain Travel/Sobeck, "The Adventure Company," brochure for 1992 Seminars in Wilderness Medicine.

7. Bista 1993, 5.

8. Kapstein 1993 and Leon 1994.

9. Lanier 1994, 57. Also in this issue of the journal is the article on Michael Roach, the Western Buddhist monk and diamond dealer, explaining why it was he came to Buddhism in the first place, which again resonated with my insights on Sherpa relationships: "What attracted me to Buddhism was not what you'd expect—it was the approach to personal relationships. My parents were divorced in a rough way, and it was traumatic. A Buddhist principle is that the seed of the destruction of the relationship is born when the relationship is born; it doesn't require an outside force to destroy any existing object, it's simply their starting

which destroys them. And I saw that relationships, no matter how nice they might be, would always fall apart—and that's a Buddhist principle, impermanence." Tonkinson 1994.

10. This insight is useful despite the overwhelming tendency of Pico Ayer to treat those he observes as "different" in a manner reminiscent of the perspectives that authorize a nostalgic romanticism.

Appendix D

1. I refer to work by Harvey 1989 and Jameson 1991.

2. I am thinking of Mintz 1985, Ong 1985, Sider 1986, and Stivens 1981.

3. Parry 1986, 458.

4. Aristotle, cited in Taussig 1980, 129. Marx noted that the rise of capitalism enabled two related processes that fundamentally altered the relationships between people and the products of their labor. First there was reification, in which commodities assume a value in money as opposed to in the labor invested in them—commodities appeared as things not associated with the labor that produced them. Second, fetishization was that process which enables commodities to assume a life of their own, which, instead of highlighting the labor relation that produced them, actually masks that relation and at the same time turns the labor of people into a commodified object.

5. Baudrillard 1988, 69.

6. Baudrillard 1981, 91.

7. Counterfeit belongs to an era (the Renaissance) in which status was fixed in social rank—for example, monarchical styles. Reproduction is born of an era in which it became possible to make reproductions of images, signs, and signifiers with ease (such as photography), and simulation belongs to a contemporary era in which it becomes possible to manufacture signs with no referents (such as video), yet it is a way of apprehending signs that penetrates the whole cultural matrix such that the simulacrum is the only truth.

8. Escobar (1988) makes useful suggestions here when he says that rather than seeing capitalism as the apparatus through which we can apprehend non-Western societies, we ought to think in terms of a Western economy, which operates according to a logic not only of capital but also of culture. I also think that Comaroff 1985, Taussig 1987, Ong 1991 also contributed to this perspective shift, though not by a reading of Baudrillard.

9. Following the usage of the notion of postmodernism of Harvey 1989 and late capitalism of Jameson 1991, who both resort to metanarratives of Marxism to understand the contemporary.

Glossary of Sherpa Terms

N. — Nepali
S. — Sanskrit
Sh. — Sherpa (usually, no Tibetan spelling)
T. — Tibetan

adakche — N. *adakche* — political ward representative
amchi — T. *amchi* — doctor
bardo — T. *bar-do* — intermediate state after death and before rebirth
bodhicitta — S. *bodhicitta* — altruistic motivation
boksi — N. *boksi* — witch
'byung po — T. *'byung-po* — category of demons and elements
chamba — Sh. — a cold or flu
chang — T. *chang* — home-brewed rice or barley beer
chellup — T. *byin-rlabs* — blessing; holy substance offered by lamas, believed to
   be medicinal
chi nang sang sum — T. *phyi nang gsang gsum* — inside outside secret three
chiwa — T. *phyi-ba* — outside one (from *phyi*, outside)
chongo trung sum — T. *mchod ngo drung? gsum* — three offerings for a shrine
chupa — T. *chur/phyu-pa* — layperson's traditional formal-dress robe or coat
   (for Sherpas, refers to men's robes only)
churpey — Sh. — dried hard cheese
chusam — Sh. — shrine or small altar in a home
devachen — T. *bde ba can* — heaven; a celestial abode
dge lugs pa — T. *dge lugs pa* — the most modern of the schools of Tibetan
   Buddhism
dharma — S. *dharma* — T. *chos* — religion (refers to the Buddha's teachings)
dikpa — T. *sdig pa* — sin; demerit; action that is not virtuous
domang — T. *mdo-dmangs* — one of the sutra texts used commonly in *kurims*
don dam bden pa — T. *don dam bden pa* — absolute truth; holy meaning
dorje — T. *rdo rje* — thunderbolt; small brass *vajra*, the scepter held by an officiant
   at a ritual
dozonggup — T. *rdo dzong bkug* — exorcism ritual
drultzi — Sh. — spirits riding into a home on the backs of visitors
duk — T. *'brug* — dragon
Fangnyi — Sh. — annual picnic celebration
garsu — Sh. — butter offering
garuda — S. *garuda* — the mythological bird-god Garuda
gdon — T. *gdon* — powers that bring about illness
gek — T. *bgegs* — obstructions; obstacles
glud — T. *glud* — ransom
gnyan — T. *gnyan* — spirits

gomba — T. *dgon pa* — monastery

gter-ma — T. *gter ma* — discovered text

gunsa — Sh. — winter field for livestock

gu sung thu la chu pa pul — T. *sku gsung thugs la mchod pa phul* — to give offerings with body, speech, and mind

gyaptak — Sh. — a spirit attached to oneself

gyelbo — T. *rgyal po* — king

gyeshe — T. *dge bshes* — a Buddhist monk scholar, with the equivalent of a Ph.D.

gyurpa — T. *brgyud-pa* — lineage

iwi — Sh. — mother-in-law

jhankri — N. *jhankri* — Nepali shaman

jiktenba — T. *'jig rten pa'i* — of the transmigratory existence; destructible

jindak — T. *sbyin bdag* — sponsor

jutho — N. *jutho* — pollution

karma — S. *karma* — T. *las* — karma; literally, work

kata — T. *kha btags* — felicity scarf

kenney — Sh. — a depiction of the deceased used in funerals

khadewa — Sh. — "mouth-sharing"; those with the same (high) status with whom one has commensalism

khamendewa — Sh. — "mouth-not-sharing"; those with low status with whom one does not have commensalism

kherang ming la khang sii? — T. *Khyed rang ming la gang zer?* — What is your name?

khondup — Sh. — not talking

khonjok sum — T. *dkon mchog gsum* — the three jewels (Buddha, dharma, community)

khonjok sum la chu pa pul — T. *dkon mchog gsum la mchod pa phul* — to give offerings to the three jewels

kuma — T. *kug-pa* — female cretin

kun rdzob bden pa — T. *kun rdzob bden pa* — truth that obscures

kurim — T. *sku rims* — effigy ritual; the category of rituals that use effigies

kuwa — T. *kug-ma* — male cretin

lamii — Sh. — "work person"; wage work

leka — T. *las ka* — work

lha — T. *lha* — god

lhabeo — T. *lha babs* — god descending; possession

lha khang — T. *lha-khang* — god residence

lhang — Sh. — god residence

lhawa — T. *lha ba* — god one; shaman

lu — T. *klu* — water goddess

lus — T. *lus* — body

luzongu — T. *glud rdzong bkug* — exorcism ceremony

Mādhyamika — S. *mādhyamika* — school of Buddhism associated with Nagarjuna

makpa — T. *mag-pa* — son-in-law

mana — N. *mana* — measurement of volume (a little more than a cup) *mandala* — S. *mandala* — mandala; an idealized array of the universe created as an offering; divine circle

Mani Rimdu — T. *mani ril sgrub* — an annual ceremony celebrating Tibetan Buddhist history and cosmology

mi che — T. *mi che* — big person (in status)

minung — Sh. — seer, diviner

mogyo — T. *mo-rgyab* — "hunting"; divination

mohani — N. *mohani* — a spell

mudras — S. *mudras* — ritual hand gestures

naljorpa — T. *rnal-'byor-pa* — yogi

nama — Sh. — daughter-in-law

namdok — T. *rnam-rtog* — thoughts

nangwa — T. *nang-ba* — inside one (from *nang*, inside)

ngalok — T. *nga gla/lags* — self-labor; reciprocity labor

ngyug ma'i lus — T. *gnyung ma'i lus* — innate, peculiar body

nor — Sh. — things

norpa — Sh. — ghost

nying — T. *snying* — heart

nyombu — T. *smyon pa* — mad; madness

oung — T. *dbang* — empowerment; empowerment ritual

pagin — T. *bad kan* — phlegm humor

pang — Sh. — depression illness

payin — S. *punya* — merit; virtuous action

peca — T. *dpe-cha* — book; religious text

pem — Sh. — witch

pharchya lamsum — T. *bar chad lam sel* — removing obstacles from the path (a *kurim* ceremony)

phembu — Sh. — the container of holy water used by lamas during blessings

pradhan pancha — N. *pradhan pancha* — elected representative (mayor)

Prajnaparamita — S. *Prajnaparamita* — Perfection of Wisdom teaching

rag pa'i lus — T. *rags pa'i lus* — body of touch; sense

raksha — S. *raksha* — ogre

raksi — N. *raksi* — distilled *chang* or liquor

rgyud bshi — T. *rgyud bzhi* — root tantra Buddhist medicine

rigi — Sh. — potato

rinpoche — T. *rinpoch'e* — supreme one

rlung — T. *rlung* — wind humor; vibratory power

rlung rta — T. *rlung rta* — wind horse; prayer flags that are offered in order to gain religious knowledge or protection; also, religious knowledge or protection itself, in folk use; also luck

rnying ma pa — T. *rnying ma pa* — oldest school of Tibetan Buddhism

rongbas — T. *rong pa* — persons from southern regions

samsara — S. *samsara* — endless cycle of rebirth

sangwa — T. *gsang-ba* — secret one (from *gsang*, secret)

saptak — T. *sa bdag* — earth spirit

sems — T. *sems* — sentient mind

sems nagpo — T. *sems nagpo* — "black mind"; a mind filled with bad thoughts

senge — T. *seng ge* — snow lion

serkyim — T. *gser skyems* — religious community

shakpa — Sh. — Sherpa potato stew

shashu — Sh. — offerings made to spirits (from *sha*, meat)

sheru — T. *zhabs spro* — Sherpa dancing

shinying du dok — T. *sher snying bdud bzlog* — the stages of repelling demons based on the Heart Sutra

shrindi — Sh. — spirits

shunga — T. *srung-ba* — a protective amulet given by lamas, worn around the neck

sodene — Sh. — a second marital "asking ceremony"

sojung — T. *gso sbyong* — worship to remove faults; taking vows

sonam — T. *bsod nams* — merit; also, what Sherpas call "fate"

stupas — S. *stupas* — T. *chorten* — large shrines symbolizing the mind of the Buddha

sungdok — Sh. — lama's acts of protecting or repelling obstacles, thought of by Sherpas as a lama's divination

tag — T. *stag* — tiger

takgyu — T. *khrag-skyug* — vomiting of blood

tangdak — T. *gtang-rag* — offering of thanks to one's personal gods

Tengboche — T. *steng po che* — name of monastery in the Khumbu

thangka — T. *thang ka* — religious painting

thawa — T. *grwa pa* — monk

theep — T. *sgrib* — pollution

thorgyap — T. *gtor-brgya* — effigy ceremony

thuk — T. *dug* — poison

thurmu — T. *'dug-mo* — togetherness; closeness

tiple — N. *tiple* — measurement (a pitcher-full)

tiwa — T. *mkhris-pa* — bile humor

torma — T. *gtor ma* — effigy figurine made of dough

tromo — T. *grogs mo* — ritual sister

trowo — T. *grogs po* — ritual brother

trulku — T. *sprul sku* — emanation body; sentient rebirth

tsampa — T. *rtsam-pa* — mixed-grain flour

tsawi — T. *rtsa ba'i* — root, as in root lama

tshe-oung — T. *tshe dbang* — category of empowerment ceremonies

tsung di — T. *srung-mdud* — protective string given by lamas, worn around the neck

tuchey — T. *thugs rje che* — thank you

vajra — T. *rdo-rje* — thunderbolt; double-orbed scepter

yab — T. *yab* — male principle; father

yang — T. *gyang* — luck; wealth; an augmentative principle

yangdze — T. *gyang rdzas* — luck-bearing gift

yang gyou — T. *gyang 'gugs* — luck-calling ceremony

yersa — Sh. — summer field for livestock

ye shes lus — T. *ye shes lus* — body of primordial wisdom

yid lus — T. *yid lus* — mental body

yum — T. *yum* — female principle; mother

zee — T. *gzi* — valuable striped agate bead

zendi — Sh. — wedding

zopkyok — T. *mdzo-khyo* — male cross-breeds between cows and yaks

zum — T. *mdzo-mo* — female cross-breeds between cows and yaks

zungshii — T. *gzungs-shing* — essential center pole of the universe; internal essence of a person made up of external things

Bibliography

Abrams, Gary. 1994. "Temptation Comes to Shangri-La." *San Francisco Chronicle*, October 12.

Adams, Vincanne. 1989. "Healing Buddhas and Mountain Guides: The Social Production of Self within Society through Medication in Nepal." Ph.D. diss., University of California, Berkeley.

————. 1992a. "Reconstituted Relations of Production in Sherpa Tourism." *Annals of Tourism Research* 19, no. 3.

————. 1992b. "The Social Production of the Self and the Body in Sherpa and Tibetan Society." In *Anthropological Approaches to the Study of Ethnomedicine*, edited by Mark Nichter. New York: Gordon and Breach.

Ahlgren, Calvin. 1991. "Datebook: William Shatner Stars in Odd Ode to the Earth." *San Francisco Chronicle*, February 17.

Allen, Nicholas J. 1992. Review of *High Religion: A Cultural and Political History of Sherpa Buddhism*, by Sherry B. Ortner. *American Anthropologist* 94:967–68.

Appadurai, Arjun. 1986. "Theory in Anthropology: Center and Periphery." *Comparative Studies in Society and History* 28, no. 2:356–61.

————. 1990. "Disjuncture and Difference in the Global Cultural Economy." *Theory, Culture, and Society* 7:295–310.

Aziz, Barbara Nimri. 1978. *Tibetan Frontier Families*. New Delhi: Vikas.

Bachelard, Gaston. 1984. *The New Scientific Spirit*. Boston: Beacon Press.

Bahktin, Mikhail. 1981. *The Dialogic Imagination*. Translated by C. Emerson and M. Holquist. Austin: University of Texas Press.

Barth, Frederic. 1969. *Ethnic Groups and Boundaries: The Social Organization of Culture Difference*. London: Allen and Unwin.

Baudrillard, Jean. 1981. *For a Critique of the Political Economy of the Sign*. New York: Telos Press.

————. 1983. *Simulations*. New York: Semiotext(e).

————. 1988. *Selected Writings*. Edited by Mark Poster. Stanford: Stanford University Press.

Benjamin, Walter. 1969. "The Work of Art in the Age of Mechanical Reproduction." In *Illuminations*, edited by Hannah Arendt, translated by Harry Zohn. New York: Schocken Books.

————. 1978. *Reflections: Essays, Aphorisms, Anthropological Writings*. Edited by Peter Demetz. New York: Schocken Books.

Bernstein, Jeremy. 1986. "The Himalaya Revisited." *New Yorker*, February 3.

Berreman, Gerald. 1972. *Hindus of the Himalayas: Ethnography and Change*. Berkeley and Los Angeles: University of California Press.

Beyer, Stephan. 1978. *The Cult of Tara: Magic and Ritual in Tibet*. Berkeley and Los Angeles: University of California Press.

Bhabha, Homi. 1984. "Of Mimicry and Man: The Ambivalence of Colonial Discourse." *October* 28 (spring): 125–33.

Bhabha, Homi. 1985. "Signs Taken for Wonders: Questions of Ambivalence and Authority under a Tree outside Delhi, May 1817." In *"Race," Writing, and Difference*, edited by Henry Louis Gates. Chicago: University of Chicago Press.

Bharati, Agehananda. 1978. "Actual and Ideal Himalayas: Hindu Views of the Mountains." In *Himalayan Anthropology: The Indo-Tibetan Interface*, edited by James Fisher. The Hague: Mouton.

Bishop, Barry. 1962. "Wintering in the High Himalayas." *National Geographic* 122, no. 4 (October): 503–47.

Bishop, Peter. 1989. *The Myth of Shangri-La: Tibet, Travel Writings, and the Creation of Sacred Landscape*. London: Athlone.

Bista, Sichendra. 1993. "A Unique School in Sherpaland." *Independent* (Kathmandu), August 11, 5.

Blondeau, Anne-Marie. 1977. "Le Tibet, aperçu historique et géographique." In *Essays sur l'art de Tibet*, edited by A. Macdonald and Y. Imaeda. Paris: Centre national des recherches sociales.

Bonnington, Chris. 1973. *Everest: South West Face*. London: Hodder and Stoughton.

Boon, James. 1992. "Cosmopolitan Moments: Echoey Confessions of an Ethnographer-Tourist." In *Crossing Cultures: Essays in the Displacement of Western Civilization*, edited by Daniel Segal. Tucson: University of Arizona Press.

Bourdieu, Pierre. 1975. "The Specificity of the Scientific Field and the Social Conditions of the Progress of Reason." *Social Science Information* 14, no. 6: 19–47.

———. 1977. *Outline of a Theory of Practice*. Cambridge: Cambridge University Press.

———. 1979. "Symbolic Power." Translated by Richard Nice. *Critique of Anthropology* 13–14, no. 4:77–85.

Brentano, Robyn. 1993. "The Wheel of Time: Symbolic Transformation in the Cross-Cultural Transmission of Tibetan Buddhist Ritual." Master's thesis, New York University.

Brower, Barbara. 1991. *Sherpa of Khumbu: People, Livestock, and Landscape*. New Delhi: Oxford University Press.

Brubaker, Rogers. 1985. "Rethinking Classical Theory: The Sociological Vision of Pierre Bourdieu." *Theory and Society* 14:745–75.

Carrier, Jim. 1992. "Gatekeepers of the Himalaya." *National Geographic* 182, no. 6 (December): 70–89.

Chattopadhyaya, Debiprasad. 1976. *What Is Living and What Is Dead in Indian Philosophy*. New Delhi: People's.

Chow, Rey. 1993. *Writing Diaspora: Tactics of Intervention in Contemporary Cultural Studies*. Bloomington: Indiana University Press.

Church, George. 1985. "No French Connection." *Time*, May 13, 20–24.

Clifford, James, and George Marcus. 1986. *Writing Culture: The Poetics and Politics of Ethnography*. Berkeley and Los Angeles: University of California Press.

Cohen, Abner. 1969. *Custom and Politics in Urban Africa*. Berkeley and Los Angeles: University of California Press.

Cohen, Eric. 1988. "Authenticity and Commoditization in Tourism." *Annals of Tourism Research* 15:371–86.

Comaroff, Jean. 1985. *Body of Power/Spirit of Resistance: The Culture and History of a South African People*. Chicago: University of Chicago Press.

Crick, Malcolm. 1985. "'Tracing' the Anthropological Self." *Sociological Analysis* 17:71–92.

Das, Chandra. 1983. *Tibetan-English Dictionary*. Kyoto: Rinsen.

Dash, Bhagwan. 1976. *Tibetan Medicine*. Dharamsala: Library of Tibetan Works and Archives.

de Certeau, Michel. 1984. *The Practice of Everyday Life*. Berkeley and Los Angeles: University of California Press.

———. 1989. *Heterologies: Discourse on the Other*. Minneapolis: University of Minnesota Press.

Des Chene, Mary. 1991. "A Cultural History of the Gurkhas, 1815–1987." Ph.D. diss., Stanford University.

———. 1992. "Traversing Social Space: Gurung Journeys." *Himalayan Research Bulletin* 12, nos. 1–2: 1–10.

Desjarlais, Robert. 1992. *Body and Emotion: The Aesthetics of Illness and Healing in the Nepal Himalayas*. Philadelphia: University of Pennsylvania Press.

Dhonden, Yeshe, and Jampha Kelsang. 1983. "The Ambrosia Heart Tantra." *Tibetan Medicine*, no. 6.

Doig, Desmond. 1966. "Sherpaland, My Shangri-La." *National Geographic* 130, no. 4 (October): 545–77.

Douglas, Mary. 1986. *How Institutions Think*. Syracuse, N.Y.: Syracuse University Press.

Escobar, Arturo. 1988. "Power and Visibility: Development and the Invention and Management of the Third World." *Cultural Anthropology* 3, no. 4:428–43.

Evans-Pritchard, E. E. 1947. "The Nuer of Southern Sudan." In *African Political Systems*, edited by Meyer Fortes and E. E. Evans-Pritchard. Oxford: Oxford University Press.

Fabian, Johannes. 1983. *Time and the Other: How Anthropology Makes Its Object*. New York: Columbia University Press.

Fanon, Frantz. 1965. *Studies in a Dying Colonialism*. New York: Monthly Review Press.

Fisher, James. 1986a. "Tourists and Sherpas." *Contributions to Nepalese Studies* 14, no. 1 (December): 37–61.

———. 1986b. *Trans-Himalayan Traders: Economy, Society, and Culture in Northwest Nepal*. Berkeley and Los Angeles: University of California Press.

———. 1990. *Sherpas: Reflections on Change in Himalayan Nepal*. Berkeley and Los Angeles: University of California Press.

Foucault, Michel. 1973. *The Birth of the Clinic: An Archaeology of Medical Perception*. London: Tavistock.

———. 1979. "On Governmentality." *Ideology and Consciousness*, no. 6 (autumn): 5–21.

———. 1980. *The History of Sexuality*. Vol. 1. New York: Vintage.

———. 1986. "Of Other Spaces." *Diacritics* 16, no. 1:22–27.

———. 1988. "Technologies of the Self." In *Technologies of the Self: A Seminar with Michel Foucault*, edited by L. H. Martin, H. Butman, and P. H. Hutton. Amherst: University of Massachusetts Press.

Freidman, Jonathan. 1990. "Being in the World: Globalization and Localization." *Theory, Culture, and Society* 7:311–28.

Furer-Haimendorf, Christof von. 1964. *The Sherpas of Nepal: Buddhist Highlanders*. New Delhi: Sterling.

———. 1975. *Himalayan Traders*. New York: St. Martin's Press.

———. 1984. *The Sherpas Transformed*. New Delhi: Sterling.

Geertz, Clifford. 1982. "Deep Play: Notes on the Balinese Cockfight." *Interpretation of Cultures* 412–53.

Gilman, Sander. 1988. *Disease and Representation: Images of Illness from Madness to AIDS*. Ithaca, N.Y.: Cornell University Press.

Goffman, Erving. 1959. *The Presentation of Self in Everyday Life*. New York: Doubleday.

Goody, Jack. 1977. *The Domestication of the Savage Mind*. Cambridge: Cambridge University Press.

Graburn, Nelson. 1977. "Tourism: The Sacred Journey." In *Hosts and Guests*, edited by Valene Smith. Philadelphia: University of Pennsylvania Press.

Greenwald, Jeff. 1990. *Shopping for Buddhas*. New York: Harper and Row.

Greenwood, David. 1977. "Culture by the Pound: An Anthropological Perspective on Tourism as Cultural Commodification." In *Hosts and Guests*, edited by Valene Smith. Philadelphia: University of Pennsylvania Press.

Gupta, Akhil, and James Ferguson. 1992. "Beyond 'Culture': Space, Identity, and the Politics of Difference." *Cultural Anthropology* 7, no. 1:6–23.

Habermas, Jurgen. 1974. "The Public Sphere (1964)." With an introduction by Peter Hohendahl, translated by Sara Lennox and Frank Lennox. *New German Critique* (fall): 45–55.

Haraway, Donna. 1989. *Primate Visions*. New York: Routledge.

Harvey, David. 1989. *The Condition of Postmodernity*. Oxford: Basil Blackwell.

Hillary, Edmund. 1962. "We Build a School for Sherpa Children." *National Geographic* 122, no. 4 (October): 548–51.

———. 1964. *Schoolhouse in the Clouds*. New York: Doubleday.

———. 1982. "Preserving a Mountain Heritage." *National Geographic* 161, no. 6 (June): 696–703.

Hillary, Edmund, and George Lowe. 1956. *East of Everest: An Account of the New Zealand Alpine Club Himalayan Expedition to the Barun Valley in 1954*. London: Hodder and Stoughton.

Hitchcock, John, and Rex Jones. 1976. *Spirit Possession in the Nepal Himalayas*. New Delhi: Vikas.

Hochschild, Arlie Russell. 1983. *The Managed Heart: Commercialization of Human Feeling*. Berkeley and Los Angeles: University of California Press.

Holmberg, David. 1989. *Order in Paradox: Myth, Ritual, and Exchange among Nepal's Tamang*. Ithaca, N.Y.: Cornell University Press.

Hopkins, Jeffrey. 1979. Introduction to *The Buddhism of Tibet: His Holiness the Dalai Lama*. Ithaca, N.Y.: Snow Lion.

Hunt, John. 1954. *Our Everest Adventure*. New York: E. P. Dutton.

———. 1955. *The Ascent of Everest*. London: Hodder and Stoughton.

Jackson, John A. 1955. *More than Mountains*. London: George G. Harrap.

Jameson, Frederic. 1991. *Postmodernism; or, The Logic of Late Capitalism*. Durham, N.C.: Duke University Press.

Jeffreys, Bruce. 1985. *Sagarmatha, Mother of the Universe: The Story of Mount Everest National Park*. Auckland, New Zealand: Cobb/Horwood.

Kapadia, Harish, and M. H. Contractor, eds. 1990–91. *Himalayan Journal* 48.

Kapstein, Matthew. 1993. "Sherpas: Religion and the Printed Word." *Cultural Survival Quarterly* 7, no. 3:42–44.

Karmay, Samten. 1975. "A General Introduction to the History and Doctrines of Bon." MTB Offprints Series No. 3, *Mémoires of the Research Department of the Toyo Bunko*, no. 33.

———. 1985. "The Rdzogs-chen in Its Earliest Text: A Manuscript from Tun-huang." In *Soundings in Tibetan Civilization*, edited by B. Aziz and M. Kapstein. New Delhi: Manohar.

———. 1987. "L'âme et le turquoise: Un rituel tibetain." *L'ethnographie* 83, no. 100–101:97–130.

Kelly, John. 1991. *A Politics of Virtue*. Chicago: University of Chicago Press.

———. 1992. "Fiji Indians and a Commoditization of Labor." *American Ethnologist* 19, no. 1:97–120.

Kleiger, P. C. 1988. "Accomplishing Tibetan Identity: The Constitution of a National Consciousness." Ph.D. diss., University of Hawaii.

Kohn, Richard. 1988. "Mani Rimdu: Text and Tradition in a Tibetan Ritual." Ph.D. diss., University of Wisconsin, Madison.

Kunwor, Ramesh Raj. 1987. *Fire of Himal: An Anthropological Study of the Sherpas of Nepal Himalayan Region*. New Delhi: Nirala.

Lalou, Marcelle. 1952. "Rituel Bon-po des funérailles royales." *Journal asiatique* 240, no. 3:339–62.

Lama, Udaya. 1993. "Sherpas: Mountain Men of Nepal." *Rising Nepal*, May 20.

Lamar, Jacob V., Jr. 1986. "A Summit of Substance." *Time*, May 19, 15–16.

Lang, S. D. R., and Ann Lang. 1971. "The Kunde Hospital and a Demographic Survey of the Upper Khumbu, Nepal." *New Zealand Medical Journal* 74, no. 470:1–8.

Lanier, Jaron. 1994. "Comparative Illusions." *Tricycle: The Buddhist Review* (summer): 57.

Latour, Bruno. 1986. "Visualization and Cognition: Thinking with Eyes and Hands." *Knowledge and Society: Studies in the Sociology of Culture, Past and Present* 6:1–40.

Leon, Lydia. 1994. "Tengboche Cultural Center in Nepal: Project Reports." *Cultural Survival Quarterly* 8, no. 3:69–70.

Lessing, F. D. 1951. "Calling the Soul: A Lamaist Ritual." In *Semitic and Oriental Studies*, edited by Walter Fischel. Berkeley and Los Angeles: University of California Press.

Lopez, Donald S., Jr. 1996. "The Heart Sutra as Exorcism Text." In *Elaborations on Emptiness: Uses of the Heart Sutra*. Princeton: Princeton University Press.

———. Forthcoming. "The Stages of Repelling Demons Based on the Heart Sutra, the Summary of the Vast, Intermediate, and Condensed Mothers." In

Religions of Tibet: In Practice, edited by D. Lopez. Princeton: Princeton University Press.

Lyotard, Jean François. 1989. *The Postmodern Condition: A Report on Knowledge.* Minneapolis: University of Minnesota Press.

MacCannell, Dean. 1973. "Staged Authenticity: Arrangements of Social Space in Tourist Settings." *American Sociological Review* 79:589–603.

———. 1992. *Empty Meeting Grounds: The Tourist Papers.* New York: Routledge.

Macdonald, Alexander W. 1973. "The Lama and the General." *Kailash* 1, no. 3:225–33.

———. 1979. "The Writing of Buddhist History in the Sherpa Area of Nepal." In *Studies in the History of Buddhism,* edited by A. K. Narain. Delhi: B. R. Publishing.

———. 1983–87. *Essays on the Ethnology of Nepal and South Asia.* Vols. 1 and 2. Kathmandu, Nepal: Ratna Pustak Bhandar.

———. 1984. "Religion in Tibet at the Time of Srong-Bstan Sgam-Po." *Bibliotheca Orientalis Hungarica* 29, no. 2:129–40.

Malartic, Yves. 1954. *Tenzing of Everest.* New York: Crown.

Matthiessen, Peter. 1978. *The Snow Leopard.* New York: Penguin.

Mauss, Marcel. 1937. *The Gift.* London: Cohen and West.

McCallum, John D. 1966. *Everest Diary.* New York: Follett.

McHugh, Ernestine. 1989. "Concepts of the Person among the Gurungs of Nepal." *American Ethnologist* 16, no. 1:75–86.

Messick, Brinkley. 1992. *The Calligraphic State: Textual Domination and History in a Muslim Society.* Berkeley and Los Angeles: University of California Press.

Meyer, Fernand. 1988. *gSo-Ba Rig-Pa: Le système medical tibetain.* Paris: Centre national des recherches sociales.

Miller, Robert. 1965. "High Altitude Mountaineering, Cash Economy, and the Sherpa." *Human Organization* 24, no. 3:244–49.

Mintz, Sydney. 1985. *Sweetness and Power: The Place of Sugar in Modern History.* New York: Penguin.

Mitchell, Timothy. 1991. *Colonising Egypt.* Berkeley and Los Angeles: University of California Press.

Morris, James. 1958. *Coronation Everest.* London: Faber and Faber.

Mumford, Stan Royal. 1989. *Himalayan Dialogue: Tibetan Lamas and Gurung Shamans in Nepal.* Madison: University of Wisconsin Press.

Nandy, Ashis. 1983. *The Intimate Enemy: Loss and Recovery of Self under Colonialism.* Delhi: Oxford Publications.

Nepal. His Majesty's Government. 1985. *Nepal Tourism Statistics.* Kathmandu, Nepal: Ministry of Tourism.

———. 1986a. *Festivals of Nepal.* Kathmandu, Nepal: Ministry of Tourism.

———. 1986b. *Nepal Tourism Statistics.* Kathmandu, Nepal: Ministry of Tourism.

Newman, John R. 1987. "The Outer Wheel of Time: Vajrayana Buddhist Cosmology in the Kalachakra Tantra." Ph.D. diss., University of Wisconsin, Madison.

Ong, Aihwa. 1985. *Spirits of Resistance and Capitalist Discipline.* Albany: State University of New York Press.

———. 1991. "The Gender and Labor Politics of Postmodernity." *Annual Review of Anthropology* 20:279–309.

Ong, Walter. 1982. *Orality and Literacy: The Technologizing of the Word*. New York: Routledge.

Oppitz, Michael. 1973. "Myths and Facts: Reconsidering Some Data concerning the Clan History of the Sherpa." In *The Anthropology of Nepal*, edited by Christof von Furer-Haimendorf. London: Aris and Phillips.

Ortner, Sherry. 1978a. "The Decline of Sherpa Shamanism: On the Role of Meaning in History." Department of Anthropology, University of Michigan. Typescript.

————. 1978b. *Sherpas through Their Rituals*. Cambridge: Cambridge University Press.

————. 1978c. "The White/Black Ones: A Sherpa View of Human Nature." In *Himalayan Anthropology: The Indo-Tibetan Interface*, edited by J. Fisher. The Hague: Mouton.

————. 1984. "Theory in Anthropology since the Sixties." *Journal of Comparative Studies in Society and History* 26, no. 1:126–66.

————. 1989. *High Religion: A Cultural and Political History of Sherpa Buddhism*. Princeton: Princeton University Press.

Parry, Jonathan. 1986. "The Gift, the Indian Gift, and the 'Indian Gift.'" *Man* 21, no. 3:453–73.

Paul, Robert. 1976a. "The Sherpa Temple as a Model of the Psyche." *American Ethnologist* 3:131–46.

————. 1976b. "Some Observations on Sherpa Shamanism." In *Spirit Possession in the Nepal Himalayas*, edited by J. Hitchcock and R. Jones. New Delhi: Vikas.

————. 1979. "Dumje: Paradox and Resolution in Sherpa Ritual Symbolism." *American Ethnologist* 6, no. 2:274–304.

————. 1982. *The Tibetan Symbolic World: Psychoanalytic Explorations*. Chicago: University of Chicago Press.

Pawson, I. G., D. Stanford, and V. Adams. 1984. "Effects of Modernization in Nepal's Khumbu Region: Changes in Population Structure, 1970–1982." *Mountain Research and Development* 4, no. 1:73–81.

Pawson, I. G., D. Stanford, V. Adams, and M. Norbu. 1984. "Growth of Tourism in Nepal's Everest Region: Impact on the Physical Environment and Structure of Human Settlements." *Mountain Research and Development* 4, no. 3:237–46.

Pearl, Max. 1965. "Kiwi in the Khumbu." *New Zealand Journal of Medicine* 64: 584–88.

Pigg, Stacy Leigh. 1992. "Inventing Social Categories through Place: Social Representations and Development in Nepal." *Comparative Studies in Society and History* 34, no. 3:491–513.

Rechung Rinpoche Jampal Kunzang. 1973. *Tibetan Medicine*. Berkeley and Los Angeles: University of California Press.

Richardson, Hugh. 1949. "Three Ancient Inscriptions from Tibet." *Journal of the Royal Asiatic Society* 15, no. 1:45–65.

————. 1952–53. "Tibetan Inscriptions at Zva-hi Lha-khang." Parts 1 and 2. *Journal of the Royal Asiatic Society* (October): 143–54; (April): 1–11.

————. 1963. "Early Burial Grounds in Tibet and Decorative Art of the Eighth and Ninth Centuries." *Central Asiatic Journal* 8, no. 2:73–92.

Ricoeur, Paul. 1981. *Hermeneutics and the Human Sciences.* Edited by John B. Thompson. Cambridge: Cambridge University Press.

Ridgeway, Rick. 1982. "Park at the Top of the World." *National Geographic* 161, no. 6 (June): 704–25.

Rona-Tas, Andras. 1955. "Social Terms in the List of Grants of the Tibetan Tun-Huang Chronicle." *Acta Orientalia Hungarica* 5, no. 3:249–70.

Sahlins, Marshall. 1976. *Culture and Practical Reason.* Chicago: University of Chicago Press.

———. 1988. "Cosmologies of Capitalism: The Trans-Pacific Sector of 'The World System.'" *Proceedings of the British Academy* 74:1–51.

Samuel, Geoffrey. 1982. "Tibet as a Stateless Society and Some Islamic Parallels." *Journal of Asian Studies* 41, no. 2:215–29.

———. 1985. "Early Buddhism in Tibet: Some Anthropological Perspectives." In *Soundings in Tibetan Civilization*, edited by B. Aziz and M. Kapstein. New Delhi: Manohar.

———. 1993. *Civilized Shamans: Buddhism in Tibetan Societies.* Washington, D.C.: Smithsonian Institution Press.

Sandrock, Mike. 1988. "Teacher Makes Trek from Nepal to CU." *Colorado Daily*, October 6.

Schein, Louisa. 1993. "Popular Culture and the Production of Difference: The Miao and China." Ph.D. diss., University of California, Berkeley.

Sherpa, Lhakpa Norbu. 1992. "The High-Profile Dump." *Himal* (Kathmandu), November–December, 28.

Sherpa, Mingma Norbu. 1982. *Sherpa Culture: Sagarmatha National Park.* Khumbu, Nepal: National Park.

Shoukang, Gu. 1984. "The Sherpas: Hardy Folk of the Himalayas." *China Tourism* (Hong Kong) 35 (December): 10–14.

Sider, Gerald. 1986. *Culture and Class in Anthropology and History: A Newfoundland Illustration.* Cambridge: Cambridge University Press.

Silver, Mitchell. 1991. "Another Good PC Cause." *PC World*, September, 2.

Skafte, Peter. 1990. "Lessons with a Nepalese Shaman: Where Rivers Meet." *Shaman's Drum* 19:54–59.

Snellgrove, David. 1987. *Indo-Tibetan Buddhism.* Vols. 1 and 2. London: Serinda.

Snellgrove, David, and Hugh Richardson. 1968. *A Cultural History of Tibet.* New York: Frederick A. Praeger.

Spivak, Gayatri Chakravorty. 1988. "Can the Subaltern Speak?" In *Marxism and the Interpretation of Culture*, edited by Cary Nelson and Lawrence Grossberg. Chicago: University of Illinois Press.

Stein, Aurel. 1957a. "L'habitat, le monde, et le corps humain en Extrême-Orient et en Haute Asie." *Journal asiatique* 245, no. 1:37–74.

———. 1957b. "Le linga des danses masquées lamaiques et la théorie des âmes." *Sino-Indian Studies* 5 (parts 3 and 4): 200–234.

———. 1972. *Tibetan Civilization.* Stanford: Stanford University Press.

Stevens, Stanley F. 1982. "Tourism and Development in Nepal." Departments of Anthropology and Geography, University of California, Berkeley. Typescript.

———. 1985. "Tourism Development and Impacts in Sagarmatha National Park:

A Preliminary Report." Department of Geography, University of California, Berkeley. Typescript.

———. 1993. *Claiming the High Ground: Sherpas, Subsistence, and Environmental Change in the Highest Himalaya*. Berkeley and Los Angeles: University of California Press.

Stivens, Maila. 1981. "Women, Kinship, and Capitalist Development." In *Of Marriage and the Market*, edited by K. Young, Carol Wolkowitz, and Roslyn McCullagh. London: CSE Books.

Stoner, Charles. 1955. *The Sherpa and the Snowman*. London: Hollis and Carter.

"Taking the Pain Out of Design Data Management.' 1986. *PC* (fall).

Taussig, Michael. 1980. *The Devil and Commodity Fetishism in South America*. Chapel Hill: University of North Carolina Press.

———. 1987. *Shamanism, Colonialism, and the Wildman: A Study in Terror and Healing*. Chicago: University of Chicago Press.

———. 1993. *Mimesis and Alterity: A Particular History of the Senses*. New York: Routledge.

Tengboche Rinpoche, with Frances Klatzel and Tsering (Ang Kunchie) Sherpa. 1987. *The Stories and Customs of the Sherpas*. Khumbu, Nepal: Tengboche Monastery.

Thompson, Sue. 1993. "The Everest Legacy." *Shangri-La* (Kathmandu) 4, no. 2:24–31.

Tonkinson, Carole. 1994. "A Diamond Cutter Like No Other: The Many Facets of Michael Roach." *Tricycle: The Buddhist Review* (summer): 64–69.

Trekking Agencies Association of Nepal. 1988. *Nepal Mountain Tourism: News and Views*, July.

Tsing, Anna. 1993. *In the Realm of the Diamond Queen: Marginality in an Out-of-the-Way Place*. Princeton: Princeton University Press.

Tucci, Guiseppe. 1955. "The Secret Characters of the Kings of Ancient Tibet." *East and West* 6, no. 3:197–205.

———. 1970. *The Religions of Tibet*. Translated by Geoffrey Samuel. London: Routledge and Kegan Paul.

Turner, Victor. 1964. "Betwixt and Between: The Liminal Period in Rights of Passage." In *Symposium on New Approaches to the Study of Religion*, edited by J. Helm. Seattle: American Ethnological Society.

Ullman, James Ramsey. 1955. *Tiger of the Snows: The Autobiography of Tenzing of Everest*. New York: G. P. Putnam's Sons.

Urry, John. 1990. *The Tourist Gaze: Leisure and Travel in Contemporary Societies*. London: Sage.

Vaughan, Megan. 1991. *Curing Their Ills: Colonial Power and African Illness*. Stanford: Stanford University Press.

Wolf, Eric. 1982. *Europe and the People without History*. Berkeley and Los Angeles: University of California Press.

Index

adventure companies, ownership of, 215
agriculture, 25
amchi medicine, 126, 128, 131–32, 154–55
Ang Rita Sherpa, 16, 234
Appadurai, Arjun, 28, 229, 241
Armington, Stan, 223
authenticity, 10, 23, 27, 63, 66, 76, 118, 167, 269n53; anthropological, 8, 22, 29–31, 37, 66–68, 70, 172; Buddhism's, 36, 125, 162; commodification and, 72, 73, 74; desires for, 37, 169, 229, 237; in intimacy, 175; modernity and, 84; shamanism's 172, 183, 200; symbolic capital and, 225
Avalokiteśvara, 267n22
Ayer, Pico, 241
Aziz, Barbara, 264n33

Bachelard, Gaston, 163, 251, 254
Bahktin, Mikhail, 252
bardo, 160, 179
Barth, Frederic, 75, 269n48
Baudrillard, Jean, 225–29, 252, 258–61, 270n55, 281n8
Benjamin, Walter, 205, 276n11, 266n42
Berreman, Gerald, 71, 267n30
Beyer, Stephan, 161, 274n27
Bhubha, Homi, 19, 21, 264n20
Bharati, Agehananda, 8, 267n30
biomedicine, 80, 83; clinical encounters, 94, 100, 151; education in, 92, 98; and expeditions, 85, 207, 271n4; interventions of, 36, 84, 90, 103, 107; research for, 86–88, 206; of Sherpa physicians, 206; and specialization, 99; technologies of, 99, 100
biopower, 104, 270n1
Bir Hospital, 206
Bishop, Peter 264n29
blood, 100, 207–8
bodhicitta, 147, 155
body, 133; in biomedicine, 84, 99–102, 118; in Buddhism, 140, 148–49, 154–55, 157, 160; and commodification, 101; expansive, 161, 169, 204; and modernity, 109; and mountain climbing, 111; and shamanism, 174; and subjectivity 274n19
boksi. See witches

Boon, Jim, 276n10
boundaries: of the subject, 156, 169, 174–76, 180, 183; Westerners and, 203
Bourdieu, Pierre, 29, 196, 278n9
Brentano, Robyn, 275n33
Brubaker, Rogers, 278n9
Buddha, 15, 132, 135, 138–39, 141, 247, 275n48
Buddhism, 11, 19, 22, 123; history in the Khumbu, 126–29; history in Tibet, 131, 273n15; and lay perspectives, 139–41, 146–56; reality and truth in, 25, 131, 154, 158, 167; and transnationalism, 52, 54, 125; and Westerners, 36, 55, 128, 164
Buddhist spirituality, 47–49, 54, 62, 85, 121–31, 161–70
Bumtsho, 130, 212

capitalism, 45, 50, 72–73, 229, 279n13
cash-value documents, 225
charitable development, 10, 26, 79, 94, 105, 124
chi, 141, 174, 175, 183, 195. See also *nang*
chiwa, 123, 125, 168
Chow, Rey, 13, 67
Cleanup Treks, 233, 235
Clifford, James, 71, 197
Cohen, Abner, 269n48
Cohen, Erik, 72, 73
Comaroff, Jean, 281n8
commodification: of cultural difference, 229, 281n4; and tourism labor, 277n2
compassion, 15, 124, 130, 147, 161, 223, 243
conscious mind. See *sems*
cosmopolitanism, 177
cretinism, 91, 108–9
Crick, Malcolm, 72
Cultural Survival Quarterly, 236
culture: as capital, 232; distinction of, 23, 65, 75, 90, 93, 113, 204, 208; loss of, 32; preservation of, 63–64, 92–93, 96; as productive, 37, 215; work, 215, 219

Dalai Lama, 51, 161, 164
Das, Chandra, 139